PROS AND CONS OF THE EMU AND EU

Emmanuel Stiakakis

MINERVA PRESS
LONDON
MIAMI RIO DE JANEIRO DELHI

PROS AND CONS OF THE EMU AND EU
Copyright © Emmanuel Stiakakis 2001

All Rights Reserved

No part of this book may be reproduced in any form,
by photocopying or by any electronic or mechanical means,
including information storage or retrieval systems,
without permission in writing from both the copyright owner
and the publisher of this book.

ISBN 0 75411 676 X

First Published 2001 by
MINERVA PRESS
315–317 Regent Street
London W1R 7YB

Printed in Great Britain for Minerva Press

PROS AND CONS OF THE EMU AND EU

With thanks to the editor of *Asiaweek* for kind permission to reproduce the table of movement of currencies from the issue of 10 January 1997.

With thanks to the editor of *Arab News* for kind permission to reproduce in Part Four of this book twenty-nine excerpts from various 1997 issues of the newspaper.

*To all those who believe that they should
have a say in their future,
and to Socrates, Aristotle and Plato*

Preface
WHAT THIS BOOK IS ALL ABOUT

This book examines the pros and cons of a single currency (euro) for the fifteen countries (sovereign nations) of the entity called the EU (European Union). It also examines all the associated issues, including the issue of participating in the EU itself.

In Part One of the book, the economic arguments for and against the euro are considered in a scientific way. The science of economics will be employed as it is taught today (standard textbooks) in all the universities of the democratic countries. It should be stressed that the economic theory employed is common to books from both left-leaning and right-leaning schools of thought. This part of the book is strictly scientific since only the science of economics plus any empirical results available will be used.

In the next section of Part One of the book, the political arguments for and against a single currency will be examined. This section builds on some scientific results derived from economics and is rational since simple logic and experience are used.

The rest of Part One is clearly philosophical. It examines the basic argument whether it is at all necessary all over the world for the existence of many governments, parliaments and justice systems or whether we would do better to strip them of their powers and live under a world government for all people, with one world parliament and one world justice system.

Part Two of the book examines the arguments for and against participating in the EU. It is structured, as in Part One, into economic, political and philosophical arguments and tries to compare the EU model with an ideal alternative.

Part Three gives a number of specific examples and facts which try to disprove the argument that the EU is a collection of independent nations and reinforce the view that the EU is already an independent and sovereign entity.

Part Four of the book tries to answer the question why and by whom the EU was created, while Part Five tries to predict the final long-term outcome of the EU experiment. One of the basic ideas, throughout the five parts of this work, is that sometimes experiments fail, but even when they fail they are nevertheless beneficial, and occasionally necessary, for the progress of humanity.

It is hoped that this book treats as completely and scientifically as possible the subject of a common currency for the fifteen countries of the European

Union (EU) as well as the general subject of the EU itself. I have never written a book before, but I believe that truth, justice and freedom cannot be compromised.

Contents

Part One	About the EMU	11
Part Two	About the EU	77
Part Three	What the EU Is Today – The Simple Facts	247
Part Four	How and Why the EU Was Created – A Rational Approach	301
Part Five	Epilogue and What Lies Ahead	321

Part One
About the EMU

Chapter I
HOW THIS BOOK WAS STARTED

> 'Begin at the beginning,' the king said gravely, 'and go till you come to the end, then stop.'
>
> Lewis Carroll[1]

It all started for me in the spring of 1994. I was then working as a civil engineer with a Greek construction-maintenance company in a very small town named Rabigh, 150 kilometres north of Jeddah in Saudi Arabia. I saw there an advertisement in *The Economist* for studying with the University of London as an external student for the 'Postgraduate Diploma in Economic Principles'.

Although a civil engineer by profession I had always wanted to study economics but for various reasons until that day I had not had the opportunity to do so. Now I had the chance to study economics as an external student at a reputable university without abandoning my work. I had been working in the construction industry in Saudi Arabia since 1980 and I felt that now was the time to fulfil one of the dreams of my life, to study the 'dismal science'. I took that chance. I enrolled as an external student.

By the end of January 1995, I had received the first books in microeconomics and macroeconomics from the university by mail and I started my studies. I had already moved to Jeddah on the Red Sea coast of Saudi Arabia and my workload was considerable – a minimum of sixty hours of work per week – but I managed to find three hours every day for my studies (one and a half hours during lunch break and one and a half hours staying in the office after everybody had gone home).

In the summer of 1995, I read in the local newspapers that there was a plan for all the currencies of the European Union countries to be replaced by one common currency. I realised immediately that this was contrary to what I was being taught in the subject of macroeconomics, at least according to the books that the university had sent me.

When in the autumn of 1995 I went on vacation to Athens, Greece, I bought three different books in macroeconomics from other also widely recognised authors (mainly Americans). My conclusion after reading those books was the same: under all schools of thought (left or right leaning) and for any country in Europe, Asia, Latin America or elsewhere, the money supply

---

[1] From the book, *The Road to Virtue: resolutions for daily living*, by Michael L Loren, MD, published by Avon Books, 1996.

and the interest rate were economic policy tools which were essential for the economic progress and well-being of the citizens.

So, according to the science of economics, abandoning a currency (abandoning the monetary policy tool) was not only unacceptable and wrong scientifically, but it was also against the economic interests of the citizens of the fifteen countries which comprised the European Union. I was astonished! How could governments do such a thing contrary to the well-being of the very people who had elected them? Were they working against the interests of their voters? No, I could not accept that and still I cannot accept it. No government willingly will work against the interests of its country and no rational politician will try knowingly to do harm to his people. So what was going on?

From that time until January 1997, I became preoccupied with the matter. I started collecting information from all possible sources on the subject although I was in Saudi Arabia. It became for me an obsession to find the answer to the following two questions:

Question One:
Is abandoning a currency and adopting a common one with many other countries good or bad for the short, medium and long term well-being of the average citizen of any country?

Question Two:
Which forces (if any) are behind this very serious move?

By January 1997 I had received my Postgraduate Diploma in Economic Principles, having successfully completed all assignments and written examinations with the university. I felt equipped to write a book to treat the matter in a complete and scientific way. The rest of the book treats and answers only question one above. Question two remains to be definitely answered.

This book is addressed to the average person who has not necessarily studied economics (or any other science). So the arguments for and against the single currency are presented in a popularised manner. More detailed treatments of some arguments are given in the appendices of this book for those readers who have studied macroeconomics, microeconomics and international economics.

Chapter II
THE GRADING SYSTEM

> Every truth has two sides. It is well to look at both, before we commit ourselves to either side.
>
> Aesop (Ancient Greek)

> You must speak straight, so that your words may go like sunlight to our hearts.
>
> Cochise of the Apaches

> When you are right you cannot be too radical; when you are wrong you cannot be too conservative.
>
> Martin Luther King, Jr[1]

What Aesop tells us is that the matter of EMU (Economic and Monetary Union) has two sides and we have to look at both sides before we make our decision. But looking at both sides of a proposition does not mean that both sides carry equal weight in our final judgement. In other words, the fact that there will be arguments for and against EMU does not mean that the final conclusion will be a draw and hence make the choice immaterial. I will give grading points to each argument and the final assessment will be based on the algebraic sum of all those points. Algebraic sum means that some points might be negative as well as positive for any one of the two sides.

In order to give points to each side, we will examine an argument's merits and not only those of the economic effect on the life of a citizen of any country. The implications of merging currencies obviously will have consequences (good or bad) on material well-being, but since we differ from animals in that we have a brain (and maybe a soul), I will also give points for anything that will be found to affect our mental or psychic well-being.

In other words, the economic arguments will be of great importance and will be given great weight. But we will give weight to the political and philosophical arguments associated with abandoning one's currency. I say arguments associated with abandoning one's currency because, as will be shown very early in the book, the proposed single currency goes with other phenomena that are indispensable and will have to follow sooner or later with mathematical certainty.

---

[1] Ibid.

Another very important point of our grading system will be the time dimension. We all, whether we know it or not, live in a four-dimensional world. Three dimensions are the usual length, width and height that all of us know. The fourth dimension of our space is time. We all live and die in it and any respected physicist or mathematician can confirm this. So, when giving our grades we will consider the short-, medium- and long-term effects of merging currencies i.e. we will consider the element of time. It may be proven that what we do today may have greater consequences for future generations (good or bad consequences) than the consequences for this generation. It is a privilege of human beings only to be able to judge their present actions in relation not only to themselves and to their parents and children but also in relation to the children of their children and on into the future. (Someone would say that the future is purchased by the present).

In order to be accurate and as detailed as possible on the grading system, our minimum unit will be 1 over 10,000 (1/10,000). In other words 'full marks' on a matter (100% of the grade) will be 10,000/10,000.

Chapter III
THE FACTS AND NOTHING BUT THE FACTS

Money talks and often just says, 'Goodbye'.

There is only one good, knowledge; and only one evil, ignorance.

Socrates, Greek philosopher
5th century BC

1. The facts

Before we proceed to the arguments for and against abandoning a country's currency and adopting the euro we all need to know the basic facts so that we all understand that we are talking about the same thing and that we understand it. I say facts, because they are not opinions, but actual events that have to take place, as confirmed by any economist.

1.1 FACT NO. 1

The central bank of the country (say, the central bank of France) must cease to exist.

1.2 FACT NO. 2

Printing of money (euro notes and coins) will be done in effect by a central bank stationed in Frankfurt. No euro will be printed unless the central bank in Frankfurt does so (or says so).

1.3 FACT NO. 3

The interest rate of the euro (say in France) will be determined solely and exclusively by the central bank in Frankfurt. The interest rate will be the same for all the countries that have abandoned their currency.

1.4 FACT NO. 4

The participating countries will in effect transfer the foreign reserves that exist today in their central banks to the new central bank in Frankfurt. For example, the foreign reserves (foreign government bonds and gold) that exist today in the central banks of Holland, Belgium and France will be transferred in effect to the central bank in Frankfurt. Thereafter, they will be under the absolute control of the new central bank, which will decide when to sell or buy foreign reserves. No single government will have control over those foreign reserves (including the German government!).

1.5 FACT NO. 5

The question of who gives instructions to the new central bank in Frankfurt is, for our introduction here, irrelevant. The new central bank could be influenced to a smaller or larger degree by the participating governments, but the fact remains that the governor of the new central bank in Frankfurt will be ultimately the person to set the interest rates or to print money for the citizens of the participating countries. The question whether Germany adopts the euro or not is also irrelevant for our analysis. One can very easily imagine the board of directors at the new central bank being in a building in Frankfurt while only France, Belgium and Holland adopt the euro and the German people decide to keep their own currency, the Deutschmark!

1.6 FACT NO. 6

The physical location of the new central bank is irrelevant. It could be in a single location in Germany or could have branches in cities of the participating countries. With branches or without branches the fact is that only the new central bank will be able to print money. If, for example, money is printed at a physical location in France, this will be done only on the instructions of the new central bank (there will be only one new central bank) located in Frankfurt and the quantity of money printed in France will be strictly controlled by the headquarters in Frankfurt. The physical location of the headquarters of the new central bank inside Germany is, I must stress, irrelevant at this point. The headquarters could theoretically be in any location inside the participating countries, or even in a location in a country which chooses not to abandon its currency. (We ignore here as insignificant any security considerations.)

2. What exactly is and what exactly does the central bank of any country on earth do in very simple terms?

Before we proceed further it is absolutely necessary to understand what exactly the central bank of *a* country is (I emphasise the letter *a* because I have not seen in the definitions and descriptions of economic textbooks of the central bank of *many* countries. The economics books all over the world speak of the central bank of *a* country).

The central bank is usually a government-owned bank which performs the following many functions:

- It is the banker to the government of the country.
- It is the banker to all other banks of the country.
- It manages the supply of money (or, alternatively, the interest rates) of the country. The management of the supply of money (or the interest rates) can be done under the full instructions of the government of the country (like, for example, in the United Kingdom) or can be exercised

completely autonomously by the board of directors (approved by the government) who have predetermined targets regarding the country's inflation rate (or money supply) as is the case today, for example, in New Zealand. The degree of independence of the management of the supply of money varies today from country to country all over the world but the common characteristic is that the central bank is always owned by the public, it is accountable to the people of the country (and hence their government) and its directors are always appointed by the government of the country.

- It is the government's broker in its borrowing and lending operations, issuing and dealing in government bonds and treasury bills to underpin the government's year-to-year budgetary position and the management of the country's National Debt.
- It holds the country's stock of international reserves which are used in financing the country's balance of payments deficits and repaying any outstanding National Debt.
- It manages the country's exchange rate by buying or selling international reserves according to day-to-day or year-to-year targets or instructions from the government. It is important here to note that the government may prefer not to interfere at all with the exchange rate of the currency or try just to smooth out excessive day-to-day fluctuations.
- It acts for the country's banks (privately or government owned) as a lender of last resort, i.e. it can lend to banks facing massive capital outflows as much as they need to satisfy their depositors' claims, thus avoiding frequent panics caused by the commercial banks' inability to repay their depositors (bank run), which could easily create general financial panic.

It is very illustrative to see a typical balance sheet of a central bank of any country in a very simplified manner. Let's look at Figure 1 where the balance sheet of the central bank of an imaginary country named SWC[1] is presented in a very simplified form. The currency unit is named SM[2] and all figures are in billions.

---

[1] For anyone wishing to know the exact name of the imaginary country and its currency, the initials SWC stand for Sovereign and Wealthy Country.
[2] Initials SM stand for Sovereign Money.

Figure 1: *Simplified form of the central bank of SWC Balance sheet for June 1997 (All figures are in billions of SM)*

Assets (Sources)		Liabilities (Uses)	
Type of asset	Amount of asset	Type of liability	Amount of liability
Foreign reserves	60b SM	Deposits held by commercial banks in central bank	80b SM
Government bonds	940b SM		
		Currency in circulation	920b SM
Total Monetary Base – M_O – (Sources)	1,000b SM	Total Monetary Base – M_O – (Uses)	1,000b SM

It is very instructive to see here by an example one of the ways (the word one must be stressed here) the central bank of SWC creates money in circulation (currency in the hands of the citizens). At the end of June 1997 the board of directors of the central bank decides to increase the amount of currency in circulation by 1% (to increase the monetary base M_o by 1%).

During July 1997, the central bank buys 10 billion worth of bonds from the government of SWC. These bonds were previously held by the citizens, or even by foreigners. In order to pay for these bonds the central bank prints 10 billion SM in notes and coins and pays those who held the government bonds. In this way the currency in circulation is increased during July 1997 by 10 billion and now at the end of that month the balance sheet of the central bank is as in Figure 2.

Figure 2: *Simplified form of the central bank of SWC Balance sheet for July 1997 (All figures are in billions of SM)*

Assets (Sources)		Liabilities (Uses)	
Type of asset	Amount of asset	Type of liability	Amount of liability
Foreign reserves	60b SM	Deposits held by commercial banks in vault of central bank	80b SM
Government bonds	950b SM		
		Currency in circulation	930b SM
Total Monetary Base (Sources)	1,010b SM	Total Monetary Base (Uses)	1,010b SM

Comparing Figures 1 and 2 we see that both the left and the right side of the central bank's balance sheet over a period of one month were increased by exactly the same amount of money. The assets of the central bank are now 1,010 billion SM, but the liabilities too of the central bank are now 1,010 billions of SM. This is always true of any balance sheet: the assets must be equal to the liabilities (you cannot create liabilities without increasing your assets by an equal amount and vice versa).

For those readers who have studied macroeconomics or international economics a somewhat more detailed account of the central bank of SWC is given in Appendix 1. Going through Appendix 1 is not at all necessary for maintaining continuity and understanding the arguments presented in the rest of the book.

Chapter IV
MACROECONOMIC ARGUMENTS ON THE EMU

The truth is rarely pure and never simple.

Oscar Wilde

1. What is macroeconomics?

There are three main branches of the science of economics: macroeconomics, microeconomics and international economics.

Macroeconomics is concerned with the overall performance of an economy. It considers the economy's total output of goods and services (Gross Domestic Product or GDP), the rate of growth of that output year after year, the rate of inflation (the percentage rate by which prices change every year), the unemployment rate (the percentage of citizens able and willing to work but who cannot find work), the balance of payments or the balance of the total payments made to or from foreigners for any reason during a particular year (trade in goods, services, investments, repaying debts, loans, etc.) and the exchange rate of the currency of a country.

2. The role of money, interest rates and the central bank of a country in determining the national income

If we open any book in basic macroeconomics we see that a great part of the book (maybe 40%) is dedicated to the role of money and monetary policy in any country. Any government in the world in order to regulate the macroeconomic indicators of the country (rate of increase of disposable income per citizen, inflation rate, unemployment rate, balance of payments, exchange rate of currency) has in its hands practically and broadly speaking only two macroeconomic policy tools: fiscal policy and monetary policy.

2.1 FISCAL POLICY

This is concerned with the amount in taxes the government collects every year and the amount of spending by the government for services or goods produced by the public sector as well as the amount in transfer payments (redistribution of income) going every year from the government to the citizens of the country (pensions, health care, unemployment benefits, education, etc.).

2.2 MONETARY POLICY

This is concerned primarily with the quantity of money available to the economy of a country by regulating the money supply (or the interest rate). Such regulation is accomplished by changing (increasing or decreasing) the amount of currency available, or changing the interest rate under which the central bank lends money to commercial banks, or by changing the required reserves that the commercial banks should keep with the central bank or by any combination of these.

Monetary policy is implemented by the central bank of the country which is accountable to the citizens of the country who control it through their elected government. The degree of control that the government exercises over the central bank varies from country to country, but the fact remains that the central bank is always a public institution and as such is part of the wider government of any country.

Now suppose that a country (say, France) is in recession with high unemployment and an insignificant increase in real income per citizen during the past year. The French citizens demand from their government quick action. The government can use the fiscal policy tool or the monetary policy tool, or a combination of fiscal and monetary policy.

With the fiscal policy tool it can, for example, increase spending (say, for infrastructure) or decrease taxes. Any such fiscal measures will increase the demand for goods and services in the French economy and the increased demand will induce an increase in the supply of goods and services by businesses. Increasing the supply of goods and services means that more people will be employed by French businesses and that next year the economy will be in equilibrium in a higher position (increased Gross Domestic Product).

Alternatively in our example, the French government can use the monetary policy tool. It instructs (and persuades) the French central bank to reduce the real interest rate. The central bank reduces the interest rate by increasing the supply of money (the French franc). The supply of money can be increased by printing more French francs or reducing the discount rate at the central bank (the rate with which French commercial banks can borrow francs from the central bank) or even by reducing the reserve requirements of the commercial banks with the central bank.

Any of the above measures taken by the central bank means in effect increased liquidity (an increased quantity of money in the broader sense of 'money') in the French economy. Businesses, investors and households in France now start borrowing more money from the French commercial banks and this increases both private consumption and, most importantly, private investment. So the lower interest rate induces companies to borrow more (most of the companies all over the world invest with borrowed money) and expand (new factories, shops, building, cars, etc.) or set up completely new businesses (say, in the tourism, information, entertainment, telecom, transportation and power industries). Households, with interest rates reduced, are now more eager to borrow for buying new houses or for repairing existing ones. Increased demand for private investment and consumption means that there will be increased supply of goods and services in the French economy during the next year (remember that the supply of goods and services will try always to match the demand for goods and services). The end result of the action by the French authorities responsible for conducting monetary policy will be that in the next year the French economy will be in equilibrium in a higher position (increased Gross Domestic Product).

In our example we ought to stress two important things.

1. Usage of one policy tool does not exclude usage of the other policy tool. In fact all over the world governments are using one tool in combination with the other. So in our specific example with an imaginary French recession with high unemployment, the French government could use a little fiscal policy (say, only a small reduction in tax rates in order not to increase considerably the budget deficit) and a little monetary policy (say, only a small reduction in real interest rates in order not to increase the inflation rate significantly).

2. These two macroeconomic policy tools (fiscal policy tool and monetary policy tool) are only for solving short-term economic problems (say, deep recessions or high inflation, etc.). They are suitable for jump starting or cooling an economy (putting the brakes on the economy). They are not tools to deal with long-term problems of an economy. They are, however, the only two practical short-term macroeconomic guns in the armoury of any economics minister in any country on earth.

Before we depart to our first argument, let us see, in a simple diagram that any reader can understand, what happens in our example when the French government, faced with very high unemployment, tries to jumpstart the economy by using the monetary policy tool.

In Figure 3, the horizontal axis measures the total output of goods and services in the economy. It also measures the total income of French citizens (since for any economy total income and the value of total output of goods and services are roughly equal). The vertical axis measures the price level of the French economy.

The curve AD_1 stands for Aggregate Demand and measures the total demand for goods and services in the French economy. The curve AS stands for Aggregate Supply and measures the total amount of goods and services that the firms wish to supply for any given level of prices.

Originally (when in recession with high unemployment) the French economy is in equilibrium at point E_1 with price level P_1 and National Income

(Output) Y_1. This output Y_1 corresponds (for the sake of our example) to high unemployment. When the French public authorities decide to use the monetary policy tool, they lower the interest rate of the franc. Lower interest rates in the French economy cause increased demand for goods and services (for the reasons outlined on pages 23-24). Therefore the demand curve during the next several months moves to the right to the new position AD_2.

The new equilibrium of the French economy (for maybe the next couple of years) is at point E_2 (the equilibrium of any economy at any moment is at the intersection of supply and demand curves). Point E_2 corresponds to a higher level of national output Y_2 and this means lower unemployment for French citizens. It also corresponds to a slightly higher level of prices P_2. We say 'slightly higher' since we have drawn the Aggregate Supply curve AS relatively flat. This is because, in our example, we assumed that owing to the adverse economic circumstances (low Gross Domestic Product and high unemployment) there is a lot of spare capacity in the French economy (the industrial plants, the service industries, etc. all have spare capacity) and therefore the firms are willing to increase supply (produce more goods and services) without increasing their prices considerably.

Figure 3

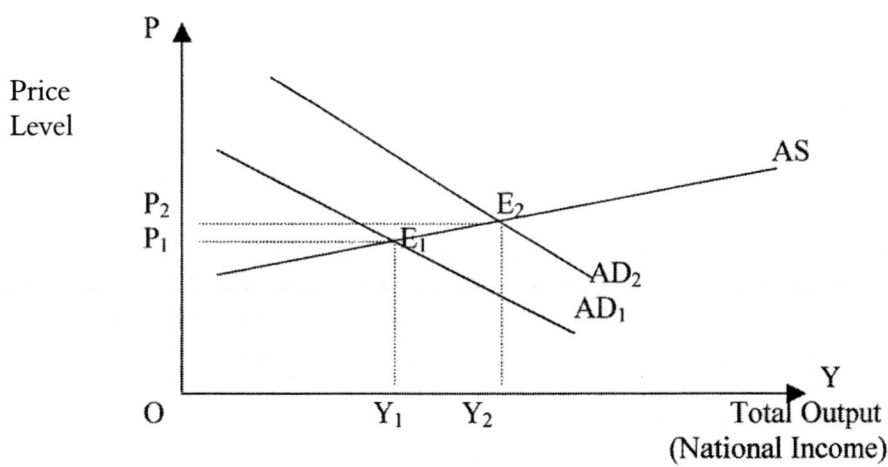

From Figure 3 we see how powerful a macroeconomic policy tool monetary policy is. It can help a country alleviate temporarily acute problems such as high unemployment. It can also help a country fight high inflation. (In the high inflation scenario the monetary authorities act in the opposite direction – they raise the real interest rates.)

For those of the readers who have studied macroeconomics, Appendix 2 shows how the Aggregate Demand curve changes position when the interest rate is reduced. The very well-known IS-LM model is used.

3. Argument No. 1 (Macroeconomic)

> Abandoning my currency means abandoning my ability to exercise monetary policy through my central bank and my elected government. Abandoning my ability to exercise monetary policy means that I lose the ability to exercise any macroeconomic policy specific to my country by about 50% (since monetary policy is about 50% of the total available macroeconomic policy tools). Losing 50% of the macroeconomic control of my country is bad for my material well-being as well as for all future generations.

Put simply, this argument says that when a country does not have its own central bank it does not have the ability to exercise any monetary policy specific for the economic needs of the citizens. The public authorities (the elected government and central bank) cannot tailor the interest rate (or equivalently the money supply) to suit the specific macroeconomic needs of the people of the country.

The argument is extremely important and serious, so we will try to look at the underlying theory as well as empirical results.

EXAMINING THE ARGUMENT

We only have to go back to pages 23-24 where the importance of monetary policy was described. If we assume that a country does not have its own currency, it also does not have its own central bank. Having lost its central bank, the country cannot regulate the interest rate (or equivalently the 'money' supply). Hence the country cannot have any monetary policy specific for it. Its elected authorities have completely lost the capability to exercise monetary policy tailored specifically for the needs of the people who elected them. They have lost at least 50% of their macroeconomic policy tools.

In order to give a concrete example, let us go back to our imaginary situation on page 23 where France was assumed to suffer from exceptionally high unemployment and the French government was urged to take some action to alleviate the problem. In addition, assume that the French citizens have now abandoned their currency and they are now using a currency in common with other countries.

Now the French government cannot use the monetary policy tool! It cannot lower the real interest rate! This means that the French government is left with only one policy tool: the fiscal policy tool. It can increase spending for infrastructure, education and healthcare, but by increasing spending it will also increase the government budget deficit and the public debt (foreign and domestic). Since the government is already highly indebted, this will make things worse.

If the government had the monetary policy tool available, it could use a substantially smaller increase in public debt combined with a considerable reduction in the real interest rate. We see here that, having abandoned the monetary policy tool, the public authorities of a country can very easily find their macroeconomic hands completely tied. To be more precise, they would be in a macroeconomic straitjacket!

Early results of this macroeconomic straitjacket have been seen during the last few years (after 1992) in many countries which, though suffering from excessively high unemployment, do not lower their real interest rates as much or as quickly as they would like to because their governments have already in effect abandoned the monetary policy tool. They had to coordinate with other governments because of ERM (Exchange Rate Mechanism) and because of preparing for EMU (Economic and Monetary Union).

The reader is in addition urged to go to his nearest library or bookshop and check randomly in any number of books in macroeconomics by just seeing the contents and leafing through each of them (no need to read them). He will find that a big part of each book is about monetary policy. This is because monetary policy is an integral part of any economy. To say that a country can exercise control over its macroeconomic performance and not issue its own currency (and not have control over its money supply through its own central bank) is contrary to the science of macroeconomics. It is at least very strange. One could easily say that it is an insult to all the scientists who have studied macroeconomics. One can argue whether the monetary authorities of a country should be concerned only with inflation or with inflation and unemployment and growth, but no one can argue that a country should not have its own central bank (its own currency and monetary policy).

There are 185 countries (members of the United Nations). Are there any two countries that have the same currency (the same central bank)?[1] There are countries using the same language like Australia, New Zealand and the USA. But each country has its own currency issued by its own central bank. This is not a coincidence. There cannot be a country with its own economy (and hence economic policies) without having its own currency (and therefore central bank)! This is why the fifteen former Soviet republics, as soon as they declared that they were becoming independent countries looking after the economic interests of their own people, immediately established their own currencies issued by their own central banks!

It is beyond any reasonable doubt that the removal of the capability to exercise monetary policy specifically suited to the needs of a country, when everything is taken into consideration (the unemployment rate, the growth rate, the inflation rate, etc. specific to the country), will have negative effects

---

[1] In fact, in West Africa there is a very small number of former French colonies using the currency issued in France. Those countries are amongst the countries with the lowest per capita income today.

for the economic well-being and progress of its citizens. In other words, everything else being equal, the citizens of the country will not be able to maximise collectively and individually their economic potential for ever (now, or after five years, or after fifty years or after five hundred years). In the previous sentence we used the phrase 'everything else being equal'. Since we will be using this phrase repeatedly we explain here what exactly is meant.

In economics, when we want to estimate the effects of a policy tool, we assume two situations in the economy. One situation is with the policy tool and the other is without the policy tool and we assume that all other factors in the economy are the same (everything else is equal, or everything else is kept constant). Then we compare the theoretical or empirical results of the two situations and come to our conclusions about the usefulness or otherwise of the policy tool on the economy. In this book we will use this method repeatedly and not only for economic arguments, but also for political and philosophical arguments.

In other words, in order to understand the possible effects of a policy tool or an event or a change in a society, we will assume two situations in the same society: one situation with the change, and the other without the change, assuming that everything else in the specific society (or even in the individual person) is the same (including the time dimension).

We are in effect doing what all positive sciences are doing: in order to analyse the effects of a specific factor we change only that factor and assume that all other factors in the society are kept the same when comparing the two situations.

We now come back to our discussion on page 26 and conclude that Argument No.1 is valid from the point of view of the existing science of macroeconomics, both at the theoretical as well as at the empirical level. According to our grading system established on page 16, we will give grades to our two options or situations as shown in Figure 4.

Figure 4

Argument No. 1 (Macroeconomic)	
Option 1	Option 2
Abandon my currency (adopt EMU – euro) Grade: 0/10,000	Retain my currency (retain monetary policy tool) Grade: 1,500/10,000

Remember that when all the arguments are added, the sum of the options should be the maximum 10,000/10,000 = 1.

4. Argument No. 2 (Macroeconomic)

With EMU (abandoning my currency and adopting a common one), I will still have a monetary policy tool, but this will be applied to all countries (fifteen countries or twenty-five countries, etc.)

EXAMINING THE ARGUMENT

What in effect this argument says is that a new central bank will take care of monetary policy for my country as well as for all of the other countries. Let us examine the argument. It is certainly true that a new central bank will exercise monetary policy for my country. The point is, will this monetary policy be equally effective as when it was exercised specifically and only for my country (everything else being equal)?

There are two things here (equally important):

1. Monetary policy roughly amounts to the management of the liquid assets of a country. If we keep all other factors equal (the skills of the labour force, the natural resources, the laws, the microeconomic conditions, etc.) it is rational to say that, everything else being equal, the management of economic agents (households or human beings) is more effective the smaller the number of the economic agents. In simple words, it is much easier for a central bank to manage the monetary affairs of, say, 83 million German citizens than to manage the monetary affairs of 500 million people. We assume here that the 500 million people are in all aspects (skills, habits, resources, know-how, etc.) identical to the 83 million German people and they differ only in number.

2. Not all economies or countries or people are the same, nor do they remain the same through time. Some countries have highly skilled labour forces (for example, the German labour force) while other countries have less highly skilled labour forces. Some countries like to save a considerable portion of their income (high savings rate), whereas others like to consume and have fun (low savings rate). Some countries are rich in natural resources (Britain in oil, for example) and some countries are poor in natural resources. Some countries have strong manufacturing industry bases (Denmark or Sweden, for example) while other countries have competitive advantages in service industries like tourism (Spain is an example). Some countries have developed considerable industrial know-how (France, for example) and some lag in both know-how and technology. Even if we assume that today all countries are endowed with exactly the same factors of production or characteristics (including even culture, work ethics, history, homogeneity, etc.), we cannot assume that during the next fifty or five hundred years those countries would be experiencing the same economic cycles

(periods of very high growth, or unemployment, or inflation, etc.). To assume that all countries starting today from the same point would experience in the future the same troughs and peaks in the economic cycles at the same time and with the same intensity is not logical and contrary to experience. To assume further that all countries would experience every year in the future (indefinitely for the next 10,000 years say) exactly (or even roughly) the same rate of growth of disposable income per citizen is contrary to human nature and assumes that some invisible hand would try to put the brakes on those countries running fast while pushing forward those countries going slowly. Moreover, it is very doubtful whether any visible or invisible hand has the fundamental right to define the collective rate of growth of the citizens of a country against their will.

To sum up: because countries are different they almost always experience different economic cycles and rates of growth and thus it is better to have different monetary policies than to have one common monetary policy.

We come now to the grading of Argument No. 2 as shown in Figure 5.

Figure 5

Argument No. 2 (Macroeconomic)	
Option 1	Option 2
Abandon my currency (adopt EMU – euro)	Retain my currency (retain monetary policy tool)
Grade: 0/10, 000	Grade: 500/10,000

5. Argument No. 3 (Macroeconomic)

With EMU (abandoning my currency and adopting a common one), I will lose the monetary policy tool specific to my economic needs, but I will retain the fiscal policy tool specific to my economic needs.

EXAMINING THE ARGUMENT

Put simply this argument says that with EMU the citizens of a country will lose their ability to set the interest rates in their own country according to their economy's specific circumstances and needs, but they will retain the fiscal policy tool with which they will be able to manage the macroeconomic characteristics of their country (unemployment rate, inflation rate, growth rate of disposable income per citizen, public debt, etc.)

The short answer to this question is as follows: it is always better to have available two policy tools than only one! To use a simple metaphor: any human being suffering from any illness (serious or not) always prefers to have available two different and completely independent ways of treating the illness than only one! This is equally true regarding the macroeconomic characteristics of a country. Any junior student of economics knows that fiscal and monetary policy tools are two completely different and independent tools, but almost always they are applied in a country in a combination because their combined effect is much greater than if each one was applied without regard to the other!

The grading of this argument is given in Figure 6.

Figure 6

Argument No. 3 (Macroeconomic)	
Option 1	Option 2
Abandon my currency (adopt EMU – euro)	Retain my currency (retain monetary policy tool)
Grade: -500/10,000	Grade: 0/10,000

Note that we have given a negative grade to option 1 because it will lead to negative economic management. We have given zero (0) grades to option 2 because option 2 is supposed to be already available to each country. This ceased to be true for the fifteen countries of the EU after 1992 when the ERM (exchange rate mechanism) and the goal of EMU were announced. It should be stressed here that under option 2 the availability of two policy tools in any country does not guarantee or imply that the tools have been or will actually be used in the future in a correct or in the most efficient way for the benefit of the citizens of that country!

6. Argument No. 4 (Macroeconomic)

> Under EMU (abandoning my currency and adopting a common one with other countries), fiscal policy as a tool of my government will be greatly diminished. Losing a great part of the fiscal policy tool is bad for my future material well-being as well as that of all coming generations.

Fiscal policy refers to how much income tax (direct taxation) plus indirect tax (Value Added Tax or VAT) a government collects per year and how much spending out of those taxes a government performs per year for (among other things): salaries of public sector employees, procurement of materials by government, education, healthcare, unemployment benefits, infrastructure, pensions, support to agricultural products, defence, foreign policy and various transfer payments to members of society which need support (income redistribution).

What, in effect, the argument says is that under EMU the ability of any government to change fiscal policy according to the economic circumstances prevailing for the citizens of a country will be greatly restricted and that this restriction is bad for the well-being of the citizens both in the short term and in the long term.

EXAMINING THE ARGUMENT

In order to make things simpler we will use an example. Suppose that a country, say Italy, is experiencing recession, which means a period of very low or even zero growth of the disposable income per citizen per year, a high unemployment rate and (most probably, but not always) a very low inflation rate. Suppose also that the Italian citizens have chosen already to enter the EMU and, having abandoned their own currency, they are now using a new one together with fourteen other countries. Suffering from high unemployment, the Italians ask their government (the government that they elected) to do something and this something has to be specific for their economic situation. We saw before (Argument No. 1 on page 26) that the monetary policy tool has already been taken away from the Italian government. So it has to use the fiscal policy tool.

Using fiscal policy in a recession means either to decrease taxes or increase government spending (including welfare payments) or both of these. Any of these measures will result in an increase in this year's government budget deficit and this deficit has to be financed by issuing government bonds. However, these government bonds cannot be financed by the Italian government issuing money (putting into circulation a slightly increased amount of currency to temporarily finance the deficit until better times arrive for the Italian people). This means that the bonds will now be considered by the markets on equal footing with the bonds being issued by the big Italian corporations. In economic jargon, the Italian government bonds have ceased being named sovereign government bonds; they are just government bonds. This means that the interest rate that the Italian government (and therefore the Italian citizens) will have to pay for those bonds will be higher than what they would have been before entering the EMU. The Italian government is now being viewed by the markets as a big corporation (as far as issuing bonds is concerned) and this makes it reluctant to issue debt (all other things being equal). This means that there will be less likelihood and capability to decrease taxes or increase spending in difficult times (in recessions).

To come back to the argument, we can say that under EMU the fiscal policy of any government will have lost one degree of freedom and it will be inevitably more restrictive and much less effective regarding income redistribution (transfer payments to weak members of the country). However, we have not established that reducing the scope of the fiscal policy tool is bad for the material well-being of the citizens of a country.

In fact, as far as we know from the science of macroeconomics as well as from experience, we cannot say whether or not reducing the scope of the fiscal policy tools during recessions or inflations (troughs and peaks of the economic cycles) is good or bad or neutral for the economic progress of the people living in a country. Deeper examination of such an argument is beyond the scope of the present discussion but in order to give a grading to the argument we can be sure that the reduction of the scope or the capability of fiscal intervention when a country enters the EMU is not necessarily a bad or a good thing for material progress. So, on purely materialistic grounds (if we consider human beings as equal to animals or plants), one should give for this argument zero grades to both options (we should be indifferent to both options).

However, on further consideration we note that under EMU the citizens of a country lose one more degree of collective economic freedom. They lose part of the capability of their elected government to borrow and spend in recessions or tax and reduce spending in expansions. Losing this one degree of collective economic freedom is contrary to human nature and we have to assume that in the long run this will reduce (even if by an insignificant amount) the happiness (welfare in the most general sense) of the economic agents of a country (the people). Therefore we conclude that, on general grounds (mental as well as materialistic), retaining the currency would be the best option in terms of this argument, and this is reflected in Figure 7.

Figure 7

Argument No. 4 (Macroeconomic)	
Option 1	Option 2
Abandon my currency (adopt EMU – euro)	Retain my currency (retain monetary policy tool)
Grade: 0/10,000	Grade: 0/10,000

Note that in this grading we have not considered happiness as a welfare criterion since we will look in depth at them during the political and philosophical arguments.

7. Argument No. 5 (Macroeconomic)

For long-term growth of per capita income in my country, the real interest rate should be low (the rental cost of capital should be low). With EMU I lose for ever the capability to set the real interest rate in such a way that it influences the capital needs (the rate of capital additions) specific to my country. This is not good for the long-term yearly increases in my income as well as for the future generations.

In simple words, this argument says that, if the citizens of my country need to attract direct capital (for direct investment) in greater amounts than some other countries also participating in the EMU, they will not be able to use the low rental cost of capital as a means to increase investment and that this can only be bad for the long-term growth of their income.

EXAMINING THE ARGUMENT

It is widely accepted that for long-term growth over many decades in the per capita income in any country, an extremely important factor is the rate in yearly additions to its capital stock (machinery, cars, aeroplanes, hotels, factories, roads, schools, etc.). The more direct investment done in a country, the higher will be the long-term growth of the country, other things being equal. One way for a country to induce increased rates of additions to its capital stock is to have relatively low real interest rates. The real interest rate here is the nominal interest rate for raising capital (for borrowing), less the inflation rate. This real interest rate is known also as rental cost of capital and gives roughly the cost for the investors to make additional direct investment. The lower this cost, the greater the investment made in a country over the long run.[2]

Now suppose that a country (say, Greece) wants to raise capital stock in increased quantities. It needs to have real interest rates relatively low. But this possibility will now depend on what the new central bank thinks. The new central bank will have in its mind not only the long-term investment needs of the Greek economy, but also of many other economies. This means that the Greek people will not be able to define their long-term investment (additions to their capital stock by direct investment) using the rental cost of capital as a tool specific for their country. This can only be bad in the long term for any economy, all other things being equal.

A very important distinction should be made here. In some previous arguments we talked about real interest rates as a tool for short-run corrections. Here we are talking of real interest rates as a tool for long-run growth of per capita income in a country. We are talking here about the rate at which an individual will become richer year after year over many decades.

The grading for the argument is in Figure 8.

Figure 8

Argument No. 5 (Macroeconomic)	
Option 1	Option 2
Abandon my currency (adopt EMU – euro)	Retain my currency (retain monetary policy tool)
Grade: 0/10,000	Grade: 100/10,000

---

[2] The underlying reason is that the firms will continue investing in a country up to the point where rc = MPK, where rc is the rental cost of capital and MPK is the marginal product of capital.

8. Argument No. 6 (Macroeconomic)

> Within EMU the Commission in Brussels will be reviewing and approving the next year's budget of the government of my country for ever. This can do only damage to my material well-being as well as that of future generations.

When a country abolishes its currency its central bank cannot spend as it likes wherever it likes. It will be necessary for the budget of, say, the Spanish government to be reviewed, altered if necessary and finally approved by the so-called Commission in Brussels before implementation the next year. And next year will be any year from here to eternity. Here there are, we believe, huge and maybe explosive political and philosophical questions. Those questions will be examined in the relevant political arguments and philosophical arguments about EMU in later chapters. We will try there to find out if anyone (including the United Nations) has the fundamental right to review, make comments on and alter the budget of any sovereign country. Here we will examine only whether this can have any adverse effect on the rate of growth of the wealth of the average citizen of any country from the macroeconomics point of view.

EXAMINING THE ARGUMENT

Let us use here a specific imaginary example of, say, any Spanish government following that rule. The first problem we see here is one of adding one more procedure to the lengthy procedure of designing, submitting for approval and approving the government's budget. Under the new procedure the Spanish government would have to add one more rather big step into all the steps for making comments and approving its budget. It would now be not only the Spanish parliament that would have to make comments on, alter if necessary and approve the government's budget. This additional step means more bureaucracy, lost time and all this is always translated into money (we have always to bear in mind that bureaucracy and lost time mean lost money).

The second problem one could see here is that the comments and possible alterations to the next year's budget of the Spanish government might not reflect the short- as well as long-term interests of the Spanish people. One could see situations where the Spanish people want their government to increase spending next year for education and decrease spending for welfare benefits, but the Commission has the opposite opinion. It is rational here to assume that the citizens know better than anyone else how best to collect money and redistribute it for public goods and transfer payments. (In economic jargon a park is a public good and an unemployment benefit is a transfer payment.)

To be specific the Spanish people have their government, their opposition parties, their parliament, their media, their public opinion, and their scientists (professors, etc., in their universities) to give advice, to comment on and judge the next year's budget. The opinion of the Commission in Brussels and, for that matter, the opinion of any other organisation (say the opinion of the Organisation for Economic Cooperation and Development known as OECD or even the United Nations!) can only complicate and make matters worse.

We are not implying here that the Commission would be biased or not have good intentions or have less scientific knowledge than the community of human beings known as Spanish citizens. We are just using a basic principle that the Spanish people know better than anyone else how to prepare their budget for next year (unless we assume that there are not enough scientists in economics in Spain today, which we believe is not the case!).

There is, however, a third much deeper and, we believe, much bigger problem here. We call this problem 'the loss of interest, loss of initiative and loss of reward problem'.

Everyone knows that for any individual to succeed in an enterprise, interest, initiative and reward are of paramount importance. Regarding the next year's Spanish budget by introducing the element of review and final approval by the Commission in Brussels we introduce a factor that takes away from the Spanish government, opposition parties, parliamentarians, etc., part of their collective interest, initiative and final reward for designing and executing it successfully. The design, examination and approval of the next year's budget is a collective effort and now all those people, with the certainty that the Commission in Brussels will claim the budget for itself, will have less interest in designing it (the budget will not be exclusively their brain child), less initiative (why initiate something if it will be rejected in Brussels?) and less reward if the budget is successful. (If, for example, next year the budget, upon execution, is finally in surplus, Spanish public opinion may not clearly attribute it to the government but assume that the design of the budget was due to some wise men in Brussels!).

It is this third problem which appears to be very important and detrimental for the budget as a macroeconomic policy tool. We are faced here with behavioural problems regarding the budget. Regarding human behaviour, the science of macroeconomics teaches us that it plays a paramount role for the long-term rate of improvement of the well-being of the people. In our case, we are facing an alteration to the human behaviour which goes contrary to human nature (even to collective human nature, i.e. the factors involved in designing and approving the budget). We are going against the fundamental characteristics of efforts by groups of human beings (government, parliament, etc.). Those characteristics tend to show that the less interest, the less initiative, and the less expected reward for a collective effort, the worse the outcome, other things being equal.

Figure 9

Argument No. 6 (Macroeconomic)	
Option 1	Option 2
Abandon my currency (adopt EMU – euro)	Retain my currency (retain monetary policy tool)
Grade: 0/10,000	Grade: 500/10,000

9. Argument No. 7 (Macroeconomic)

Within the EMU my government will be paying fines if at the end of the fiscal year the government budget deficit exceeds 3% of the Gross Domestic Product of my country. Although this appears to instil fiscal discipline in my government, when it is examined in depth from the macroeconomics point of view, it is wrong and will have adverse consequences for the collective material progress of the people of this country.

It is well known that within the EMU any country that at the end of its fiscal year (after actual execution of the government budget) achieves a budget deficit above 3% of the country's Gross Domestic Product (GDP) will be penalised by paying an amount of approximately 0.5% of GDP. For our discussion it is not of interest what the exact amount of the penalty will be, neither is the mechanism for the imposition of the penalty important (whether automatic penalty according to some predetermined rule or penalty on a case by case basis). We will not examine either the colossal question of whether any organisation on earth (and in the universe in general!) has the fundamental right to impose collectively penalties on the people of a sovereign country. This question will be examined in the political and philosophical arguments on the EMU.

EXAMINING THE ARGUMENT

Let us say here a few fundamental things regarding a government budget. The budget of a government is exactly like the budget of any family or firm. It is the yearly sum of all receipts (mainly taxes) minus the yearly expenses (mainly for buying goods and services by the government – the services of its employees and for transfer payments). At the end of the fiscal year (when the government budget has been implemented and receipts and payments have been made), the budget can be in surplus (a positive number algebraically speaking) or in deficit (a negative number algebraically speaking).

When the budget is in deficit, the government has to borrow (usually by issuing government bonds) to finance the deficit. And if the government borrows too much or too often (over many years) then the lenders (the 'markets' in economic jargon) penalise the government by demanding and getting higher interest rates. Any sensible government will try to have its budget either in surplus or at least balanced in the same way that a family tries every year to have a surplus or balance in its yearly budget. However, in difficult times, it is not unusual that a government will be prepared to run a deficit in the same way that a family in difficult times borrows to survive. But this borrowing cannot go on indefinitely, otherwise the government (the country) goes bankrupt. So having a balanced budget or a budget in surplus is a matter for any government of good housekeeping and simple logic and it is not a matter of mastering higher mathematics!

Now let us come to the macroeconomic problems imposed by the procedure of penalising a government running a high budget deficit.

The first problem is one of bureaucracy – more meetings and procedures. The government of a country will have to sit down in Brussels, discuss, argue, counter-argue, be penalised, pay, etc.[3] However, this bureaucratic procedure can be neglected as insignificant regarding the material progress of the citizens of a country.

The second problem is that, with this new procedure, the disciplining of the government with the high deficit is not imposed by the markets through the higher interest rates procedure (as happens now in all countries all over the world). It will be imposed by some committee or some rule! We have here an example where a rule or a committee tries to substitute for the markets! Any macroeconomist will find this contrary to the basic philosophy about free markets! If the economic history of human beings can teach us anything, this is that it is wrong to try to substitute the law of supply and demand (the supply and demand of the government bonds through the acts of millions of economic agents) with some man-made rule or committee! It is obvious here that such a procedure, being contrary to what is termed in economics as 'efficiency of the markets', will lead in the long run to outcomes that will be inferior to those prevailing in developed countries in the world.

A third problem we see here with the penalising procedure is again a behavioural problem for the collective behaviour of the government of a country, which we termed on page 36 as 'the loss of interest, loss of initiative and loss of reward problem'.

We saw this very important behavioural problem on page 35 when a government designs and submits the budget for approval. We see here the same problem, but from the point of view of implementation of the budget. Now a government will perceive that if the budget only has a small deficit or surplus (maybe due to efforts for efficient tax collection, spending curbs, successful laws introduced in parliament, increased economic activity, etc.) the kudos for this collective effort will not accrue to the government wholly, but only partially (if at all). It will be perceived as being the result of the 'wise rules from the Commission'. This will, in the long run, induce great behavioural

---

[3] It would also have to synchronise the end of its fiscal year with other countries' fiscal years, for obvious reasons.

change in any government participating in the EMU. There will be less interest, and hence less efficiency, in the outcome of any budget! This can only be bad for the long-run economic well-being of the people of any country.

A fourth problem is the one that we will call the 'unfairness problem'. It can be described as follows.

Assume that during a certain year the governments of most countries participating in the EMU are within the limits for the deficit (0% to 3% of Gross Domestic Product); one country runs a deficit of say 4% (beyond the limits); and two countries, having tried hard and their citizens having made sacrifices, achieve a budget surplus of, say, +1.5% of their Gross Domestic Product. (It is perfectly possible to achieve a budget surplus in any country and, in fact, there are many countries who have been running budget surpluses regularly during the past hundred years – there is nothing strange or impossible with budget surpluses.)

It is obvious that the principle behind the country running the deficit of 4% of GDP being fined is that the citizens of that country should not live at the expense of the citizens of other countries (which is absolutely correct philosophically). But by the same token, the two countries that ran the surpluses of +1.5% last year should be compensated by all the other countries by being given a fiscal reward (by predetermined rule or committee, etc.) in the form of, say, an amount of money equal to 0.75% of their Gross Domestic Product! But such a rule does not exist within the EMU! Figure 10 grades this argument.

Figure 10

Argument No. 7 (Macroeconomic)	
Option 1	Option 2
Abandon my currency (adopt EMU – euro)	Retain my currency (retain monetary policy tool)
Grade: 0/10,000	Grade: 500/10,000

10. Argument No. 8 (Macroeconomic)

> If I adopt the euro, I will have a currency that will be a first-class currency. It will be like a Mercedes car. I will have always low inflation (and therefore low borrowing costs).

This argument, in simple words, supports the thesis that if medium-sized or small countries abolish their central banks and create a new big central bank, then the resulting currency will be stronger and somehow will induce a lower inflation rate (other things being equal).

EXAMINING THE ARGUMENT

The economic theory does not make any link between the value of a currency or the inflation rate of a country with the size of the liquid assets (money) under management by the central bank. To support such a link is at least unscientific and shows maybe an effort to deceive people who have not studied economics (the great majority of the people in all countries) with arguments that appeal to intuition but are false nevertheless. To mention only a very elementary thing from the subject of international economics, the long-run and short-run behaviour of a currency are the result of thousands of factors at any one moment. Some factors of great importance are the current account of a country, the capital account, the competitiveness of the country and the expectations of the markets, but there is no factor such as the size of the central bank (or equivalently the amount of money under management)!

Empirically, one can understand this by just observing that over the past few decades there have been big economies with relatively stable currencies (like the USA), but there have also been small economies with equally stable currencies (Switzerland, New Zealand and Singapore are some examples).

The same applies to the inflation rate of a country. According to macroeconomic theory there are a number of reasons why a country has high or low inflation rate, the paramount reason being the growth of the money supply, which is at any moment regulated by the central bank of the country. Nowhere in the economic books is there a theory that the larger the size of the liquid assets (money) under management, the lower the inflation rate!

In other words, there is no link between the sum of money under management or the geographical size of a country and its inflation rate. There are big countries with relatively good inflation performance over long periods (the USA is one example), but also small countries with very good inflation performance (Switzerland, Norway, Singapore, Taiwan and New Zealand being some examples). There are also big countries with high inflation performance in the past (Brazil is one example) as well as small countries with high inflation in the past (Nicaragua). The grading for this argument is shown in Figure 11.

Figure 11

Argument No. 8 (Macroeconomic)	
Option 1	Option 2
Abandon my currency (adopt EMU – euro)	Retain my currency (retain monetary policy tool)
Grade: 0/10,000	Grade: 0/10,000

11. Argument No. 9 (Macroeconomics)

One of the roles of a central bank is to be a 'lender of last resort'. Within the EMU the participating countries would have only one lender of last resort. This could increase the chances that, during the next hundred years, a financial meltdown happens (other things being equal).

EXAMINING THE ARGUMENT

The central bank of a country functions, amongst other things, as a lender of last resort to the commercial banks. It provides, in simple words, cash to any commercial bank (it lends at the discount rate). Any bank which, for some reason, needs to borrow money urgently can do so either by asking other commercial banks or by asking the central bank.

Sometimes a commercial bank faces a so-called bank run. Some depositors with the bank believe (rightly or wrongly) that the bank will fail and rush to the bank to withdraw their money before everybody else does so. In the process, the commercial bank may close up shop temporarily or eventually fail. If other banks had lent money to the bank under attack, or they also become the target of their own depositors, the whole process can develop into a generalised bank run (general financial panic), which could theoretically lead to total financial collapse (financial meltdown). This risk is always present in all countries. A bank run happened in 1929 in the USA when many banks failed.

The crucial question here is, For my country, other things being equal, do I have a greater risk of a bank run or even total financial collapse with one central bank (and one currency) or with many central banks (and many currencies)?

Other things being equal, this means that any country will always face a risk (albeit very, very small) of total financial collapse due to, for example, economic mismanagement of some of the commercial banks or even by general economic mismanagement by the public authorities. However, within the EMU, in addition to this risk, I face the following possibility: a bank run or a total financial collapse can start in any of the other participating countries (due to certain banks failing there or the public authorities there mismanaging the system), but since now there will be only one central bank to support the system (not only as a lender of last resort, but also taking other supporting measures such as public statements, etc.)the panic could very easily spread to my country and create bank runs or even total financial collapse in all participating countries.

So the answer here is, yes, within the EMU the chance of total financial collapse is greater (other things being equal) because there will be, in effect, much greater interconnection of all banks. There will be no safety valves for isolating the failed banking system from the others. *Philosophically speaking, a monopolar world can fail much more easily than a multipolar, diverse world (and will develop slower as well from all points of view).* We have italicised the previous sentence because it could prove to be one of the central messages of this book.

Having said that, we must stress that the danger of total financial collapse is today very, very remote (although it exists!). Therefore we will give a very low grade to the argument, as in Figure 12.

Figure 12

Argument No. 9 (Macroeconomic)	
Option 1	Option 2
Abandon my currency (adopt EMU – euro)	Retain my currency (retain monetary policy tool)
Grade: 0/10,000	Grade: 1/10,000

12. Argument No. 10 (Macroeconomics)

In real life in every country there are macroeconomic cycles of economic expansion and contraction (recession). Within the EMU those cycles will be definitely synchronised and this may create deeper recessions than otherwise.

EXAMINING THE ARGUMENT

Past experience all over the world shows that from the macroeconomic point of view each economy follows a wave-like action where the peak of each wave is named expansion (low unemployment, high rate of growth, etc.) and the trough of each wave is named recession (high unemployment, very low or negative rate of growth, etc.). Because of free trade, communications, easy travel, etc., it is natural that the peaks and troughs of one country will influence progressively the peaks and troughs of all other countries on earth. This means that gradually the economic cycles of the various countries will tend to coincide (tend, here, has the mathematical meaning where you can tend to the infinite point, but you will never reach it!).

Now if a country participates in the EMU its economy will have to follow in the future (say for the next thousand years) the same (coinciding) economic cycles with all other participating countries. This is a direct consequence of having exactly the same interest rates with all other countries.

The question is: is forcing the economic cycles of different countries to coincide for ever a good or a bad thing for me and future generations?

The answers are as follows:

1. 'Forcing' the economic cycles to coincide instead of letting them to 'tend' is equivalent to replacing a natural phenomenon (tendency or overlapping) with an unnatural one (man-made force or rule).

Economic history has proven that replacing natural laws with man-made rules is not good in the long to very long run!

2. One country can never have exactly the same cycles with another due to a myriad factors (natural resources, technology, geographic location, culture, etc.). It is much better having each one making its own economic cycles since this will let it exploit its maximum potential over time.

3. From the mathematical-physics point of view, if we imagine the economic cycles as waves with peaks and troughs by synchronising the waves (the oscillations if you wish) we run the risk of resonance with very low troughs (recessions bigger than otherwise!). It is as though we replaced a number of natural waves with a larger man-made tidal wave (or tsunami). We come again here across the philosophical point which we saw first on pages 41-42 that plurality in economics is better than singularity, diversity better than homogeneity.

There is an additional point here: *natural procedures should not be replaced by man-made procedures (even by procedures made by men who are wise or think they are wise)*!

One final point is that the fact that there have been economic cycles in the past does not guarantee that there will be in the future! But whatever happens in the future with respect to the economic cycles is better left to the natural economic forces than to man-made enforcements. My personal view on the matter is that the surest way to perpetuate steep cycles is to try to replace many economic policies with one (and many governments with one eventually!). We will come again to this point in the philosophical chapters. The argument is evaluated in Figure 13.

Figure 13

Argument No. 10 (Macroeconomic)	
Option 1	Option 2
Abandon my currency (adopt EMU – euro)	Retain my currency (retain monetary policy tool)
Grade: 0/10,000	Grade: 10/10,000

13. Argument No. 11 (Macroeconomic)

Only within the EMU would my government be obliged to follow the convergence criteria stipulated by Maastricht. These criteria are very good for the economy of my country.

EXAMINING THE ARGUMENT

From the macroeconomics point of view, there is nothing wrong with the Maastricht criteria as such. However, a country does not need to be within the EMU or even within the EU to meet the criteria. There are many countries in Asia, America and Europe which at this moment meet the criteria. Norway, outside of the EU, meets all of them! Any sensible government is in fact supposed not only to try to follow the criteria but try to follow what science and common sense suggest, i.e. that:

1. The inflation rate in a country should be kept very low.
2. The yearly budget of the government should not be in deficit but rather balanced or even in surplus! (The Maastricht 3% of GDP deficit criterion has no scientific foundation but it is rather an arbitrary point of reference or starting point.)
3. The total government debt (to foreigners and citizens of the country) should be minimal and in the long run zero! (The Maastricht 60% of GDP criterion again has no scientific foundation but it is rather an arbitrary point of reference.)

Any government suggesting that only within the EMU can a country follow correct criteria is just not telling the scientific truth. Additionally, any government suggesting that it follows economic policies advocated by macroeconomic science and by common sense which some outside criterion or organisation or source is imposing on it cannot claim those policies are for the benefit of the people who elected it. It is not worthy of the name of government. Hence the grading in Figure 14.

Figure 14

Argument No. 11 (Macroeconomic)	
Option 1	Option 2
Abandon my currency (adopt EMU – euro)	Retain my currency (retain monetary policy tool)
Grade: 0/10,000	Grade: 10/10,000

There is no right way to do a wrong thing.

Chapter V
MICROECONOMIC ARGUMENTS ON THE EMU

> We report on what has occurred or is anticipated, not on what will make us look good.
>
> Aramark

> We have found a common sense, and it's your money!
>
> Johnny Rotten of the Sex Pistols
on why the 1970s punk band decided
to reunite for a 20th anniversary tour.

> Common sense is not so common.
>
> Voltaire

> You can make even a parrot into a learned political economist – all he must learn are the two words 'Supply' and 'Demand'.
>
> Anonymous

1. What is microeconomics?

In this chapter we will examine arguments for or against abolishing one's currency and adopting one common for many different countries from the point of view of the science of microeconomics.

Microeconomics deals with the choices of individuals, including individual households or individual firms (the word 'micro' means in the Greek language 'small'). Such choices are taking place continuously within our everyday life. Some examples are:

- Will an individual go to university after high school?
- Will an individual marry?
- Will an individual buy a Toyota or Mercedes car?

Firms also are making choices continuously every day:

- Whether to expand output.
- Whether to close down a plant.
- Whether to enter a new type of activity.

Microeconomics is also concerned with relative prices (beef versus chicken, apples versus oranges, holidays abroad or at home) of relatively homogenous products or services. Words such as choice, scarcity, resources, household, individual, producer, consumer, firm, entrepreneur, competition, monopoly, etc. are of paramount importance. Moreover, microeconomics analysis investigates how scarce economic resources are allocated between alternative ends and seeks to identify the strategic determinants of an optimally efficient use of resources.

2. Argument No. 1 (Microeconomics)

> When travelling over the countries of the EU I always lose a small portion of my money when selling my national currency in order to buy the currency of the country I am visiting. When I abolish my currency and adopt a common one with others, this inefficiency will stop.

Today any individual wishing to change his currency to another one loses a small percentage during the transaction changing from one currency to another. The argument says that by having the same currency this transaction cost is eliminated.

EXAMINING THE ARGUMENT

The transaction costs for individuals changing relatively small amounts of money are today a few percentage points of the total amount. This transaction cost reflects the labour cost of the trader doing the transaction, the rental cost of the building or shop where the transaction is made, the cost of depreciation of the machines of the bank, etc. It is true that this transaction will not be needed if I use the same currency over various countries. However the following points are also true:

1. The recent advances in technology (computers, cash machines, office automation, credit cards, debit cards, smart cards, etc.) and many more, which are all coming with great speed, plus the intense competition between the banks in any country will over the medium, long and very long run make this transaction cost insignificant (i.e. the 'spread' between buying and selling a currency even in small quantities will be compressed to near zero). This has already happened for large amounts of money being transferred between banks. (It is estimated by the University of Georgia economist Lawrence H White that new payment technologies have already lowered the cost of wiring money from $20 to 2 cents per transaction.) In many countries all over the world tourists use cash cards that are valid in almost every other currency (i.e. one can have a cash card issued in Japan and withdraw cash from a cash machine in Rome, Paris, New York, etc.) In East Asia today,

experiments are in progress with 'smart cards' (not cash cards) which can be 'loaded' with five different currencies to be used as cash in five different countries!

During late 1996 and early 1997, Mondex, a refillable electronic money card that was backed by MasterCard, holding up to five currencies, was used by thousands of Hong Kong residents. It was the first large-scale experiment by Mondex and it was part of the competition that had just started against Visa cash and other cards that were trying to become a substitute for coins and cash.

In general, in the cashless markets where all countries are tending today with great speed, one expects that the transaction costs between currencies will very soon be practically zero even for small quantities of money.

2. Even if we had the same currency as others in Europe, we would still need to change to other currencies when travelling because there are 185 sovereign countries, unless we assume that we will restrict our travel to certain countries (which we will not because we are in general inclined to travel everywhere). Nevertheless, the argument is graded as in Figure 15.

Figure 15

Argument No. 1 (Microeconomic)	
Option 1	Option 2
Abandon my currency (adopt EMU – euro)	Retain my currency (retain monetary policy tool)
Grade: 500/10,000	Grade: 0/10,000

3. Argument No. 2 (Microeconomics)

When as a consumer I will be touring a country participating in the EMU I will not need to make multiplications to translate the foreign prices into my country's prices, so it will be a little easier for me to find the 'bargains'. When, as a buyer in the procurement department of a private company or a governmental organisation, I search for the offers of vendors from countries participating in the EMU, it will be a little easier for me to compare their prices. This is good for me since it makes my life a little simpler.

EXAMINING THE ARGUMENT

Yes, the argument is generally correct. Participating in the EMU will make the comparison of prices in cross-border shopping a little easier for the citizens of countries participating in the EMU (even if this 'little easier is a very small quantity). There are, however, the following reservations:

There will still be more than 170 sovereign nations with more than 170 currencies to shop with as a tourist.

For professional shopping for an employee in the procurement department of a firm, future market research will be done mainly through computer networks and the Internet and there the translation from all the various foreign currencies to the local currency will be done continuously and online by the pre-programmed computers which will be connected to the dealing room of the foreign exchange market all the time.[1]

The argument is graded in Figure 16.

Figure 16

Argument No. 2 (Microeconomic)	
Option 1	Option 2
Abandon my currency (adopt EMU – euro)	Retain my currency (retain monetary policy tool)
Grade:1,500/10,000	Grade: 0/10,000

4. Argument No. 3 (Microeconomics)

As an individual person or firm, my intertemporal decisions regarding consumption and production are based on the market interest rate. Within the EMU this market interest rate will reflect the supply and demand for funds not only in my country but within all participating countries. Hence my behaviour regarding future consumption and/or production will be influenced by the behaviour of borrowers and lenders in many countries. Since this behaviour of borrowers and lenders is basically different from country to country, I see here the introduction of an unnecessary distortion in the markets. Theory as well as common sense say that distortions in the markets are not good in the medium to the very long run.

EXAMINING THE ARGUMENT

In each country the market interest rate is at any moment defined as the intersection of two curves: the supply of funds curve (money from savers deposited in the banks) and the demand for funds curve (money requested by borrowers for investment, houses, etc.). Knowing at any moment the individual person or firm, the market interest rate makes its choices regarding present and future consumption or production of goods and services.

---

[1] Systematic Internet shopping is already established on the Internet. Large corporations buy materials from all over the world using their website and receive offers electronically. There is also at least one website where a 'virtual world market' is set up and where anyone who wants to buy something electronically posts his 'request for quotes'. The request, using custom software, is sent out to thousands of suppliers and bidders from all countries electronically post their offers.

These choices are very important because they in essence reflect how the individual citizen of a country values the utility of future consumption in relation to abandoning some present consumption and vice versa. They also in essence reflect how the individual businessperson values the utility of future production of goods and services in relation to present production of goods and services. In other words, there is always a trade-off between future and present consumption (of goods and services) as well as a trade-off between future and present production (of goods and services). This trade-off is to a very great degree a function of the individual character. However, this individual character is slightly different from country to country reflecting differing behaviours, customs, values and habits of various groups of people. There is certainly a difference between the behaviour of the average German and the average Spaniard towards sacrificing present consumption for future consumption. This different behaviour is reflected in the prevailing market interest rates (supply and demand of funds for borrowing).

Within the EMU, the market interest rate will be defined by the joint behaviour of the two groups. However, the individuals will continue to be essentially different and this is equivalent to having introduced a microeconomic distortion in both markets regarding intertemporal choices. Theory and experience tell us in principle that we should avoid introducing market distortion whenever possible. In other words we should not interfere with nature unless there are compelling reasons to do so. The conclusion is that within the EMU the intertemporal choices of individuals will be slightly distorted (for ever) and this certainly is not good. However we will not give any grades to this argument since on page 43 we examined a very similar argument from the macroeconomic point of view.

Chapter VI
INTERNATIONAL ECONOMIC ARGUMENTS

> One of the fundamental ways in which we make sense of the world is through comparing and contrasting – looking for similarities and differences.
>
> *Imprimis*

> If the chief problem of economic decisions is one of coping with inevitable ignorance, the task of a science of economics (trying to explain the joint effects of hundreds of thousands of such decisions on men in different positions) is to deal with an ignorance, as it were, of a second order of magnitude, because the explaining economist does not even know what all the acting people know, he has to provide an explanation without knowing the determining facts, nor even knowing what the individual members in the economic system knew about these facts.
>
> Friedrich A Hayek (1899–1992)
> *The Road to Serfdom*
> As quoted in 'Coping with Ignorance',
> *Imprimis*, July 1978, Vol. 7, No.7

1. What international economics is about

International economics is about trade (in goods and services) and investment between citizens and firms of independent nations. The fundamental motives and behaviour of individuals and firms are the same in international trade as in domestic transactions. However, there are special issues raised when economic transactions are between sovereign states. The main themes of international economics are the gains from trade, the pattern of trade, protectionism, the balance of payments, exchange rate determination and the international capital market.

2. Argument No. 1 (International economics)

> If I adopt a currency common with a number of other countries, then I will not face exchange rate fluctuations in my trade in goods and services. This certainly is very good for me as a producer of goods or services or as a trader.

EXAMINING THE ARGUMENT

Put simply, the argument says that if I somehow fix the exchange rates of my trading partners with the exchange rate of my currency, I will have trading advantages or, at least, I will not suffer the disadvantages associated with continuously fluctuating exchange rates. The argument seems very plausible to anyone who has not studied international economics and also appeals to intuition. However, the argument about fixed exchange rates is not supported by the science and we believe it is philosophically wrong.

The first thing that one should remember is that, even if a few countries fix their exchange rates one with another, they would still have to trade with a great number of other countries in different currencies. We are facing today a world where trade is being done increasingly with all nations on earth and that trade, progressively and in the long run, will be done with countries from all continents (Asia, Africa, America, Oceania and Europe). To assume that because I fix my exchange rate with that of my main trading partners I will avoid exchange rate fluctuations in my trade is self-defeating and very dangerous.

It is self-defeating because every country is trading increasingly with all other countries (not only with the EU countries) and the trade with non-EU countries is definitely going to increase much faster than up to now. In fact, all economists agree that growth in trade will come in the next century not from within the EU, but from the so-called emerging markets. However, the main problem is that, by fixing the exchange rate with other countries, traders, producers and individuals will be biased in the long run towards those EMU-participating countries and they will tend to ignore or neglect or underestimate the trading opportunities presented by the rest of the world.

Secondly, the argument that fixed exchange rates are superior to floating exchange rates is not supported by the economics literature. Fixed exchange rates prevailed in almost all countries until 1973, but after 1973 most countries in the world adopted floating exchange rates. Each system of exchange rates (fixed or flexible exchange rates) has its pros and cons, but both economic theory and evidence suggest that floating exchange rates are either superior or at least as good as fixed exchange rates. Since the arguments for and against fixed exchange rates are crucial regarding the EMU, we present them here below very briefly as they appear in the literature.

Short-term policies

For fixing the short-term problems of a country fiscal policy is more effective under fixed exchange rates whereas monetary policy is more effective under flexible rates. On theoretical grounds we cannot say that one tool is preferable to the other. However, we have to note here that fiscal policy in the long run tends to create more interventionist and bigger government sectors than monetary policy, other things being equal. Whether bigger or smaller government sectors as a percentage of Gross Domestic Product of a country is a good or a bad thing is beyond the scope of this book but we feel that the tendency in the twenty-first century will be for smaller public sectors and bigger private sectors for all countries. Hence, on the grounds of general tendencies in all countries, we have to note that fixing the exchange rate is going against the tide.

Uncertain prices for exporters-importers

For the traders of any country uncertain prices due to exchange rate volatility are a destabilising factor. On the other hand, almost all traders today buy 'forward' foreign currencies and use other hedging techniques available in the capital markets to minimise the risks.

It should be stressed here that, on theoretical grounds, the exchange rate fluctuations should be going, in the long run, upwards and downwards to the same extent. So, for example, for an exporter a currency overvaluation during one year may be a problem, but this can become a currency depreciation during another year and then is a benefit. In the long run, other things being equal, a currency should go up or down equally and have a neutral effect overall on the traders.

On empirical grounds, one could mention that after 1973, when in almost all major countries in the world flexible rates were introduced, there has not been noticed any consistent decrease in the growth rates of the volume of world trade despite two adverse energy shocks. Hence floating rates do not impede trade growth.

Price stability

Since monetary policy is much more suitable as a policy tool (and under more control) with a flexible rate regime and since inflation in the long run is a monetary phenomenon, we believe that there should be more price stability over the long run under a flexible rate regime for any country. Regarding imported inflation due to a depreciating currency, we see no reason why a country should have a depreciating currency (assuming that 'everything else is equal') and not a randomly fluctuating currency (causing random deflation – lowering prices of some goods – as well as inflation).

Demand or supply shocks – stability

Regarding stability to external or internal shocks in the demand or supply sector, the following should be noted. In general, flexible exchange rates provide more stability to an open economy (an economy with trade) in relation to disturbances that originate in the foreign sector, such as autonomous changes in exports and imports. Fixed exchange rates provide more stability to the open economy in the presence of disturbances that originate in the domestic flow of spending, such as autonomous changes in domestic investment, consumption and government spending.

Accordingly, there are pros and cons regarding stability for each regime. We would like, however, to note that a flexible rate may be more appropriate (regarding stability) for an individual country due to the following:

1. Since an individual country is one and the plan is that there will be several countries in the EMU the probabilities are (statistically

speaking) that during the next decades or centuries disturbances will originate more frequently from the 'other countries' participating in the EMU than from domestic factors. For example, considering the Netherlands' population (labour force, consumers) or geographical size (natural resources, energy, etc.), the chances are that disturbances will originate more frequently in the other participating countries than within Holland itself (always considering the statistical point of view).

2. The government of any country obviously has more control and more policy options in order to face and resolve internal shocks while it cannot exercise control over what is happening in other countries. Hence, any government needs something to absorb outside disturbances. This something is more readily available under flexible exchange rates than under fixed rates.

The exchange rate as a microeconomic signal
We left for last an argument which we did not meet in the economics literature but which we believe is by far the most important argument against fixing the exchange rate even with your best friends and trading partners!

The exchange rate of a currency being the 'price' of the currency in terms of all other currencies is continuously signalling to the economic agents (individuals, households, firms, traders and governments) the resultant of thousands of economic forces, efficiencies and inefficiencies. As such we believe that a floating rate can be used as an early indicator to both government and individuals for economic action (or inaction). It can signal very effectively inefficiencies (and even wrong economic policies) and can be used as a signal for structural change in a country. Any countries participating in the EMU will automatically lose this extremely effective microeconomic (and why not macroeconomic) indicator specific for the efficiencies and inefficiencies of the country. The economic agents and the political opposition parties of any participating country will lose one very important and very effective source of information about the 'health' of the economy of their particular country. And it is obvious that political parties and individuals in any country make better economic assessments and decisions both at individual as well as collective level the more information they have available in their hands. Moreover, if more information is more wealth, then less information is less wealth, especially in today's information society. Suppose, for example, that the people of a country (including their government) inside the EMU for some reason become suddenly less productive than the people in other countries inside the EMU. With flexible exchange rates this inefficiency would be reflected sooner or later in their currency. But having lost their own currency, they will have to realise this inefficiency exclusively from other micro or macro indicators which may come later (for example, unemployment, etc.). They would have thus lost one crucial indicator about their own economic health and efficiency.

From the foregoing discussion it is apparent that 'fixing' the exchange rates does not 'fix' the problem! Or, to put it more simply, he who believes that by fixing the exchange rate of his currency he will hide his individual inefficiencies is reminiscent of a shopkeeper in a free market who believes that when losing his customers he can fix the problem by arbitrarily fixing the price of the goods he is selling. The truth of the matter is that in competitive and free markets the price of anything can go up as well as down and no man-made rule can change this! The relative merits of the argument are shown in Figure 17.

Figure 17

Argument No. 1 (International economics)	
Option 1	Option 2
Abandon my currency (adopt EMU – euro)	Retain my currency (retain monetary policy tool)
Grade: 300/10,000	Grade: 700/10,000

3. Argument No. 2 (International economics)

In many instances a depreciating or an appreciating currency can be used as an instrument for solving economic problems in the short run. By not having my own currency, I lose this instrument specific for the economic circumstances of my country.

EXAMINING THE ARGUMENT

Suppose that a country suffers very high unemployment. One of the ways that the government can try to face the problem in the short term is by promoting (pushing) exports of goods and services to other countries by letting its currency depreciate. However, if the country is within the EMU it does not have its own currency any more. So it will not be able to use this tool unless all other participating countries have the same problem to the same degree and all agree to use the exchange rate as a short-term policy tool (which is very unlikely). We see here that any country abandoning its own currency abandons at the same time the exchange rate policy tool for promoting exports of goods and services (from manufacturing to tourism to transportation) and thereby reducing unemployment in the short run. For the same reasons the exchange rate cannot be used any more for reducing 'imported' inflation or even cooling down the economy of any particular country if this country does not have its own currency.

However, we have to note the following: the exchange rate can be used as a policy tool for a country only in the short run. It cannot solve the long-run (structural') problems.

INTERNATIONAL ECONOMIC ARGUMENTS

Whether it is desirable to use such a policy tool, and how and when it should be used are value judgements and hence debatable for any country. What is not debatable is that a country, by not having a currency specific for its economic circumstances, is abandoning for ever the exchange rate as a policy tool.

Figure 18 gives the grading for this argument.

Figure 18

Argument No. 2 (International economics)	
Option 1	Option 2
Abandon my currency (adopt EMU – euro)	Retain my currency (retain monetary policy tool)
Grade: 0/10,000	Grade: 10/10,000

4. Argument No. 3 (International economics)

If I do not have my own currency I will not be able to know the balance of payments position of my country. This is no good because I will not be in a position to know if year on year my country is becoming collectively wealthier or not.

EXAMINING THE ARGUMENT

The balance of payments of any country for the past year is the algebraic sum of the current account (roughly, trade in goods and services plus long-term investment to or from abroad plus official receipts and private profits to and from abroad) plus the capital accounts (short-term or 'hot' money in or out of the country basically for buying government bonds and minority shares). This algebraic sum is always equal and opposite in sign to the change of foreign reserves of the country. Within the EMU no country will have foreign reserves specific to that country so there will be no balance of payments for the country. There will be no meaning in the phrase 'balance of payments for Germany', for example.

However, the indicator of total (collective) wealth accumulation for any country is not its balance of payments. It is the current account of the country that indicates to the citizens of the country if their net worth has increased or decreased during the past year. This indicator (the current account) will continue to exist even within the EMU, one hopes.

55

Figure 19

Argument No. 3 (International economics)	
Option 1	Option 2
Abandon my currency (adopt EMU – euro)	Retain my currency (retain monetary policy tool)
Grade: 0/10,000	Grade: 0/10,000

5. Argument No. 4 (International economics)

Within the EMU part of the foreign debt of all participating countries will in essence become 'internalised' and the rest will be claimed equally from everybody regardless of which government created the debt originally. This amounts to an unauthorised transfer of burden.

EXAMINING THE ARGUMENT

The government of any country has accumulated over recent decades a certain total amount of debt. This is called the government debt and, practically speaking, it is the total amount of outstanding government bonds and loans. Some of these outstanding government bonds and loans are in the hands of citizens and constitute 'internal debt' (claims by citizens on their own government), and some are in the hands of citizens of many other countries and constitute 'external debt' (claims by foreigners on the government of the country).

There are countries that are heavily indebted at the moment (Belgium is an example with a total government debt of around 150% of GDP, i.e. 150% of the total value of goods and services produced by Belgium within one year) and there are countries that are less heavily indebted at the moment (Germany, for example, has a total government debt of around 62% of GDP).

Now let us assume that both Belgian citizens and German citizens have abolished their own currency and they have now a common one called the euro. The foreign debt of the Belgian government owned by Germans (citizens or banks of Germany holding Belgian bonds and loans) will not show as foreign debt in the balance sheet of the new central bank in Frankfurt. This part of the debt will be considered by the central bank as an 'internal' debt owed by a big corporation–organisation (the Belgian government) to various holders of euros (German as well as Belgian citizens).

However, any outstanding loans or bonds of the Belgian government being held by anyone not in the EMU (for example, a Japanese citizen) will be still considered as 'foreign debt' by the new central bank. But, in the calculations, policies and balance sheet of the new central bank there will be only one foreign debt item common for both the Belgians and the Germans!

In other words, the foreign debt of any participating country in the EMU will, in practical terms, be distributed equally to all participants whereas up to now it was on the shoulders of those who created it!

From the moral point of view, there are people who are prepared to say that 'if a Belgian carries permanently on his shoulders a debt of 150 kilograms and a German carries a debt of 62 kilograms, why not distribute equally this weight so that from now on each one is carrying an equal debt of $150/2 + 62/2 = 106$ kilograms?'

However, this approach is economically wrong because it creates the so-called 'free rider problem'. When a ride is free everybody tries to get a ride on the bandwagon without realising that someone has paid to create and run the bandwagon. It also creates the mentality that 'I get a loan today and you will pay back part of my loan', which I believe is economically wrong, although morally the practice can be acceptable provided that my partner agrees.

The foregoing discussion concerns existing debt. But equally important is the fact that any debt created in the future by any EMU-participating government and being held by citizens of any other country not participating in the EMU will put equal pressure on the euro for all citizens of the EMU zone. For example, if after ten years the German government issues new debt (in bonds or loans from a bank), this debt, unavoidably, when it is cashed in by, for example, an American, creates pressure on the new central bank managing the euro. But since the Belgians are also using the same currency they will bear part of the debt pressure. In other words, any debt created in the indefinite future by any EMU country will fall equally on the shoulders of all the others.

The problem with the system is not a moral one. It is a problem of practical attitude and mentality. It is well established in economics that we can have free rides, but only when there are compelling reasons in a society to have available a free 'public good'. We do not need to have free rides without good reason. It is also well established in human history that human beings and human communities make faster progress when they know that they will be responsible for their own actions only and not for the actions of others or other communities. This should not be confused with humanitarian assistance, which is a voluntary, temporary case-by-case act (and which I am deeply for).

The argument's grading is given in Figure 20.

Figure 20

Argument No. 4 (International economics)	
Option 1	Option 2
Abandon my currency (adopt EMU – euro)	Retain my currency (retain monetary policy tool)
Grade: 0/10,000	Grade: 300/10,000

INTERNATIONAL ECONOMIC ARGUMENTS

6. Argument No. 5 (International economics)

Only relatively large countries should have their own currency. Small countries like Greece, Portugal, Ireland, Denmark, Sweden, Finland, etc. should not have their own currency because it is impractical.

EXAMINING THE ARGUMENT

The argument is answered in the science of international economics under the heading 'optimum currency area'. If you have an 'economy' you can have a currency however small the country. Even city states like Hong Kong or Singapore (both of them are big cities) have their own currencies and their economies are extremely successful. They trade a great part of their products and services with the rest of the world, the growth rates of their Gross Domestic Product have been for the past twenty years roughly three times that of any West European country and the income per head of the population is one of the ten highest in the world today. Any country larger than a city can have its own currency without any adverse effect on the rates of wealth creation and wealth accumulation by its citizens, so we can grade the argument as in Figure 21.

Figure 21

Argument No. 5 (International economics)	
Option 1	Option 2
Abandon my currency (adopt EMU – euro)	Retain my currency (retain monetary policy tool)
Grade: 0/10,000	Grade: 0/10,000

7. Argument No. 6 (International economics)

Every government, when issuing paper money, benefits some real resources that are known in economics under the term 'seignorage'. If I participate in the EMU the government of my country (and therefore myself) are losing this seignorage.

EXAMINING THE ARGUMENT

To highlight the argument we will use an example. When the central bank of Belgium creates 1 Bf (Belgian franc) in the domestic economy of Belgium, practically no interest is paid on cash and the central bank (i.e. the government of Belgium) benefits by 1 Bf of resources for every 1 Bf created). If that 1 Bf were invested it would earn, say, i% per annum, so i/100Bf represents the income flow generated by creating 1Bf.

In the international monetary system the Belgian government does pay interest for its debt issued (money) but because this debt is short term and liquid, it is usually below the long-run rate of return on investment. If the latter is i_L%, but the government pays i% on its own money debt, resources of i% accrue to the foreign holders of Belgian currency and (i_L-i)% to the Belgian central bank (i.e. to the Belgian government and hence to the Belgian people).

Within the EMU the Belgians will not have a central bank and all the seignorage (profit from issuing paper currency) would accrue to the new central bank in Frankfurt. So the answer to the argument is that for any country abolishing its currency there will be loss of the seignorage (profit to the central bank from issuing currency). However, we will assume that the new central bank in Frankfurt will be distributing each year any profits from seignorage to all the participating countries in some 'just way'. It should be also noted that the annual profits from seignorage are a very small percentage of any country's GDP, so we will give no grades to the argument, as in Figure 22.

Figure 22

Argument No. 6 (International economics)	
Option 1	Option 2
Abandon my currency (adopt EMU – euro)	Retain my currency (retain monetary policy tool)
Grade: 0/10,000	Grade: 0/10,000

8. Argument No. 7 (International economics)

If I abandon my currency there will be costs to the banks, insurance companies, government agencies, etc., of my country in replacing paper forms, computer programs, machines, etc., and these costs finally will be extracted from me.

EXAMINING THE ARGUMENT

The answer to the argument is, yes, there will be costs for any country abandoning its currency translated into man hours, materials or equipment. However, the costs in proportion to the GDP and especially if one distributes those costs to the next, maybe, one thousand years are negligible and hence we will not give any grade to the argument in Figure 23.

Figure 23

Argument No. 7 (International economics)	
Option 1	Option 2
Abandon my currency (adopt EMU – euro)	Retain my currency (retain monetary policy tool)
Grade: 0/10,000	Grade: 0/10,000

9. Argument No. 8 (International economics)

Within the EMU there will be no official reserves owned specifically by my country (including Germany). I feel that this is not good for my material well-being.

EXAMINING THE ARGUMENT

Materially, the absence of reserves specific for any country does not alter for better or worse the fortunes of the citizens of any country. However, the official reserves are used as a 'war chest' and for enforcing legal tender. Since both these subjects are political (and philosophical) and not economic, we will examine them in the political arguments chapter and grade the argument as in Figure 24.

Figure 24

Argument No. 8 (International economics)	
Option 1	Option 2
Abandon my currency (adopt EMU – euro)	Retain my currency (retain monetary policy tool)
Grade: 0/10,000	Grade: 0/10,000

Chapter VII
POLITICAL ARGUMENTS

> Minds are like parachutes – they function only when open.
>
> Aramark

> Half the world is composed of people who have something to say and can't, and the other half have nothing to say and keep on saying it.
>
> Robert Frost

> The bad thing about good things is that they come to an end; and the good thing about bad things is that they also end.
>
> Annamaria Rabate Cervi

> If we ignore our spiritual needs, then we may also lack a sense of purpose in life, and have no profound sense of why we are here. We may, without realising it, be very afraid of death.
>
> *Imprimis*

1. A few simple things about politics and countries

Politics, very roughly, is the way a particular group of people tries to govern itself. Politics is concerned about the way people issue laws for themselves (in a legislative body or parliament or congress) and execute the laws (executive body or government) and how they try to impose justice to any one of their group that violates the laws (judicial system).

A country contains a group of people that tries to govern itself without being subjected to punishment, persecution, etc., from other groups of people unless it goes to war with them. Hence, a country is necessarily sovereign and independent from the will of other countries. We often talk indiscriminately of a country or a nation.

The word 'nation' is equivalent for our purposes to a country but should not be confused with the word 'nationality'. There can be many nationalities in a country, but if they follow some common laws, way of life and sense of purpose then they all constitute a country (or nation).

Today, there are 185 nations (or countries). They are all members of an organisation named the United Nations (UN) and they all share one common characteristic. Each member of the UN is sovereign, i.e. it can govern itself as it likes as long as it does not go to war with others.

The size of a country is not related to sovereignty. A country can be very small (Singapore is just a city), small (Greece is a small country), medium sized (Germany), large (Argentina is an example) or huge (China is an example).

2. Argument No. 1 (Political)

> If I abolish my currency then the government of my country will be paying huge fines if in any one year the budget deficit exceeds 3% of GDP. I feel that this is not good for me and future generations from the psychological point of view.

EXAMINING THE ARGUMENT

On page 37 we saw the financial-material aspects of disciplinary action taken against any government in the EMU. We saw there that the penalties mechanism tries to replace the discipline imposed by the free markets on governments with a man-made mechanism and we concluded that in the long run the man-made mechanism is inferior to the market mechanisms from the material wealth point of view. However, human beings have also psychological needs which are extremely important. Human beings do not need only food, water and shelter (the material needs that are everything for animals). They need also things such as love, freedom, dignity, sense of purpose, identity, feeling of belonging to a community, entertainment, scientific knowledge and many other things. In fact, the history of humans is one of paying progressively more attention to the needs of mind (and soul, if such exists) than to the needs of body.

Now let us see what the implications are of a government being disciplined by others in an imaginary example. Suppose that French citizens have abolished their currency (the French franc) and have adopted the euro and that after x years in the EMU their government's budget deficit exceeds 3% of GDP. Then a huge financial penalty will be imposed on their government and therefore on the French citizens (since the French citizens pay for their government through direct and indirect taxation). The French government will suffer the indignity of paying fines, not to the French people but to others. But indignity for the French government necessarily means indignity for the whole of the French people since the government represents the whole of society (it is another matter, irrelevant for our discussion, whether this representation is successful or correct or not). But dignity is one of the fundamental things that an individual needs from life.

The second huge injustice with the concept of punishment is about democracy. If the French government makes mistakes or does not perform well, who should be the one finally to discipline and punish the French government? The only body that should be entitled to discipline the French government should be the French public with their vote. At least, this is what is supposed to happen in a democracy. Unfortunately, with this concept of discipline, in the long run the mentality that will be instilled in the French people will be that they and their political parties, parliament, media, etc. are not necessary for the successful functioning of their government, at least regarding the very important matter of budget deficit. We have here the seeds of the destruction of a democracy whereby the people elect their government and if the government is unsuccessful they punish it with rejection at the ballot box. Whether less democracy is a good or a bad thing is a normative issue but we assume that human beings like in general to have as much control as possible over their own affairs so we feel that less democracy will in the long run make the French citizen more unhappy.

The third huge problem with this disciplinary action concept concerns collective freedom or sovereignty. In particular, and still using our imaginary situation of the French government paying fines, we raise the following point: apart from the individual freedom of the French citizens there exists their collective freedom, the ability of French society to follow through time as a group any peaceful path and way of life without being punished by anyone.

This collective freedom is simply known as sovereignty and is the cornerstone of the existence of any country. This collective freedom does not exist for sub-areas of countries. It exists only for individual countries as whole units and is the building block of the organisation known as the United Nations.

No one can imagine, for example, Argentina or Japan or Malaysia or Canada or even Singapore paying fines to other governments for the way they run their own budgets and affairs in general, regardless whether the implementation of their budget is correct or not. We see here that by simply accepting the possibility of punishment (automatic or not) the French people are immediately losing their sense of collective freedom or sovereignty. Collective freedom is a recognised complement of individual freedom and hence loss of collective freedom means less total freedom. Whether less freedom is a bad or good thing is again a normative issue but, considering human nature, we will assume that people like to have as much freedom as possible, so less freedom means less welfare (in the more general sense) and hence less happiness. The question now arises: what is the value of happiness? The answer is that no one can calculate it, but I believe that any political or economic system should strive to achieve the maximum happiness for its individual members. Material wealth creation (cars, food, house, clothes, etc.) is a necessary but not sufficient condition for the happiness of human beings. People need to be as wealthy as possible, but they also need to be proud, with dignity (and not humiliated unnecessarily), have a sense that they control their own government and have the maximum available amount of freedom. But we saw before that disciplinary action by others means humiliation, less democracy (less sense of control of our own government) and complete abandonment of collective freedom.

Concluding this argument we can say that abolishing one's currency means less happiness for ever and this is an extremely important point. Its importance is reflected in the grading of Figure 25.

Figure 25

Argument No. 1 (Political)	
Option 1	Option 2
Abandon my currency (adopt EMU – euro)	Retain my currency (retain monetary policy tool)
Grade: 0/10,000	Grade: 2,000/10,000

3. Argument No. 2 (Political)

Without its own currency, my country is not sovereign, neither is it independent. This makes me unhappy and will have huge consequences for the material as well as mental well-being of all future generations.

EXAMINING THE ARGUMENT

It is beyond any reasonable doubt that no country can be independent or sovereign without having its own currency and central bank. In order to understand this point one would normally have to know the fundamentals of the science of economics. However, for the simplicity of our discussion we can prove that with the following simple statements (facts):

- In all cases in the past where there was a currency merging this has been always accompanied by the peaceful or violent acquisition, or the dissolving of the existence, of the country as an independent and sovereign entity.
- Today, out of 185 independent and sovereign nations, no two countries have the same currency. An exception is a very small number of West African and very poor francophone countries which are former French colonies whose currency is the French franc issued by the French central bank. It is questionable whether those countries are truly independent or sovereign.
- The former fifteen Soviet Republics, when they declared their independence and sovereignty, immediately created their own central banks and issued their own currencies.
- Can anyone imagine an organisation suggesting to the American people that their central bank should cease to exist, that a new central bank will be created, say, in South Korea, issuing a new currency for Americans, South Koreans and Japanese, but that nevertheless no one in America should worry? The American nation would, according to the suggestion, continue to be an independent and sovereign country with its own economic policies. Would the American government or the American Congress accept

such a proposition as true? Would they think that their country was still independent and sovereign? Would the Japanese government accept a similar suggestion regarding the currency of the Japanese people? Would, in fact, any South American or Asian or African government accept that, having lost the ability to issue its currency, it would continue to be an independent and sovereign country?

- It is a fact of life in the science of economics that you cannot have independent economic policies unless you have your own money supply, your own interest rate, your own central bank and therefore your own currency. Without having a specific and exclusive central bank and currency you are not an independent or sovereign country. You can be a province or region, a prefecture, a county or a state, but you cannot be a country. By definition, countries are independent and sovereign entities able to design and apply their own economic policies according to the will of their people (if they are democracies). Provinces, regions, prefectures, counties or states can have some specific economic policies but those policies are not independent. They are dependent and constricted by the general policies and laws of the country.

- What is the legal status of a currency common to many governments? If there are some common currencies circulating which government is responsible to tackle a currency problem?

- Without its own exclusive currency no country has foreign reserves (including Germany). But the foreign reserves are, amongst other things, the war chest of any country in case it is attacked by others. So, without foreign reserves no country can go to war independently of the other participants. Hence, it is no longer an independent country (it is not, in fact, a country!).

But having established that, for example, Germany, when abolishing its currency (the Deutschmark), ceases to be an independent and sovereign country, this does not automatically and necessarily lead to the conclusion that Germans will be worse off! There are many individuals who would be willing to give up independence and sovereignty in exchange for a wealthier life. But will the German citizens be wealthier when they abandon their own currency, the mark? We have seen in previous chapters that, from the economics science point of view and from experience, there is no reason to believe this and that in the long run rather the opposite is true ceteris paribus (other things being equal). Hence, German citizens will be left with the complete loss of their sovereignty, i.e. the complete loss of their collective freedom. This loss of collective freedom will not last for five or ten years. It is supposed to last for ever! Assuming that humans value their collective freedom (their ability to go through time peacefully as a community the way they choose to go), this loss of freedom will make them in the long to very long run unhappy or, to be more precise, less happy than if they had kept their collective freedom.

The importance of this issue is reflected in the grading of Figure 26.

Figure 26

Argument No. 2 (Political)	
Option 1	Option 2
Abandon my currency (adopt EMU – euro)	Retain my currency (retain monetary policy tool)
Grade: 0/10,000	Grade: 3,000/10,000

4. Argument No. 3 (Political)

Our government during the past few years, in order to prepare the budget deficit, total public debt and inflation rate for compliance with the targets of entering the EMU, has taken harsh but necessary measures that are good for the finances of the country. I feel that this is good for me, even if it is a one-off measure.

EXAMINING THE ARGUMENT

The argument has two sides. It is correct because many governments, by trying to meet the Maastricht criteria for entering the EMU, have been able to apply some difficult policy measures.

It is also wrong because a government should always try to do what is right for the people who elected it, regardless of Maastricht or the EMU. If an executive measure or the passing of a law is beneficial for the country, it should always be undertaken by any government that respects its name, regardless of any outside criteria. Again, if an executive measure or the passing of a law is not beneficial for the country, it should not be undertaken by any government. Politicians should always remember that they are elected by the people to do what is right for the people and not because others are imposing criteria on them.

In order to make this point clearer, one could refer to an item of news in a newspaper of 23 January 1997 which said that the government of a member country was very happy to see interest rates being eased. Many of that government's hopes, according to the press report, rested with lower interest rate bills in order to bring the economy into compliance with the terms of the planned launch of the single European currency in 1999. The government of the member country estimated that it would save $12.6 billion a year in debt servicing costs for every percentage fall in the discount rate.

The question that any rational individual should ask when reading this is: were it not for the EMU, would the government not try to save $12.6 billion a year in debt servicing? In other words, without the EMU would the government not try to do what is correct and beneficial for the people who elected it? Why did it ask the people for their votes (and got them)? If, on the other hand, those measures are not beneficial for the people, and the government normally would not take them without the EMU, then why is it taking them now? To harm the people who elected it? See, now, Figure 27.

Figure 27

Argument No. 3 (Political)	
Option 1	Option 2
Abandon my currency (adopt EMU – euro)	Retain my currency (retain monetary policy tool)
Grade: 0/10,000	Grade: 0/10,000

5. Argument No. 4 (Political)

Many governments are cheating in order to appear at the end of 1997 to satisfy the Maastricht criteria. I feel that this is not good for the creation of a new currency.

EXAMINING THE ARGUMENT

It is a fact that many governments are fudging and cooking the figures. Some elementary examples are:

- In order to reduce the budget deficit the assets of state-owned companies are included in the government books, but not their associated liabilities.
- Gold reserves owned by the central bank (i.e. the people of a country) are sold.
- Pension liabilities are government obligations as surely as Treasury bonds. However, they are not included in the total government department calculations. If they were included they would almost double the total debt of many governments.
- Raising of special taxes (named 'Eurotax') just in order to get the numbers right for only one moment.

It is beyond any reasonable doubt that the Maastricht criteria were being fudged almost everywhere by accounting methods which would lead to jail terms for any private company or organisation employees.

However, my point is not what happens in the short run. It is what happens in the long run, i.e. in the indefinite future. Suppose that an invader came tomorrow from another continent and occupied with his army all the countries in the continent of Europe. The first thing that the invader would do in order to stay permanently in Europe would be to abolish all currencies and oblige everybody to use his currency. The invading forces would not ask about any satisfaction of Maastricht criteria. They would simply give their new currency to everybody. What the citizens of the various countries would have to consider in this hypothetical situation of an occupying force is not just the initial shock of how they got to have a new common currency (although these are also things that greatly matter). The main point would be the long-term consequences for both their material progress (to make progress as fast as possible) and their attaining of the maximum possible state of happiness.

Therefore I will not give any grades to this argument in Figure 28.

Figure 28

Argument No. 4 (Political)	
Option 1	Option 2
Abandon my currency (adopt EMU – euro)	Retain my currency (retain monetary policy tool)
Grade: 0/10,000	Grade: 0/10,000

Chapter VIII
PHILOSOPHICAL ARGUMENTS

> We can easily forgive a child who is afraid of the dark; the real tragedy of life is when men are afraid of the light.
>
> Plato, Greek philosopher
4th century BC

> If we don't speak against what we feel is wrong, then often our silence may be interpreted as agreement with what was said or done.
>
> *Imprimis*

1. Philosophy as a discipline

Philosophy is probably the most important of the disciplines of human activity. The word philosophy comes from the Greek words 'philo' which means 'friend', and 'sophia' which means 'wisdom'. As a mental activity, philosophy is at the roots of higher mathematics and every other positive or theoretical science. As a discipline, philosophy is concerned with the most fundamental questions (many of which remain unanswered) such as:

- What is the meaning of life?
- Should a human being try to maximise wealth or happiness or both of them? Is wealth related positively or negatively to happiness or is it independent of happiness?
- Why does the universe exist at all?
- Are there natural rights for man such as liberty, property and pursuit of happiness, or are all rights made by human laws and as such are not natural, but under the control of those who created the laws, i.e. society at large?

In the second part of this book we will examine a number of philosophical arguments related to the EU. Those arguments are extremely important and constitute the main reason why this book was written.

In this chapter we will examine only one or two philosophical arguments regarding the so-called EMU.

2. Argument No. 1 (Philosophical)

Wouldn't the world be better if instead of having 180 currencies we had only four or five currencies and then, at a later stage, only one currency?

The argument is extremely serious and is part of the following more general argument: 'Wouldn't the world be a better place if, instead of 185 different countries (members of the United Nations), there was only one country and one government? Wouldn't we thus avoid all wars, spend nothing on defence and all be better off?' I will attempt to examine this more general argument later in this book and I will try to give my point of view on this matter, which in effect is the core subject of this book.

Here, however, I will attempt to examine only the 'narrow' argument regarding currencies.

EXAMINING THE ARGUMENT

We saw in Chapters Four through to Seven that from the point of view of the science of economics the avoidance of transaction costs is a negligible advantage compared to the advantages that a nation gains when it has its own currency. We saw that, according to theory and experience, each economy should have its own currency (optimum currency areas) provided that the economy is at least the size of a city (like Singapore or Hong Kong). We saw also that the size of an economy is not related to the strength of its currency. Russia is a huge economy but its currency is at present (1997) weak. The same is true for Brazil or India. In contrast, Switzerland, New Zealand, Norway, Singapore and Taiwan are 'small' countries (population-wise or area-wise) but their currencies are very strong. The size of a country (or an economy) does not produce strong currencies by itself. It is the correct economic policies (at the microeconomic and macroeconomic and political levels) that produce strong and stable currencies and low levels of inflation.

However, there is a more fundamental reason why to have 170 currencies is better than having just four or five. The reason is given in the following two words: *transparency* and *competition*.

By transparency I mean that, without its own currency, an economy is not signalling to the market participants (domestic as well as foreign) all the possible pieces of information regarding the relative (to all other trading partners) figures of the economy (efficiency of labour force, efficiency of capital, natural resources, government policies, etc.). Without its currency an economy loses one of the most crucial signals and this means much less transparency.

By the word competition we mean that an oligopolistic situation is always inferior to a perfectly competitive situation.

In the science of economics, an oligopoly is a situation where only a very small number of participants (three to five firms) completely dominate a market. A monopoly is a situation when only one player firm participates and dominates the market and competition (or perfect competition, if you wish) is a situation where a large number of participants compete in the market.

If the science of microeconomics teaches anything, this is that *monopolies and oligopolies should be avoided whenever possible.*

Today the world financial market (foreign exchange markets) is a market with around 170 currencies competing with each other to attract capital. Some competitors are big (e.g. US dollar) and some are small (e.g. Israeli shekel). The situation can be compared to a competitive situation with 170 participants. Maybe the competition is not always perfect, but undoubtedly there is competition. To try to reduce the participants from 170 to four or five is philosophically and practically equivalent to trying to change a competitive market into an oligopolistic market. *This is philosophically and morally wrong*!

If anything, we should all strive to keep and increase competition and not to reduce it! It is more natural to imagine a future world with even more currencies (maybe 300 reflecting some 'real' economies) than to envisage a world with just four currencies or even one currency. One could argue that the small-sized participants (e.g. Swiss franc) are at a disadvantage relative to the big participants (e.g. US dollar). This simplistic view is wrong. Smallness or bigness regarding currencies has nothing to do with the strength of the currency, low inflation and attracting foreign capital (per head of the population). With each country having its own currency, wrong policies sooner or later are reflected in the foreign exchange market and this is good for governments, opposition parties, media and the people in general. This is good, after all, for democracy.

There is, however, one more aspect to the oligopolistic view of the foreign exchange markets. It is the dynamic view. By dynamic is meant the addition of one more dimension to the foregoing static discussion, the addition of the dimension of time. Assume that someone could convince us that an oligopolistic market is better than a competitive market today. But the world does not exist only today. The world will exist also tomorrow (and for thousands of years). The world is not static (without the dimension of time), it is dynamic (with the dimension of time). We cannot escape the existence of this dimension, even if some people would like to! So, with an oligopolistic situation and with the passage of time, the few big participants would gradually 'collude' and stop competing. There would be less transparency and certainly no competition, ceteris paribus. Profligate or wrong policies could not be disciplined by the markets (as happens now) and the people would be less informed about their own progress relative to the other nations.

Some (very few) economists argue that in certain industries (e.g. power generation) monopoly (one firm – the monopolist) or oligopoly (very few firms – the oligopolists) are more efficient than having many competitors. My view on the subject is that when we add the time dimension (dynamic considerations), perfect competition is in the long run much better than monopoly. This, I believe, is especially true for the foreign exchange markets, which are perfectly competitive. I can also add that if the foreign exchange markets are not competitive, then no other market in history has been competitive! It will be wrong to attempt to destroy competition where it exists instead of trying to create competition where it does not exist. Moreover, if for some industries there are technical or economic reasons where size matters (and hence oligopoly or monopoly should not be dismissed easily) this is not true regarding currencies where size does not matter.

3. Argument No. 2 (Philosophical)

> In the past the politicians and central bankers in my country have often produced high inflation currency. Maybe it is better to give control of the currency to politicians and central bankers from other countries who appear to be more competent.

EXAMINING THE ARGUMENT

It is a fact that in many countries wrong monetary policies (setting the real interest rate very low or, equivalently, systematic high growth of the money supply by the monetary authorities) have produced periods of high inflation rates with all the well-known bad consequences, although, in some instances, high inflation is a product of abrupt increases in the prices of natural resources over which the monetary authorities of the country have no control (e.g. two energy shocks during the seventies). It is also true that for any country a high inflation rate in the long run is a monetary phenomenon over which the monetary authorities (government and/or central bank) should exercise proper control. But to jump from these facts to the conclusion that the people of a country should give permanent control of their monetary affairs to others (even if these others are extremely well qualified, competent and well intentioned) is wrong for the following very simple and important reasons:

1. It is very difficult to imagine today any country – however small that country might be – that does not have within its population a few well qualified economists to run correctly its monetary affairs (and the Ministry of Economics). It is a simple matter for the voters of any country to vote for governments that are using qualified and hard-working economists and punish with their vote any government that produces high inflation rates (or does not put qualified personnel in the central bank in case the central bank is semi-independent). It should be noted here that to produce low inflation rates and stable currencies does not require a Nobel prize in economics. It requires adherence to a few very simple (elementary) rules regarding monetary and economic policy in general. It does not require high-powered computers, advanced mathematics or nuclear physics! Voters should vote for governments that put the correct people in the correct positions and not for governments that put people in public positions because they just happen to have the right connections or networks. Meritocracy is a

PHILOSOPHICAL ARGUMENTS

word that should be constantly applied by governments and not be found only in the dictionaries.

2. In the extreme case where a nation judges that it lacks well-qualified people to run its monetary affairs (for any reason whatsoever), it should follow the example of basketball or football teams. It should recruit, on a temporary basis, foreigners who can reinforce the team and teach the rest to produce new local talent. There are many well-qualified economists in many countries who can be transferred to the central bank of a country on a contract basis to run the monetary affairs of the nation. It is better to know your own weaknesses, accept them and then bring others from abroad on a temporary basis to train your population (until you can confidently take over) than to give permanent control of the monetary affairs of your country to people outside the country.

3. For a nation to come to the point where it accepts that it is unable to run its monetary and economic affairs properly is equivalent to denying itself. The lowest point that an individual person can ever come to in life is where he or she (for whatever reason or tragic circumstances) totally loses his or her self-confidence. There can be no lower level in human life than when an individual comes to this conclusion and it is always a wrong conclusion. It is the same for nations (groups of relatively homogenous people with common history, culture, language, habits, laws, etc.). For a nation to accept that it cannot run its monetary affairs properly is equivalent to denying its ability to exist and to make progress in dignity and peace. One cannot imagine, from the moral and psychological point of view, anything worse than this. God (or nature, if you wish) created humans to live in peace, dignity and pride and not to consign themselves to oblivion either individually or collectively.

4. Argument No. 3 (Philosophical)

> The EMU is for me a matter of war and peace. Within the EMU, my country cannot go to war ever and this is definitely very good.

When a country does not have its own central bank and currency, then necessarily the country does not control any foreign reserves (mainly foreign treasury bills, gold, positions in the IMF and special drawing rights or SDRs). For any country to go to war it is necessary to have gold and other foreign reserves in order to finance the war. Thus the argument runs that since a country in the EMU will not have foreign reserves it will not go to war alone. The argument is very serious and is part of a more general and fundamental argument that will be examined in detail later in the book. Here we will examine the narrow aspect of the argument, the aspect of foreign reserves and currency.

EXAMINING THE ARGUMENT
First some facts:

1. Everyone wants peace but everyone also wants dignity and the preservation of values. There were in history wars that were aggressive, but there were also wars that were purely defensive. Life is a dynamic phenomenon and no one can exclude in the indefinite future the possibility of others attacking their country. The ability to defend the values of a democratic country is a philosophically and morally legitimate purpose.
2. The existence of a common currency and of a central bank does not eliminate the possibility of war, as we saw during the 1990s in the former Yugoslavia and in Chechnya.
3. The bottom line of the argument is because you are a country (independent and sovereign nation) you might in the future go to war, so I will transform you into a province (or region or prefecture) so that I can remove the ability to go to war again.
4. To transform the argument to the individual's level, we can say that because individuals or families, although they are generally and usually very peaceful, sometimes fight each other, it is very effective to cut off the hands of everybody as a precautionary measure!
5. During the last fifty years peace has been attained by military alliances and not by abolishing countries. My feeling is that the keys to peace in the future will be better education, full democracy, prosperity and, for particular nations that still feel threatened, defensive military alliances.
6. Peace will not come from eliminating or uprooting the feeling of groups of people that they have an identity or a culture or a common purpose or a common destiny.

5. Argument No. 4 (Philosophical)

> I am fed up with my currency after so many years. I want to try the euro, which is something new and hence it must be progressive and exciting.

EXAMINING THE ARGUMENT
It is in the nature of human beings to want to try new things, new habits, new laws, new relations. Our life would become extremely boring (and most probably suicidal) if everything in the world was static. Thus it is natural for every citizen of any country to be positively inclined to explore new things. In fact, human progress in all fields (material, scientific, psychological) has come due to the drive pushing humans to explore new avenues.

Nevertheless, the opposite is not true at all. Not every new idea that someone suggests to us is beneficial. Not everything that comes into our minds should be adopted without due examination about its short-term, medium-term and long-term consequences. This is, after all, a crucial difference between the human race and animals. Humans have the ability to think critically first and then decide.

If today someone suggested I tried hard drugs, this would certainly be a new thing for me. It would give me pleasure to taste something new and exciting and even give me a hedonistic pleasure in both body and mind. But would this action be good for me both in the short and in the long run? Would this action be good for society at large? The answer is (for most people) a simple big no. Human progress comes almost always from exploring new things and adopting new ideas, but not all new things or ideas are good.

Chapter IX
THE VERDICT ON THE EMU

Ye cannot serve God and mammon.

Matt. 6:24

If you do not ask, the answer is no.

Owen Laughlin

It has recently been discovered that research causes cancer in rats.

Anonymous

In previous chapters we examined the pros and cons of adopting the EMU from both the materialistic as well as psychological point of view. We included the dynamic effects (the dimension of time) in our considerations (short-run, medium-run and long-run considerations). By adding the grades given in all previous pages we come to the final grade in Figure 29.

Figure 29

Option 1	Option 2
Abandon my currency (adopt EMU – euro)	Retain my currency (retain monetary policy tool)
Final (total) grade: 1,800/10,000	Final (total) grade: 9,131/10,000

It is obvious that retaining one's currency (retaining the monetary policy tool and central bank) is preferable to abolishing one's currency (especially in the long to very long run).

The subject of the EMU is a typical economic-political and philosophical subject where the advantages are easily understood by everybody (mainly the elimination of transaction costs when changing currencies), but where the colossal disadvantages are not very easily understood by anyone who is not a trained economist. This was the main reason why Part One of this book was written.

Part Two
About the EU

Chapter X
INTRODUCTION TO THE EU

1. How I came to examine the subject of the EU

Until 1992 I was a very strong supporter of the concept of the European Economic Community (EEC). I thought that the EEC was about establishing completely free trade in goods, services and capital (currencies) all over the continent (geographical area) of Europe. My instinct was that unimpeded exchange of goods, services and capital (and ideas, I may say) was in the best interests of everybody. When later I studied international economics I found out that my instinct on the matter was absolutely correct.

I also thought that the EEC was about more competition and about free markets. My instinct was that fair competition and free markets are basically good things in the long run. When later I studied microeconomics and macroeconomics I found out that my instinct on that matter was also absolutely correct.

At some point at the beginning of the 1990s, while I was working as a civil engineer in some rather remote place in Saudi Arabia, I read in the newspapers that the EEC had changed to the EU (European Union). I thought at that time that it was just a change of name. Then I heard about the ratification of the Maastricht Treaty. The main aspects of this Maastricht Treaty as I understood it at that time were:

- People could go to work freely in any of the fifteen countries comprising the EU.
- There would be an effort to install fiscal discipline in all governments to substantially reduce public debts, budget deficits and inflation rates.
- There would be some transfer of funds (structural funds) to relatively poor countries.

At that time (1992), I didn't find anything objectionable to all this. On the contrary, I loved the idea that if I were unemployed in Greece I could freely go to Britain or Germany or France to look for work. Thus, I continued being a strong supporter of the whole idea of the EU. I also loved seeing, together with the Greek flag, a new flag (blue with stars) in the roads in Athens when I went there on holiday. The idea of the peaceful coexistence of fifteen democratic countries on the continent of Europe was marvellous.

Unfortunately, those feelings turned sour in 1995. While studying macroeconomics, I started critically investigating the subject of not having a specific currency for a specific country. While doing that investigation, I started thinking critically also about the whole concept of the EU. What exactly was the EU? What were the basic consequences and detailed mechanisms of the EU for the progress, well-being and happiness of the individual citizen of any of the fifteen countries? Was it maybe something painful in the short run but very good in the long run? What were the results of the EU for democracy, freedom, wealth creation, peace, justice, etc.? Was the EU a trading bloc or was it a new country? And if the EU was a new country where had all the other fifteen countries gone? I always kept in mind the old saying that 'you cannot be a country within a country'.

These were puzzling questions of immense importance to me. I started buying newspapers and magazines from the nearest news-stand in Jeddah. I started listening very carefully to the satellite television stations. I soon realised that something extremely serious was happening for all the citizens of the EU. By December 1996, I had made all my conclusions on the subject.

In Part Two of this book I present an examination of the subject of the EU from every possible point of view (economic, political, cultural, psychological) for both the short and the long run, for the citizen of any member country.

2. A very rough and very important definition of a democratic, independent and sovereign country

Since it will be essential for all our discussion about the EU, we give here some very simple but also extremely important definitions.

In a democratic country there exist three different powers:

- The first power is the legislative power (parliament or congress or senate). It is the body of wise people elected for the main purpose of making the laws for the whole society. Everyone living inside the country is subject to the laws drawn up by the representatives of the people (members of parliament, or congress or members of the senate).
- The second power is the executive power or government. The members of government can act only according to the laws passed by the legislative body. In other words, the prime minister (or president) and the ministers can execute their programme only if every act is in accordance with the laws of the legislature.
- The third power is the judicial power or judiciary. Anyone living in a country and violating the laws of the legislative power is tried by the judges (the justice system). It is important to mention that no one living in such a country is above the laws of the country, including the members of the government, the members of parliament and the members of the justice system.

It is extremely important to note that for a country there can be no power above the three powers. For example, there can be no legislative body sending laws to the legislative body of Japan, or South Korea or Chile. There can be no executive power (government) giving instructions (governing) the government of Thailand or New Zealand or the Philippines or South Africa. There cannot be a justice system annulling decisions of the justice system of Australia or India or Zimbabwe. If there can be any power above the three powers of a democracy, then we do not speak about a country (or roughly a nation) but about a province or a region or a district or a prefecture or even a state, but in no way we can speak about a country.

A democratic country is defined as independent if the government of the country is able to participate or withdraw from any international body or alliance (for example, the United Nations or NATO). The government of an independent country can judge today that it is to the benefit of the people who elected it to participate in NATO and the same government (or another government) can judge after ten or twenty years that it is no longer beneficial to participate in NATO. Then and only then we talk about an independent country.

Regarding sovereignty, we can define it in very simple terms as the ability of a group of people to live according to the way of life they have chosen for themselves without being obliged to accept interference from others. They can change their laws and, in general, their way of life only because they wish to do so and not because somebody else imposes it on them.

According to this definition and what was said on page 80 a country is always sovereign, but this is not so for a district or prefecture or county or state.

3. Some preliminary findings regarding the fifteen countries of the EU

Having seen in section 2 what a democratic country is, the first and most striking finding is that the fifteen member countries of the EU are not countries any more! They have been downgraded to states! The real country de facto is a country named the EU.

This is the result of the following three very simple facts:

1. The legislative power of any member state is subordinated to a legislative power (parliament) in Strasbourg and Brussels.
2. The judicial power of any member state is subordinated to a Court of Justice in Luxembourg.
3. The executive power (government) of any member state is subordinated to a Commission in Brussels.

However, the fact that fifteen countries have been downgraded to states in favour of a new country named the EU does not mean by itself that this is bad for the average citizen (neither of course does it mean that it is good). This will be dealt with in detail in the next few chapters. What can be said now is that the colossal transition from fifteen countries to one country has been performed in effect roughly since 1985 in a careful, skilful, slow and wise manner, step by step in such a way that it is very doubtful whether the average citizen has realised the extent of the short-term and long-term consequences of the change.

4. Which situations will be compared? What is the alternative?

In the course of the following chapters we will examine a great number of arguments regarding the fundamental question: is participation in the EU beneficial to the average citizen of any country?

But in order to get concrete results we need to compare participation in the EU with something specific, an alternative. This alternative will be:

1. Completely free trade in goods and services for the country with all other countries on earth.
2. Completely free transfer of liquid assets (money, bonds, shares) from country to country.
3. Completely free investment of capital and know-how in any country.
4. Complete control by the citizens of a country over their geographical area regarding:
    - making laws for themselves (legislative power, parliament or congress or senate).
    - delivering justice to themselves (justice system, judicial power).
    - governing themselves (government).

The need arises here to clarify the alternative or option two with as much detail as possible, otherwise serious misunderstandings will occur.

So, what is the exact and detailed picture of the alternative? In other words, let us define the alternative in simple and specific characteristics (truth, wealth and happiness usually require simple and rational steps and not some complicated and sudden enlightenment!)

DEFINITION OF THE ALTERNATIVE

1. The citizens or firms of country X trade their goods freely with individuals or firms of any other country on earth without tariffs, quotas or other restrictions on trade. They can sell or buy any goods (cars, refrigerators, clothes, food, books, aeroplanes) with no duties. It should be noted that today (almost) no duties are in place between the EU countries. There are, however, considerable tariffs, quotas and other trade restrictions with the rest of the world (170 countries with a population

of around 5,000 million people).

2. Completely free trade (zero tariffs, quotas, etc.) for country X in services with all countries (telecommunications, banking, insurance, tourism, shipping, education, healthcare, entertainment, etc.). Any citizen or firm in country X is free to buy or sell services to any other individual or firm on earth without any duties. It should be noted that today trade in services is almost completely free between EU member countries but there are considerable barriers to trade in services with the rest of the world.
3. The citizens or firms of country X are completely free to send their money abroad or receive money from any country.
4. The citizens or firms of country X are completely free to buy or sell bonds or shares in any country.
5. The citizens or firms of country X are completely free to invest capital and know-how in any country. Firms are free to expand in other countries, make tactical or strategic alliances with any firm in any other country, to merge and also to de-merge or spin off.
6. The citizens of country X have full control over the laws that will be voted and applicable to their own country. The people and their elected representatives (members of parliament or congress or senate) will have full control over the lawmaking process (suggesting a law and voting for a law). There will be no other legislative body above the legislative bodies of the people of the country.
7. The citizens of the country have full control over delivering justice in their geographical area. There will be no other justice system above the justice system established by the people of country X.
8. The citizens of country X have full control of their administrative body (executive power or government). They govern themselves (self-government) as they wish and there will be no other government or organisation above their own government.

These eight characteristics of the alternative appear at first glance to be unobtainable or very simplistic or even isolationist. During the discussion of each of the arguments in the next several chapters we will examine the proposed model in great detail. For the moment we can state the basic (fundamental) principals which are behind the model:

- The maximum possible economic progress for the people in the indefinite future (short term and long to very long term)
- The maximum possible freedom and development for the people in the indefinite future.
- The maximum possible happiness for the people other things being equal

(ceteris paribus).

We should all remember that the ultimate goal of any society is the maximum happiness of its members and that human beings in order to be in a state of maximum possible happiness need maximum possible material wealth, freedom, sense of community, sense of purpose and most important of all health in its most general form which includes mental as well as bodily health. In the next few chapters we will try to find out whether the EU model or the alternative model can better achieve these very simple but very essential and fundamental principles. Simplicity, rationality and determination are the first steps for moving forward.

5. The grading system again

In the next several chapters during our discussion of each argument regarding whether participating in the EU or the alternative is more beneficial we will need a grading system since we need to be as rational as possible and not sentimental. We will use a grading system very similar to the one in Part One (about the EMU), but with a scale of 1 to 100,000 and not to 10,000. The vastly more detailed scale is needed because the subject of the EU in general is vastly larger, more important and deeper than the subject of the EMU.

Chapter XI
ECONOMIC ARGUMENTS

1. Argument No. 1 (International economics)

If my country is within the EU, then as a producer I can sell my products or services free of tariffs, quotas and other bureaucratic restrictions to the other member countries. As a consumer also, I can buy the products or services of the other member countries free of tariffs, quotas and other bureaucratic restrictions (and therefore cheaper). If, on the other hand, my country is out of the EU I will face tariffs, quotas and other non-tariff barriers (bureaucratic restrictions). Therefore I am better off within the EU.

The situation today is that there are no trade restrictions (in goods and services) between member states, but uniform tariffs and other barriers (non-tariff barriers like quotas, government procurement policies, health requirements, etc.) are compulsory for products or services coming from the rest of the world, i.e. each country is applying the same tariff (whether it wishes or not) to a product coming from, say, Taiwan or Singapore or South Africa. In general, participation in a trading bloc means no trade friction between member countries and uniform trade friction with the rest of the world.

The disappearance of trade barriers between member countries which increases trade between them is known as trade creation in economics jargon and is in general beneficial, but at the same time it decreases trade with the rest of the world. This decrease in trade with the rest of the world is known as trade diversion and generally decreases welfare. The final result (benefits of trade creation minus disadvantages of trade diversion) is ambivalent in economic theory.

Let us use an example of a Greek consumer wishing to buy a car and a German consumer wishing to buy tomatoes. Without tariffs between Greece and Germany, the Greek consumer tends to buy a German car because the corresponding Japanese car is more expensive owing to the tariff imposed on the rest of the world. So, free trade between Greece and Germany is in general beneficial to the Greek consumer because it lowers the price of the German car. But at the same time the mandatory imposition of tariffs on the Japanese car (regardless of the will on that particular matter of the Greek government and lawmakers) takes away from the Greek consumer the chance to buy an even cheaper car from Japan (or maybe South Korea or Brazil or the USA or Canada or Mexico). Similarly the German consumer wishing to buy tomatoes buys them from Greek producers because there are no tariffs on the Greek tomatoes, and not from Egypt or South Africa because there are tariffs with those countries. This situation is known in economics as the second best and it is generally ambivalent both in theory as well as in practice.

In addition, we see here another very important aspect of the concept of a trading bloc: the *inflexibility concept*. The Greek government is not free to do what it would wish to do regarding tariffs on the Japanese cars nor the German government regarding tariffs on Egyptian tomatoes. If, for example, the German government found tomorrow that it would be to the benefit of German citizens to eliminate tariffs on the Egyptian tomatoes, it could not do so. The same applies if we assume that the Greek government found tomorrow that it would be to the benefit of the Greek people to eliminate tariffs on Japanese cars (they would be cheaper automatically). So what is the best solution? To return to imposing tariffs between the fifteen EU member countries? Certainly not! The solution is a situation where each country is set free to eliminate tariffs with all other countries. This is the first characteristic of the alternative, namely that *country X eliminates all tariffs and all other non-tariff barriers to trade in all goods and services with the rest of the world*.

There are two questions here. The first is: is elimination of all trade barriers a good thing for the citizens of country X? The answer is that, according to the science of international economics, the elimination of trade barriers in all directions increases welfare. If free trade between Germany and Italy is a good thing, it must also be a good thing if it is free (with reciprocity, of course) with Japan, Singapore, Argentina etc. The consumer in Italy, for example, should be free to buy goods from the cheapest available source worldwide and not just from the cheapest available source within the fifteen member states of the EU. Equally important, the producer in Italy should be able to sell his goods or services free of any barriers not only to the fifteen member states in the EU but to any country (it is implicit in the alternative that trade barriers have fallen between country X and all other countries). Then and only then, the producer in Italy will reap the full benefits of free trade (one should remember that the population of the rest of the world is more than 5,000 million people growing economically on average two to three times faster than the average country within the EU, even after the rate of population increase has been considered).

The second question is: can a country that is inside the EU decide alone to eliminate all trade barriers with other countries once it decides that this is to the great economic benefit of its citizens? The answer here is that each country should do what is to the benefit of its people and not be held prisoner by some organisation that was set up ostensibly to facilitate free trade. There is no law in economics and no empirical evidence to suggest that free trade is good only within the boundaries of nations in a specific part of a continent or in the whole of a continent and not good with other nations. There is no law in international economics saying that countries should dismantle trade barriers between them and at the same time erect trade barriers at their periphery. The erection of external barriers economically erases all (or almost all) the benefits arising due to the elimination of the trade barriers between the trading bloc countries. Moreover, the view that fifteen countries can become a fortress and be self sufficient and protected is extremely simplistic, scientifically and empirically wrong, and in the medium and long term very damaging to the interests of the citizens.

If free trade is theoretically and empirically beneficial (and it certainly is, especially in the medium to long term), then it is beneficial in all directions and with all the reciprocating countries.

Another question that naturally arises in the mind of the reader is: given that there is free trade between my country and all reciprocating countries, what if the EU imposes tariffs on my country? The short answer to this is that this sounds like blackmail and any human being or organisation which uses blackmail does not have good intentions.

There is, however, a more rational and very fundamental answer. According to the WTO (World Trade Organisation – successor to GATT) a programme is in progress that will eliminate all tariffs and other non-tariff barriers to trade in goods and services between all countries (except some extremely poor ones with little trading volume) by the year 2010 and with the very few poor countries by the year 2020. There are already three fundamental treaties – one signed and the other two to be signed within the next year or two. The telecommunications treaty facilitates the setting up of telecom services in all major countries by companies from any other country. A Japanese or South Korean or Canadian company can set up telecom businesses in any EU country and vice versa. Upcoming within the next year is the signing of a similar treaty regarding information technology (computer hardware, software, etc.) and a treaty regarding financial services (banks, insurance, brokerage, etc.). Those treaties are covering a huge amount of the world trade and mean that by 2000 trade restrictions in the periphery of the EU will have to be eliminated anyway in these extremely important trade sectors. The rest of the barriers in trade are expected to have fallen within the WTO by 2010. Therefore, free trade of country X with all other countries is not only an entitlement of the country but it is a fact of life.

There is a corollary to the above discussion. If within the WTO (World Trade Organisation) there is going to be free trade by country X (member of the EU) with practically all other countries, what is then the meaning of the EU as a trading bloc? The answer is that after 2010 there will be no meaning in the EU as a trading bloc, nor there will be meaning in any other trading bloc. All of this leads to the grading in Figure 30.

Figure 30

Option 1	Option 2
Member of the EU	The alternative
Grade: 50/100,000	Grade: 1,000/100,000

2. Argument No. 2 (International economics)

Within the EU, I, as an individual or a firm, can make investment in real assets not only in my country but in any of the fifteen participating countries. Similarly firms or businessmen from any of the fifteen participating countries can invest in my country in real assets (buildings, factories, hotels, shops, banks, etc.) practically without any restriction. This is a very good thing for everybody.

Investment in real assets means capital expenditure on the purchase of physical assets such as plant, machinery, equipment and inventory in order to produce goods or services, i.e. physical or real investment. Physical investment creates new assets, thereby adding to a country's productive capacity. Both empirical evidence and the science of economics suggest that investment is of extremely great significance to economic prosperity and therefore the absence of restrictions to investment between fifteen countries enables business people and firms to transfer their capital and know-how to where greater opportunities (returns on capital) arise. This means for the recipient (host) country more chances of employment and the supply of a greater quantity of more sophisticated products and services to the consuming public (including even services such as education, transportation, infrastructure and health). For country X (member of the EU) freedom to invest to any of the fifteen countries is undoubtedly a very good thing.

There is one crucial point, however. The ability of a country to attract real (physical) investment depends greatly on the expected return on capital. The expected return on capital (i.e. what will be the yearly profits for the outside investors as a percentage of the total invested capital) depends greatly on the laws of the country at both the microeconomic level and the macroeconomic level (labour laws, taxation, competition policies, government size and regulations, working practices, etc.). Within the EU there is a general frame of macroeconomic and microeconomic policies imposed by EU laws on every country.

Suppose that tomorrow the people of country X want to attract a greater amount of investment from the other fourteen countries in the EU by drastically altering their laws at both the macroeconomic and microeconomic levels. They will find that they can alter their laws only within the limits of some 'common standards' of the EU, which are already very strict and very narrow. This means that, practically, the people of country X and their lawmakers are unable to make any meaningful change in their attractiveness to outside investment. The situation is much worse if they decide to alter their laws in order to attract investment from the rest of the world. They will find that they can move only within specific very strict limits imposed by the various EU institutions in all kinds of activities. In the long run this is a very large disadvantage because attracting investment (especially from the rapidly progressing and growing rest of the world) is, economically speaking, an extremely important matter and because each country should be able to fully exploit its competitive advantages, geographic location, culture, special or historic links and, most important of all, country X should be able to quickly apply the special ideas and willingness of its people to drastically alter its attractiveness to investment from outside.

Let us now see what the alternative provides regarding foreign investment.

CHARACTERISTICS OF THE ALTERNATIVE REGARDING OUTSIDE INVESTMENT

- The citizens and firms of country X are free to invest in physical assets not only in any of the fifteen member states of the EU but in any reciprocally acting country.
- The firms of country X are able to make tactical or strategic alliances or merge with any firm not only in any of the fifteen EU member states but also in any reciprocally acting country.

The advantages of the alternative are obvious, but how feasible is it as a solution? The answer is that today most countries are continually lowering their barriers or restrictions to physical investment in goods or services. The World Trade Organisation (WTO) as well as the reality of good economic governance are forcing even the poorest of the poor countries to dismantle barriers to foreign physical investment. We see that companies from Japan, South Korea, Taiwan or Switzerland (not a member of the EU) have invested in more than fifty or even one hundred countries. We see firms from Switzerland merge with firms in the USA and create giants operating and investing everywhere. There is no reason, either in economic theory or in practice, to restrict a company, say, from France to merge only with companies in the EU countries. A firm should be able to merge or invest anywhere in the world where it believes there are greater opportunities. The notion that somehow the firms in the EU should invest or merge only between themselves is theoretically and practically wrong (it is also another form of mercantilism).

Concluding this section, one can say that we are maybe only twelve years away from the date when all physical investments anywhere in the world will be almost without any practical restriction. The argument is graded in Figure 31.

Figure 31

Option 1 Member of the EU	Option 2 The alternative
Grade: 1,000/100,000	Grade: 2,000/100,000

3. Argument No. 3 (International economics)

> Within the EU, every year my country receives from Brussels considerable amounts of money in the form of support for agricultural programmes, structural funds, research funds and cultural exchange funds. These yearly sums of money are especially important for the less developed member states. Certainly this is a very good thing for the average citizen of any country within the EU.

The argument is practically very powerful. Before we see if it is correct or incorrect, let us consider the facts.

FACT NO. 1

The Commission in Brussels every year automatically collects from every government of every member country an amount of money equal to 1.43% of its GDP. Since on average, taxation (income taxes, value added taxes, property taxes, inheritance taxes, capital gains taxes, business taxes, etc.) is approximately equal to 0.45% of GDP, then it is evident that the amount of money collected by Brussels is roughly equal to 3.18% (1.43/0.45 = 3.18%) of the taxation of every citizen of any country within the EU. To make it very simple: for every 100 German marks, or French francs, or Italian lira, or Spanish peseta, etc. paid as taxation to any government, 3.18 money units go automatically from the national government to the Commission in Brussels. The amount thus collected for fiscal year 1996 was equal to 91 billion ECU (about US $103 billion).

FACT NO. 2

This money, after it is collected by Brussels, is spent by the Commission as follows:

- Salaries and other expenses for about 20,000 direct employees of the EU at the main institutions (Brussels, Strasbourg, Luxembourg), expenses for running buildings, capital expenditures (e.g. for computers), travel expenses of EU officials, etc.
- Salaries and other expenses for people and institutions residing locally within each country but paid directly by the EU.
- Expenses for direct advertising of the aims and philosophy of the EU. For fiscal year 1995 those direct advertising expenses were equal to US $375

million. We will see later on in other arguments and chapters that there are also expenses for indirect advertising of the aims and philosophy of the EU.

- Support of the prices of various agricultural products (Common Agricultural Policy or CAP).
- Expenses for various EU directed programs in many countries in the fields of scientific research, education, cultural exchanges, computerisation, environmental protection and energy preservation.
- Expenses for various infrastructure projects (roads, airports, railways, marinas, sewage treatments, etc.), especially in the less developed countries (Greece, Portugal, Ireland, Spain) and in poor regions of more developed countries.

It is worth noting that all these programmes, funds and projects come together with some nice public relations announcements to the media, big board signs on the roads, flags (blue with fifteen yellow stars) and national government discussions.

COMMENTS ON THE ABOVE FACTS

In the light of the foregoing facts, let us now re-visit the argument critically. The process in rough lines is:

Step 1: Automatic collection from each national government of an amount equal to 3.18% of the taxation of the average citizen and transfer of this to the commission in Brussels.

Step 2: Payments by the commission in Brussels for activities of its employees and its other fixed assets (buildings etc) and for advertisements.

Step 3: Return by the commission in Brussels of the rest of the money to the various national governments in the form of agricultural support and in the form of various programs and funds. The latest amount (programs and funds) are distributed by the commission in such a way that the bulk of the money flows to the governments of the less developed countries.

From the economics point of view, step 1 is considered as directly unproductive activity. There is no economic benefit or meaning for the average citizens of country X when their tax money goes to Brussels and then returns from Brussels. To be more precise, this activity can be characterised as directly unproductive power-seeking activity because concentration of vast sums of money by any organisation creates real power for the organisation: the power to distribute money to people who will be grateful and thankful to and dependent on the organisation (without realising that it is their money).

Step 2 (payments for employees, buildings, travel, computers, committees and advertisements) is, from the economics point of view, an indirectly unproductive activity for the very simple reason that whatever is done by the Brussels employees could be done by the various national government employees. The fifteen national governments do not lack employees and there was no need to have created an additional body of in effect public sector employees (since they are paid by tax money). In addition, the money spent on direct advertisement of the EU philosophy and political aims is clearly a directly unproductive activity seeking political aims. In later chapters we will examine what those political aims are, whether they are correct and if spending public money to promote political aims is compatible with democracy and the constitution and laws of any EU member country!

The biggest inefficiency, however, is with step 3. The so-called Common Agricultural Policy suffers from the following fundamental, practical and philosophical flaws:

Flaw No. 1
Because money comes back to the farmers of each country from Brussels, the farmers consider it (logically) as somehow 'foreign aid' and some of them try to absorb as much as possible by devising various ways to bend the rules and deceive the officials. The newspapers of the past five years were full of such stories in almost every country. In this way, a portion of the farmers support money is lost to fraud.

Flaw No. 2
Each national government also considers the money going to farmers from Brussels as foreign money and not only does not try to minimise the fraudulent losses, but turns a blind eye. The same applies to the opposition parties in each country. Everyone tries to absorb as much money as possible for the nation's farmers, and everyone forgets that this money is in effect coming from the taxpayers of their own country. The national government should try to distribute the money to the farmers according to laws, ethics and appropriate principles, while the opposition of the country should try to make sure that the government behaves politically and ethically correctly.

Flaw No. 3
The whole principle of creating a command economy over fifteen nations regarding agricultural products is scientifically and practically wrong from both the microeconomics and international economics point of view, i.e. the principle on which the Common Agricultural Policy was founded is wrong.

By the CAP, the Commission tries to create a common price for each agricultural product each year by regulating on a supranational level the produced quantities of each product over the vast area of fifteen countries. It creates thus within the EU a monopoly for each product and a command economy in agriculture. Monopolies are theoretically and practically wrong and are generally condemned because they make the producer inefficient (especially over the long run) and the consumer always pays a higher price. The command economy is also a wrong concept when it is applied on a supranational level by people in Brussels having very little contact with, knowledge of or interest in what is being cultivated by the farmers in fifteen nations.

Worst of all, the Common Agricultural Policy, if it were followed in the future by other trading blocs, would result in a worldwide oligopolistic situation where the prices and quantities of the agricultural products all over the world would be determined by a few oligopolies (the trading blocs). The science of microeconomics is very clear that competition (perfect or not perfect) is far superior to oligopoly. If such an oligopolistic situation arose worldwide, then consumers would suffer and the producers (the oligopolists) would become inefficient. The seeds of inefficiency have already been seen during the past twenty years in the mountains of surplus dairy and farm products all over the EU being stocked, destroyed or dumped in the world markets. Moreover, it is unfair to all other trading nations (rich and poor, large and small) if the Commission in Brussels tries to create in a pan-EU market a situation where, for each agricultural product, there is in effect one seller producing a predetermined amount of product and thus trying to manipulate the world price by gaining market power. This is theoretically and practically wrong and damaging for all citizens of the EU, contravenes the spirit and rules of the WTO (World Trade Organisation), is against the spirit of fair competition and is unethical. In the long run (and we have already entered the long run because the Common Agricultural Policy is a few decades old), it is greatly damaging producers and consumers everywhere and confirms that regulation of quantities or prices for agricultural products on a supranational level is theoretically and practically wrong.

We have noted the problems and inefficiencies in step 3 when the Commission in Brussels sends back money to the farmers. There are bigger problems and inefficiencies, however, with the rest of the money that the Commission sends to the national governments for various structural programmes like infrastructure projects, scientific research, cultural exchanges, energy preservation and environmental protection. The funds always come with nice flags, billboards, announcements to the media and signs on the roads, and appear to be coming from some outside source. They are perceived by everyone as foreign aid, i.e. the average citizen believes that some machine printing money is sending him or her aid. The reaction to the funds (which are actually taxpayers' money) is as follows:

1. The private firm of recipient country X (say, a construction firm) getting an infrastructure project, or the public institution of country X (say, a university) getting a research fund, tries in most cases to absorb as much as possible of the funds using legal or illegal methods regardless of the produced result. For example, the construction firm tries to absorb money over and above the budgeted amount without regard to

the quality and quantity of the final work and without regard to the time limits.

2. The government of recipient country X, perceiving that the money coming from Brussels is 'foreign' money, tries to absorb not the minimum but the maximum amount of money for any specific project! Moreover, it is not interested in supervising the project efficiently (regarding cost or quality). Maybe the poorer or more backward the country appears next year to the Commission, the more money the government will get for structural and other funds (to be distributed in many cases to the political friends of the government). Money means power and any government on earth naturally seeks the power to distribute foreign money.

3. The opposition parties of country X, perceiving also that the money coming from Brussels is 'foreign' money, have no interest in checking how efficiently the money is run through each specific project. On the contrary, the opposition parties not only do not check on the government (as they ought to do), but they too are very happy if the country absorbs as much as possible.

What is the end result of this procedure regarding the various EU-supported programmes? It is a huge cycle of inefficient work, some corruption, some outright fraud, delays, extremely poor results and a perpetual beggar mentality for whole nations or regions.

Some people will agree that the system is on balance totally inefficient but assert that it is beneficial to the relatively poor countries or regions where it creates jobs, even if temporarily. Let us examine a typical relatively poor country X.

The citizens of the country send to the Commission in Brussels approximately 3.2% of their tax money. Suppose that they receive back from Brussels an amount equal to 7% of their taxation. This 7% all comes as EU aid and not as the net difference between the 7% they received and the 3.2% they contributed (which is 3.8%). In other words, the citizens see nice flags and signs, and announcements not on the net amount they receive from outside (which is equal to 3.8% of their taxation), but on an imaginary amount of 7%. There is thus a kind of systematic deception of the average citizen of country X to make him believe that he or she is assisted from outside by an amount approximately double the real one.

The story, however, does not end here. From the amount of 7% returning should be deducted the amount that was lost during the travels of the funds from country X to Brussels and then back to country X in advertisements, meetings and expenses of officials, salaries of EU employees, expenses of EU institutions, etc. How much might this amount be? It is roughly 1% of the taxation of country X. So the true calculation for a citizen of country X would be:

7% (coming from Brussels) − (3.2% sent to Brussels) −
1% (lost to inefficiencies and bureaucracy) = 2.8%

So, finally, 'poor' country X receives from the Commission a net amount equal to 2.8% of the tax of its citizens. But this amount is perceived by its citizens (and political parties) to be equal to 7% of the total taxation. But let us forget the grand and systematic deception to change a number from 2.8% to 7%. Do the citizens of the country on balance get the benefit of even this 2.8%?

The answer is no because this net and real 2.8% comes with strings attached regarding all kinds of policies (fiscal and monetary policies). For example, the government of country X is not in practice free to set the interest rate or the exchange rate of its currency according to the circumstances of the local economy. This results in job losses (in, for example, manufacturing or tourism or shipping). Another example is the conditions on how much money the government can spend on all kinds of activities (health, education or social insurance) known as fiscal policies. The government is in practical terms not free to lower or increase taxes. It is free only within certain limits which cannot reflect the special characteristics of the economy or the location of country X. We thus see that this actual and real 2.8% coming from Brussels creates temporary jobs in the sectors of the specific projects undertaken but destroys an equal or greater number of jobs in other sectors of the economy. In effect, country X is in a straitjacket. By destroying jobs, however, in those other sectors it also destroys tax collection money greater than the 2.8%. Additionally, and equally importantly, this assistance by deception creates a mentality of dependency on a grand scale and destroys the morale and the will of the people of country X to make progress. They start believing that somehow they are unable to grow economically unless some outside official source sends them money every year! A vicious circle on a national and supranational level has been established where temporary jobs are created in, say, construction or research, and permanent jobs are lost in tourism, manufacturing, shipping, etc.

If this is what happens regarding EU budget procedures or structural funds to poor country X, what is really happening to the rich country Y? Let us follow the path of money from rich country Y to the Commission and then from the Commission to poor country X and also to the farmers and other categories of citizens of country Y.

The government of rich country Y sends to the Commission automatically an amount of money roughly equal to 3.2% of the taxes paid by its citizens in all forms. Out of this 3.2% an amount roughly equal to 1% is lost to advertisements and expenses for running the various institutions and paying salaries of direct employees of the EU. The rest of it is sent:

- Back to the farmers of the same country for support of their products (Common Agricultural Policy), but now the farmers perceive it as coming not from their own country, not from their own government, not from their own taxpayers, but from an outside source, namely the Commission in Brussels or Brussels or the EU. Naturally, the farmers feel dependent or thankful, not to their fellow taxpayers but to an entity called the EU. We come again across a phenomenon mildly characterised as 'systematic and carefully engineered deception on a supranational level'.
- Back to a poorer region of country Y as structural or infrastructure funds. Again the receiving end (citizens or firms of country Y) perceive the money as coming from 'The Commission' and not from their fellow taxpayers. Naturally, they tend to feel grateful to this benevolent outside source of money.
- The rest of the money goes to 'poor' country X as structural funds, research funds, etc. The recipients (citizens or firms or public institutions of country X) naturally tend to be obliged, not to the taxpayers of country Y but to an entity called the EU. Again deception on a grand scale.

In addition, all the recipients of this 2.2%, regardless of where they reside (being farmers in rich country Y, or citizens of a poorer region of rich country Y or citizens of poor country X), do not have the slightest incentive to use this money efficiently. No one is really interested on how this money is allocated or spent because, in effect, nobody knows exactly where this money is coming from. No governmental party or opposition party is really interested to make any check.

If this is the situation with the so-called budget of the EU, what is to be done? Does the alternative have anything to say regarding this vast annual amount of money?

The alternative regarding this money is to stop sending it to Brussels. The 3.2% of taxation money is spent directly by the government of country X to support its farmers and to give structural or research funds to its regions. Naturally, country Y is free to send official assistance to 'poor' country X at any level it deems proper every year.'

Now, let us see the characteristics of the alternative in some detail and see if it has any merits compared to the present system.

Merit No. 1

Glasnost (transparency). The citizens (and voters) of country Y know where their tax money is going. They know precisely how much is going to the farmers of their country, how much to undeveloped regions of their country and how much is going to less developed country X. They are able to instruct their government through their votes to increase or decrease any of these amounts of money every year. They are able to know what exactly is happening to their money and how it is used every year. The opposition parties and the media of country Y are constantly in a position to check the efficient allocation and usage of this 3.2% of tax money.

Merit No. 2
Efficient and responsible allocation and usage of resources (money) because now the factor of self-interest affects everybody (government, opposition parties, lawmakers, justice system, public institutions, universities, private firms and the simple men and women of country Y). Because the allocation of money is now done by the people of country Y through their elected government, everyone behaves more responsibly than before.

Merit No. 3
No money is lost in advertisements of the political and philosophical aims of the EU, in announcements, in TV programmes, or in TV, radio or newspaper commercials. Advertising political aims is, from the economics point of view, a directly unproductive activity.

Merit No. 4
No money is lost in paying for salaries, buildings, computers, travel expenses, etc. of those 20,000 EU employees. All their necessary tasks and functions are done by public employees of country Y residing within country Y, paid by the taxpayers of country Y and accountable to the voters of country Y. If the public sector employees of country Y are not sufficient to undertake those additional tasks, then the citizens are free to instruct their government to employ more people to deal with their international relations. Increasing the government size or employee numbers is a legitimate (though not necessarily correct) measure in a country as long as the risk, responsibility and reward is undertaken by the informed citizens of the country.

Regarding the question of how those 20,000 employees of the EU can be distributed and work from within each country and still function, the answer is twofold. First of all, the actual number needed is not 20,000 or 40,000, but very near to zero according to the alternative. Second (and most important) someone should speak to the supranational institutions about the advent of the Internet, electronic mail and especially video-teleconferencing. Any international function, committee, meeting, conference etc can be done very effectively by people residing each one in his/her own country and communicating via videoconferencing and the Internet. No need exists for lavish buildings, expensive travel and hotels. We have to make use of the exploding new technologies in communications in order to save money. It is high time that the new IT technologies were used in international relations in order to eliminate unnecessary costs.

Merit No. 5
The yearly aid for structural funds given to country X by country Y is pre-announced and known to everybody. The citizens of country Y know whom and by how much they are assisting every year and they can observe the efficient use of their money by the relative progress of country X. They can

thus reduce the amount the next year if they see (through their media and political parties) that there is systematic mishandling of their money by country X's government. On the other hand, the citizens of country X know very well where the official aid is coming from and they feel grateful to the citizens of that particular place and not to a vague entity called the EU. They also know that the official aid can be decreased or eliminated if the use of the funds is not efficient.

Merit No. 6
There are no strings attached to the official aid given to country X. Since the aid is going directly from specific country to specific country, there is no practical reason why conditions should be attached to the official aid or structural funds. The government of country X is set free to put the money to the best possible use for the benefit of its people. It knows very well that if this use proves not to be good, then sooner or later the citizens of country Y will stop sending anything.

There is, however, a deeper principle to this no strings policy regarding foreign aid. Why should foreign aid to poor or less developed countries be without conditions attached? The moral reason is that when we see someone (an individual, a family, an organisation or a whole country) honestly in need of help to stand on his or her own feet, we decide either to assist him or not, but never on the condition that he or she does what we want. Assistance under conditions loses its moral value. It is enough for us to see the humiliation which the individual family or nation is suffering and decide honestly and wholeheartedly either to give or not to give. Moreover, the conditions imposed do not usually allow the recipient nation to make the maximum use of its own potential. What the donor nation can do, however, if it sees repeated mismanagement of its own funds is very simple: reduce or eliminate the structural funds. This is certainly more straight and honest than behaving as if whole nations are children not knowing what is best for them.

These considerations are reflected in Figure 32.

Figure 32

Option 1	Option 2
Member of the EU	The alternative
Grade: 0/100,000	Grade: 1,000/100,000

4. Argument No. 4 (International economics)

The larger the market that I live in, the higher will be my income. Also, the larger the market that I live in, the higher the rate of increase (the growth) of my income. Therefore, being within the EU, which is a very large market, I am better off than being outside the EU in my own market.

The theory of economics does not support any such claim. The theory of international economics indicates that it is very beneficial to have access to as many markets as possible, i.e. it says two things:

1. That individuals and firms should be able to sell their products or services to as many markets as possible. For example, the Portuguese should be able to sell their products and services to France or Germany or Sweden or Finland and vice versa.
2. The selling of products or services from country to country (international trade) should be completely unimpeded, i.e. without tariffs (a form of taxation), quotas (quantitative restrictions) or any other bureaucratic restrictions erected especially to restrict the entrance of foreign goods or services.

Once an individual or a firm has unimpeded access to a market, he can reap all the benefits of free trade. You don't need to be a US citizen to reap the benefits of the US market. You need to be able to sell your product or service to the US without tariffs or other non-tariffs barriers. In summary, the theory says that you need free access to trade with all markets in the world, but you don't need to be part of a huge market in order to reap the benefits of trade.

Economic theory (microeconomics) says also that each market should be internally free, which means that the laws applying to the market should promote competition as much as possible with relatively little government interference.

To put it in a few words, economics as a science speaks about *free trade access to free markets*. It does not say that an individual has to be living in a huge market in order to get the maximum possible economic benefits.

Now let us see the empirical evidence regarding the absolute level of per capita income and the rate of growth (rate of increase) of per capita income year after year. The per capita income of an individual living in the huge US market is surely high. But equally high is the per capita income of an individual living in Switzerland, Norway, Singapore or Hong Kong which are all small markets (not one of those countries is a member of the EU). In fact, according to most statistics, the per capita income in any of those small markets is higher than the per capita income in the US market. What is the secret of each of those small markets with a population each of five to seven million inhabitants? How can they be rich since they don't belong to a huge market? The answer is very simple: *free trade*. Once you have access for investment or trade to a market then you can reap all the benefits of that market.

On the opposite side, we see other huge markets like the Chinese or Indian or the Russian whose participants (citizens) have at present an average low per capita income.

Conclusion: there is no direct or inverse relationship between a huge market and high per capita income.

Regarding yearly growth of per capita income, i.e. the rate at which the living standards of the average citizen increase year after year, again the economic theory does not support that the rate of growth has anything to do with the size of the market. City states like Singapore or Hong Kong have had, for the past ten years, rates of growth two to three times the rates of growth of big markets like France or Germany (or even the USA). There are huge markets like China with growth rates of 8% yearly, but there are also small markets with equally high (or even higher) growth rates (like Malaysia, South Korea, Taiwan).

Conclusion: there is no direct or inverse relationship between a huge market and the rate of growth of per capita income.

Finally one can easily support that free access (free trade) to free markets is what provides high incomes and high growth rates to the average citizen and this has no relation to the size of the country.

It is worth mentioning here that the rate of growth of the per capita income of the EU countries has not accelerated since they formed the EU. On the contrary, the rate of growth of the EU participating countries for the past ten years at least has been much lower on average than in other industrial countries like Japan, Canada, Taiwan, South Korea, Australia, New Zealand, Switzerland and the USA.

So, what is the position of the alternative regarding the subject of a huge market? The chief characteristics of the alternative are that the citizens of the country trade freely in all markets large and small and the size of their own market is irrelevant to their economic well-being. The argument is graded overall in Figure 33.

Figure 33

Option 1 Member of the EU	Option 2 The alternative
Grade: 1,000/100,000	Grade: 1,000/100,000

5. Argument No. 5 (Economic)

Only within the EU can I be in a free market.

By the words 'free market', in very simple terms, one means a market where there is a lot of competition, as little government regulation of economic activities as possible and a relatively small public sector as a percentage of the GDP.

In a more general sense, we can define the degree of freedom of a market as the degree to which the laws of the country allow the natural economic laws to function. The most important natural economic law is the law of supply and demand.

The argument that if someone wants to live in a free market he or she has to be within the EU is obviously wrong. The freedom of a market is defined by the laws being in effect in the market and those laws are made by the people through their representatives. The lawmakers of any country can legislate at any time to make the market as free as the people who elected them wish. In fact, the degree of economic freedom of the EU is rather small today. Countries like the USA, New Zealand, Chile, Singapore, Hong Kong, Australia and Switzerland enjoy much higher degrees of economic freedom than the EU. Every week, the Commission in Brussels sends to the various member states a great number of regulations to be applied everywhere within the EU. In addition, the government sectors in the various countries are quite big as a proportion of Gross Domestic Product. So the EU is not a free market in principle. What is the alternative offering?

CHARACTERISTICS OF THE ALTERNATIVE

The alternative does not presuppose that free markets have to be imposed on the citizens of a country through laws coming to them from outside. The citizens of the alternative decide every four years how much free market they wish to have and give instructions accordingly to their lawmakers. They enjoy the flexibility of being able to make laws drastically reducing the size of government or drastically reducing regulation, for example, but they are perfectly able to reverse course at the next election.

To put it very simply, the citizens of the alternative have the opportunity to change their laws regarding degrees of economic freedom as time passes according to the findings of the science of economics, according to the change in technologies, according to what they see happening in any other country in the world (successes or failures) and according to their own experiences and wishes. They remember that time is a dimension that they cannot escape and that a practice that appears today to be correct may appear wrong after twenty years. The world is not static but dynamic and therefore a market should be able to change quickly.

When the citizens of the alternative want to change economic legislation or regulation in their market they have to convince only themselves and not the people living in other countries. Suppose, for example, that they want to reduce the size of government from 50% of GDP to 32% of GDP and then from 32% of GDP to 20% of GDP because they see that countries with very small governments have the highest rates of growth. This means that they will have to reduce taxation and spending, reduce regulation and so on. The citizens of the alternative are completely free to do just that, regardless of what is happening elsewhere and regardless of any regulations coming from Brussels. They are, however, equally free to increase the size of their government from say 38% of GDP to 45% of GDP and then to 55% of GDP if they so wish. They are free to experiment with themselves and their market as time passes by. What today is scientifically and practically correct may be equally scientifically and practically wrong after 150 years, but at the time when they want to change the degree of freedom of their market they will not have constraints imposed on their market by others and also they will be able to change quickly since they will have to decide and convince only themselves within a relatively small market.

Suppose, for example, that today the citizens of Ireland want to reduce the size of their government sector by, say, 10%. They will have to reduce taxation by 10% and government spending by 10% of GDP. In order to reduce taxation, they will need to reduce Value Added Taxes drastically, the taxes on income, taxes on firms' profits and maybe eliminate the taxes on the savings accounts in the banks. Unfortunately, they cannot do that. They have to convince the Europarliament and the Commission first. In effect, they have to convince 360 million people, pass the same legislation through the Europarliament and then receive this as instructions from Brussels. In practical terms, they cannot set their market as free as they wish.

These considerations lead to the grading in Figure 34.

Figure 34

Option 1 Member of the EU	Option 2 The alternative
Grade: 500/100,000	Grade: 2,000/100,000

6. Argument No. 6 (Microeconomic)

> The larger the market, the greater the competition. Therefore, within the EU I can reap the benefits of competition.

The discipline of microeconomics teaches us that for every product or service sold in a market the greater the competition the better for everybody, especially in the long run. Competition is dependent basically on the number of competing firms producing the same product or service and on the laws prevailing in the market (ease of entry into the market, anti-monopoly laws, bureaucracy, regulations, taxation, etc,). It is obvious that, in a very large market (like the EU), initially there will be more competitors than in a small market (say Switzerland or Norway).

However, as time passes, there is a tendency in every homogenous market (large or small) for consolidation so that in the long run a very small number of competitors prevail (say three to five firms). We have then the so-called oligopolistic situation, which is generally bad for the consumer since the oligopolists tend always to collude one way or another at the expense of the consumer. Therefore, theoretically, what counts for competition is not the size of the market, but the existence and application of anti-monopoly and pro-competitive laws (absence of barriers to enter the market, checking that the market power of each firm does not exceed a certain limit, and restricting bureaucracy and unnecessary regulations). Empirically, we can see that small markets like Hong Kong, Singapore, Switzerland, Norway or Australia have more competition internally than the large market of the EU or are at least equally pro-competitive. What, therefore, is important regarding competition in a market is not the size of the market itself but the continuous existence and application of pro-competitive laws.

Let us see now what the alternative offers regarding competition.

CHARACTERISTICS OF THE ALTERNATIVE

- Any foreign firm can enter the market of the alternative (always with reciprocity and with respect for the environmental regulations, labour laws, etc. of the country) by investing their capital and know-how.
- There are strict anti-monopoly laws in full force.
- All firms of the country are free to merge or make alliances with foreign firms, but no firm or alliance can at any time have a share of the market of the country greater than a specified amount (say, 5% of the market for the particular product or service). The percentage amount is specified by the citizens of the country through their lawmakers and nobody else. The amount can also vary with time according to the circumstances.

As defined above the alternative has the following advantages regarding competition:

- It allows full competition since any foreign firm or individual can enter the market in the form of investment in fixed assets, liquid assets and know-how.
- It supervises effectively the enforcement of competition since the supervision is done on a national level and not on a supranational level and is done by those interested in having results and not by outsiders without specific interests.
- It allows the companies to exploit economies of scale (if such economies exist in their field) by making alliances or mergers on a supranational level but in such a way that the alliance or the merged company cannot have market power in any national market higher than a specified small percentage.

To give a simple concept of the pro-competitive effects of the alternative one can ask: is it easier in the long run to produce oligopolistic situations over a huge geographical area when this area is one homogeneous market or when it consists of fifteen smaller markets, each one of which tries to be fully vigilant over competition? In both cases, you can have big players (if there is economic necessity for big players), but by having fifteen smaller markets no particular player can exploit any particular market by concentrating market power. To use a very simple example: by having one huge market (over the EU) in the long run a firm can have monopolistic power in, say, Germany but by not being active in the rest of the EU, it can be considered as not having sufficiently large market power. In effect, what could be an unacceptable monopoly over Germany can be considered as an acceptable oligopolistic player over the whole of the EU. This inherent disadvantage of a huge homogeneous market regarding competition is removed by the alternative, and this is reflected in Figure 35.

Figure 35

Option 1 Member of the EU	Option 2 The alternative
Grade: 500/100,000	Grade: 2,000/100,000

7. Argument No. 7 (Microeconomic)

In a huge market the firms can grow very large and hence can exploit economies of scale as well as face the tough competition from worldwide competitors. This can be achieved only within the EU.

We speak about economies of scale when a firm, by becoming larger, manages to reduce the cost of a unit of product or service sold (unit cost). There are certainly specific industries where economies of scale are present. However, this is not true for most industries and also varies with time and technology. There are many industries where size is immaterial and other industries where there are 'diseconomies of scale' (i.e. largeness is a disadvantage).

Let us concentrate now on a firm which is active in an industry where there are economies of scale present. What the firm needs in order to become large is the ability to sell its product or service in all fifteen member states of the EU and beyond. If the firm originates from country X within the EU, then the firm can certainly sell its products or services in every other country within the EU and if successful become large. By becoming large, the firm theoretically also has a better chance in facing competitors from South Korea, Taiwan, Japan, the USA, Canada, etc.

Let us now see the same firm originating from country Y which is following the alternative.

The firm is perfectly able to sell its products or services to any of the fifteen

EU member states. We have assumed free trade with all reciprocating countries and certainly the EU countries are supposed to promote free trade. Therefore the firm is perfectly able to expand and grow in all the EU countries and reap economies of scale. It is also in a position to merge with any firm it wishes to merge with provided that it does not get an excessive market share (and hence market power) in any of the fifteen countries. Examples of such a firm are large Swiss firms in the pharmaceutical, banking or electrical engineering businesses which have grown huge by participating in the markets of more than one hundred countries each and being successful in the tough competition of each market or even merging with firms from other countries. Other examples are highly successful firms from Japan, South Korea, Taiwan or Canada which have become large not because they originated in a huge market, but because they competed successfully in a great number of markets all over the world. No one of the above countries (including Switzerland) is a member state of the EU.

What is then the difference (if any) between the alternative and the EU regarding this particular argument of economies of scale? In both cases a firm, if successful, can grow, but with two significant differences in the long run:

Difference 1
Within the EU the firm will somehow have a false sense of security that it is shielded through trade or legal barriers from competitors of countries outside the EU. This false sense of security is becoming increasingly evident and will be absolutely clear during the next ten years when, according to the World Trade Organisation, all barriers to free trade (in services as well as in goods) will be totally eliminated almost everywhere in the world. However, within the alternative the firm knows that reciprocal free trade and competition is the name of the game in all directions and on all continents.

Difference 2
Within the EU in a particular industry, the firm can grow finally so large that the whole industry is dominated finally by two or three players (oligopolists) who exercise market power at the expense of the consumer all over the EU. The worst aspect with the oligopolists is that in the long run they get used to colluding amongst themselves, they get year after year a specific percentage of the market and they become 'lazy', i.e. their ability to improve with time (technological or managerial motivation, cost-effectiveness, etc.) is greatly reduced whereas in a competitive market (with a large number of players) they keep being 'fit' (innovative and efficient) in order to survive.

Under the alternative in each country, no firm can have market power greater than a specified percentage per industry (say, 5% of the market of the country). In this way the firm can expand or merge in all 185 countries on earth and become large globally (exploiting any existing economies of scale) but at the same time it cannot become an oligopolist in the particular market of the alternative. It will be forced always to compete against a great number of competitors and this is certainly very good, especially in the long run for both the consumers (prices) and the producers (innovation–cost-effectiveness).

The aspects of the argument are reflected in Figure 36.

Figure 36

Option 1 Member of the EU	Option 2 The alternative
Grade: 1,000/100,000	Grade: 2,000/100,000

8. Argument No. 8 (Economic)

Within the EU the citizens of individual countries have lost the flexibility to innovate by introducing important new laws at both the macroeconomic and microeconomic levels. This is extremely damaging, especially in the long run.

No human society is static. Societies (and their cultures) are dynamic in the sense that they change with time. This is the result of many factors, some of which are technology, the education level of the average citizen, the income level of the average citizen, developments in other societies, ease of travel and telecommunication, environmental degradation, health awareness and changes in customs and ethics. No human society was the same fifty years ago compared with what it is today, neither will it be the same after fifty or one hundred years. Not all changes are for the better, but in democratic societies the failures are spotted sooner or later and corrected or reversed. In practical terms societies progress through what is termed trial and error, i.e. they try something new and if it is successful they establish it as a permanent change. Some of the new ideas come from within a society and some (maybe the majority) come from other societies where they have been born or already successfully implemented.

A change in the economic affairs of a country usually presupposes the enactment of a new law by the lawmakers. Now let us imagine country X within the EU whose citizens decide to innovate by taking specific steps in either the macroeconomic sphere or microeconomic sphere. Suppose that they want to enact the following changes:

1. Scrap the minimum wage law (because this minimum wage produces unemployment according to elementary microeconomic theory)
2. Increase value added taxes from an average of 12% to an average of 20%
3. Reduce by 50% all income taxes (for the rich and the poor)
4. Eliminate the taxes on deposits in the banks, on inheritances and on capital gain.

5. Increase taxes on anything that pollutes the environment or causes serious health problems by 100%.
6. Eliminate all restrictions on the total hours of dependent work per week.
7. Let all shops and firms open and close according to their commercial needs without restriction.
8. Give monthly to all parents with children less than eighteen years old a considerable amount of money (child allowance) that will really permit all children to develop in approximately equal conditions regardless of how rich or poor their parents are.

From the scientific point of view, the first seven changes are in the microeconomic and macroeconomic spheres and the last change is in the philosophical sphere. No one in this imaginary country X knows for sure whether the changes will be successful and when (if ever). Maybe the changes will cause pain in the first five years but will start producing great results after ten years. Maybe the changes will fail altogether and will have to be reversed after twelve years of experiment. Some people agree with the proposed changes and some disagree but a slight majority of the country are for the changes and finally the citizens of country X decide to try.

Unfortunately, they cannot try! They find out that they cannot even legislate because all of the above laws contradict general laws or regulations of the EU! The only thing they can do is to force the EU to change its laws. But to do that they find that they have to persuade another 360 million people of different cultures, economies, geographic locations, histories and languages. They also find out that if today they have to persuade 360 million people, after fifteen years they will have to persuade around 500 (or even 600) million people. So, what do the citizens of country X do? They finally do nothing because in practical terms they can do nothing fundamental to change their lives (for better or worse). They can take very small measures similar to those taken by a local council or a mayor (a little more money for education, small increases in property taxes, some decreases in income taxes, some decreases in defence expenditure, build some roads and hospitals) but nothing substantial or really fundamental. They can move only within the given small degrees of freedom and small limits of flexibility.

What is the end result of all this for the citizens of country X? It is that they cannot move forwards (or sometimes backwards – who knows?) at the pace they wish. They can make progress in their living standards only at the slow pace that others have defined, not at the pace they would like to move forward (or at the pace they are actually capable of moving forward). *A big human society is rigid and slow to move forward. A small human society is flexible and quick to move forward.*

Some might think that maybe the citizens of country X would be luckier if they tried to introduce other measures. The truth of the matter is that within the EU there is today legislation and regulations on almost any kind of human activity (economic or non-economic) and the freedom of manoeuvre for the citizens of any specific country is zero on important economic matters and limited on secondary or tertiary matters.

The consequences of all this are that the pace of growth of the economy of country X and the pace of the improvement in living standards will be much less than they would have been without those restrictions.

In the long run human societies make the maximum possible progress when they are absolutely free to experiment, to try, to innovate and to reap the fruits of their successes as well as the consequences of their failures. Then and only then they develop their maximum potential!

Let us now see if the alternative has anything to offer on this very important matter.

CHARACTERISTIC OF THE ALTERNATIVE

The lawmakers of the country are completely free to introduce and enact any law that the citizens have instructed them to introduce. They are bound only by international treaties with the World Trade Organisation regarding free trade.

It is obvious that the citizens of the alternative have no problem moving forwards (or even backwards!) as fast or as slowly as they wish to. Hence the grading in Figure 37.

Figure 37

Option 1 Member of the EU	Option 2 The alternative
Grade: 500/100,000	Grade: 7,500/100,000

9. Argument No. 9 (Economic)

> Within the EU I am free to seek work in any of the member states. This is undoubtedly good for me because it increases my chances of employment.

We are talking here not of the freedom to stay in other countries for tourism, education, health treatment, investment in real assets and cultural exhibitions. We are talking here about the freedom to work legally (or to seek work) in all EU member states.

Let us see first what the discipline of international economics says on this matter. In a world where there is labour mobility within a country, but no labour mobility between countries, and where there is free trade, it is easily proved that *free trade equalises factor rewards (labour and capital rewards) between countries and thus serves as a substitute for external factor mobility.*

This proposition is known as the 'Factor-Price Equalisation theorem' and full proof of this theorem can be found in any book on international economics. Intuitively we can describe it with the following example.

Assume that Germany is more abundant in capital and Greece is more abundant in labour in relative but not in absolute terms. This means that the labour-intensive tourist service is 'exported' from Greece to Germany (German tourists visit Greece) and that the capital-intensive car manufacturing industry is being exported to Greece (Germans sell cars to Greece). By exporting a labour-intensive service (such as tourism), Greece (the relatively labour abundant country) indirectly exports a net amount of labour in exchange for a net amount of capital; and Germany being a relatively capital-abundant country does the opposite. This indirect exchange of labour raises the real wage rate in Greece (and lowers the real wage rate in Germany) and also raises the rental rate of capital in Germany (and lowers the rental rate of capital in Greece).

Thus, with free trade in goods and services, both labour and capital do indeed migrate between countries, not directly but indirectly through the exports and imports of goods and services. In the process the real factor rewards (the real rewards to both labour and capital) tend to be equalised between countries. This is indeed a very important condition for the efficient allocation of resources worldwide.

A casual look, however, at the real world can convince us quickly that factor prices (labour and capital rewards) are not actually equalised among nations. Construction workers, software engineers, doctors, bankers and so on do not earn the same wages in India and Pakistan as they do in Germany or France. No doubt some of these differences reflect disparities in skill (or human capital).[1] But not all factor price (wage rate and capital rent) differentials between countries can be explained away in this fashion. It appears, therefore, that freer factor movements can enable the world economy to enjoy large gains in potential welfare – in addition to the gains from free trade in commodities (goods and services). In summary, free trade is a substitute, albeit imperfect, for factor movements (labour or capital movements) between countries.

This is as far as the theory goes. Now let us see some empirical results.

Switzerland is outside of the EU but trades freely with all EU member states. The unemployment rate in Switzerland is one of the lowest in the continent of Europe (and in the world).

Greece is a member state of the EU. The convergence of Greek wages to German wages was much higher from 1950 to 1992 (i.e. before the Greeks could settle legally in Germany without requiring any invitation) than from 1992 to 1997 (when the Greeks could work legally in any of the other fourteen

---

[1] Some of the differences also reflect the very important fact that until recently there was no free trade (neither does it exist today).

member states of the EU). Similarly the unemployment rate in Greece was much lower from 1950 to 1992 than from 1992 to 1997.

Hong Kong is a city state with 6.5 million people trading freely with their giant neighbour, China, but without freedom to work in China (at least until 1997). The unemployment rate is negligible and per capita income the highest in the world (about thirty times the per capita income of the giant China!)

Singapore is a city state of 5.5 million people trading freely, with unemployment rate and per capita income roughly the same as Hong Kong!

The empirical evidence is therefore that *free trade is a substitute for inter-country labour movement, especially when free trade is coupled with correct economic policies within the country.*

There is, moreover, a flip side to the free movement of workers and professionals from country to country which is not examined in the ideal world of economics where minimum wages, maximum working hours, work environment laws, unemployment benefits, free or subsidised health care and social insurance are either non-existent or at least neglected for the sake of simplicity.

Let us use an imaginary example. Today (summer 1997) in Germany, the unemployment rate is high at around 11% of the workforce. Now suppose that the German people, by taking some extraordinary measures among themselves, managed tomorrow to reduce their unemployment rate to just 4%. There is no importance as to what exactly the extraordinary measures or sacrifices or legislation were that the German citizens used to achieve this very low level of unemployment. We just assume that tomorrow their unemployment rate has become just 4% and practically everybody in Germany has a job. What would happen the next day, the day after tomorrow? Unemployed citizens from the other fourteen member states of the EU, realising that they would have some good prospects to find work in Germany, would flock into Germany looking for a decent job in all disciplines and professions (from unskilled labourers to plumbers to physicists to software engineers).

They would be ready to offer their services for a little less than German citizens and this would mean that very soon the unemployment rate in Germany would go up towards 11% again. This is a result of the simple fact that after 1992 (Maastricht Treaty) all fifteen member states became, in effect, communicating vessels as far as the employed and unemployed are concerned, and practically no individual state can hope to have considerably less unemployment than its neighbours. If we add here the fact that the incoming citizens of other countries are unavoidably using the infrastructure and the public services of the recipient country such as schools, hospitals and police stations (for which the Germans have paid through their taxes), then the picture is clear that in our imaginary example the German citizens cannot hope to reduce seriously their unemployment rate to a level much lower than the average of the other fourteen member states. To put it in a few very simple words, *my freedom to seek employment in any of the other fourteen member states means at the same time that all citizens of the other fourteen states are free to seek employment in my country.*

Is this on balance good or bad? No one really knows when both microeconomic and macroeconomic considerations are taken into account.

Is it good for the USA to open its southern borders and permit all the citizens of Mexico to work legally in the USA today? According to theoretical economics the free movement of labour (any kind of worker from scientists to manual workers) would be slightly beneficial to everybody, but on practical grounds it is doubtful. Is it good for Germany if 980 million decent citizens of India are permitted tomorrow to work legally in Germany and in the EU in general? Again, according to theoretical economics it is slightly beneficial for everybody, but on practical grounds it is doubtful.

So what is the alternative offering on this very important matter?

CHARACTERISTIC OF THE ALTERNATIVE

In country X the export and import of labour (of any specialisation) is done through:

1. completely free trade in goods and services with all 184 countries on earth
2. completely free flows of capital
3. completely free investment in financial assets (stocks, bonds, etc.)
4. completely free investment in real assets (factories, service firms, etc.)

The philosophy behind these characteristics is that the four degrees of freedom are almost equivalent to the freedom to work legally anywhere and the freedom of others to work here especially when combined with correct economic policies within country X, without, however, the drawbacks of uncontrolled labour movements. The citizens of country X retain fully their ability to control and correct all economic indicators within their country especially the indicators of unemployment and budget deficit. (Note: uncontrolled immigration necessarily has consequences on public services like hospitals, schools, etc., and this in turn affects the budget deficit.)

Now let us turn our attention to two imaginary situations in country X showing the effect of the alternative regarding unemployment.

Situation 1: high unemployment in country X

If the unemployment is cyclical (i.e. due to some economic cycle or disturbance from within or from abroad), it is the government of the country that has to act with temporary fiscal or monetary expansion (or both).

If the unemployment is structural (i.e. the labour force of the country is for some reason not competitive or expensive), it is structural measures that have to be taken by the citizens of the country through their lawmakers (legislature). What exactly those structural measures would be depends on the circumstances (point in time, political atmosphere, etc.) and on the will and determination of the people of the country to solve their unemployment problem. One thing is certain. Structural unemployment in the country needs structural measures to be solved (and also lawmakers who understand economics). Those structural measures can be taken once the people of the country take the decision (and find the suitable leaders). There is no other solution to the structural unemployment problem. The solution of bringing legal cheap labour (of all specialities) into the country in order to push down the general level of wages is like what the ostriches do (put their heads in the sand thinking that there isn't a problem). The final outcome is that the structural problems remain, the citizens of the country become unemployed and draw benefits and the problem perpetuates indefinitely. Even if all the unemployed citizens of country X could today move to another country to work legally without solving the structural problems in their country, it is certain that, after a few years, the high unemployment within the country would reappear through the labour force that would have entered the working age population in the meantime.

Unless you remove the cause (or causes) you cannot remove the effect and unemployment is the effect. All other propositions are simply wrong.

Situation 2: very low unemployment in the alternative country X

Suppose that we are in the unusual situation of country X 'suffering' from very low unemployment, i.e. firms cannot easily find people to employ. What then do the citizens of country X do? Since they live in the alternative and they cannot be automatically flooded with decent people from other countries looking for work what do they do? Their economy needs extra hands and brains and lack of sufficient numbers of hands and brains is economically as bad as having surplus hands and brains.

The citizens of country X should conduct every year an electronic referendum on the following single subject: how many legal immigrants, citizens of other countries, do you wish your government to allow to settle in this country during the next twelve months? (Choices should be between specific numbers such as: 0 thousand, 10 thousands, 30 thousands, 100 thousands)

The electronic referendum would cost virtually nothing to the taxpayers and would be done through the Internet. All legal immigrants taken each year into the country should automatically become citizens of the country after three years of residence.

Details about the introduction of the electronic referendum principle will be given in later chapters, but for the time being it suffices to note that:

1. Electronic referenda are perfectly possible with today's technology.
2. They cost virtually nothing.
3. They are the most democratic means of deciding on the important matter of immigration.
4. They take the controversy of immigration (and all associated responsi-

bilities) away from the governments and the opposition parties directly to the people.
5. No one can suggest that any government or lawmaker or opposition party knows better than the simple citizens of country X how many new immigrants (if any) they need each year within their country.
6. Such an immigration referendum covers only economic immigrants and not asylum seekers.

Some clarifications are necessary here regarding the method of deciding by electronic referendum. Immigration for economic reasons is generally a very good thing for any society because it helps the society to fill voids in the workplace, to receive extra brains, know-how or muscle power when it needs them, to renew gradually or develop its culture and indirectly to avoid wars since people and cultures gradually get to know and trust each other better. But this is so only when this happens with the full knowledge and consent of the citizens of the recipient country and in a manner and at a pace that does not make them feel disoriented or pushed aside or as though they are losing their identity or their culture.

Immigration for humanitarian reasons is a completely different matter. A person persecuted in his or her own country and trying to find shelter in country X deserves extra consideration completely outside of economic logic (cost-benefit analysis). It would be a characteristic of the alternative that, for people trying to settle in country X owing to persecution, the government would decide quickly to assist them following the fundamental principle: when someone knocks on our door and asks for shelter because he or she is threatened, we bring him or her in and try to help to the best of our ability and with the whole of our heart.

On page 111 it was suggested that for the alternative free trade, combined with free investment in real assets, financial assets and with free flows of capital, is for all practical purposes equivalent to free inter-country movement of labour and it was mentioned that free trade is applied worldwide, provided that it is reciprocal. A serious question arises here: completely free trade between rich countries with high labour costs and poor countries with very low labour costs may be very dangerous in the sense that it is unfair and therefore will lead by itself to unemployment in the rich country. It may also be very dangerous to the poor country because its factories and firms are not yet very efficient and will be swallowed up by the efficient sharks of the rich countries. If the wages in India are so much lower than the wages in Greece, then Greek real wages will be drastically reduced if Greek workers are subjected to the competition of Indian cheap labour through completely free trade in goods and services. If Japan's efficiency is so great, then its producers will undersell Greek producers in every line of production. How could Greek producers, who are technically inferior to their Japanese counterparts, compete? Accordingly, in order to protect Greek producers and workers from ruinous foreign competition, import tariffs are required against Japanese and Indian products or services.

According to the science of international economics both these arguments are wrong. They are pseudo-arguments that do not stand up to scientific scrutiny. Full proof of this can be found in any elementary book of international economics in the chapters relating to what is known as the law of comparative advantage. However, a very brief example is given below to illustrate the matter.

Suppose that the Japanese producers are six times more efficient than the Greek producers in the production of automobiles and twice as efficient as the Greek producers in the production of tourist services (running hotels, etc.). In absolute terms, the Greek producers are at a disadvantage in both activities, but in relative terms they have a comparative advantage in tourist services and a comparative disadvantage in car manufacturing, while the opposite is true for the Japanese producers. Under completely free trade, the Greeks will specialise in tourist services (where they enjoy a comparative advantage), and the Japanese producers will specialise in car manufacturing (where they enjoy a comparative advantage). The final situation will be that Greek tourist services will be exchanged for Japanese cars and the total potential output of both countries for both cars and tourist services increases. The fact that Japanese producers have an absolute advantage in tourism (i.e. they can run tourist resorts twice as efficiently as the Greeks) is irrelevant. Moreover, the law of comparative advantage has much general validity. For instance, it applies to the division of labour between individual persons. Examples are not difficult to find. A physician, though a great bookkeeper himself, employs somebody else to do his bookkeeping because his comparative advantage lies in medicine. The same is true of a business manager who employs a secretary to do his typing, a lawyer who hires a gardener and a teacher who has an assistant to grade the students' papers.

Another wrong idea is that a large country, because of its sheer size and economic power, can reap all the gains from free trade by taking advantage of a small nation. This rational feeling is incorrect. In the arena of world trade the rules of the game are not the same as those that prevail in a wrestling arena, where a big guy can push around a weak wrestler. Indeed, in international trade the opposite is true. When two trading countries are of unequal size, all the gains from free trade may accrue to the small nation, with the large country gaining nothing. An obvious example of this is tiny Singapore (city state of 6 million people) trading with giant China (a country with 1,200 million people) with the Singaporeans having one of the highest per capita incomes in the world today!

Where does all this discussion finally lead us? Is the alternative a better model than the classic member of the EU model regarding this particular argument of movement of labour?

My opinion is that if there were not existing governments, minimum wages, unemployment benefits and what is called 'the safety net of a modern country' the model of the EU is slightly superior. This is because it permits a slightly quicker exchange of labour in both the high unemployment case and the very low unemployment case. In other words, on purely theoretical economics grounds (completely flexible labour, no safety net, etc.) the model of member of the EU is slightly superior. However, on practical economics grounds, I believe that the alternative is slightly superior. When we deal with economics we have to consider the real world circumstances and not an imaginary world (which may prove finally a utopia). Therefore I will give equal grades to both options as in Figure 38.

Note that associated with the above argument there are cultural, political and philosophical aspects which are maybe a million times more important than the economic aspects. Those will be examined in later chapters.

Figure 38

Option 1 Member of the EU	Option 2 The alternative
Grade: 1,500/100,000	Grade: 1,500/100,000

10. Argument No. 10 (Economic)

> Within the EU I can enjoy the single market where the rules of the game are the same for everyone and therefore competition is 'fair'. This is certainly good for me as an individual producer (businessman or member of a firm), consumer or worker.

The concept of 'single market' is the core concept of the EU and is an extremely serious subject, mainly from the philosophical and political points of view. The philosophical and political aspects will be examined in later chapters. Here we will examine only the economic ideas behind the single market.

Economics as a science speaks about 'free markets' and not about a 'single market'. Either by unintentional mistake or intentional manipulation of the language, someone (or a group of people) has replaced the word 'free' with the word 'single' and changed the word markets from the plural to the singular. Economics as a science refers to each market trying to be 'as free as possible'. It does not say that each continent on earth should have one single market. We are confronting either a colossal misunderstanding or a colossal deception.

The economic theory says that each market works more efficiently if it is free, i.e. without unnecessary or excessive government intervention, without restrictive labour laws, without excessive taxation or regulation and so on. This free market is nevertheless subject to the political wishes of the citizens of the country since politics (i.e. the wishes of the people) is above economics and not the other way around. To put it in a few simple words the theory states that each country should have its own free market (subject to the will of the people) and not that the countries on the European continent should merge their markets into one single market (which, incidentally, could not be so free!).

But let us forget about the established economic theories and try to see, on practical grounds, the single market from the economic point of view.

First of all, the single market means common laws on any kind of economic activity. Only then we can have a single market. But since almost all human activity is more or less related to economics, single market means single set of laws for all participating states. Common laws on maximum working hours, common laws on the minimum wage, common laws on opening hours for shops, common laws for workers compensation, common laws regarding labour unions, common laws regarding social insurance, common laws on environmental protection, common laws on support to farmers, livestock growers and fishermen, common laws on protection of the unemployed, common laws on protection of the old, common laws on protection of the disabled. The list is endless and this is only natural because the majority of all decisions or choices by human beings are, in essence, economic decisions (materialistic decisions or choices) and all decisions have economic consequences. Now the question arises: are common laws good or bad?

As a quick answer, human beings are moving forward not due to singularity or uniqueness but due to diversity and plurality. Singularities in advanced mathematics are points of anomaly and for the advanced astrophysicists the black holes are singularities. At the singularities the laws of mathematics and physics break down. By its very concept the single market tries to replace diversity and plurality with singularity and uniqueness. This is not good for the material progress of human beings.

Now let us give a more down-to-earth answer on the common laws question.

In a static world (i.e. in a world where time is still), the 'one size fits all' theory creates the following problems:

1. In order to make a single law (a common law) for fifteen countries, usually the lowest common denominator is taken, or maybe the path of least resistance. That means that usually the worst of all fifteen alternatives is applied to all fifteen member states.
2. The single law cannot take into consideration the differing geographic locations of each country, the different structure of each economy, the different stage of development of each economy, the differing cultures, etc.
3. The single law is slow to be enacted because, by definition, it is con-

ceived as an idea by a legislator in one country, then it has to be a convincing idea for the legislators in the Europarliament in Brussels or Strasbourg and, after it is voted by some majority, it has to be ratified by the national parliaments.

4. The single law means that the citizens of any particular country cannot make the law to 'fit their size', to fit their preferences, peculiarities or desires. Their elected representatives in the national assemblies are actually reduced to discussing things of a third level of importance. That means that the common laws are necessarily reducing the legislative ability of any particular nation and are being made in a centralised manner in Strasbourg or Brussels to suit the needs of 360 million people and not only the needs of the people of a particular country. In the age of decentralisation, Internet and flexibility, we have centralisation, rubber stamping of incoming laws by the national parliaments and rigidity. Where we had a picture of valleys and hills, lakes and forests, we have a flattened out field, the same for all, regardless of their particular needs or wishes.

Another aspect of the single laws is the judicial aspect. *Common laws mean a single justice system.*

If the laws are common, then it is natural that judgements about violations of laws are common and this in effect means a single justice system. If an action breaks the single law in Finland, then it is necessarily so in Portugal or Spain too. This means that the primary justice system is that residing in Luxembourg and that judges in all countries have, in one way or another, to take their decisions in accordance with the single judgement.

We saw before how the single market means that the legislative processes of fifteen countries become one and the same goes for the judicial processes. What then about the third pillar of any democracy, which is the executive body (or government)?

First of all, the most important public body for any nation in order to have economic progress is not the executive (i.e. government) but the legislative body (parliament).

Second, a very important aspect of the single market is not only the common laws, but also the common everyday parameters or policies. In a single market, by definition you have to have a single currency and a single currency means a single monetary policy. But monetary policy is at least 50% of what any contemporary government does ('government' in its most general sense, inclusive of all public institutions) regarding economic policy. But economic policy is the main task of any executive body (government). In addition to the above, a single monetary policy heads sooner or later to a single fiscal policy (no doubt about this). But fiscal policy is the other 50% of the tasks of any government.

In a single market you need to have more or less common conditions for participation by economic agents (i.e. by individual human beings or firms). But common conditions mean a single tax rate on income, a single tax rate on property, common value added taxes, common tax rates on profits by firms or individuals, a single capital gains tax, a single tax on deposits in the banks, common unemployment benefits, common social insurance rates, common inheritance taxes, common health care contributions, common rules regarding military service, common taxes on those polluting the environment, common agricultural, livestock and fisheries support, common borders control, a single police force, a single fire-fighting force, common support to married couples, common support to those with many children, common educational procedures, common health care procedures, common tests for new drugs (and new ideas maybe!), common trade policies, common tariffs, a single aviation policy, common foreign affairs policies (including single embassies in third countries), common national day holidays, common religious holidays, a single land and sea transportation policy, common teaching materials and methods, a single level of infrastructure facilities, a single day of the year for changing our clocks, common dates for elections, common trade unions, common scientific or professional associations, common government procurement policies, common support to cultural events or artists, common rules for the stock markets, a single team in the Olympics, a single basketball or football league, unified athletics associations, a single passport form, a single identity card form, a single national anthem and common flag.

I am not sure what constitutes a single government but I believe that the set of all the above commonalities constitutes a single government.

Someone might object to the above list in terms of whether all of these exist today or whether they are going to exist in the future. If one accepts (and this is a very big if) that fifteen countries should live in a single market, then all the above common things follow or will follow in the future as a natural consequence of the single market concept. In fact, in a single market the actual list of common features is maybe 10,000 times bigger than the above list. Let us see some examples:

- In a single market, students in Greece are disadvantaged compared to the students in Britain because those in Greece have to spend thousands of hours learning a difficult language (the Greek language) and then they have to spend additional thousands of hours (and their parents' money) learning English as a foreign language. If changing money from one unit to another is a little inefficient, what about all those millions of French, German, Italian, Spanish, Belgian students spending thousands of hours (and money) studying English? What about all those hours and money spent during conferences and symposia for translations? What about all those inefficiencies in translating books into various languages? It is obvious that in a single market you have to have a single language (or no more than two or three

common languages).
- In a single market, the number of teaching hours in all schools at all levels must be the same, otherwise the students receiving fewer hours of teaching per week are at an economic disadvantage. For the same reasons, the teaching methods must be the same and, in general, the amount of money spent by the state for each student must be the same.
- In a single market, if in a particular country the deposits in the banks are not taxed, then this is unfair competition. Moreover, the tax rate applied to the deposits should be the same otherwise there is no single market.
- In a single market, the level of the unemployment benefits must be the same otherwise any significant differentials will send waves of unemployed people to the country with the highest benefits and this is unfair to the taxpayers of the particular country paying a higher proportion of their income for support of the unemployed.
- In a single market, the contributions for pensions must be the same otherwise individuals and firms living in the country with the highest contributions are at a competitive disadvantage during their working lives.
- In a single market, the public care for the disabled must be the same otherwise the disabled from all countries will tend sooner or later to migrate to the country offering the best care, straining unfairly the budget deficit of the high standards country (and reducing unfairly the budget deficit of the low standards countries).
- In a single market, property taxes and inheritance taxes must be the same otherwise people from all other countries will tend to own property, live and die in the country offering the lowest property or inheritance taxes, distorting the property market, straining the infrastructure and the budget of the lowest tax country (and crowding its cemeteries!).
- In a single market, military service must be done everywhere by professional soldiers or must be compulsory everywhere, otherwise the young men and women of any country serving by law in the armed forces say for 1½ years are at a disadvantage with the others entering the labour force 1½ years earlier. In general, the amount of tax paid for defence must be the same otherwise the citizens of the country paying for a relatively big defence budget are at a disadvantage.
- In a single market, the taxes and regulations for individuals, firms, products or services polluting the environment must be the same otherwise economic agents living in the country with the stricter controls (highest taxes) are at an unfair disadvantage.
- In a single market, the support for any agricultural product (and the taxes associated with this support) must be the same everywhere otherwise the economic agents (farmers, livestock growers or fishermen) in the country

with the lowest support are at a disadvantage.

- In a single market, the control of the borders must be the same, otherwise economic immigrants from third countries will tend to enter through the country with the laxest border controls and then spread absolutely free to all other countries. This means that the authority and body for checking the borders of a country must be centralised and absolutely under the control of Brussels so as to make sure that the same standards for security, illegal immigration, drug trafficking and weapon smuggling are applied to all countries and that no country lives at the expense of others. This necessarily means that all those people associated with border control (including armed forces, coast guards, border police, etc.) must be paid by the central authority (otherwise no effective and fair control can be effected).

- In a single market, the inter-country policing must be under a central authority (Europol) otherwise it will be very easy for individuals or firms who for some reason break a law, to migrate to another country unnoticed (or even welcomed if they are financially attractive). Furthermore, the level of policing within each country must be roughly of the same standard otherwise a country may choose to ignore tax offenders (big or small) or other illegals creating conditions of unfair competition. If we accept different policing standards, then light or heavy illegals (from people simply smoking marijuana to people being sought for arson or murder) will tend to concentrate on the country with the lowest policing standards. This necessarily means that the centralised police (Europol) must be directly employed (and paid) by Brussels, otherwise there can be no effective and fair police control.

- In a single market, the customs clearance of goods coming from third countries must be done from the same central authority otherwise in one country it may be that some goods are taxed at low tariffs and then distributed freely to all other countries. This would create a situation where the particular country with the low tariff would collect tariffs from a huge volume of goods (everybody would send their goods through that country because of low tariffs) and this country would be at an unfair advantage (collecting more taxes from the big volume of incoming goods). The same applies if the customs officers of a particular country happen to suffer from a higher than normal level of corruption. That means that the customs authority should be centralised and all personnel under the full control, payment and budget of the Commission.

The list of common features is almost endless. Therefore, in a single market not only the set of laws (legislative power) has to be common, not only the judicial system has to be common, but also the economic policies have to be common. Economic policies are basically the monetary policy and the fiscal policy, but actually all kinds of policies must be common because everything has economic consequences. Foreign policy, defence policy, trade policy, immigration policy, internal security policy, educational policy, pensions policy, public works policy, health policy all are directly and indirectly related to economics and to the sense of competition under the same conditions. But common policies mean a common government.

Now the question arises: is a single government (single set of executive policies) for fifteen countries a good or a bad thing on purely economic grounds?

In a static world (remember that we are still in a world where there is no time), a single set of executive powers has the efficiency of bringing down the cost of government. In other words, instead of running fifteen ministries for each kind of activity in each country, there should ideally be only one ministry of each kind centralised in Brussels and each individual country should run only a skeleton ministry. This cost saving, however, is negligible in relative economic terms. The economic disadvantages of centralising the executive bodies are, however, very large. Some of them are:

1. Central government means necessarily that the economic policies (fiscal policy, monetary policy, trade policy, level of taxation, pensions policy, etc.) will always try to suit the needs of fifteen different countries trough the lowest common denominator or the path of least resistance. As a natural consequence of that, the common policies, by definition, will never reflect the will of the citizens of any particular country to improve their lives as much as they wish or maybe as much as they are prepared to change their lives. The citizens of any particular country will be shopping government policies from a general merchandise superstore instead of shopping from a boutique.

2. By definition, a centralised government can never cater for the needs of the citizens of each country as much as a national government can, other things being equal. A centralised government will be always something distant from the economic needs of the people.

3. A centralised government necessarily creates centralised lobbies. It is already a fact very well known to everybody that a huge army of lawyers and thousands of other lobbyists are permanently lobbying the European Commission in Brussels and the Europarliament in Strasbourg. The lobbying is done for various industries, companies, institutions and professional associations. These lobbies acting now on a supranational level are first of all very strong and secondly not accountable and checked by anyone. This means that the economic policies are now influenced by strong lobbies and not by what the citizens of each particular country wish for themselves. Centralisation of power and strong lobbies means less efficient policies than with decentralised government and necessarily small lobbies.

We see, therefore, that in a single market and a static world there has to be a single set of laws, a single judicial system and a single executive body (government) which are associated with a number of economic inefficiencies.

But let us jump now to a dynamic world, a world where time is running. In such a world the inefficiencies associated with the common features become very great because:

1. The economic conditions do not change with time homogeneously for fifteen nations but the response (to the changing conditions) in the form of changing laws or executive policies will be, by definition, homogeneous. If for some reason next year the tourist industry is badly in recession but not the manufacturing industry, this will affect countries relying heavily on tourism (like Portugal, Spain or Greece) differently than heavily industrial countries like Germany, Sweden or Finland. But the response to the problem will be with some common policy measures which will be necessarily inferior to the measures that individual countries could take. *In a dynamic world where everything changes with time, specific economic problems need specific and targeted responses.*

   This cannot happen with single laws and policies because, for example, a measure or law that is good for the tourist industry in Portugal may very well do some damage to manufacturing in Germany and vice versa. Economies are different because of different geographic locations, different climates, different cultures, different mentalities, different population densities, different endowments of capital and, most of all, different amounts of determination on the part of the people of any particular country for sacrifices or hard work or savings or attitudes towards public goods or towards the weak members of society.

2. The rate of change of the policies or laws in a single market is definitely slower than the rate of change that each individual country could have if it were able to respond individually to the changing world. The speed of change of any economic policy is necessarily lower in a single market because of the centralised structures, the size of the populations involved and the necessary study of the possible consequences of any particular measure to every country. *A very long economic train is in general slower than a train having only its engine and one wagon (other things being equal).*

3. Finally, in a single market, when a single law or single policy finally changes with time, it will most probably change to a form with the least consequences for 360 million people and not to the best possible form, even if we assume that the people of a particular country know what this best possible form is and they are willing to dare proceed with the change.

Suppose, for example, that regarding taxation of savings in the banks the best possible form is a zero rate of tax because this increases the savings rate and, in turn, the higher savings rate increases investment. This, in turn, decreases unemployment and makes everyone better off. Assume further that the citizens of country X want to make zero the tax on savings and instruct their government to do so. Unfortunately their national government cannot make the change because in a single market taxes on savings have to be the same!

We have seen up to now in this argument the fundamental economic disadvantages of a common legislature and executive body. But aren't there any advantages? Yes, there are mainly two.

One is possible economies of scales by eliminating or reducing by, say 80% to 90%, the size and scope of the national legislatures and governments. These economies of scale presuppose, however, that there will be no duplication of power and conflicts of interests so that once the central power or authority decides then decisions are implemented quickly and without resistance from the national authorities (local authorities or powers). In practical terms, things get very complicated because the national (or local) bodies (governments and legislatures) are in general uninterested in the implementation of the central power instructions since the instructions or changes are initiated by others in response to problems that may have appeared in other countries.

The second and most important economic advantage of a single market is that the economic agents (firms or individuals) do face less friction when active in many states. The reduced friction when setting activity in different states is a direct result of the common laws, executive body policies and justice systems. A company or individual wishing to set up shop in any state knows beforehand what laws and government policies it will have to face and this is positive for any kind of economic activity. It is generally much easier to set up shop in a different state in the EU than to go to Argentina or South Africa or India and start business there.

Having discussed the advantages and disadvantages of the single market, let us see the alternative.

The objectives of country X under the alternative are the following:

- single market within country X and not necessarily outside country X.
- ability of the market of country X to change laws or regulations or government policies according to the wishes of the citizens of country X in the shortest possible time in order to respond to national or international developments.

In order to achieve the above objectives the imaginary country X is organised upon the following concrete measures:

1. The legislative power, the executive power and the judicial power are completely separated. Any member of the government cannot be lawmaker (member of parliament or congress or senate) or judge.
2. There is no legislative body above the legislative body of country X.
3. There is no judicial system above the justice system of country X.
4. There is no executive body above the executive body of country X.
5. The lawmaking body receives officially through electronic means (fax, e-mail, Internet) all laws passed (enacted) every day by the legislative bodies of all other 184 countries on earth.
6. The lawmakers of country X are not voters. Voting on any new law is done one day of the week at the same time (say, every Saturday at 4 p.m.) by the citizens of country X through electronic referendum via the Internet. Before voting electronically, the citizens of the country read on their computer/television screens through e-mail all the pros and cons of the law as discussed during the week by the lawmakers.
7. The top body of the judges are all elected every four years.
8. The whole government is elected every four (or five) years and not just the prime minister.

Let us now discuss the above eight measures of our imaginary alternative in some detail, giving special emphasis to their economic consequences or merits.

Measure 1: separation of the three powers
Since the members of parliament cannot be members of government and vice versa, this gives incentives to the lawmakers to think only of their job (to propose laws suitable for the citizens who elected them not because they are beautiful but because they are wise and honest) and gives incentives to the members of government to govern only to the best of their abilities and according to the laws voted by the citizens of the country without interfering with the lawmaking or judicial process.

Also since the judges cannot be members of the government or the legislating body, they have every opportunity to judge independently, without any interference by government members or legislators.

The complete separation of powers in country X results in better specialisation and concentration on a particular elected position, no interference by others and therefore a better outcome. Government, legislature and judges perform their functions better.

Measure 2: no lawmaking body above that of country X
By being truly independent of any other lawmaking body, the lawmakers of country X are able to legislate according to what they perceive to be just and correct and beneficial for the citizens who elected them. So independence from others means in general better judgement and better performance in the lawmaking process. But it means also greater speed and flexibility, and greater

ability to respond to the special needs of the citizens of country X and to adapt to a rapidly changing internal and external environment (economic developments worldwide, technological developments and cultural developments).

In addition, independence in the lawmaking process means greater accountability of the lawmakers, i.e. the members of congress or the senate will not be able to say to their fellow citizens that they are making a law because this law came as an instruction from other lawmakers (in the Europarliament). All the above advantages in lawmaking (better judgement, better performance, greater flexibility, better response to a rapidly changing world and absolute accountability to the citizens of the country) mean a better economic environment for everybody in country X (especially in the long run) because it is the set of laws that permit the citizens of any country to achieve their maximum economic (and mental) potential. Of the three powers (legislative, government and judges), the legislature is in practical terms by far the most important power of any country.

Contrary to what is believed by the average citizen of the average country, it is the lawmakers who make or break the country and not the government.

Measure 3: judicial system supreme in country X
The complete independence of the judges from other justice systems means that they are free to judge according only to the laws voted by the citizens of the country and that they are fully and completely accountable to the citizens of the country. All these in turn mean that the judges exhibit better performance and efficiency and judgement in their job. A better justice system means in turn that the economic agents of the country (households, individuals, firms, organisations, etc.) have greater confidence in the administration of justice in general. This confidence in the justice system produces in general better economic performance by everybody (and a greater amount of happiness for everyone in the country).

Measure 4: government is supreme in country X
The government of the alternative does not receive instructions or regulations for execution from any other body except its own legislature. This means that the government is able to govern to the best of its ability, according to what it perceives as the wishes of the citizens who elected it, reacting quickly to developments or events and without excuses of the form: this is a common policy measure or this is a directive from the Commission (in other words, the government elected by the people is fully accountable to the people and to nobody else and cannot project excuses for failures of policies or incompetent behaviour).

Measure 5: legal dynamism
Inside the parliament of the alternative there is a computer which performs a very strange and very critical task: the computer is connected to the legislative bodies of all other 184 countries on earth and receives by electronic mail automatically the contents (full description) of any new law passed. The task is

technically very simple, costs nothing and requires only the consent of the sender legislature under a mutual permanent agreement. The electronic mail thus coming to the computer of our imaginary country X is then distributed automatically to all the lawmakers of the country.

In this very simple manner the lawmakers receive automatically the contents of any new law passed in any legislature on earth. They have therefore the opportunity to know about any new law that other countries on any continent are adopting and think carefully whether this new law could be beneficial for the citizens of their own country. In this automatic way the good or even brilliant ideas of lawmakers of other countries are very quickly made available to all lawmakers of country X (regardless of each one's specific political affiliation). The pool of ideas becomes richer as the laws of the total human population are available for the evaluation of the (supposedly) wise lawmakers of country X. Each lawmaker can very easily forget the great majority of the new laws coming from other countries that are either considered wrong or not applicable to country X, but at the same time he or she can note any law coming from other countries that appears to be correct or could be applied to country X. The lawmakers can thus suggest the specific new idea coming from another country be discussed by the legislature. What are the advantages of this procedure?

The main advantages are:

1. The pool of new lawmaking ideas becomes much bigger.
2. New ideas for lawmaking are not drawn from just one continent, the continent of Europe. Bright new ideas naturally come from all 185 countries on earth and should be exploited for the benefit of the citizens of country X regardless of the country of origin.
3. Since the incoming new laws are not coming from a superior legislative body they are not considered by the lawmakers of country X unless the lawmakers truly see that they (the laws) could be applicable and beneficial for the citizens who sent them to the legislature to serve their lawmaking needs to the best of their abilities (for a specific period of time – no one should forget that). The phenomenon of rubber-stamping a law coming from the Europarliament is thus eliminated.

The long-run economic consequences of such a process are immense because country X would obviously enact the best laws in the world specially tailored for its needs and requirements. At the same time, if many countries become alternatives, they will gradually converge to have similar sets of laws since, by definition, in a freely communicating world the best ideas are sooner or later adopted by everybody (with the necessary small differences from country to country).

The final outcome will be that:

1. Each country becomes as free a market as its citizens wish and at the pace they wish. (Note that the pace could be reversed if this is required after, say one hundred years, because nothing is permanent in business societies and nothing can stop the alternative from changing its laws).
2. Each country is a single market.
3. The laws in alternative countries are in the long run similar (but not identical). The firms of country X, when economically active in other markets, have to comply with the laws of the other markets utilising the human resources of the host countries.
4. The game is fair in the sense that when a firm from country X sets up shop in country Y it faces the same laws that all other firms active in the market of country Y are facing.

Measure 6: the electronic referendum

The citizens of our imaginary country in the alternative exploit the electronic revolution that started just a few years ago with the Internet to vastly improve the lawmaking process since the set of laws is the most crucial element in each society for material progress, the growth of knowledge and happiness. They use their lawmakers only to prepare, suggest, discuss and examine new laws but not to vote on new laws. Voting is done by the common citizens (here the word 'common' appears to be properly used!) through very quick and cheap electronic voting.

Let us see first very roughly the technicalities of a typical arrangement for the electronic voting in our imaginary country X.

1. Electronic voting takes place every week on the same day, say, every Saturday from 2 p.m. to 10 p.m.
2. All citizens of the country are eligible to vote.
3. Voting is done from inside each person' house through his or her PC station connected to a special set-top box and by using a special smart ID card.
4. Confidentiality of the vote is ensured through encryption (if we can send money or other messages digitally by encryption, we can certainly send our votes too).
5. Citizens who do not yet happen to have a PC at home can use the nearest home or shop that has one or the nearest ATM machine (in the next five to ten years almost all homes in at least the developed countries will have a TV-PC station).
6. Counting of the votes is done automatically through central computers (supervised by all political parties) and the results announced a few minutes after closing the electronic polls.
7. Full descriptions of the contents of the proposed new law are available

to every citizen at a special address on the Internet and also in a special TV station broadcasting teletext for the full seven days prior to voting.

8. Full descriptions of what any of the lawmakers said regarding this new law are available in text form at a special address on the Internet and also from the special TV stations broadcasting teletext for the full period of seven days prior to voting. The same is available in the form of video on demand through Internet or cable TV for those citizens who wish to hear and see the lawmakers in action.

This is the procedure of the weekly rolling Electronic Voting System in our imaginary country X. The first question that might arise is whether such a procedure is technically feasible today. The answer is that with the existing technology it is absolutely feasible. Once a country decides to follow this new voting method it will be a matter of one to three years for the system to be up and running.

The second question is whether this law voting system is costly or not. The answer is that electronic examination by every citizen of any law, and then voting and counting votes costs virtually nothing in the form of explicit costs. Implicitly, the costs may be the time each week that each voter will lose to go through the law. However, implicitly each voter gets satisfaction by fully participating in the law process, being proud that he or she decides for his or her own laws and in the process greatly enhancing his or her education in real life. Therefore, in a broader economic analysis, explicit costs are zero and the implicit costs are outweighed by the implicit benefits (cost-benefit analysis as it is known in economics and business theories).

The third and most crucial question is whether the voting system for country X has more advantages than disadvantages when compared with the existing voting systems.

First, the disadvantage. There is the danger that less educated citizens would not properly understand the content or true meaning of a proposed new law if it is complex. But the counter-arguments to this are that:

1. If we accept that less educated citizens cannot understand a proposed complex new law, then how in the first place can the same citizens be expected to vote for or against the lawmakers at the national elections and on what grounds?
2. It is up to the lawmakers to explain the pros and cons of any new law with simple words during their discussions in the legislature and all those explanations and discussions will be available to the citizens in the form of video or text in the Internet and on TV.
3. In most developed countries the greater proportion of the population is today quite well educated and it will be more so in the future.

Now let us see the advantages of the Electronic Voting System:

1. Participation of the whole body of citizens in the voting process means that each law will reflect their wishes in the best possible form.
2. The various lobbies with their special interests will not be able to influence the introduction of any new law. Their influence will be almost eliminated. All citizens are equal when they vote regardless whether they have a special interest in the specific law or not.
3. When any new law proves after a few years to be bad or impractical or ineffective the citizens will have to blame themselves and not the lawmakers or political parties or others. Power comes hand in hand with responsibility.
4. The whole process of studying the text of a new law could easily become interactive with the political parties explaining their position even on pre-recorded video transmissions through the Internet.
5. Phenomena of corruptions in public life at least as far as the lawmakers are concerned will be greatly reduced or even wiped out (there will be very few reasons for influencing the legislators' body).
6. Each citizen will at least feel that he or she is really 'in power' regarding the legislating procedure when at the moment feels that this power is in practical terms far removed from him or her. This will certainly make the average citizen happier, other things being equal. But happiness is the final target of any organised human society.
7. Past experience has shown that deepening and widening democracy and the participative process have always resulted in improved lives especially in the long run.

It is obvious from the above discussion that the rolling Electronic Voting System will lead to an introduction of better laws in the alternative and this will certainly help the economy.

Measure 7: the top body of the judges directly elected every four years
In practical terms the separation of the judicial power from government and the legislature can never be made complete and real unless the top judges are directly elected by the people. In our alternative the citizens once every four or five years vote electronically to elect directly the best three or five or ten amongst, say, their two hundred highest-ranking judges. The curriculum vitae of all judges are published on the Internet and on the special TV stations transmitting teletext continuously. The citizens are also able to read or see in the media any comment about the efficiency and capabilities of any candidate judge. Participation of judges in any organisation that has any kind of political aim is strictly prohibited. Since voting takes place electronically, the actual cost of voting is zero in practical terms.

This system completely and truly makes all the judges dependent only on the electorate and independent of the executive or legislative bodies. Any young judge wishing to climb all the way up the career ladder will know that any misjudgement or corruption at any stage of his professional life will appear in the comments on the Internet when he is eligible for re-election. This will make all judges more careful when dispensing justice and will greatly reduce any kind of corruption.

By making the administration of justice better, the system indirectly improves the economic performance of every firm or individual because they know that now justice is truly blind and justice is the same for everybody, rich and poor, powerful and weak, celebrities and unknown men and women. Apart from improving economic performance, the system obviously makes every citizen in country X happier (which is the final target).

Measure 8: executive elections every four or five years

In the alternative, the executive body (government) is elected through the EVS (Electronic Voting System), which costs next to nothing (in both time and money) and is much more informative and participative because it is done basically through the Internet and the home PC-TV. The advantages of the EVS when electing a government by using the Internet are many. The main advantage, however, is that any political party which has something to say can say it (and push it or advertise it) on the Internet very, very cheaply. Pictures, sound and text are already part of the Internet and anyone can publish his or her ideas or programmes for government and put them to the judgement of the ultimate judge, which is the electorate. The need for huge sums of money in order to make your party, programme or even ideas known is almost eliminated. The grip of some parties in government owing to the power of money and not ideas is over. The political 'market' (to use terms from microeconomics) changes and from 'duopoly', 'oligopoly' or even 'monopoly' becomes 'perfectly competitive'. If perfect competition is the best form of economic market (the market where people exchange goods and services) the same perfect competition is the best form of political market (the market where people exchange ideas and public affairs governors).

There is, however, one more peculiarity in the alternative regarding voting for the executive power (government). There is not just the candidate for head of the government from every party. Each party submits to the electorate the names of all the team, i.e. in the team of political party Z candidates are named for all positions that will change with the change of government. Thus, the list of party Z contains not only the name of the prospective prime minister (or head of government), but all the ministers, deputy ministers and, in general, the name of anyone who will be in the new government. So the list says, for example, that Mr WM is candidate for the education ministry, Mr XY is candidate for deputy education minister, Mr KP is candidate for defence minister, etc. Once the whole team of the prospective prime minister (or president, as the case may be) is elected by the voters, no changes in names can be made or transfers between ministries. In case of resignations or deaths there are predetermined 'spare' people included in each voting list. The advantages of such a system of 'team choosing' instead of 'person choosing' are:

1. The voters know well before the elections who will be responsible for each ministry and can judge each one as well as the whole team accordingly before giving their votes.
2. The possibility that the prime minister (or head of government) once elected gives nasty surprises to the electorate by appointing people thought to be unsuitable is eliminated.
3. Government becomes truly teamwork and not a one-man show or one-man empire.
4. The party and the prospective prime minister know that if they include unsuitable people they will be voted down.
5. Public scrutiny of each prospective member of government takes place before taking office not after (when usually it is very late for the average citizen). Phenomena such as the education minister being someone who has never taught anything, the defence minister being someone who has never passed out from an armed forces barracks, or the trade minister being someone who knows nothing about international economics are either eliminated or greatly reduced. Also, anyone who is, even slightly, suspected of corrupt or unethical behaviour in the past knows very well that they cannot hope to achieve membership in the list.

It is obvious that the whole process for electing a government in the alternative is structured in such a way that, other things being equal (ceteris paribus), government is better and this leads to better public policies and hence superior economic outcomes for the country as a whole.

Now, let us summarise the alternative as described in this argument only from the economics point of view. The alternative is:

- A free market as 'free' is defined in the current microeconomics literature.
- A homogenous market in the sense that the same set of laws, justice system and government policies are available to all its participants (local and foreign participants).
- A dynamic market in the sense that its regulations, laws and government policies can change very quickly with time to adapt to both the changing world and the wishes of its citizens. In this dynamic market even the term 'free', which in essence is the principle of the market, can very easily change if the citizens so wish. For example, today's economic thinking and practice

is undoubtedly for maximum competition, deregulation and privatisations. But if after, say, one hundred years, owing to any technological, economic or political development the citizens wish to change to any other form of market organisation (for example, nationalising industries, expanding government size and activities, etc.), then they can make the change for themselves without unnecessary delays or obstacles or restrictions. Given today's data, free markets are by far the best solution from both the theoretical economics point of view and the experience point of view. But no one can say whether or not the same will be true after fifty, one hundred or one thousand years. As the ancient Greek, Heraclitus, said, 'All is flux, nothing stands still.' And he was certainly correct. Cultures are changing, the climate is changing, the technology is changing, tastes are changing, human races are changing, philosophies and religion are changing, the sun is changing (it burns continuously itself, reducing its mass and eventually cooling down) and the universe itself is changing (it expands for the time being!). Nothing is static. Everything is dynamic because everything is existing or happening within the dimension of time.

It is only natural that by now some could face the dilemma: which is better: a single market over fifteen countries or fifteen free markets?

The main advantage of a single market is the ease of access to the economic agents (individuals or firms). The main disadvantage is its rigidity in both the geographical sense (in the three-dimensional sense) and in the dynamic sense (in the fourth-dimensional sense – time sense). The main advantage of the alternative is its ability to adapt to geography and time. Its main disadvantage is that the conditions (laws, policies, justice system) are not everywhere the same. They are similar but not the same. However, access and participation to the economic agents is assured owing to the words 'free markets' (which mean free trade, free investment, competition, etc.).

On the above purely economic grounds, I will give more marks to free markets than to a single market as shown in Figure 39.

Figure 39

Option 1 Member of the EU	Option 2 The alternative
Grade: 2,500/100,000	Grade: 5,000/100,000

11. Argument No. 11 (Economic)

Within the EU every year the Commission will check and approve or disapprove the budget of my country for next year (every year). This is not good from the microeconomics and macroeconomics point of view.

It is very well known and published that vis-à-vis the EMU the Commission in Brussels will review and reject or approve the yearly budgets of all participating states. The macroeconomic implications of this are basically that the general levels of taxation and government spending are decided by others and not by the elected government of the country. One could suggest that the Commission will review and approve only the stated budget, but not define the size or kind of budget. The simple truth is that if you can approve something, you can also reject it until this something is more to your liking. Since we have discussed the macroeconomic implications of this in a similar argument in the EMU part, we will stop only at the microeconomic consequences of such 'approvals'.

Suppose that the government of country Z wants to increase spending on education and in order to find the money intends to dramatically increase next year the value added tax on petrol and cigarettes. Its budget will not be affected on average (outlays are equal to receipts), but this increase in the value added taxes is rejected by the Commission in Brussels when it reviews the budget. It is rejected because within the EU all products or services are supposed to have identical value added taxes. The Commission suggests to the government of country Z that it find the required money elsewhere. The government of country Z then decides to increase income taxes. The budget then is approved. The final result is that the size of the budget (in essence the size of government) is the same as the one first suggested by country Z. This means that macroeconomically Brussels has not altered anything. Microeconomically, however, Brussels has altered a tax. Instead of taxing consumption of a product or service (which country Z, believes rightly or wrongly, should be taxed because it damages the environment and the health of the people), it taxes income, i.e. the work effort (which country Z believes, rightly or wrongly, should be taxed as little as possible).

We see here that the approval or rejection of government budgets have not only macroeconomic but microeconomic consequences as well. Whether the Commission or the states government are wiser is not easy to answer. However, it is believed that on average a government of a specific country is nearer the problems of the citizens of the country. What is, however, beyond any doubt is that government budget approvals by the EU unavoidably introduce macroeconomic and microeconomic distortions to each country. Figure 40 reflects this assessment.

Figure 40

Option 1 Member of the EU	Option 2 The alternative
Grade: 0/100,000	Grade: 5,000/100,000

12. Argument No. 12 (Economic)

> Within the EU my country cannot have any trade policy of its own at all. This is generally not good.

It is a fact today that matters like trade policies, agreements for tariffs reductions, quotas and anti-dumping monitoring are pursued by the EU solely through its Commission (executive power or body). No individual country can negotiate with any third country regarding trade policies. In all international meetings regarding trade, no trade minister from any individual EU member country participates. Only the trade commissioner of the EU represents the fifteen countries.

The examples are plentiful. During 1996, two very important trade agreements were concluded between more than one hundred countries under the auspices of WTO (World Trade Organisation). One agreement liberalises telecommunications services and products and the other information technology products and services. In other words, starting in 1998, any phone company can set up shop in any of the participant countries without tariffs and on equal terms with the host country's telecom companies (but following always the laws of the host country regarding employment, investment, etc.). The same applies to manufacturers of telecom equipment, computers, modems and software.

During all the discussions preceding those very important (and, may I suggest, very beneficial) agreements, there were negotiators from countries like Japan, South Korea, Chile, Malaysia, Brazil, Singapore, Hong Kong, Australia and New Zealand. However, there was no negotiator specifically from Germany, the United Kingdom, France, Italy, Spain, Portugal, Greece, Holland, Belgium, Sweden, Denmark, Finland, Italy or Ireland. There was only a negotiator from the EU. The same is happening almost every week with some international conference or meeting or agreement on trade. This is only natural since, by definition, no state in the EU can set its own terms of trade (tariffs, quotas, bureaucratic restrictions).

Now we come to the important point: is it better for an individual country to have no trade policies of its own or is it better to have its own trade policies suited to the needs of its citizens? Obviously, it is better to have its own trade policies even if on any particular trade matter the stance of a country is identical to the stance of other countries. In a sense, no country in the EU should have a trade ministry today since there is the Trade Commissioner in Brussels who is its trade minister in disguised form!

Another question is that maybe it would be more economical if the trade ministries of all fifteen EU member states were tomorrow abolished and all states used the services of the Trade Commissioner in Brussels. Again we come to the subject of cost-benefit analysis. Trade policies certainly impose some running costs on any country (ministry building, salaries of minister and assistants, etc.). However, there are certain benefits from having individual trade policies. If there were no benefits then all countries on earth would have abolished their trade ministries and used instead the trade ministry of Japan or the USA on their behalf! Free trade is one thing and abolishing a country's ability to have any trade policies is another thing. Unfortunately, within the EU this 'another thing' has already happened! Within the EU you cannot increase trade barriers on your own and you cannot lower your trade barriers on your own. Increasing barriers is generally a bad thing, but lowering the trade barriers is generally a good thing. The freedom to fail is the flip side of the freedom to succeed. Remove the freedom to fail and you remove the freedom to succeed! Every nation in the EU has certainly lost the freedom to succeed (without any guarantee that it has also lost the freedom to fail because the EU is keeping unnecessary barriers to trade with third countries using the protection argument, which is an illusion, a misunderstanding and an excuse).

But let us see the alternative on this particular matter of trade policies.

Our imaginary country X believes in completely free trade in goods, services, investment in real assets, investment in liquid assets and in currencies in all directions, i.e. free trade not only with the countries in the continent of Europe but with any country on earth. It believes in expediting the process of reducing all barriers to trade so that within the next five to ten years (say, by 2005) trade is free everywhere. It believes in free trade with any country that agrees to that either in a bilateral or multilateral way. Tariff (and other barrier) reductions can be achieved through the World Trade Organisation (multilateral agreements). But reductions of barriers can be also achieved in bilateral agreements between country X and any other country Y. If, for example, the government of country X believes that all barriers to trade with Argentina should come down today, then it does not need to wait for the WTO. It just negotiates through the trade ministry with Argentina and signs a free trade agreement beneficial to the people in both countries. If the theory of international economics as well as the empirical worldwide evidence suggest that completely free trade is good for both countries, then instead of waiting for some multilateral agreement through the WTO, country X proceeds to the agreement today in order to gain benefit today for its people.

If free trade is beneficial to the people of country X, then the sooner this happens the better for the people of country X. There is no reason for the trade minister and the government of country X to wait for a number of years until it receives instructions from some 'outside wise source' to proceed to trade negotiations and agreements. However, any expediting of this process through the WTO is welcome.

In all these processes, negotiations and agreements the trade ministry plays a very important role in safeguarding that the vital interests of the citizens and firms of the country are properly served and that the other party or parties will observe the agreed rules. Observing the agreed terms is of vital interest to the citizens of the country and cannot be left to some outside wise source. In all international agreements country X is properly represented by its trade minister, who is responsible, together with the rest of the government, to the people of the country. Thus if a trade agreement fails or does not prove beneficial, it will be the government of country X who will be penalised by the voters of the country and not the outside wise source. This certainly makes the trade policies of the government more responsible and more reflective of the wishes of the electorate. Accountability of the trade ministry to the people of the country is part of the democratic process, which in general is much superior to the 'command and control from a Trade Commissioner in Brussels' process. Recapitulating, and before grading as in Figure 41, the main advantages of having specific trade ministers with full powers to negotiate anything are:

1. The pace of any negotiations can be increased (or decreased) according to what is considered at the moment to be beneficial to the people of the country.
2. The trade negotiations can be pursued with any country on earth regardless of stage of development, size of country or continent. The only valid criterion is whether the interests of the citizens of the country are being promoted or not.
3. The negotiations can be multilateral (between many participating countries) or bilateral (between only two countries).
4. There is full economic accountability of the government (and especially the trade minister) to the people who elected them in order to promote their economic interests. No excuses can be made of the style: 'You see, these are the wishes (instructions) from Brussels.'
5. Since country X retains full control over its trade policies, it can reverse them easily in the future. If, for example, owing to some economic or technological or natural resources developments the citizens of country X see after one hundred years that free trade is no longer beneficial to them, they can easily reverse course and make other agreements. They still have their own trade ministry and they still do not need the permission of any outside force to proceed peacefully to bilateral or multilateral agreements.

Figure 41

Option 1	Option 2
Member of the EU	The alternative
Grade: 0/100,000	Grade: 5,000/100,000

13. Argument No. 13 (Economic)

> If you abolish the various ministries of your country and centralise the ministries in one place (say, Brussels), then you will reap economies of scale. The costs of running governments will be reduced and this is generally a good thing.

A very quick answer to the argument is that if this were true then within each individual country there should not be local councils or mayors for the cities. Instead, everything should be done from the capital of the country, but, on the contrary, the opposite is happening because decentralisation is the name of the game and not centralisation.

Let us see the argument in some more detail. First of all, according to the standard economic theory only some economic activities (industries) exhibit economies of scale. The rest exhibit diseconomies of scale or maybe are neutral to the size of the firm. Government, as an economic establishment with revenues and expenses, exhibits increasing costs, i.e. increasing the size of the government increases the cost of a unit of delivered service (or product).

Assume for a moment that the fifteen ministries of economics were abolished (or merged) and a new powerful ministry of economics was created in Brussels. One could very convincingly suggest that by such a merger of the ministries the running costs would be reduced because one would need only one economics minister and one deputy economics minister instead of fifteen for each post. This is true, but it is also true that you would still need all the other employees of the ministries to collect taxes, to distribute welfare payments, to collect statistics, etc. The savings are, in practical terms, zero. On the other hand, the delivered product (the services offered by the employees of the ministry and the efficiency of the minister) would certainly suffer because it is much easier to manage the economy of Finland from Helsinki than from Brussels.

An economics minister in Helsinki is certainly in a better position to know the economic problems of the Finnish people than a ministry in Brussels. He can collect the taxes in a better way (and maybe in a more equitable way) and distribute the unemployment benefits more efficiently simply because he knows the Finnish people and conditions better and is accountable to them.

If by centralising the fifteen economics ministries in Brussels, the running costs are reduced by say 1%, but at the same time the quality of services is reduced by say 20%, then obviously to the average citizen the cost per unit of service or product has been substantially increased as the ratio

$$\frac{100\% - 1\%}{100\% - 20\%} = \frac{99}{80}$$

which is greater than one (1)!

The worst of all is that if from a static world (a world where time does not exist) one moves to a dynamic world (a world where time exists), then the inefficiencies with centralising fifteen ministries of the same kind become very big. In order to be specific let us transfer ourselves into the world of microeconomics which (amongst other things) teaches that in certain industries (for example, in electricity production and distribution within a country) it is better to have only one big producer (public or private) because this producer, by being huge, can reap economies of scale, i.e. owing to its size the cost of a unit of electricity is lower than if there are many smaller producers. But this happens only in a static sense. If the monopolist is allowed to exist for many years without other competitors then the firm, becomes complacent, lazy (fat cat syndrome), uninnovative and, in the long run, inefficient.

A monopoly, even if it is efficient because of its size at a point in time, will be inefficient over a period of time and the fact is that all monopolies live in a period of time. Governments and ministries are not exceptions to this rule.

When fifteen economics ministries become one then immediately coping with successful ideas from the other fourteen ministries (and avoidance of unsuccessful ideas or practices) disappears. The one ministry of economics becomes in a sense the monopolist of ideas or economic practices and the result is great inefficiencies (or, equivalently, inferior product or service) in the long run.

Now, let us see what the empirical evidence is on the subject of centralisation of a government activity.

For the past fifty years all governments have promoted decentralisation. If a government activity can be done locally (through local councils, boroughs or mayors) it has been decentralised (sent to the periphery – to the concerned people). This has been true for both large and small countries, developed and developing ones. Even the breaking up of the Soviet Union was (amongst other things) a decentralisation phenomenon! In the United States today, in spite of the fact that the USA has one country, one culture and one language, both main political parties (Republicans and Democrats) compete with each other to decentralise and send as much power as possible from Washington to the states. Only recently, for example, the responsibility (and financial resources) for welfare payments have been passed from the centre (Washington) to the states.

Now the question arises: if I am within the EU, will this centralisation of ministries take place? The answer is: the centralisation of ministries has already started and is well under way, and it is only natural that a single market concept leads sooner or later to the single ministry concept. After all, those various commissioners in Brussels (Trade Commissioner, Competition Commissioner, Agriculture Commissioner, Fisheries Commissioner, etc.) are central ministers in disguised form! This leads to the grading in Figure 42.

Figure 42

Option 1	Option 2
Member of the EU	The alternative
Grade: 0/100,000	Grade: 2,500/100,000

14. Argument No. 14 (Economic)

> If taxpayers' money spent by my national government is spent inefficiently, then the same taxpayers' money when spent by the European Commission is spent many times more inefficiently. On purely economic grounds, then I should not send any of my money to Brussels. My tax contributions should be all given to and spent by my government.

The reason why any money spent by the European Commission is spent less efficiently than if the same money is spent directly by a government is not a superficial or irrational reason or belief. The people in the Commission are no more corrupt or less capable than the people running any of the fifteen governments (neither, of course, is the opposite true). The inefficiency on practical and philosophical grounds has to do with the following:

1. *An outsider can never know the problems and needs of a country as well as an insider (someone who lives in the country).*

    Example: a person in Brussels can never know the true infrastructure problems in Portugal, Greece, Finland or Sweden as well as someone inside the governments of those countries.

2. *The allocation of funds is always done more efficiently if it is done at a local (national) level than if it is done at an international (supranational) level.*

    The underlying philosophical reason is that since the government of a country knows the problems of its citizens better it can allocate more efficiently any taxpayers' money in its hands. For example, the minister of public works in Germany, in principle, knows better than anyone in Brussels which areas of his country have priorities regarding infrastructure projects.

3. *The lack of accountability in using taxpayers' money is by definition greater in Brussels than in any national government. Greater lack of accountability means by definition greater possibility for misuse of taxpayers' money, other things being*

equal (ceteris paribus).

In Brussels there are already established mechanisms for control, accounting and checking. However, even with the best system of controls, a huge organisation will be always more difficult to check and control than a smaller organisation. If we assume that both a nation's government and the European Commission are an organisation differing only in size (on philosophical or practical grounds we cannot assume that the people in Brussels will be, for example, more corrupt or less competent than the government people in Paris) then it is only natural to say that: controls and accountability are greater the smaller the size of the organisation other things being equal (ceteris paribus).

How many people in France or Germany know today the total amount of money that was sent to Brussels last year? How many French or German citizens know the total amount of money sent by all fifteen countries that was spent for all kinds of purposes by the Commission last year? How many French or German citizens know what percentage of the Commission's budget went to cultural events, or to infrastructure, or to agriculture, or to direct or indirect advertisements? Furthermore, what percentage of the members of the parliamentary houses in France or Germany can answer correctly any of the above questions?

4. *The lack of incentives and disincentives makes the European Commission less effective in the use of other people's funds.*

The 20,000 or so people in the various EU organisations in Brussels and using money coming from many countries do not have by definition any incentive (or disincentive) to perform their tasks efficiently or to supervise efficiently how the money is spent when it goes to various countries for infrastructure or research in universities, support to farm product prices or to cultural events. The only incentive they have is a relatively well-paid and secure job in an organisation which collects other people's money and immediately uses the same money to pay its way. The end result is phenomena associated with bureaucratic habits like luxurious offices and big signboards advertising the organisation.

It is not the particular people or the particular system that are producing this bureaucracy. It is the existence of the system that is producing bureaucracy.

When there is no underlying economic reason for a system to exist, then the system produces bureaucracy through which it reproduces itself, i.e. bureaucracy is here a by-product of the system that exists without any real economic necessity. However, not all bureaucracies are by-products of such schemes.

5. *The 'foreign money illusion' is the most prominent reason why the public funds spent yearly by the Commission will be always abused at the point of delivery.*

Abuse of public funds at the point of delivery (i.e. by the recipient individual person, government, private firm, contractor, research organisation or university) definitely happens in all countries to a lesser or greater extent. However, when the recipient perceives, correctly or incorrectly, that the money is 'foreign', i.e. other countries' money then the abuse of the public funds is statistically increased manyfold.

We all know, for instance, that in general the funds given to various underdeveloped, developing or developed countries by organisations like the United Nations (and its various affiliated sub-organisations or parallel organisations) or by the World Bank are statistically speaking abused to a much higher degree than private funds and investments.

We also all know many instances of farms in various countries that have been receiving funds from Brussels through the Common Agricultural Policy (CAP) while the farms did not exist at all!

In both examples, the national governments and the recipient public or private organisations or persons perceive the money as foreign and simply (and maybe naturally) try to absorb as much of this foreign money as possible!

Where does all this lead us? Is there any solution to the problem? The simple answer is there is no solution to the problem with the EU model!

Does the alternative provide any solution to the problem? The alternative model provides a solution to the problem because the alternative is simply a country which does not send any money to Brussels! It sends direct foreign aid to any country on earth to the degree that its citizens wish it to do so and watches through the Foreign Affairs Ministry the use or misuse of the money. If the money is misused it simply cuts off the aid next year! (One could suggest that sometimes extremely complex problems have very simple solutions!) Hence the grading in Figure 43.

Figure 43

Option 1	Option 2
Member of the EU	The alternative
Grade: 0/100,000	Grade: 2,500/100,000

15. Argument No. 15 (Economic)

> During the decades to come my country's trade with third countries is expected to increase much faster than trade with EU member states. Within the EU I have the false impression that the market is the EU. However, the real market is the globe.

All prognostications (and common sense) are that for any one of the fifteen states of the EU future expansion in trade lies with the various fast-developing countries in every part of the world much more than with any of the other member states. Firms and individuals that realise this fact quickly will make much faster progress than those who think that the future in trade is only with their immediate neighbour. The model of the EU provides to the average citizen of any member country the illusion that he or she can trade within the single market only and somehow be secure indefinitely. The simple truths, however, regarding trade (in goods and services) are that:

1. The trade of any EU country will need to expand much more with countries in Asia or Africa or South-Central America than with any other EU countries for the simple reason that the former countries are developing with a rate of growth of 5% to 10% per year, whereas the average EU country (since they are mature markets) is developing with a rate of growth of 1% to 2% per year. When India or Pakistan experience an 8% rate of growth this means that their needs for imports are on average increasing much faster than the needs for imports of an EU member country with a 2% rate of growth.

2. Within the next five to ten years all barriers to trade (tariffs, quotas and bureaucratic artificial restrictions) will fall completely between the vast majority of countries on earth. This is already happening with various multilateral or bilateral agreements, many of which are done through the World Trade Organisation (WTO). All countries have more or less realised that everyone benefits from free trade and all are very rapidly reducing the tariffs and other non-tariff restrictions. For the moment, some people think that they can somehow hide inside a 'fortress EU' which is imposing tariffs on the outsiders so that the insiders are secure. This is a completely false sense of security.

You can be secure only by being lean, mean and efficient through free trade. You cannot be secure by keeping barriers to trade.

According to the WTO, by 2010 all EU tariffs with the rest of the world will be zero. However, most of the tariffs will have been eliminated much sooner. Thus any particular EU country is actually five to ten years away from complete elimination of its tariffs with third countries.

Given the above facts, a firm, individual or even country within the EU suffers the danger of thinking in terms of the internal market when the market is the global market and of thinking in terms of protection and self-sufficiency instead of thinking in terms of free trade and expansion to fast-developing markets.

In this regard the alternative provides a model of unbiased and reciprocal free trade with any country on earth and has the following advantages:

1. It does not give to its citizens a false (and sometimes fatal) sense of security regarding free trade. Free trade is in theory as well as in practice beneficial to all participants, but it is done to the extent that the citizens of the country wish it to be done.
2. It does not give to its citizens a false sense of the direction of trade. There is not any natural law saying that free trade is beneficial in that direction and not beneficial in other directions, or that free trade is good if done between countries on the same continent but not between countries on different continents, or that free trade is good between countries of similar cultures but not beneficial between countries of different cultures.

There is not a closed trading system in the EU or anywhere else. The only closed trading system is the whole world! (Until human beings either start living on other planets or until they discover the existence of aliens in other galaxies and start trading with them). The argument is graded in Figure 44.

Figure 44

Option 1	Option 2
Member of the EU	The alternative
Grade: 250/100,000	Grade: 1,000/100,000

16. Argument No. 16 (Economic)

In the European Commission, the Europarliament and the European Court thousands of man hours (therefore money) are spent yearly on translations. This money lost is, in essence, mine (it belongs to the average taxpayer) and can be saved if I choose the alternative.

It is a fact that each year an amount of money is spent in Brussels (Commission), Strasbourg (Europarliament) or Luxembourg (Court of Justice) in the form of man hours and paper for official and unofficial translations. These translations are required solely because of the existence of these branches of power where people with different mother languages are required to work together every day. The total amount of money thus lost in absolute terms is maybe rather large, but in relative terms (i.e. compared to the total budget of the Commission) is surely negligible. Therefore, in economic terms, the argument is correct but of negligible importance and we will not give it any marks.

17. Argument No. 17 (Economic)

> Within the EU there will be sooner or later a single tax code system, a single pension system and a single health care system. This is wrong from the economic point of view.

In the newspapers of 16 January 1997 we read that the European Commission did not rule out the possibility of a single European tax code.

Such announcements are not strange and are a direct and natural consequence of a single market. As was explained earlier, a single market requires (sooner or later) single sets of laws and a single government (executive branch). But the tax system, the pension system and the health care system in every country are defined by laws and the laws are applied by the government of each country. If both the set of laws and the government are common, then it is only natural that taxes, pensions and health systems will be common too. The important question is whether such a mixing of systems is a good or a bad thing.

The most important defect of the idea of having a common pension system is that the present and future liabilities of each system are distributed to all other systems. In simple words, every system carries a different burden of debt (in proportion to its total size) and when the systems are intermixed liabilities are transferred from the relatively weakest (those with a present debt of, say 60%) to the strongest (those with a present debt of, say 10%, or maybe with a present surplus). The same applies to the present or future liabilities of the health system of each country. Such a transfer of liabilities from country to country is economically wrong because it creates and reinforces the so-called 'free riders problem'. Everyone is pushed to believe that he can have a free ride at the expense of other countries' taxpayers.

The most important problem of such an approach is, however, not a static one, but a dynamic one. By having a common pension system the citizens of any particular country cannot in the future easily change their country's system if they wish to do so. They can change their system only if they convince the other 360 million people to follow them. Imagine, for example, that the citizens of country X came to the conclusion that they wanted to privatise their pension system following the successful examples of Chile or Australia. They could not do the change by themselves. They would have to convince the rest of the EU first.

In general, even within the same country, mixing of liabilities of different groups of citizens is practically wrong (it penalises the 'tidy' group), philosophically wrong (it gives the wrong signals) and reduces the present and future flexibility of each group to follow the best and quickest possible solutions to each problem.

However, when the mixing of liabilities is done between different countries, it becomes a recipe for permanent inefficiency.

These considerations are reflected in Figure 45.

Figure 45

Option 1	Option 2
Member of the EU	The alternative
Grade: 0/100,000	Grade: 500/100,000

18. Argument No. 18 (Economic)

> I am better off today than I was in 1992 when the single market actually started to operate in practical terms. Therefore, the EU and its single market are at least economically good things.

For any country and for any economic system it is not the absolute level of disposable income per person that counts as a judgement of the system or of the government. *It is the rate of growth of disposable income per citizen that counts.*

Every country experiences each year some growth in its Gross Domestic Product (roughly the sum of all goods and services produced within the country during each year). The growth is negative only in times of recession but most of the time and in the vast majority of countries growth is positive. However, the rate of growth varies greatly from country to country, even amongst developed countries. A developed country might experience growth of say 1% per year or 3.5% per year. The difference between 1% and 3.5% growth may seem insignificant, but the truth is that 3.5% is 3.5 times the rate of 1%!

Assume that a country starts in 1992 with a level of Gross Domestic Product equal to 100 units (base year) and that for the next six years it experiences a rate of growth of 1% per year. Then at the end of the sixth year its Gross Domestic Product will be 106 units (to be more precise, it will be 106.15 units). Now assume that the same country starts in 1992 with 100 units GDP but experiences a rate of growth of 3.5% per year. Then at the end of the six-year period its Gross Domestic Product will be 122 units (to be precise, it will be 122.92 units). We see that in both cases the country six years after 1992 is richer, but in the second case it is approximately 16% richer than the first.

So, it is not the absolute level of wealth that counts when we compare the present with the past. It is the rate of growth of the wealth that counts. All countries on earth experience positive rates of growth year after year with very few exceptions (say, for ten or twenty countries out of 185) so all countries, when they look back and see their starting point six years ago, will naturally observe that today they are richer. This should not be the criterion because, except for severe economic recessions, most of the countries will find themselves richer. The criterion should be the rate of growth. Has the country been growing richer with a growth rate of 0.5% per year or with a 3% per year growth rate?

It is not the absolute level of improvement, it is the speed of improvement that counts.

Furthermore, a more exact measure of the rate of growth is the rate of growth of income per capita in a country. If, for example, during a certain year the country's total income increased by, say 1%, but at the same time the working population increased by 2% (due perhaps to people from other countries coming to work legally or illegally), then the per capita income of the average worker decreased instead of increasing.

In conclusion, the criterion for the success of a government or of an economic system or of a set of economic policies should be the rate of growth of the per capita income including all the people living during a particular year within a country.

Having said that, what is the empirical evidence in the fifteen EU member states since 1992 regarding rates of growth? The evidence is that the rates of growth were generally very small and that the average citizen of the average country feels that he or she is making some material progress, but very, very slowly, especially compared with the past. What is more important is that there is not any statistically significant evidence to suggest that participation of any country in the EU has increased its rate of growth of GDP or that it has increased in any significant way the rate of improvement of the disposable income of the average citizen.

Note that since we don't know what any of the fifteen countries would have done after 1992 under the alternative, we will not give any grades to the options.

19. Argument No. 19 (Economic)

> Brussels sends too many regulations to my country. This is no good for my economic well-being.

Undoubtedly any country needs a set of regulations in order to perform as an organised society. But a country within the EU is bound to receive additional regulations from Brussels. The reasons for this are twofold:

1. Sending regulations to the countries is one of the main reasons for the existence (raison d'être) of the Commission. It is one of the best ways to reinforce itself and to reinforce the EU as an entity de jure.
2. Assume that the fifteen countries have fifteen more or less different

sets of regulations in the mathematical sense of the word set. Assume further that owing to the concept of a single market, out of those fifteen different sets a common one must be found. Then it is easier to establish a common set using a union of sets instead of the intersection of sets. In other words, the easiest thing to do is to impose on each individual country all the regulations of the other fourteen countries that do not exist in it already. Furthermore, if anyone of the fifteen countries has a regulation it must also have some reason for introducing the regulations in itself. The reason is usually rational and hence it is only natural that it should be applied to the rest of the countries.

3. Those two main reasons for regulation exist regardless of the specific people who happen to run the Commission at any one time. Apart from this, however, there is a far more fundamental reason for a big regulation set from Brussels. It is the size of the subject population that is being regulated. It is only natural that, other things being equal, a large population of say 360 million people spread over a large geographical area will need a larger set of regulations than a small population living in a small geographical area.

So, it is beyond any reasonable theoretical doubt that within the EU the population of a country will always live under a much larger set of regulations than it would without the EU. The empirical evidence of regulations coming to all governments from the Commission is that every year hundreds (or even thousands) of new regulations are imposed.

If this is so, is it a good or a bad thing for any economy to have more regulations than it could live without? Here all economic theories regarding growth are very clear. Unnecessary or excessive regulation is bad for the growth of the economy of any country. To put it simply, the less regulation the greater the growth of the economy of any country, other things being equal.

Now, let us see the alternative regarding regulations. In the imaginary alternative the citizens are free to impose on themselves as much regulation as they wish to, but they do not accept regulations coming from other sources. If they are a society which lives with too much regulation in any field, they can impose on themselves a lot of regulations. If they are a society which prefers in certain areas fewer regulations, they can deregulate as much as they like. Moreover (and more importantly), they can reverse any regulatory or deregulatory course quickly and according to their specific needs. Hence the assessment in Figure 46.

Figure 46

Option 1	Option 2
Member of the EU	The alternative
Grade: 0/100,000	Grade: 2,500/100,000

20. Argument No. 20 (Economic)

In today's global economy with continual liberalising conditions of trade, there is no meaning in the EU as a trading bloc. Neither any other trading bloc has meaning. Trading blocs had meaning in the past, but today they only serve to divert the natural flow of trade, to give a false sense of security and keep alive the last remaining tariffs and other barriers.

Global trade in goods and services is being liberalised with increasing speed owing to the willingness of all countries (rich and poor, large and small) to benefit from free trade. The volume of world trade is increasing year after year at a rate of 5–10% (per year). The last remaining tariffs between more than 140 countries are scheduled to be eliminated in five to ten years' time. There is no economic rationale in the thought that any nation in Europe should trade freely with nations only in Europe and continue imposing tariffs on goods or services coming from other countries. Consumers in any European country should be able to buy goods or services from the cheapest source, regardless of where this source is. Producers in any European country should be able to sell their products or services freely to consumers in any part of the earth. Free trade does not recognise geographical directions or continents and its benefits accrue regardless of skin colour or culture.

In a world where manufacturers often discount their prices for hardware by 20% or more and the average logistics costs of moving a product around the globe are less than 10% of its end-user price (TVs, for example, are 7% and automobiles less than 5%), physical distance has become economically irrelevant. With the increasing use of the Internet any European consumer should be able to find the cheapest product or service around the world and buy it regardless of source, and any European producer, again through the Internet, should be able to sell his product or services to any consumer or firm around the globe. To pretend that there is somehow something special about the EU as a trading bloc (or any trading bloc for that matter) is irrational (to say the least) and counterproductive since the digital bits of the electronic information flow do not register anything when passing the borders of the trading bloc. Nevertheless, since theoretically the EU is supporting global free trade, we will not grade the argument.

21. Argument No. 21 (Economic)

The basic microeconomic goals of efficiency and equity can better be achieved through the alternative model than through the single market model.

Broadly speaking, microeconomic policies have two objectives: efficiency and equity. By efficiency is generally meant the efficient allocation of resources (labour, capital and natural resources). The allocation of resources is done through the price mechanism and this price mechanism is efficient when there is competition and reduced regulation. By equity is meant general equality of opportunities, not equality of rewards. However, the concept of equity is one of normative substance and varies from country to country according to the wishes of its citizens.

Now we will attempt to compare two models regarding efficiency. One model consists of fifteen alternative countries, each one trying to be as efficient as possible. The other model consists of a single market of fifteen countries. By our assumption, the citizens in both cases wish to be as efficient as possible. What are the main possible reasons for inefficiencies in each model?

The first possible reason for inefficiencies is the creation of oligopolists or monopolists (in any industry). Under the alternative each country has legislation whereby, for example in industry Z, no producer can have market power larger than T%. For example in the television industry no service provider could have more than 30% of the market and in the banking industry no bank could have more than 5% of market power. Under the single market model, if we assume the same anti-monopoly percentages for the whole market we are left with the possibility that in a country like Greece a producer could have 90% or 100% of market power (i.e. be in effect a monopolist) but still be compatible with the anti-monopoly laws of the single market if the monopolist in Greece is not active in the rest of the EU. In general, within the model of the EU the tendency in many industries (those that exhibit economies of scale) will be to create a small number of oligopolists, each one having considerable market clout over the whole of the EU, but who could be at the same time a monopolist over a specific area, say over Germany. On the other hand, with a model of fifteen alternatives, there will be a tendency in the same industries to create (through mergers or alliances usually) the same oligopoly over the whole of the EU, but this time there can be no monopolist in any individual country because, by definition, there is anti-monopoly legislation in each alternative.

It must be said here that monopoly in an industry is an inefficient form of production and inefficiencies should be avoided. Oligopoly is a less inefficient form of industry structure, but still much inferior to perfect competition where there is a large number of players, each having a very small market power. However, the nature of some industries is such that oligopoly is unavoidable, but with the alternative model it is up to the citizens of the alternative to legislate the maximum market power that they want an oligopolist to have in a specific industry within their country. It should be noted here that, owing to rapid technological developments, industries where oligopoly was the name of the game may become industries where perfect competition might become better. One such case is the telecom industry where after ten years the service providers on the Internet could also be telecom providers and within a specific country (say Finland) one could have tens (or even hundreds) of such telecom providers instead of just two or three big telecom players. An industry, then, that today is characterised in Finland as oligopolistic could be under perfect competition in ten years (or even earlier) simply because of technological developments.

Another form of possible inefficiency is when, in a specific industry, economies of scale are present (i.e. a firm has to be large to lower its product costs), but owing to legislation or other circumstances it cannot grow. Under the alternative model a firm can grow large by expanding in all other EU countries. It could just expand by itself or use mergers, acquisitions, strategic alliances or tactical alliances. Under the alternative, investment in real assets, mergers, etc. are free between any mutually agreeing countries. Under the EU model the same expansion can happen but with one difference: in the EU model the players-firms somehow get the impression that they have an internal market where they are protected from outside competition, and in this internal market they have to grow first, be good players and then maybe expand into other countries. In the model of the alternative the firm knows that in real life there is no protection and there is no internal market. The firm can expand into any mutually agreeing country. Economic considerations dictate where to expand or invest not some divine logic of 'us' and 'them'.

Regarding the efficiency of the economic structure of a country, there are in general many factors determining how efficient an economy is. Some of those factors are the extent of farm product price support, minimum wage laws, the power of the trade unions, income subsidies, income taxes, housing subsidies and health care subsidies. All these factors can be summarised in the phrase 'degree of economic freedom of the country' or 'degree of free market'. Here there is also a considerable difference between the alternative and the EU model. Under the alternative, free markets are generally an extremely good thing but only to the extent that the citizens of the country want them. It is the citizens who decide how much free market they wish to have and not others who decide for them. Eventually, if the citizens of any alternative make wrong decisions regarding how much of a free market they want their country to be, they will be left behind by other countries and will change their minds and give instructions to their legislators accordingly. In the alternative, politics and culture (i.e. the wishes of the people) are above some kind of divine economic logic imposed by others.

In the EU model, the same degree of economic freedom and the same considerations of efficiency are applied over all the states indiscriminately. This frequently leads to legislation or regulation which may or may not be agreeable to an individual country and which may or may not be correct according to the science of microeconomics. I will give below three examples:

Farm support

For many years the Commission has been giving farm support by supporting the prices of agricultural products (using, of course, money collected from the fifteen states). According to standard microeconomic theory, it is not efficient to tinker with the prices, even the prices of farm products. It is much more efficient for the same funds to be given to farmers in the form of income support.

An individual country, if it was given the ability to handle its own farm support money, could have done the right thing. Of course, an individual country could have chosen to do the wrong thing like the Commission, but it would be its choice and at its own risk. It is not the extent of support to the farmers that is under discussion. It is the kind of support that is under discussion. If an individual country had given its farmers income support instead of price support in 1985, then it is probable that its practice would have been imitated by other countries to the benefit of everyone. Unfortunately, within the EU, it is Brussels that is using the taxpayers' money for farmers' support and not an individual government.

Minimum wage laws

It is generally accepted in microeconomics that any minimum wage law is inefficient because again it tinkers with the price system. This time price is the price of labour or wages. It is generally true that minimum wage laws produce unemployment. However, it is also generally true and absolutely legitimate that a nation may choose to enact minimum wage laws on the grounds of equity. The subject of equity is highly normative and it varies from country to country according to circumstances and the mentality of its people. It is perfectly plausible that a nation can choose less efficiency in order to gain more equity. But it is also perfectly plausible and possible that a nation may understand equity as equality of opportunities and not equality of rewards (or equality of outcome) and hence a nation may choose not to have minimum wage laws or scrap the existing laws. Within the EU no individual nation can do that. It has to have minimum wage laws!

Official assistance to poor areas

Every country has areas which for some reason are poorer than the rest of the country and tries to find ways to lift them through various programmes. But this assistance can be given in various ways. One way is using public funds (i.e. taxpayers' money) directly for special infrastructure projects, research grants or cultural events. But using this method of direct handouts is only one possible method to help poor regions. Other ways may be to use the same public funds in the form of reduced income tax in those poor areas or reduced investment and profits tax, establishing free trade zones (the lost tariffs are the equivalent of public funds injected) or even deregulation. All this can be done when the matter is in the hands of an individual government which decides every time according to the instructions of its citizens (through their votes).

This is not possible, however, with the official assistance programme when it is done through the EU. There is only one system for official assistance to poor regions for all countries. The system is that the Commission collects money from the taxpayers of all countries and then sends the money to the poor areas in the form of direct handouts. Some people may see merits in this system, but other people see that the system produces the mentality of the beggar or dependent or addict, which in the long run has bad or catastrophic consequences for the ability of poor regions or poor countries to lift themselves out of poverty. Thus we see today whole countries like Greece with the addict mentality dependent on the EU structural funds, having lost economic dynamism and any belief in their own ability to lift themselves and move forward.

One can agree or disagree with the form of direct handouts for poor areas, but the problem is that the one who disagrees cannot use another form because his or her tax money has gone already to Brussels and Brussels does not like any other forms of assistance to poor regions. (One reason for this is that the other forms of official assistance through reduced taxation in a poor region or a special export-import regime or deregulation are contrary to the single market concept and to the consequent single set of laws concept, but the main reason is that with the direct handouts the people in poor regions will come sooner or later to believe that the economic power is with the Commission and the other EU institutions and not within their own country.)

Where does all the above discussion lead us? Regarding efficiency, an individual country under the alternative can in principle fight inefficiency better than if it suffers the constraints of the single market. Regarding equity, an individual country under the alternative can follow its own normative definition of equity according to the mentality, culture, history and circumstances of its own citizens who express their wishes with their votes. This normative definition of equity is at the risk of the citizens of the alternative but can also be modified or completely changed upon their votes. The whole discussion leads to the grading in Figure 47.

Figure 47

| Option 1 | Option 2 |
Member of the EU	The alternative
Grade: 2,500/100,000	Grade: 5,000/100,000

22. Argument No. 22 (Economic)

> My country has a huge social security (pension) problem, which is a time bomb waiting to explode. The solution to this problem is much more difficult within the EU model because of regulatory restrictions which reduce greatly the available options.

Most countries face a huge problem regarding the solvency of the pension (social security) system. The degree of the intensity of the problem is not the same for any two countries, even amongst the developed ones. However, everyone realises that something has to be done today in order to make sure that people who will retire in the next ten to thirty years will have a pension above the subsistence level. This is well known to all political parties, all lawmakers and even to the average citizen. There are many possible options or models available for each nation's lawmakers. Unfortunately, some of those options or schemes are contrary to regulations or laws from Brussels or Strasbourg. This means that the citizens of a country within the EU have limited their options to solve this huge pension problem.

Under the alternative model the citizens of a country have no limitations to the available schemes for solving the problem. They can choose amongst all the systems that exist today or they can use the imaginations of their lawmakers to devise a scheme that best suits their economy, the age mix of the population, the immigration trends and, more importantly, the degree of debt of their social security funds. Since having more options to choose from is better than having a much smaller number of options to solve any problem, it is natural that the alternative is clearly superior regarding this argument as shown in Figure 48.

Figure 48

Option 1 Member of the EU	Option 2 The alternative
Grade: 50/100,000	Grade: 500/100,000

23. Some popular arguments (Economic)

In this section some 'popular' or 'simple' arguments on the EU will be presented. All the arguments refer to economics and will be examined in a brief manner since they have been already examined in depth in previous sections. Therefore the arguments will not be graded. A common characteristic of the arguments presented here (apart from their 'simplicity') is that they ignore the long-term consequences of the EU.

> The EU is where our country sells the bulk of its products or services, boosting our companies, winning profits and creating jobs.

We need only free trade and free investment to do that. The EU is not at all necessary. Under the alternative there is the same degree of freedom for exports of goods or services or investment. Swiss or Norwegian companies are also exporting goods or services in the EU without any problem and without being members. Moreover, the companies of a country should be oriented for exports otherwise in the long run they will not survive.

> Our people can live or work anywhere in the EU with practically no restrictions.

True, but all other people from the EU can also live and work in this country with practically no restrictions.

On balance, this arrangement creates rapid changes in our labour force instead of gradual changes through free trade and investment. Gradual changes are in general superior because they give the chance to the labour force to retrain and become employed again instead of remaining permanently unemployed.

> Our country receives many billions of dollars per year from common EU funds to create jobs, help local economies and safeguard the environment.

It is a zero-sum game since the EU does not have any funds of its own (there has not been invented as yet a machine producing real money). Whatever funds a country receives are either its own funds or the funds of countries that are net contributors. Even if a country is a net receiver of funds (in theory) most of the funds are unused and ineffective. Moreover, the funds, during their travels from the national capitals to Brussels and from Brussels to the recipient capital, are diminished (mainly through advertisements, propaganda, salaries of EU employees and travel expenses for officials). Therefore, in theory the game with the EU funds is not even a zero-sum game. Due to 'friction' it is a negative-sum game.

> Our country has greater bargaining power in free trade agreements as part of the EU. The latest agreements in which EU member states negotiated as one save every household $500 over ten years.

No one knows the interests of a country better than the government of that country (or at least no one should know better). A country should sit in on all trade negotiations for itself using its trade minister (that's why its taxpayers pay to have a trade minister). If a country believes in free trade there are not many things to bargain. Free trade is free trade and there is not semi-free trade. When countries form trade blocs all over the world instead, we are moving in a sense to an oligopolistic situation, which is in general much inferior to a competitive situation. Under WTO during the next eight to fifteen years, almost all trade in the world (in both goods and services) is scheduled to be absolutely free. This makes the idea of 'trading blocs' completely redundant because in such a situation the whole world is one trading bloc.

Moreover, a country which really believes in the benefits of free trade does not need advisers (in the form of the EU) or does not even need to wait for WTO. A country can proceed at any time to free trade completely with any other country on earth through bilateral (or even unilateral) negotiations. A government elected democratically does not need the permission of any outside organisation to proceed to free trade if it perceives that this is in the interests of the citizens who put it in office.

> Our country's companies are thriving in the EU.

We need only free trade and investment to achieve that. If any company thrives, this is because it is competitive not because it is from an EU member state. Preferential treatment of a company because its country of origin is within the EU is not compatible with the interests of the consumer. The consumer should be able to buy from the cheapest source on earth. Japanese, Swiss, Norwegian, Korean, Taiwanese, American and Canadian companies are also thriving in the EU, but none of these countries is a member.

> Our country's women have equal pay with men through a 1976 European Court ruling.

The same can be achieved through a domestic law made by our parliament. This is why we have a parliament. If the lawmakers of our country believe that a proposition will benefit us they should make it into law. If they believe that a proposition will not benefit us they should not make it into law. To have rulings of outsiders imposed on our lawmakers (regardless of their correctness or not) makes our lawmakers unnecessary and consequently makes us spectators of the democratic process – not participants.

> People across our country benefit from high environmental standards agreed across the EU. Ten years ago half of our bathing beaches failed to meet EU standards. Today nine in ten fly the 'blue flag' to show they now meet them.

Environmental protection is an extremely important issue. Exactly for this reason it should be a matter for the people of our country to impose on themselves the highest standards they wish to have. We do not need the EU to set our environmental standards of cleanliness in the same way that a person does not need others to impose the standards of cleanliness within his or her own house. The fact that today we are cleaner than ten years ago does not prove anything, in the same way that the fact that we are richer today than ten years ago does not prove that this is due to EU membership. We do not know how much cleaner (or richer) we would have been if we were following the alternative model of development.

In general, all nations become more environmentally conscious year after year due to education, general awareness, higher living standards and efforts by various environmental groups. It is the rate of growth in cleanliness that counts, not the level itself. What if tomorrow, we, the citizens of this country decided to impose environmental standards three times stricter on all firms and factories operating within our country? We simply could not do that because some companies operating within this country (local or foreign) would go to the Court of Justice in Luxembourg and complain that they are at an unfair disadvantage compared to their competitors in the single market. Therefore, in the very important matter (economically, psychologically and philosophically) of environmental standards, we cannot set them as high as we wish. It is the EU that sets them.

Under the alternative model, the people in a country are free to set their environmental standards as high as they wish, targeted more specifically to the sectors they wish and they can increase the standards year after year as rapidly as they wish. Environmental awareness in general does not come from top to bottom but from the bottom up through education and proper incentives.

> Shoppers get a better deal as we're in the EU. Take children's toys. The EU's power means it can insist that toys from around the world sold within it meet its tough safety standards.

Whatever was said above regarding environmental standards can be said here regarding consumer protection or safety standards. Both consumer protection and safety standards are matters too serious to be left to the EU. These matters, together with the environment, concern both the economic productivity of our firms (and hence employment) and our health, living standards and level of happiness. If lawmaking in these matters is left to the EU, then our parliamentarians are implicitly made unnecessary or redundant and by implication our own role as citizens, wishing to set actively the standards in our daily lives, becomes completely eliminated. (Some may say that our role in the lawmaking process and in the process of setting the standards in daily life have been eliminated already.) Under the alternative, the ability of the people in a country to set their standards (environmental, consumer protection, safety) is radically upgraded through the introduction of the rolling electronic referendum scheme.

> Our country's exports to the EU have risen substantially.

The same can be achieved simply by free trade. The EU is unnecessary in that respect. Specifically, the EU is creating trade between its members (trade creation), but diverts trade between its member states and outside countries because it keeps tariffs erected against those countries. Under the alternative, the era of trading blocs is approaching the end of its useful life. The twenty-first century will be the era of completely free trade with all countries. Only in this way will the people of this country reap the benefits of really free trade.

> The single market means lower costs for exporters – a lorry travelling between distant member states saves a day in time and $60 in costs compared with ten years ago.

A very valuable improvement, but in order to achieve that we don't need the EU. We need only free trade and the elimination of bureaucracy.

> Consumers benefit when companies compete. For example, the air ticket from Brussels to Nice has been brought down to a third of the previous level.

We need only free trade in goods, services and free investment to achieve that. The EU is unnecessary.

> Less red tape equals more orders for our country.

The EU is creating more red tape through its regulations than the red tape it eliminates. Under the alternative, elimination of red tape is done by the government of the country under pressure from the citizens who elected it, not from the pressure of others.

> Our telecom firms are winning in the EU. They have been forging partnerships across the EU to make the most of the single market, ahead of 1998 when the telecommunications networks will be opened to new competition.

We need only free trade in goods, services and free investment to achieve partnerships in telecom and competition. As for the wave of more competition in telecom as of 1998, this was due to GATT not the EU.

> Up to $500 billion worth of orders can now be won by our country's firms as all firms have the right to compete for contracts with councils and public bodies across the EU.

We need only bilateral agreements between governments to achieve that. Under the alternative, the country will make such bilateral agreements with any reciprocating country. What is good between two states in the EU is also good between a member state of the EU and a Middle Eastern or a North African or an Asian country. Reciprocating is the name of the game, not some superficial idea of fifteen countries having some common destiny or having discovered a divine meaning to bidding for contracts.

> Our pensioners can stay in other EU countries as long as they can support themselves.

No need for the EU to achieve this. We need only intergovernmental agreements.

> EU law protects holidaymakers. Tour operators must give comprehensive and accurate information and deliver.

This should have been done by national legislation. There is no need for the EU to define the quality of the tour operator services because, in essence, with such legislation the EU says that it knows better than the national parliaments.

> Part-time women workers have the right to maternity leave and keep their jobs under EU rules. Disabled people will soon have better access to buildings, thanks to rules promoted by Euro-MPs. A European Court ruling abolished the limit on the compensation that a victim of sex discrimination at work can receive.

All these are matters for the national parliament of a country to decide according to the wishes of the citizens of the country. With such EU legislation the national parliament of any country is in effect abolished and its citizens are alienated from the legislative process.

> The EU sponsors research on how women can reach the top in the professions.

The EU does not have its own money to sponsor any research. The money belongs to the taxpayers – citizens of this country – and should be spent directly by our government on the same research.

24. Argument No. 23 (Economic)

> Within the EU, there is harmonisation of fiscal policies, welfare policies, pension policies and regulatory policies. This, in the long run, stifles government competition and innovation and is generally very damaging to the economic interests of the people.

Because of the concept of a single market all tax rates have to be the same sooner or later. For example, if a particular country tries to decrease substantially value added tax (VAT) on any item, this goes against the concept of a single market because it will put sellers of the same product or service in other countries at a disadvantage. If, on the other hand, the same country tries instead to increase substantially value added tax on the same item, this also goes against the concept of a single market because it will put its sellers at a disadvantage. In both cases, the firms can go to the Court of Justice in Luxembourg and overturn the decision of the government as going against the letter or spirit of a single market.

By similar reasoning the tax rates on interest from deposits in the banks, the capital gains tax rate, the firms profits tax rates and the individual worker's tax rates have to be the same. Regulation policies also have to be more or less the same and sooner or later welfare policies and pension policies would have to be very similar.

This convergence is known as 'harmonisation' of fiscal policies due to the single market concept. Here 'harmonisation' is another word for 'single' or 'common'. But is harmonisation of fiscal policies a good thing for the average citizen of any country?

Governments spend around 40–50% of the wealth created by the citizens of a typical country, so their policies are of great interest to everybody. A government has to be in continuous competition with all other governments to come up with the best products, the best services and especially with the best ideas. Governments should compete with other governments in innovations that will make them year after year more efficient. And we all know that the best way to be efficient and innovative is to be in a competitive environment where you are free and independent to pursue your own cost-cutting or innovative ideas.

But with harmonisation of fiscal policies no government in the EU is able to pursue its own ideas or policies because it is continually constrained by the 'singularity' principle. This obviously removes permanently any sense of competition, effectiveness and innovation amongst governments and it certainly militates against the fast pace economic progress of any country. And if this is so today, it will be much worse in the long run as the world changes as time passes by.

In our alternative model the government of the county does not have any predetermined constraint on its fiscal policies. It is free to innovate, try new (or even old) ideas, increase spending or decrease spending, increase regulation or decrease regulation, produce a budget deficit or produce a budget surplus. It is free to apply its policies and it knows that if the policies are successful it will be rewarded with good public opinion (this is the only benefit that honest politicians should hope for if they serve their country well). It also knows that if the policies are unsuccessful it will be penalised by the voters at the ballot box.

In the meantime, until the election comes there are daily adjudicators from the financial markets who penalise or reward good governments instantly in the form of buying or selling government securities (and thereby decreasing or increasing interest rates) and buying or selling the nation's currency. In this sense the financial markets act as automatic stabilisers as well as automatic adjudicators for the alternative's government, while the ballot box every four or five years acts as the final and irrevocable judge.

In such a system, as the various governments clash with one another in an exciting peaceful competition to come up with the best system, everyone wins, as indicated in Figure 49.

Figure 49

Option 1	Option 2
Member of the EU	The alternative
Grade: 250/100,000	Grade: 5,000/100,000

25. Argument No. 24 (Economic)

We have entered the era of globally networked markets. In such an era the concept of trading blocs like the EU is obsolete and will soon become counterproductive.

During the past few years we have witnessed the emergence of networking of all traders everywhere in the world. With the spread of information technology, computers, telecommunications, e-mail and the Internet, we are seeing increasingly every trader (a firm or an individual) being able to communicate with customers or traders anywhere in the world with the speed of light and with the cost of communications almost zero. Where will all this lead us?

Undoubtedly, it will lead us into a networked world where trade in goods, services, information or even ideas will be with the best source or the best customer regardless of geographical distance. Individual trading floors will fade into a global market that will run twenty-four hours a day, 365 days a year. Money will move at the speed of light while investors will be able to shift limitless funds anywhere at a moment's notice in search of the best possible returns.

In an interconnected world, information and ideas are spread quickly and cheaply to those who express a demand for them, regardless of any trading bloc boundaries. Most importantly, connectivity, in every sense of the word, promises to change international trade into a multilateral free-for-all. The result is a daisy chain of growth, where one emerging nation pulls another, which pulls another and so on. Where does this picture leave the concept of trading blocs? Supply makes them initially obsolete and later on counterproductive simply because the electronic communication ignores the boundaries of any trading bloc. When a trader seeks a customer or vice versa they are not interested whether the other is located within a specific trading bloc or continent. They are only looking to derive maximum utility from the trade or the exchange (including the exchange of information or ideas). It is obvious that in such a world a trading bloc is meaningless and if it applies common external tariffs (otherwise it is not a trading bloc) it is counterproductive because it goes contrary to worldwide free trade.

In this context, the alternative model pays attention to unilateral free trade and not to trading blocs. It lets the citizens of the country (individuals or firms) trade freely in goods, services, investment, capital, information and ideas with anyone else on earth willing to proceed to the transactions. If free trade is good it must be good in all directions, over all continents and with all human beings.

Figure 50

Option 1	Option 2
Member of the EU	The alternative
Grade: 100/100,000	Grade: 250/100,000

26. Argument No. 25 (Economic)

> The EU is in effect a merger of countries. This must create synergies similar to those created by huge diversified firms known as conglomerates. Therefore, in the long run the EU is economically a good thing.

There are two faults with the above simplistic argument. The first is related to the fact that mergers of firms in different fields of economic activity have in most cases failed and they usually end up in the de-merger, spin-off or break-up of the diversified conglomerates. In the past few decades it was thought that it would be beneficial for a company to build an empire. Diversification into unrelated fields would help to expand through synergies and bigger was certainly better. The result was the creation of business empires resembling dinosaurs that were lagging behind in profits and growth in sales. Finally, most of the multibusiness companies de-merged into targeted-business companies that focused on specific sectors, and much faster growth in sales and profits followed. The few remaining successful conglomerates (of multibusiness companies) all happen to have very capable leaders, but in business you cannot build a paradigm on the assumption that you will always have an absolutely extraordinary person as a chief executive officer. In business (as well as in politics) you have to set up the system and principles in a correct and efficient way and, regarding the running of the system, you have to assume that the CEO will be very good but not always extraordinary or visionary or illuminated. The conclusion of this business story over the past twenty years is that if size matters in a business field (which is not at all always the case in spite of the popular conception that bigger is better), and if increase in size is permitted by the competition policies in the various markets (which in general should be strictly limited), then merging in order to be beneficial has to be between companies in identical or very similar or related fields of activity (focused business). Now if this can be said for firms, then certainly for national economies there are on balance and in the long run no gains to be made from the merging of fifteen national economies because by definition each national economy is not even a firm, it is a set of thousands or millions of firms or individuals working in thousands of different economic fields.

The second fault of the argument for merging is a simpler but more fundamental one. Countries are not firms to merge or de-merge. Countries are political and cultural entities which want to achieve maximum growth rates in material wealth and happiness. National parliaments, judicial systems and governments are not commercial firms that they should merge. They are (not for profit) organisations serving the interests of a group of people known as a country or nation or even culture. We will examine this point of view in more depth later on in the political and philosophical arguments chapters.

What about the alternative? In our imaginary country X, merging is very easy, but only between firms, not necessarily between countries. In the alternative, there is no forced and unconditional merging of whole economies from above. Firms of country X are absolutely free to merge (or de-merge as the case may be) with any other firm of any nation on earth provided that:

- strict anti-monopoly laws (regarding market share) are applied in the market of country X, and
- the merged (or de-merged) companies observe fully and operate within the laws of country X (which laws are in effect the set of rules that the citizens of country X have established for themselves).

In the alternative, there is no such thing as 'conglomerate illusion'. Figure 51 rates the argument.

Figure 51

Option 1 Member of the EU	Option 2 The alternative
Grade: 50/100,000	Grade: 250/100,000

Chapter XII
POLITICAL ARGUMENTS

Introduction to political arguments regarding the EU

Human beings differ from the animals and the plants in that they have not only material needs but also psychological and mental needs. People do not need only food and shelter. They need also freedom, a sense of justice, self-determination, identity, a sense of purpose, a sense of social integration, love, and a system of moral values. Politics as a discipline and in practical terms is concerned with both the material needs as well as the psychological and mental needs of the people. In other words politics starts with economics but then continues with other higher aspects of human life. It is those higher aspects that will be examined in the political arguments regarding the EU.

Before going into the discussion a few very important points should be made:

- Notions like freedom or justice or self-determination are extremely important. Whether they are more important or not than economics depends on the judgement of the individual. However, for most of the people they are of utmost importance.
- There is not a dilemma between 'material progress' and 'spiritual satisfaction'. In fact, one kind of progress cannot exist in the long run without the other kind of progress. In the short run, a nation can be wealthy without freedom but only for a while (maybe a few decades). In the long run, the nation without freedom will be less prosperous than other nations simply because its people and its leaders will feel unhappy and unhappy human beings cannot work efficiently. In the long run, spiritual satisfaction and material progress go hand in hand for any group of people (a household, an individual or a nation).

1. Argument No. 1 (Political)

Within the EU the legislative body is in effect outside my country. This is bad for me.

In a democratic country there are three powers: the legislative (lawmaking body, parliament, congress or senate), the government (executive power) and the judicial power (justice system). In a democratic country today, the ordinary citizen believes wrongly that the most important power is the government. The truth is that by far the most important power is the legislative body which discusses and votes on any new law. The government then has to govern according to the law and the judges have to judge according to the law.

For any country within the EU, all important laws come from a multi-country (supranational) parliament, the so-called Europarliament. The vast majority of the laws to be followed by the citizens of Germany or France or Finland come from the Europarliament and are simply confirmed in the national parliament. There are very few areas of human activity where a member country's parliament can make new laws and, even if the parliament makes a new law this definitely cannot contradict any law of the Europarliament on the same subject. Let us see some examples and try to stretch the examples to the limit and in a very-long-run context.

Assume that the parliament in Britain wants to extend the maximum permitted employees' hours of work per week from forty-eight to fifty-two per week (including overtime). It cannot because the Europarliament says that forty-eight hours is the maximum.

Assume that the parliament in Spain wants to introduce a law to halve or eliminate the value added tax on gasoline. It cannot.

Assume that the parliament of Finland wants to eliminate tariffs in car trade between Finland and Russia. It cannot.

Assume that the legislators in Italy want to decriminalise the use of cannabis. They cannot.

The list is endless. In the long run, almost every law has to be made in the Europarliament. Stretching the above to the limit, if the Europarliament says that there should be no official religion. then no country can have an official religion and if the Europarliament says that there should be taught everywhere one common language, then in the long run no country could have its own official language.

The purpose is not to illustrate pieces of correct or incorrect legislation, but to show that within the EU a country (any individual country) cannot in real terms have its own laws.

So the legislative power has moved from the parliament of individual countries to the Europarliament. Let us see now whether this is a good or a bad thing.

First of all, a group of people, a country or a nation cannot be sovereign unless its legislative body can produce the laws that its own people want to have imposed on themselves. Sovereignty is not about making wars. Sovereignty is first of all the ability of a group of people to impose on their country the laws that exclusively they wish to have. This is not at all a superficial notion. This is the cornerstone of successful legislation. It is the people of the individual country who know best which legislation is good for them. Sometimes they may pass (impartially speaking) wrong legislation. But it is better to be able to produce wrong legislation sometimes than to receive legislation from others. The people of a sovereign country sooner or later realise a wrong law has been passed (because they usually pay for their mistakes) and change it to a correct one. So the first and very important point is that *the people of a country know better than anyone else which laws are good for them and which laws are not good for them.*

The second point is about freedom. For a group of people, a country or a nation to be free this first of all means to be able to produce for themselves the laws that they wish to have even if some of those laws are wrong. Freedom is the ability to make your own decisions, enjoy your own values and your own way of life. Most of all, freedom is the ability to take even wrong decisions for yourself and then try to correct those wrong decisions. A country which receives its laws from others is by definition not free.

The third point is that freedom produces responsibility and with responsibility comes effort and productivity. A country that loses its ability to legislate as its own (and only its own) people wish sooner or later realises that it is no longer responsible for itself. The people of the country sooner or later realise that their legislators are in reality not able to produce laws according to their wishes. They are no longer responsible for their legislation, so there is no reason to try to be productive or effective in legislation. Eventually, everyone becomes indifferent to the legislative process. But indifference regarding the legislative process is one of the biggest blows against true democracy. To vote for legislators every four years knowing that the legislators will in effect be bound to accept the laws coming from another lawmaking body (in Strasbourg or Brussels) is not democracy. Maybe it is farce, a theatre, a parody, a talking shop, but certainly it is not democracy.

The fourth point is one of time-inclusive consequences (dynamic consequences). Assume that a law imposed on a country by the Europarliament today is absolutely correct. No one can guarantee that this law will always be correct because as time passes everything changes. Now, if the people of the same country in year 2008 wish to change that particular law, which at that time they find unsuitable for themselves, they simply cannot change the law. They will have to convince not only themselves, but around 360 million other people, which may be possible but it will certainly take a lot of time and effort, or it may be impossible. So in a dynamic world (not a static one), the people will have lost their ability to change their laws. But changing the laws is absolutely necessary for any country because the world is not static. The world is dynamic. We do not live outside the dimension of time. We live in time whether we like it or not, whether we know it or not and whether we accept it or not. Economies, conditions, people, products, services, cultures, knowledge, technology, human values, attitudes and almost everything else change as time passes by. The laws of today will have to change tomorrow.

The same argument applies not only for changing an already existing law, but for introducing a completely new law. If a citizen of a country has a fine idea regarding introducing a new law, then he or she has to convince not only the people of their country but he or she will have to convince a majority in the EU. This is a recipe for suppressing new legislation, not a recipe for dynamic progress.

The fifth point is about the centralisation or decentralisation of law making. Decentralisation of power is one of the most basic characteristics of any modern country. In fact, human history is characterised, in the last few centuries at least, by a gradual (or sometimes abrupt) decentralisation of power. Almost all countries started from some central and usually authoritative source of making laws and gradually evolved a system where the people of a nation elected their representative legislators with the power to legislate in the name of the people and for a specific period of time. However, even with this system of legislation in many countries the average citizen feels that the legislators are far away from him or her. So the feeling and the effort logically should be that the legislative process should come nearer to the citizen, nearer his or her problems, i.e. towards a more participatory form of legislative process, towards a more direct and a wider based form of democracy. Instead of this, for members of the EU the legislative process has become very, very distant. It has become something that is 'abroad' stemming from 'aliens'. If before the EU there was one legislator per x number of voters, now with the EU there is one Eurolegislator per 10x number of voters. On top of this even if all the Eurolegislators of an individual country agree on something it is highly unlikely that they will be able to pass it into Euro-law because, by definition, the Eurolegislators of any country are a small minority in the Europarliament. So instead of the legislative process becoming closer to the average citizen of a country, it becomes in real terms completely foreign to them. Instead of more legislative power going to the building block of society (which is the individual person), we have much less legislative power going to the individual. Instead of more decentralisation of the legislative process, we have complete centralisation in Strasbourg or Brussels. It appears to me that centralisation instead of decentralisation is going against the history of civilisation.

The sixth point is that of the accountability of the legislators to the voters of a country. While the national legislators are theoretically fully accountable to the citizens of the country, in practical terms they are only partially accountable. The Eurolegislators are accountable to nobody because most citizens do not know what each legislator is doing in Strasbourg or Brussels and what his actual contribution to each law is. The only people who know exactly what each Eurolegislator is doing are the thousands of lobbyists, special interest groups and their lawyers who are continually pressing and following the Eurolegislators in Strasbourg or Brussels. This is certainly not a truly democratic legislative process. However, the results of such legislation have to be followed by every person in every corner of every member country of the EU!

The seventh point is one of flexibility and speed in the lawmaking process. When legislation is made in a national parliament with a population base of, say, 5 to 85 million people, then it is natural that a law will be discussed and implemented faster than if the same law were discussed in the Europarliament with a population base of 360 million people. And not only is the size of the population base a factor. It is the character of the population base (different cultures, languages, civilisations, histories, attitudes and even values to issues such as environment or education or health) that varies widely and this in a natural sense would require different kinds of legislation.

Moreover, geographic location, the nature of the countryside (mountainous or flat, rich or poor, type of agricultural products, inland or coastal), in many cases requires modified legislation. For example, the farmers producing olives in Spain require different legislation to the cattle farmers of Holland, and the pollution problems in Athens or Rome require different legislation to the pollution problems in Helsinki or Dublin simply because the pollution problems and causes (car intensity, climate, etc.) are different.

Finally, and most important of all, the economies of the countries are different and normally require legislation adapted to particular circumstances. The development levels are different, the nature of the economies is different (manufacturing-based economies or service-based economies). The knowledge levels are different, the skills of the people are different, the ethics or attitudes of the people towards employment vary, and the extent of social protection is different. This normally requires different legislation adapted to the needs of the particular economies (and to the wishes of the particular people). One could instinctively and very logically question here why there are differences between economies and whether all economies should not be the same. This is really a very important question which will be taken in the philosophical arguments chapter, but for now we can say the following two things quickly:

- Differences in economies at this moment are a fact and not a wish or a desire. Legislation should first of all start from the facts and not from some unrealistic or imaginary situation.
- Regarding the desirability of differences, or even whether they are natural or not, one can say that if the existence of many different individuals is a good thing, then differences in economies are a good thing. If the existence of different individuals is a bad thing, then differences in economies are a bad thing. If the existence of different individual persons is a natural thing, then differences in economies are a natural thing. If the existence of different individuals is an unnatural thing, then differences in economies are an unnatural thing.

But isn't there any positive aspect in this transfer of the legislative power from the national parliaments to the Europarliament? The truth is that, yes, there are two points:

- Since the population base of the Europarliament is much bigger than the population base of the Bundestag in Germany, it is natural, statistically speaking, that there will be a greater number of new proposals (or ideas) to be discussed to become law. However, any new idea having to pass through the Europarliament will have to be 'cut to size' to be acceptable to everyone and usually this means 'the lowest common denominator' not the best idea for moving quickly forward. In spite of this drawback, it is a positive fact that the mathematical probability of new ideas coming from the Europarliament is much greater than the mathematical probability of the same new ideas coming from the legislature of even a populous country like Germany (84 million people), simply because ideas are drawn from a much larger population.

- We said earlier that in the Europarliament there is less flexibility in changing a law when compared to a national parliament. But less flexibility means by definition more rigidity and sometimes rigidity is a good thing contributing to stability. There are some countries which, in the past, for various reasons, have changed the law on the same subject very often. This causes dissatisfaction and instability because the average citizen feels that the rules of the game are changing too often (Greece is probably one of the champion countries in this respect in the past).

So, this is the situation with the legislative power for any country within the EU. In one sentence, the legislative power of the country has been transferred and is residing at the Europarliament.

Let us now try to go to our imaginary country X, the alternative, and see where the legislative power of its people is and what their legislative procedure is.

The people of country X have not only decided to have 100% of the legislative power for themselves, but also have decided to move forward and use technology to distribute the legislative power to the individual citizen. They have decided that the time has come for complete decentralisation of the legislative process to where it belongs, to its building block: the individual person. They have decided that the average citizen is educated to a sufficient level that he or she can vote on any proposed law and that the technological developments of the past several years make this possible and affordable. At the same time they have decided to include in their process the two positive aspects of the Europarliament mentioned earlier. *They are using a system known as Athenian democracy.*

Let us now see the basic principles and practices of their legislative process (the phrase 'legislative system' is being avoided by the people of country X because once you are in a system it may become difficult to change it or it may become some form of untouchable and divine prison into which everyone is finally locked!)

ATHENIAN DEMOCRACY IN VERY SIMPLE LINES

Principle no. 1

The people of the country have 100% of the legislative power themselves. Others cannot impose laws on them. Only citizens of country X can vote for any legislation.

Principle no. 2

The people of the country do not wish, neither try, to impose their laws on other countries.

Principle no. 3

The members of parliament are lawmakers not law voters. They prepare and discuss in detail any new law, but when voting for the law their voting power is the same as every other citizen of the country.

Principle no. 4

Any group of citizens in country X can propose for discussion in the parliament any law provided that they collect a sufficient number of signatures (say, at least 1% of the country's population). The signatures can be collected electronically through the Internet via the Electronic Voting System described on page 127.

Means for electronic collection of signatures are television sets with special set-top boxes to make them access the Internet, or home computers, or ATMs. Each citizen uses a special code number for electronically secure identification.

Upon collection of the necessary number of citizen signatures (electronic or paper signatures), it is compulsory that the legislative body will discuss extensively the proposed law and bring it to the electorate for national electronic voting.

Principle no. 5

All discussions about a law in the legislature are recorded and stored as video film in a special site on the Internet. Any voter can retrieve the video film on demand at any time through his or her TV-computer appliance by just pressing a few buttons in the remote control of the TV-computer.

It is important to note that:

1. Any TV has also become a very simple computer giving ready and easy access to the Internet even to the oldest or least educated person simply by the addition to the TV of a simple set-top box plus a modem for connection to the phone line.
2. A publicly owned TV-radio station strictly supervised by all political parties is continuously transmitting the discussions in the legislature about any law. This is necessary for any voter who for some reason cannot or does not wish to use a computer.
3. Regarding the viability of the electronic distribution of legislation discussion as video on demand, on 3 September 1997 a software company

announced and exhibited in operation computer servers that can distribute video film on demand to thousands of people through the Internet. Each user can electronically watch the same film at the same time with thousands of other users, but the film is at a different stage for each user, i.e. while a viewer of the same film is at the beginning of the film, another is at its end, another is rewinding the film and another is unwinding it! Conclusion: if we can have video films on demand, we can certainly have video with lawmaking on demand (films and lawmaking are at least equally important for our happiness!)

Principle no. 6
Voting for any law takes place not in the parliament but over the whole country! Law voters are the citizens, i.e. all eligible voters of the nation.

Voting takes place electronically through the Internet. Conduits for voting are the TV sets (having already become suitable for access to the Internet) or home computers or the computers of the neighbours or the ATMs at the corner of the street.

Identification for voting is done through special ID cards using the same procedure with which many people already withdraw money from their bank account while they are in front of their home computer!

Confidentiality for voting is achieved through encryption software. The same encryption software is used already by people when using their smart cards at home, withdrawing money from their bank accounts and loading the smart cards with cash. Votes are collected electronically in a central computer supervised by all political parties, the police and representatives of the justice system. Voting takes place the same day every week (if any law is up for voting), say every Saturday or Sunday. The results of the voting on any law are announced a few minutes after the electronic ballot boxes are closed, say on every Sunday at 8 p.m. One might ask: is it possible for this to happen with today's technology? It is absolutely possible.

If we can withdraw money from our bank account while we are at home, if we can load our smart cards with cash while we are at home, if we can browse through books in Internet bookshops while we are at home, if we can order books and pay for them while we are at home, it is then possible to browse through a debate on a law in parliament and then vote on that law from home using the same technology regarding encryption and identification. No more special interest groups; no more lobbies; no more suspicions of low morals or corruption; no more manipulation of the wishes of the people by powerful organisations. The lawmaking process has been totally decentralised to the building block of any nation: the individual citizen, the individual from whom all legislative power emanates.

Some questions may arise at this point regarding the practicality of such a legislative process as exhibited in the alternative. How can the citizen decide on a new law? Is he or she sufficiently educated to vote on the laws? Is the process expensive? What then in the alternative is the role of the elected lawmaker? Is this process time-consuming for the citizen? Let us see the answers to those questions:

1. In all democratic nations, referenda are used for voting on the constitution or very important legislation. If the people can decide through referenda on complex issues such as whole constitutions, they can certainly decide on a specific law on a Saturday afternoon.
2. Regarding the ability of the average citizen to understand a proposed new law which may be of a complex nature:
   - the average citizen can see and hear the full debate on the law on her TV-computer-radio set on demand.
   - it is up to the political parties to present on the TV-computer a concise and simplified description of the law giving the viewers the pros and cons of the proposed new law (according to their opinion).
   - the education level of the people in almost all countries in the world has been increased and they are certainly in a position to understand the consequences of any new law.
   - to suggest that the people cannot decide themselves on a new law is not compatible with democracy and certainly not compatible with the simple fact that it is the people who will suffer the consequences of a wrong law and it is the people who will benefit from a correct law.
3. Regarding the cost of the process: in very simple terms it costs nothing to perform an electronic referendum over the whole nation every Sunday!
4. Regarding the role of the elected lawmakers in the alternative: they are lawmakers not law voters! They spend all their ideas, energy and time hearing the problems of the citizens, conceptualising laws and presenting the laws to the parliament and to the people at large in simple terms. They have to convince the people about the correctness of any new law, not themselves. The function of the legislators in a truly democratic society is one and only one: to make laws. It is not their function to bow to pressures from anyone or to try to exercise power not given to them (and sometimes – I believe very seldom – to be tempted to participate in scandals and corruptions).
5. Is the electronic voting a time-consuming process? For each new law the voter will have to watch the simplified arguments for and against the law in a ten-minute (at most) broadcast, say every Saturday, and then vote electronically, which takes another one minute. The ten-minute broadcast could be about the view of only his of her political party

or it could include the views of other political parties. The more interested voters could spend more time in front of their TV-computer and see and hear more detailed discussions or statements on the law from political parties or particular lawmakers.

We saw above the six basic principles and practices of the legislative process in our imaginary country X. Certainly there are many other details, but they are of minor importance. The basic feature of the process in the alternative is that the legislative power, instead of being centralised in a far away centre, is fully decentralised and distributed to the people. This is done in a way to reflect the wishes of the people and the abilities of late twentieth century technology. Twenty-five centuries ago, the ancient Greeks were exercising in Athens exactly that form of legislative process in principle, but with the ancient technology. Now, the people in the alternative are coming full circle and are using again the Athenian democracy, but with contemporary technology!

Let us now see the two practices that the people in the alternative have incorporated in order to take real advantage of the special Europarliament features that we saw on page 168?

Legislation is most of all a matter of successful new ideas. If, however, the pool of ideas is drawn from a group of 360 million people then, statistically speaking, a greater number of successful new ideas will come up than if the pool of ideas was drawn from a smaller group. In order to take advantage of this simple mathematical fact, the people in the alternative have introduced the following very simple principle.

Principle no. 7
The legislative body in our imaginary country X has made permanent bilateral arrangements with all the legislative bodies of all sovereign countries such that any new law passed and enacted in the parliament of any other country is automatically sent by fax or e-mail to the secretariat of the parliament in the alternative and is automatically distributed to all its members. They can thus get new legislative ideas from anybody. If they find them inapplicable to the needs of their people, then they simply put them into their files. If they find the idea relevant to the needs of their country, then they can modify the law or follow the process of electronic voting by the whole electorate at once.

In this very simple way the pool of new legislative ideas for the alternative is extended over the whole human race.

With this system, the people of the alternative have not delegated their legislative powers to any other human group but themselves. It is up to their parliamentarians (and to the people of the alternative at large) whether a new law voted in another parliament in another nation is suitable for their circumstances or of any interest at all. The legislative power is emanating only from the citizens of the alternative, but the legislative ideas are emanating from the whole globe!

We have said that the inability of the people of a country within the EU to change significantly any law or to introduce a completely new one, apart from the many very important negative consequences, also has a positive side. The set of laws becomes more stable and more permanent and this impression is conveyed to the average citizen (and especially businessman). In order to take advantage of this EU feature, the people in the alternative have introduced the following principle.

Principle no. 8
Any law enacted today cannot be changed or modified for five years. If, owing to changing circumstances (which is perfectly possible), the same law needs to change within the initial five-year period, then the majority required for passage by the electorate is increased from, say, 50% to 60% of the electorate. This arrangement discourages the legislators in the alternative to attempt to continually change the same law because of pressure groups or opportunism. On the other hand, it allows the electorate to change a law when there is widespread consensus that the circumstances demand deviation from the stability and experimentation period of five years.

This stability and experimentation period of five years as well as the increased majority of 60% are only illustrative in the alternative and can constitutionally change depending on the wishes, wisdom and desire for stability and flexibility of the citizens of country X.

The graded outcome of this discussion is in Figure 52.

Figure 52

Option 1 Member of the EU	Option 2 The alternative
Grade: 0/100,000	Grade: 5,000/100,000

2. Argument No. 2 (Political)

Within the EU, the judicial power of the people of my country has in effect been transferred to others. This is bad for me.

The second pillar of power in a democratic country is the judicial power. It is the whole set of judges who dispense justice according to the set of laws established by the legislative power. For any nation within the EU it is true that its judicial power has largely been transferred to the EU Court of Justice residing in Luxembourg. Any citizen of the nation who feels that he or she has been treated in an unjust manner can go to the EU court and hopefully try to overturn any wrong decision taken by the courts in his or her country. But by the same token, any correct decision of the courts of an individual country can be overturned by the EU court. The EU justice system in practical terms supersedes (and where necessary nullifies) the decisions of the courts of any individual state.

These are the facts in simple and generalised terms. Let us now see if there is anything wrong with these facts.

The first wrong is that we have centralisation of the judicial power of the individual states instead of more decentralisation. In general, decentralisation of power, not centralisation, is what characterises the evolution of human history and here we are again going against history.

The second wrong is about directness of democracy. The judicial powers are one of the three fundamental powers of the citizens in any democratic country and these powers should exist directly under the concerned group of people (the nation). Direct democracy is always preferable to indirect one.

The third wrong is one of trust by the citizens of a country in their judicial system. The mere existence of another judicial system above the one established and controlled by them as a group implicitly means that they somehow mistrust their own system and all its various stages. But if a group of people mistrust their own judicial power, then it is as if they mistrust themselves. Even if this is the case, then the therapy is not to transfer their democratic power to other people but to correct their system.

To mistrust ourselves as a group is as bad as to mistrust ourselves as individual human beings. If this is the case, then the way forward is not to reduce ourselves to pathetic receivers of the wisdom of others, but to find the courage to improve and correct ourselves as well as the whole system.

The fourth wrong is one of spending taxpayers' money for unnecessary travel over greater distances than necessary. The people need to travel to Luxembourg instead of remaining at home for a service they are supposed to have within their country since the taxpayers have paid for that. There is also an additional cost element involving the salaries and overheads of the judges in Luxembourg, buildings and so on.

The fifth wrong is one of the mentality of the judges. For each judge everywhere there is always the objective part of dispensing justice, i.e. the judge decides as if he were a computer having within its memory the 'specification' (the law) and running the programme according to the particular 'data' introduced to the computer (the facts about the innocence or guilt of the individual person or other legal entity under trial). However, there is a part of any decision by a judge which we can call it the subjective part. This is unavoidable because every judge is a human being and as such carries his personal values within himself. But the personal values of the judge usually reflect the general values of his country (culture, civilisation, history, morals and attitudes). It is then natural to say that when the judge is from the same country as the alleged offender the possibility, of misjudging the cultural and ethical parts of the alleged offence is minimised.

But aren't there any good aspects of the system of transferring a great part of the judicial power of a member country to the EU Court of Justice? Yes, there are!

One good aspect is that if a citizen feels deep inside himself that he has been treated unfairly at all the levels of justice in his or her own country, he or she can go to one other higher level of justice. An injustice done at all previous levels can be corrected at the last level. However, the opposite is also true: justice done at all previous levels can become injustice at the last level.

For example, a citizen of country X, having actually committed a tax fraud in his country and correctly found guilty by the courts, can in theory be found innocent in the EU Court of Justice. In principle, there is no reason why dispensing justice from Luxembourg should be more accurate or wiser than dispensing justice from within the home country at all available levels since a person or legal entity is subject to the laws of the country where the alleged violation of law was committed and not to the laws of others. However, the mere fact that the EU Court of Justice in Luxembourg represents one more (and higher) level of justice is in general positive or comforting.

The other positive aspect of the EU Court of Justice is simply that because it is far away, in many cases there is some sense of greater impartiality. It is possible, both in theory and in practice, for the judgement at any level of the national courts to be incorrect, usually owing to local political reasons, pressure from the media or public opinion. In such a case, which I must say is generally unlikely but not at all impossible, the average person or other legal entity feels relieved to know that there is one higher court in Luxembourg where he or she might go and be judged in an impartial way without any pressure from anyone. This is certainly very comforting and very positive.

So, those are the negative and positive points associated with the transfer of judicial power from the people of a country to the EU Court of Justice.

Let us now see the alternative. Let us go to our imaginary country X and see what its judicial system is. When setting up their judicial system the people were influenced by some basic principles which we shall see in a little while. However, the strange people of the alternative were particularly influenced by an event that happened in ancient Greece and specifically in ancient Athens. It is the story of a great philosopher named Socrates who was wrongly accused, condemned, sentenced to death and executed by drinking hemlock. Let us review very briefly the main points of this story.

Socrates (469–399 BC) taught philosophy in ancient Athens. His teachings were great and really very important. However, when he was very old (seventy years old) the Athenians accused him of 'introducing new and bad morals'. He was wrongly condemned, tried and sentenced to death. He was put in jail to await the day of his execution. While he was in jail his devoted students came to him. They told him that he had done nothing wrong; he was absolutely innocent; he had been judged wrongly. He was urged to escape from prison and the students offered him a safe and sure way for escaping from prison. However, Socrates refused to escape. He said that he had to obey the laws of his country and the judgement of the people of his country, even if that particular judgement was totally wrong. He had been preaching obedience to the laws of his country all his life and he could not now put himself above the laws of Athens. He stayed in prison, drank the hemlock and died.

From this story the people of the alternative have retained the following basic morals:

1. We have to obey the laws of the country we live in, whether we like a particular law nor not. If we believe that a particular law is wrong (and this may be perfectly true) then we have to use all legal means to change the law. But until and unless a law changes we have to obey the existing law.
2. If we live in a country and get all the public services and benefits, we implicitly assume that we accept the justice system of the country whether we like a particular judgement or not. We cannot assume that the justice system is generally correct and impartial when our fellow citizens are tried but when it comes to us to be tried believe that the justice system is wrong. If we feel that a particular judgement is wrong, we can fight it by all available legal means. But to believe that we have to go out of our justice system to be tried correctly is equivalent to nullifying our justice system.

Now let us see the basic principles and practices of the justice system of the alternative.

Principle no. 1
All residents of the country are subject only to the justice system of that country.

Principle no. 2
The people of country X do not wish to impose their justice system on other people.

Principle no. 3
There is not anywhere on earth any other justice system that supersedes the justice system established by the people of country X.

Principle no. 4
The judicial power in country X is completely and truly independent from the legislative power and executive power. The judges are not subject to pressures from anyone including parliamentarians, government officials, political parties, media, pressure groups and public opinion.

Principle no. 5
The top ten judges are not appointed by the government or the legislature. They are elected by the people of the country every ten years from amongst the highest in the hierarchy of judges in the country. Those ten judges are

solely responsible for the whole judicial system (like promotions of other judges) and make sure that the judicial system is functioning according to the laws voted by the people and only according to those laws. During the election of the top ten judges every ten years, the detailed curriculum vitae as well as the education of the candidates are distributed to the people of the country via the Internet, newspapers, etc. The judgement of each judge in past difficult cases is given to the media. No judge can have any kind of political party membership or other official affiliation. No judge can be at any time a member of government or parliament. Any person being paid with public money (government official, parliamentarian, public sector employee) can communicate with a judge for any matter only through letter which must pass through a central register. This central register will automatically make the letter available to the legislators, government officials and the media. The election of the top ten judges is done through the EVS (Electronic Voting System) only for one term. After their term expires they retire.

Principle no. 6
The elected top ten judges constitute also the highest court of appeals for any citizen of the country. Their judgement cannot be superseded or overturned by any other judicial body. Only if the people of the country have lost their collective freedom and are under occupation, only then can their highest court of appeals be subservient to another court and only for as long as the people of the country are under occupation.

Occupation by others is unimaginable in today's civilised and peaceful world, but theoretically it is possible if for some reason the people of country X commit a collective crime like aggressive war.

Commenting briefly on the above judicial process of the people of the alternative we see that it has the following advantages (and the grading is given in Figure 53):

- It establishes practical complete independence of the judges from the executive power and legislative power.
- It establishes complete independence of the judges from interest groups, lobbies, political parties, etc.
- It establishes accountability of the top judges to the power of the people (Athenian democracy in the judicial system).
- It reinforces the impartiality of the highest court of appeals to pressure from anywhere. The laws of the country (voted directly by the people of the country) and the conscience of the judges are the only criteria.
- It establishes the principle that as long as we live in a society we are all subject to its laws.

- It makes clear that there is not (and there cannot be) any judicial power above the collective judicial power of the people living in a country, at least as long as the country is free.

Figure 53

Option 1 Member of the EU	Option 2 The alternative
Grade: 500/100,000	Grade: 2,500/100,000

3. Argument No. 3 (Political)

> Within the EU the government of my country is virtually eliminated by the de facto government in Brussels (wrongly named the Commission). This is bad for me.

In any democratic country the executive power is one of the three fundamental and inalienable powers of the people. It is an elected group of citizens who govern according to the laws enacted by the parliament and subject to the controls of the judicial system just like anybody else in the country (at least in theory!). The government cannot act contrary to the laws of the national legislature. It is supposed to govern absolutely within the laws of the legislative body and its mandate from the electorate of the nation is usually for four or five years.

Today, for a member of the EU the ability of the government to govern according to its own will (which is supposed to coincide with the will of the majority of the people) is by definition and by the very structure and purpose of existence of the EU institutions reduced by a proportion as great as 80%. The Commission performs all the functions that a government performs, i.e. it directly employs about 20,000 people (paying for their salaries, health care and pensions), it has all kinds of ministers but under the name of Commissioner; it collects money from all taxpayers every year indirectly through their national governments (around $100 billion at the moment) and spends the same amount of money for various purposes. This government sends a great number of instructions or regulations to all the national governments for immediate implementation (instead of instructions or regulations, one could more accurately use the words 'executive orders'). Those instructions go directly to the national governments but indirectly they go to all the citizens of each individual country. As a result of all this procedure, the power of any government of any individual nation to apply policies in any ministry has been almost wiped out. The real power for policies resides in Brussels. In effect, a national government can do almost nothing to improve the lives of its people the way it sees proper and the way the citizens of the state voted it in for. It has to try to improve the lives of the people the way the Commission sees proper with a small degree of 'differential flexibility'. Let us see some characteristic examples where a national government cannot follow the mandate given to it by the people who elected it.

Economic activities

- No government can abolish the value added tax on any goods or service.
- No government can abolish the tax on the interest from deposits in the banks.
- No government can essentially change the exchange rate of its currency relative to other currencies (and maybe some governments will not have any exchange rate to think about in the future).
- No government can distribute money to its farmers. It has to send the money of its taxpayers to the Commission and the Commission will send the money back to the farmers (Common Agricultural Policy).
- No government can set quotas for the amount of fish its fishermen can catch per year near its shores. The quotas come from Brussels ((CFP)).
- No government can nationalise any industry (including industries such as health care or education or social insurance) even if the voters of the country have instructed it to do so.
- No government can increase the upper limits of the working hours per week. It can decrease the working hours per week, but cannot increase them even if its voters have instructed it to do so.
- No government can abolish the minimum wage even if the voters have instructed it to do so.
- No government can increase the budget deficit beyond a certain upper limit (set at 3% of Gross Domestic Product).
- No government can increase or decrease tariffs on any products of any third country.
- No government can make any substantial trade agreement with any third country.

Other activities

- No government can make foreign policy treaties with any third country. The foreign policy is common, i.e. defined by Brussels.
- No government can have its own immigration policy.
- No government can have its own colour, size or appearance of passport.
- No government can control the nationality (citizenship) of the public

sector employees.
- No government can have its own citizens' rights standards. It has to follow the standards coming from Brussels.
- No government can make any military alliance with any third country.
- No government can have its own environmental standards. It has to follow the standards of Brussels.
- No government can give instructions for the labelling of products. The labelling instructions are for Brussels to decide.
- No government can issue its own identity cards for the citizens; they have to be the same for all member countries.
- No government can exercise control effectively over the borders of the country except borders with third countries.
- No government can keep within the country the intelligence data collected by its foreign ministry employees. It has to share these data with Brussels because of the common foreign policy.
- No government can exercise control over customs clearance employees, procedures and organisations. Customs clearance has to be under the control of the Commission and the personnel have to be direct employees of the EU.
- No government can disapprove a new medicine once the Commission has approved it.
- No government can disapprove a new product or service once the Commission has approved it.
- No government can teach the students that there are multiple cultures and civilisations in Europe. The education system has to present history in a unified way so that every new generation is brought up with the view that there has been and there is only one European culture, one European civilisation, one European history, one European identity, one European human being: the European.

The list of examples in the form of regulations, standards, policies, advice, instructions (or executive orders to be more precise) is lengthy, going into the thousands or hundreds of thousands. It is almost endless!

Before proceeding further two clarifications should be made. One clarification is that the administrative instructions coming from the Commission are not necessarily wrong (neither, of course, are they unnecessarily right!). They are, however, coming from a source outside the individual country and outside the administrative power of the people of the particular country.

Second, in the particular examples given above some people may think that there is still some scope for the national government. One might suggest that an individual nation, say Austria, retains control over the number of immigrants coming yearly from third countries. Suppose that Austria sets a limit of say 30,000 new legal immigrants coming from third countries and tries to observe that limit. The truth is that, for example, France or Spain can decide (for their own perfectly legitimate and democratic reasons) to accept a great number of legal immigrants from third countries. Those new immigrants coming to France or Spain today will certainly become French or Spanish citizens after five years. At that time, when they will be French or Spanish citizens, they can legally decide to emigrate to Austria. The government in Austria will have no right to stop them. They will not be new immigrants from third countries. Hence the immigration policy of the Austrian people can be circumvented by the immigration policy of the French people (or Spanish people) and vice versa.

There comes the next step (as a natural consequence). The only way for the Austrians to exercise some control over immigration is if they have a common immigration policy with all the other member states. But having this policy common means that it will be decided in Brussels and the instructions sent to Vienna, Paris or Madrid. The argument has been proven: no individual government can have its own immigration policy!

It is beyond any reasonable doubt that the ability of any individual country to govern itself has been transferred to the Commission in Brussels and that the Commission simply sends instructions for execution to the people living in each country. The instructions go to the people through their national government. The type of instructions may be (depending on the case) common policies, rules, regulations, advice, opinions, approvals, professional associations standards, quality process standards, quotas, tariffs, controls, etc., but their true name should be 'executive orders'.

At this moment in the Commission there are Commissioners for each of the following areas of responsibility:

- Budget, personnel
- Competition
- Consumer policy and food safety, fish, humanitarian aid
- Farming
- Vice-president, North America, Far-East, Australasia, trade
- Single market, tax
- Economy and finance
- Eastern Europe and ex-Soviet Union
- Transport
- Regions
- Immigration, justice, home affairs, fraud
- Vice-president, Middle East, Latin American, South-East Asia

- Institutions, culture, audiovision
- Industry, info-tech, telecom
- Jobs and social affairs
- Energy, small- and medium-sized enterprises, tourism
- Africa, Caribbean, Pacific
- Environment, nuclear safety
- Science, research and education
- President of the Commission

If the above set of Commissioners does not constitute a government, then what does?

In real terms the Commissioners should be called ministers and the Commission should be termed a government.

So it is a fact that the power of the people of the member countries has been transferred to the Commission in Brussels. But this is not bad a priori. It is not, for example, self-evident that when the German people are governed from Brussels they have a worse government than if they were governed by their own government. It is not self-evident that twenty ministers in Brussels coming from many different countries are less able to govern the German people than their own government. It is natural to say that good, capable, active and honest politicians exist in any country and that no particular nation produces exclusively the best politicians or administrators. Furthermore, in principle, we cannot assume that any person as a Commissioner in Brussels will be badly intentioned towards the Germans (or any other group of people). So, what is wrong when the Germans are governed by the Commission? Is there any problem for the Germans if their executive body resides in Brussels instead of Bonn or Berlin?

The first negative point is that sovereignty and independence are lost. A group of people cannot be sovereign or independent when it lacks executive power. The value of sovereignty is a subjective matter, i.e. various groups of people attach quite a lot of importance to it and they consider sovereignty as a good thing. Therefore, loss of sovereignty for any individual country is a bad thing.

The second negative point is one of centralisation of the executive power instead of decentralisation. In previous arguments we examined centralisation regarding the legislative power and the judicial power of the people. In this argument the centralisation of the executive power is under consideration. It is obvious that having the executive power decentralised in the various national capitals rather than centralised in Brussels is much more efficient on the following grounds:

1. For the collection of information. It is much easier and efficient for the

government of, say, Finland to know what the needs of its people and geographical area are than for any government in Brussels, other things being equal. It is not only a matter of geographical distance or language. It is a matter of particular culture, attitudes, history, education level, work ethic, type of geographical landscape and so on.

2. For the processing of information. Once all the information about the needs of the people of the country (the will of the people) is collected by the national government, it is much more efficient and faster if the processing of the information is done on the national rather than on a supranational level. Once the needs of the people of Portugal are known to the government of Portugal (on any type of activity), it is much more efficient to process this information on the spot, i.e. in Lisbon, than to relay the information to Brussels for processing. It is more efficient to analyse a problem of the Portuguese people on a Portuguese level by a Portuguese government than to send all the data of the problem to Brussels and try to analyse the problems there.

3. For prompt decision-making. After processing the information an executive decision has to be made. If this decision is being taken exclusively in the national capital, it will be made faster than if it is made by a supranational body. It is obvious, for example, that a problem of the German people will be solved faster by their own government than by the Commission in Brussels. This is a direct consequence of the simple fact that the Commission will have to consider the same problem over the entire EU and then decide. It is not the result of any superiority regarding speed on the part of the German government officials compared to the Commission's officials! But the time frame within which a decision is made is of great importance for any group of people, i.e. a solution to a problem of the German people delivered after three years of study has a much smaller value than the same solution to the same problem of the same German people delivered after half a year of study. Or as one professor once said, 'If I give you infinite time you can solve any problem!'

4. For appropriate decision-making. Other things being equal, a problem will be solved in a more accurate way if it is solved by the government of the country concerned than by a group of people from many countries. A problem of the Swedish people in principle will be solved in a better way by their own government, who understand their attitudes on everything, than by a group of Commissioners from different countries. There is nothing wrong with the wisdom or the intentions of the individual commissioner deciding on policies for the Swedish people. It is natural to say that a Swedish government official understands the importance of every executive decision better than an official from another country.

5. For the implementation of any administrative decision. In government, as in all forms of administration (even in private companies or in armies), the implementation of a decision counts many times more than the degree of correctness of the decision. We used to be taught that 'A very good plan when implemented in a mediocre way is much less effective than a mediocre plan when implemented in a brilliant way.' When an administrative decision is taken by the Commission, it is sent for implementation to the national governments. But any national government naturally feels that this decision is not its baby. It is not a product of its own exclusive free will. It is logical, then, that the government of the country does not have the proper interest and incentives for successful implementation. The result is indifference by the national government and indifference is the best recipe for unsuccessful implementation of any plan or decision. Why should, for example, the French government try wholeheartedly to implement an administrative policy measure coming from Brussels? If the policy measure proves to be successful, the credit will most probably go to the Commission in Brussels, but if it is unsuccessful and results, say, in unemployment, the opposition parties will most probably accuse the French government, not the Commission.

The third negative point about transferring the executive power of the people of a country to the Commission is one of generalised solutions which do not necessarily reflect the particular wishes or the needs of the people of the country. By its very nature of functioning, any administrative decision of the Commission will be generalised and not specialised to the needs of a particular country. But a problem of, say, the French people should be targeted to their own needs, not to the needs of the Greeks or the Finns. Targeted administrative policies are not possible for the Commission, but are not possible either for the French government because the generalised decisions of Brussels supersede any specialised decision of the French government. The difference here is one of the quality of the administrative measure. It is the same difference in quality that exists naturally between a general merchandise store and a specialised store or boutique.

The fourth negative point is that in the long run the national government develops indifference in public policy measures. Why should a French minister spend a lot of effort to find a policy measure when he knows that any serious policy measure will come only from Brussels? Why should he or she spend some nights without sleep to develop any good measure when, even if a measure were found, this would have to be sent to Brussels and then come from Brussels to the French people as an intellectual product of the Commission and not of the French minister? When the national government of a country starts to realise that the administrative power resides in Brussels, then indifference starts developing from the part of high-ranking as well as low-ranking government officials. They start feeling more like permanent employees than as men and women with a mission, a duty, a responsibility. In the long run, those feelings of indifference (and maybe cynicism) will be overwhelming. But indifference by any administrative body (including the executive bodies of private companies or public organisations) is a guarantee for slow national growth. It is a guarantee for slow progress in general welfare, in education, in health care, in law and order, in sense of purpose as a society. The early fruits of such a situation are already visible in many countries.

The fifth negative point about transferring the administrative power of the people of any country to the Commission in Brussels is that sooner or later the average voter realises the fact that the power rests not with his country's government, but with the Commission, which is an alien thing. As a consequence, *the average voter develops apathy towards the political process in the country*. But a democratic political process rests first of all in the personal interest of the voter in public affairs or policy measures. When this personal interest is diminished, it also diminishes the value of the results of voting. In the long run, the apathy develops into a degree of cynicism about a political process that is completely alien and far away from the people. Instead of the citizen feeling that he is the 'master of his fate and captain of his soul', he feels that he is somehow foreign to the political process and decision-making. Instead of being an active participant in public policy measures or affairs he is the receiver of instructions from some far away and alien body. When apathy and cynicism prevail, a society cannot attain the maximum possible pace of growth – material or psychological.

The sixth negative point about transferring the administrative power of the citizens of a particular country to the Commission is the concentration of power and its associated negative consequences. The Commission, being above fifteen individual governments, has in its hands vast amounts of political, military, diplomatic and economic power. We will examine in a completely separate argument later on whether this concentration of power serves any useful purpose. For the moment we will consider some of its side effects.

Side effect 1
Monopolarity of administration is established over the whole continent of Europe. Having replaced many individual governments with one much more powerful government in Brussels, the EU has replaced different sets of 'administrative minds' with one. To use a term from the discipline of microeconomics, instead of having fifteen competitors in administrative performance over the continent of Europe, there is only one huge monopolist of administrative performance. But it is well known in microeconomics, in philosophy and to the general public that competition is always preferable to monopoly. If this is true for markets or for industries, it is one thousand times more true in administration policies, measures, practices and ideas, because what else are the executive policies, measures, practices and ideas, what else is

the executive branch of the power of the people, than a set of ideas and practices competing peacefully to achieve the best possible kind of a place for the people to live in? Is it preferable to have over the continent of Europe one huge monopolist of executive power in Brussels or to have many different competitor national governments, each one engaged in its own initiatives, innovations, ideas and practices?

Competition between governing practices is not about making war. It is about offering to each group of people the best ways to improve their lives. Competition of ideas and practices brings real progress at both the material and psychological levels. Monopoly brings in the long run bureaucracy, indifference, the fat cat syndrome, cynicism, slow growth and laziness. One cannot believe in competition between firms in an industry and not in competition between government practices. One cannot believe that in a certain industry in a market no firm should have excessive market share and at the same time believe that one government should have the whole market share in what is called the 'administration market'. One cannot believe that in an industry in a market the competitors should not collude, should not try to manipulate the supply of the product or service or to fix the price of the products or services and at the same time believe that governments should not compete but should all be in effect shop-windows of the same monopolist in Brussels.

Side effect 2

When the administrative power is in Brussels, the democratic control of the people over the actions of the administration is greatly reduced. When the administrative power of the people lies with their national government, it is much easier for them to check the actions of their government. But when the administrative power is with a big government in Brussels, the task of democratic controls is greatly complicated. It is relatively easy for the average voter in Italy to know what a government in Rome is doing and to try to exercise his or her democratic right of checks and controls. But it is many times more difficult for the same person in Italy to know what the Commission in Brussels is doing. What the Commission in Brussels is doing comes finally as regulation through the Italian 'local government', which in effect is a distribution channel for the decisions of the Commission. Democracy as a way of life is founded on the continuous ability of the people to check their government and this ability should be as wide as possible. However, having transferred most of their administrative power to one powerful government, the people have had this ability greatly reduced. So, instead of widening the ability of the people for controls, there is a narrowing of controls. Instead of widening democracy, there is a great narrowing of democracy.

Side effect 3

When the real policy power is transferred to Brussels to make a very powerful government, then we have one more transfer: the transfer of the various 'lobbies' or 'special interests' to Brussels. It is very well known that in Brussels at this moment there exists a huge army of lawyers, lobbyists and special interest groups trying to win favourable attention or regulations or funds from the Commission. When the real power is with the national governments, the life of the special interest groups and lobbies is more difficult than when the real power is in Brussels. Having sensed where the real power rests, the lobbies and other special interest groups moved in Brussels where they can, with one shot, kill fifteen different birds! And they can kill all those birds with complete safety because the people who would normally try to follow or check their activities are far away!

So, with a big and powerful government instead of fifteen less powerful ones the task of all the special interest groups and lobbies become immensely easier. Instead of progressively reducing the influence of all the special interest groups, we are seeing a tremendous reinforcement of their activities and power. From the economics point of view, this is not good because the aims of the lobbies and special interest groups are usually not pro-competitive. From the political point of view, the great expansion and facilitation of the role of lobbies and special interest groups is against the desire of the people for transparency and controls. It is most of all against the power of the people, which has been exercised through their vote. It is against a widening of democracy.

At this point one might think that maybe the Commission is not so powerful and any individual government is much more so. To answer this though one has to answer the following questions:

- Who wields more trade policy power, the Commission or the German government?
- Who wields more power to define the value added tax on any product or service, the Commission or the French government?
- Who wields more power in competition regulation, the Commission or the British government?
- Who wields more power in trade union and labour regulation, the Commission or the Italian government?
- Who wields more power in capital tax regulation, the Commission or the Spanish government?
- Who wields more power in agricultural policies and funds, the Commission or the Belgian government?
- Who wields more power in energy policies, the Commission or the Dutch government?
- Who wields more power in fisheries policies and quotas, the Commission or the Irish government?
- Who wields more power in environmental policies, the Commission or the

Danish government?
- Who wields more power in giving funds to East European countries, the Commission or the Austrian government?
- Who wields more power in the foreign relations field, the Commission or the Swedish government?
- Who wields more power in immigration policy, the Commission or the Greek government?
- Who wields more power in cultural policies, the Commission or the Portuguese government?
- Who wields more power in banking policies, the Commission or the Luxembourg government?

The answers are obvious. The actual power of the Commission is many times the power of any individual government because the Commission is the government! It is the de facto government. The national governments are de facto branches of the Commission and their employees are the indirect employees of the Commission, apart from the 20,000 direct employees. The matter of who pays whom is irrelevant because, after all, the Commission and the national governments are all paid by the national taxpayers. The crucial matter is who gives instructions to whom, who controls whom, who is deciding for whom?

But if all the above are negative points for transferring the real administrative power from a country to the Commission, aren't there any positive points?

One positive point could be that sometimes the officials of a national government are reluctant to take policy measures that may be desirable to them, but could prove unpopular. So they allow the policy measures to be presented to their public as 'measures which come compulsorily from the Commission or from our partners and which we cannot escape anyway'. But a government official is supposed to do what he or she considers to be correct not what others (from above) tell him to do. Otherwise he should not stand for election in the first place and he should not carry the name of prime minister or minister or president. Government officials who have not the courage and sincerity to speak their minds, to say to the electorate what they consider to be just and correct for their people, and try to implement their views (for which very views they came to power) should not stand for election and should leave politics. Democracy is about knowing what a politician stands for, voting for him and having him implement his policies. Democracy is not about voting for someone who keeps his real views secret, and then implements the instructions or views of others even if these instructions and views are not wrong. On such a basis, no human society can have maximum long-run material progress and happiness. On such a basis, society will only drift hopelessly and purposelessly in the long run like a ship without a captain.

One other positive point could be that in some countries where the government officials are not very competent or capable, it may be that the Commissioners in Brussels, coming mainly from other countries with more competent politicians, produce better or more appropriate or more just policy measures. There are some countries whose electorates believe (rightly or wrongly) that their politicians are for the moment either corrupt or incompetent or cowards. Therefore, many people in that country feel that if they were governed by 'foreign partners' they will be governed in a better way. This feeling amongst the populace is widespread in many countries. We will not examine here whether this feeling is accurate or inaccurate. We will just examine country Y under each of the assumptions.

Assumption 1
Suppose that the politicians of country Y are neither incompetent nor corrupt. Then to replace them with foreigners (in a permanent way) is an injustice to both the politicians and to the public of country Y who will be governed by others who are less qualified.

Assumption 2
Suppose that the politicians of country Y are truly incompetent or not well educated or even corrupt and that the people really need a good team of foreign administrators. Then the best, easiest, cheapest and most straightforward solution would be to accept their collective deficiency and hire foreign administrators from the best possible source on a temporary basis exactly as a basketball team does when it lures foreign talent. The people would then have competent and honest politicians to run the administration of the country for a number of years. And these administrators would not have to come from the continent of Europe, but could come from any country (say, Australia, New Zealand, Canada, Japan). They would have to be of the highest standard and well qualified. They would be looking after country Y exclusively and not, like the Commission, after fifteen countries. Most important of all, they would be temporary.

Once the people of country Y realised that they had produced educated, honest and competent politicians, they would end the contract of the foreign administrators (not like the Commission, whose contract with country Y is indefinite). So even in the case where, out of the whole population of country Y, there is not a team of competent politicians (which I honestly believe is not the case for any country) there is no excuse for transferring almost all of the administrative powers of a country permanently to the Commission (or to any other supranational body for that matter).

What then is the way forward regarding the executive branch? Is there a way that would combine full democracy with effective and responsible government that secures the aim of a country for maximum possible material progress, collective freedom and happiness?

Let us move to the alternative, our imaginary country X. In the alternative (country X) the following basic principles and practices are established.

Principle no. 1

The government is answerable only to the people of the country and to nobody else. There is no supranational body which can in theory or in practice impose its will or dictate policies to the government elected by the people of the country. In other words, the collective free will of the people of country X cannot be subjected to the dictates of any other government or international body. There is no one on earth who is above the government elected freely by the people of country X.

The desire of the people to have no other authority on earth in a position to impose policies or rules on them comes from the fact that they realise that in order to achieve through time maximum progress as well as happiness they need first of all to be collectively free. And in order to be collectively free their government must be elected only by them and be answerable only to them. In general, they believe that they can run their own country.

Principle no. 2

The people of country X do not wish to impose their way of government on other countries. Cooperation, advice and financial aid are desirable, but under no circumstances would they give instructions to their government to impose its views or policies on other human communities.

Freedom needs as its counterpart restraint and responsibility. Being collectively free could tempt a government to try to impose its views on other countries indirectly (through various diplomatic pressures or financial pressures) or directly through aggressive wars. Hence, the people of the alternative have permanently instructed their government never to attempt any form of pressure on other human communities.

Principle no. 3

In country X there is complete separation of the powers of the people. The executive power is completely separate from the legislative power and the justice system. All these powers are paid for with taxpayers' money, but none of the powers can determine how much money is allocated to the other two powers or how the other two powers are to function.

No government official (elected or unelected) can be a member of the legislature or of the judicial system and vice versa.

All three powers of government, legislature and justice system stem from the people in a democratic nation. When the same public official belongs to more than one of the three powers, then very often there is conflict of interest, no clear-cut duties, no clear-cut responsibilities and a lot of other ills. When the same person is, for example, a member of the government and at the same time member of parliament, it is then very easy for him to make a law that will permit him to distribute more money to his special constituency in the next year's budget.

The people in the alternative have therefore established the very fundamental principle that the same person cannot at the same time be a government official and a member of parliament. The same, of course, applies to a member of the justice system. Moreover, and in order for the government not to be able to dictate how much money will be allocated to the legislative body or to the justice system, they follow a very simple procedure whereby each body or power of the people has its own completely separate budget accountable directly to the people who approve or reject it yearly.

Complete separation of the powers of the people as envisioned for the first time in the American Revolution is one of the most important pillars upon which the alternative is built.

Principle no. 4
When the people vote for a government they vote always for whole teams not for only the prime minister or president. Special procedures and spare names are available for cases like sudden incapacitation of a newly elected minister. The procedure was described in some detail on pages 130-131.

The people of the alternative believe that they have the right to know before the elections not only the name of the prime minister (or president), but also the name of every official to be installed in any ministry or other public elected office. Therefore, it is obligatory for any party asking for their vote to submit to the electorate the detailed list of all persons to be installed as ministers, deputy ministers or any other public official who changes with the change of government. In other words, when they vote for government they do not vote for a single candidate from each political party; they vote for a single team of people from each political party.

Each person on the teams is destined for a specific position (say, foreign minister or economics minister or deputy education minister) and there can be no changes in the names of the ministry that each member of the prospective team will occupy after the election. In this way, after the elections the leader of the government cannot appoint into any specific position any person other than the one mentioned in the prospective team.

In this way:

- Nasty surprises to the electorate are avoided.
- There is no leeway for the head of government or the party regarding who will be appointed to what (give and take may apply within private companies but not within public organisations with public money).
- The electorate at large, including the media, can effectively scrutinise the curriculum vitae and the qualifications of any elected government official before the elections. They can scrutinise not only his or her general qualifications, but his specific qualifications for the specific job. In this way phenomena where medical doctors become defence ministers and retired police officers become health ministers are avoided!
- A real ethic of teamwork is permanently imposed on the government. The

government is no longer a one-man show or a one-woman show, but a team of qualified men and women to fill difficult and specialised public positions.

- Parties and political leaders are more inclined to 'choose the best for every post' and not to extend personal favours, or exercise personal power. Political activists within each party are also encouraged to promote the best candidates within the party and not the most powerful or influential within the party. Political activism and political power within a party are good and welcome, but are not enough for gaining a public post. They need the consent of the average voter regarding the specific suggested public post.

In each prospective government team there are special procedures and reserve personnel for cases such as accidents to ministers or the firing of a minister if he is deemed (after working in his post) to be incompetent.

Principle no. 5

All voting for a government is done with the Electronic Voting System (EVS) described in some detail on page 127.

The main merits of the Electronic Voting System (EVS) are as follows:

- Voting electronically for government costs virtually nothing to the taxpayers. There is no need for people to travel to other cities, to go to the polling stations, to print envelopes and voting lists, to pay people to operate each polling station, to pay police to guard each polling station, to transport the votes in sacks to a central register, to present special ID cards, to be subject to weather extremes, or to be subject to the inability of many people to move to the polling station (disabled people, sick people, old people, pregnant women, very poor people who do not have the money to go to the polling station or who prefer to work overtime instead of voting, etc.). The polling station is the TV-PC of every home, the TV-PC of the neighbour, the PC of the nearest shop or the nearest ATM at the corner of the road. All one needs is an electronic citizenship card and an electronic signature (to mark electronically the books of the virtual polling station).
- The results of the voting are announced very quickly. (Supervision of the electronic ID cards and electronic signatures is done at the central computer of the area by representatives of all political parties. After confirmation of the electronic signature a citizen's actual vote is transmitted to the 'electronic box' of the computer by encryption).
- The familiarisation of each citizen with the programme of each political party and with the curriculum vitae and special aspirations of each particular candidate is done through all the usual means (newspapers, TV, radio, leaflets, conferences, meetings, magazines) plus e-mail, Internet and, most important of all, the TV-PC. Each citizen is in a position now by pressing a few buttons of the TV remote control to read the full programme of any

political party or the ideas of any particular candidate. They can also watch on video at their TV-PC through the Internet a particular candidate deliver speeches at conferences. In this way the judgement of the voter is based on a more detailed and rational examination of each candidate and each political party.

- The need for each political party or candidate to spend huge amounts of money for marketing or advertising its program or ideas is greatly reduced. In practical terms Internet projections of one's ideas costs nothing. But Internet means PC and the PC is now connected in a very simplified form to the TV. Dissemination of ideas, philosophies and programmes is becoming almost costless. Any citizen who has good ideas and who wishes to ask for the vote of the people of the alternative does not need powerful economic backing (with its associated strings or influences). All he or she needs is good ideas!

- The whole pre-election process is becoming interactive. The voter is no longer passive to what his or her candidate or political party projects in its Internet address. He or she can ask through the PC any question, clarification or make any suggestion. He or she can actively shape the programme of his or her party or candidate.

- The same voting procedure can be applied internally to any political party during its annual conference. Its voters can voice their views electronically and choose their activists and leader again electronically from their homes. In this way the grassroots members of the party are the ones who define its policies and not some secret team of activists or professionals. The lower rank of the party is defining the policies of the top and not the other way round. Democracy is truly spread to the average citizen. As a side effect, membership in each party is greatly increased because the party member now feels that, for the first time, he or she has power and can exercise that power very simply and without costs!

Principle no. 6
During the government's term in office any of the following government policies or measures must be subjected to the approval or disapproval of the people through the EVS (Electronic Voting System).

- The yearly government budget.
- Any increase or decrease (during any particular year) of government spending of taxation exceeding 0.5% of GDP (Gross Domestic Product).
- Participation or withdrawal from any military alliance or other international organisation.
- Any trade treaty.
- Yearly proposed number of legal economic immigrants to be accepted into

the country (humanitarian immigrants are not included in this voting).
- Yearly proposed amount of money going from the taxpayers through their government to any international organisation such as the United Nations, the World Bank or the International Monetary Fund.

By voting often through the EVS on important governmental and practical matters the people of country X make sure that their government once in power does not abuse it. It cannot deviate too much from what it promised to deliver and it cannot consider that it received a blank cheque from the people to spend their money as it pleases for four or five years. Spending has to be approved by the people (not the parliament or congress) every year. This electronic voting also makes sure that the government does not proceed to important international treaties or military alliances without having popular consent. The same applies for the important matter of yearly quotas of economic immigrants which usually is a matter too difficult for any government to handle on its own without specific approval by the people.

Voting every four to five years is not a blank cheque to power for any team of people. On important and specific matters the cheque is filled in with words by the people and signed by the people. In the alternative, the era of blank cheques to power is over.

Principle no. 7
Through bilateral agreements the government of country X receives daily into a central register by fax, e-mail or letter all new government measures adopted by any other government. The central register is official and the correspondence is automatically distributed to the head offices of all political parties of the country. Access to this central register is available to all citizens.

The people of country X want to run their government by themselves, but at the same time want to be aware of any good governance ideas or practices taking place anywhere else. By receiving any new policy or measure as applied by other governments, they make sure that they are not mentally isolated, but remain at the forefront of human thinking and techniques regarding management of public affairs. It is then up to the current government to evaluate these new policies and find any that might be interesting or applicable to the country. In this way the people, the political parties and the government of country X remain in full control and responsible for their own destiny, but at the same time make sure that they have at their disposal and judgement any good idea springing up anywhere on earth. Some people say that you cannot be independent or sovereign and still have the most advanced methods of government at your disposal. Well, in the alternative they have the best of both worlds!

Principle no. 8
Members of all political parties (including the government party or parties) are free to contact any foreign government. However, elected government officials of country X have to record all of their communications (written or verbal or

electronic) with any government officials of other countries. The records are collected and are under the supervision of the legislative body as well as the judiciary. They are kept confidential and released to the public only after ten years. The measure concerns only the contacts of elected politicians and not the contacts of civil servants like foreign affairs personnel.

Government officials, paid by the people should govern according to their own free will and judgement subject to the continuous control of their electorate. In today's world where communications between government officials from different countries is extremely easy and cheap in all forms it is natural that there should be contacts between members of the government of the alternative and other governments on a very regular basis. Those contacts are welcomed by the people in the spirit of cooperation and peaceful coexistence. Contacts with other governments are encouraged (not discouraged) by the people in the alternative. However, these contacts can result in excessive influence by other governments and act against the free will of the people of the alternative.

In order to avoid any such possibility of excessive or unnecessary influence by others and since government officials are paid by the people to serve the public good (and not necessarily the public good of other countries), they have established the procedure of recording all contacts of elected government officials with citizens of other countries.

This makes the life of government officials in the alternative a little bit more difficult and formal, but then whoever said that serving in public office is not difficult? Such kinds of responsibilities, formalities and difficulties exist today even for employees and managers of private companies when they contact people from certain other companies. It is high time that such a procedure applied to the biggest and most important organisation of all countries: to their governments. It is high time that a proper and strict code of ethics covered the contacts of those who serve the public good (and are paid by the public!).

The assessment of the multifarious aspects of the whole argument is given in Figure 54.

Figure 54

Option 1 Member of the EU	Option 2 The alternative
Grade: 0/100,000	Grade: 5,000/100,000

4. Argument No. 4 (Political)

Within the EU my country is, by definition, not sovereign. This is bad for me.

We have seen in the previous three arguments that for a country within the EU the three separate powers (legislative power, judicial power and executive power) have been in effect transferred to EU institutions. But the sum of those three powers constitutes the collective freedom of the people, the collective ability to set their laws, the collective ability to define their present and future way of life, the collective ability to preserve, enrich or modify their culture, the collective ability to have an identity or not to have an identity. By transferring all three powers to EU institutions where their representatives will be always in a very small minority (this is a matter of simple arithmetic), this means that the people have lost their sovereignty. It means that as a human community they have lost their collective freedom to run their own country. Some people may say that sovereignty is a vague notion without practical implications. In the previous three chapters we examined many political and practical implications of the loss of sovereignty.

The most important of all practical implications, however, concerns the happiness of the people, i.e. it concerns the side of a human being known as mind and psyche. A group of people, when they realise that they cannot define their future and that they cannot control their own affairs, is bound in the long term to become unhappy. Unhappiness is the worst thing that can happen to human beings because what else other than the pursuit of happiness is their main concern in life? Sovereignty does not mean wars or desire for wars. It means the desire of a peaceful group of people to run its affairs as it pleases. There can be no happiness in a country unless its people feel that they can exercise full and democratic control over their own affairs. Therefore sovereignty is not at all an absurd or vague idea. It is a crucial fact of life for any human community. It gives to the human community a sense of purpose, of camaraderie, of common destiny and of common control over that destiny. It gives a real meaning to the very word 'community' and to the very words 'collective freedom'. Absence of sovereignty strikes back and destroys the foundation of a happy life for the individual. Unless the individual feels that he or she can exercise full democratic control over the public matters of his or her country he or she will not be really happy.

Some people will suggest that sovereignty for a country is maybe not relevant to the future of human communities. However, the opposite is true. The historical evidence points to the simple fact that sovereignty is a prerequisite and an indispensable characteristic for any successful group of people. History shows more and more collective freedom accruing to distinct groups of people starting with households, extending to villages, countries and nations. This is a direct result of the simple fact of life that people like to exercise maximum control over their own affairs and they are happy and successful when they can exercise that control. If anything, history tends to give more and more collective freedom to each distinct human group. If sovereignty means absolute freedom of a human group to define peacefully its own internal affairs, then in the near and distant future we are bound to see a greater number of human groups exercising sovereignty, not a smaller number. We are also bound to see all those countries who lost their sovereignty regain it.

In conclusion, sovereignty for a distinct group of people is of the same importance as the freedom of a family to live its own peaceful life within a society. A family needs individual freedom to function as a fundamental economic, political and social unit. A nation needs sovereignty to function as a happy and successful group of people. It should be stressed, however, that, as for a family individual freedom is a necessary but not sufficient condition for success and happiness, the same is true for a nation. Sovereignty is a necessary condition (as we say in mathematics), but not a sufficient condition for happiness and progress. But the mathematical meaning of the words 'necessary condition' here is crystal clear: *if you are sovereign it is by no means certain that you will be happy. But if you are not sovereign it is absolutely certain that you will not be happy.*

And where does our alternative stand regarding sovereignty? Is country X a sovereign country? Yes, the people of the alternative want to live in peace, harmony and cooperation with all other people on earth, but as a human community they want to run their own affairs. They believe that they can run their own affairs and they are actually running their own affairs. *They are a sovereign country.*

Since we examined in detail the three constituents of sovereignty in the previous three arguments we will not give any grades to this argument.

5. Argument No. 5 (Political)

> Within the EU my country, by definition, is not independent. This is bad for me.

A country is independent when it can conduct its own international relations and make alliances and treaties without restrictions by others. An independent country can make its own trade agreements with any other country, participate in or leave a military alliance according to the will of its people, exercise its own foreign policies according to its interests, and have its own immigration policy without consulting others. A country is independent only when it can change any of the above policies or treaties by resorting purely to the will of its people and not to the will of other people. It is obvious that any country within the EU is by definition not independent. It is an absolutely dependent entity. It is dependent on the will and decisions of the EU institutions within which the representatives of the country are by arithmetic definition always a small minority. All trade agreements are concluded today exclusively by the EU, not by any individual country. All treaties are concluded today exclusively by the EU. No individual country can have its own foreign policy because foreign policy must be common. No individual country can participate in a military alliance with a third country. No individual country can have 'warm' political relations with certain countries unless the Commission gives explicit or tacit approval.

But does independence have any value to the average citizen of a country? Independence concerns in general the external relations of a distinct group of people with other groups of people (while sovereignty refers mainly to the ability of the group to govern itself exclusively according to the collective will of its people).

As such, independence is similar to the way a family relates to other families within a society. A family can choose to have warmer relations with some specific families than with others and its ability to exercise such options is one of the ways a family feels a distinct social unit. If we remove this ability (to, in effect, be independent) from a family, we automatically remove one of the main characteristics that make the family a true cohesive social unit. But if a family loses its main characteristic which makes it an individual unit, it then loses a portion of its effectiveness, of its reason for existence and of its happiness.

It is the same with a country. When a country loses its independence it loses its ability to relate to others as it pleases. It loses its ability to choose its friends, alliances, partners and treaties, or to change all of these. It loses the collective ability of its people to relate to others in the way they wish and to the degree they wish. Losing this ability means losing a degree of freedom and at the same time a degree of distinctiveness and the reason for existence as a cohesive human community. Losing independence means losing the ability for continuous self-determination. Losing a degree of freedom, distinctiveness, the reason for existence, cohesiveness and self-determination means in general less happiness for the human group. Therefore, independence is a very valuable thing to lose with considerable long-term effects on the happiness of the people.

And what is the position of the people of our alternative regarding independence? For them independence does not mean to live as a community alone. Independence does not mean to live alone in a cave or like a lone wolf in the forest. Independence means that they exercise full and democratic control about how they choose to relate as an official entity with other official entities. Independence has nothing to do with how the private citizens of country X relate to other private citizens of any other country. It refers only to their official relations as an entity. They have reserved for themselves whether and how they will participate in international treaties, military alliances and trade treaties, and they retain their full right to change alliances or treaties as they see fit. They are very active in shaping various international treaties, but on equal footing with any other country. They have a voice in all international forums but it is their voice. They are not aggressive, but they have their positions and relations. They are peaceful, but distinct. They are simply independent.

A final question before proceeding to the next argument: can a country even in theory be a member of the EU and still be independent? Can the EU change to a union of independent nation-states as many people honestly wish? The answer here is simple.

You cannot be united and independent at the same time. Union and independence are mutually exclusive notions. A man or a woman can be independent human beings as long as they are not married (in a union under God). The moment they are married they have lost their independence. But while there is a lot of meaning for an individual to get married and start a family, there is not the same meaning for a nation to sacrifice its independence because *the nation is the family*.

6. Argument No. 6 (Political)

> By being all countries united within the EU we at least avoid wars. This is certainly very good for everybody.

The idea that independence and sovereignty bring war is philosophically equivalent to the idea that freedom of the individual creates violence or, to be more precise, that if we deprive individuals of their freedom we will have a more peaceful, orderly and tranquil society and that ideally we should put everybody in a large jail to eliminate crime from a city. We will examine the above very strong foundations of this argument in the philosophical arguments later on. However, here we will examine it only from its political angle.

It goes without saying that no sane human being wants to create or participate in a war and that everyone wants to live in peace. But is it independence and sovereignty amongst civilised and industrialised countries that create wars or does the absence of independence and sovereignty create wars? Did not Chechnya have the same currency as the rest of Russia when they were fighting? Did not the warring parties in Bosnia-Herzegovina have the same currency? By suppressing ideals like independence or sovereignty we do not avoid wars. We rather create wars. By artificially suppressing the desire for distinct identity we do not avoid violence. We create violence, especially in the long run.

In practical and historical terms, for the past fifty years peace has prevailed over the continent of Europe not because of the EU, but because of military alliances (NATO and the Warsaw Pact) which were in balance and acted as mutual checks. It has been the military alliances that have contributed to peace for the past fifty years. If one looks at today's situation, it is evident that after the change of regimes in Eastern Europe, even the need for military alliances is under question. However, one thing is certain: if a nation feels threatened, it has to look for military alliances. It does not need to look to eliminate its independence or sovereignty. A few other things regarding war are also becoming evident in today's world:

1. The more educated and the more prosperous the citizens of a country are the more unlikely they will create wars. Hence, prosperity and education are eliminating war and not the absence of independence or sovereignty.
2. The more clearly defined the boundaries (borders) of each nation are the less possibility for disputes and wars. Therefore, it is not the elimination of distinguishable countries from the map of Europe that eliminates wars, but the existence of clearly defined areas that will permit each country to live in peace.
3. It is very hard for anyone to think of conditions under which any one of the member states of the EU would attack its neighbours.
4. Increasingly today the world suffers from internal wars and not external ones. One can think of many internal hotspots like Nagorno–Karabagh, Azerbaijan, Afghanistan, Kurdistan, Algeria, Somalia, Sudan, Rwanda, the Congo, western part of China, the Sahara, Guatemala and Peru, but of very few external hotspots. In all those places the existence of a common currency and common government does not automatically create peace as long as there are differences.
5. Internal conflicts are always worse than external ones (as Bosnia-Herzegovina has shown recently). The EU in effect internalises any external conflict that could arise. It is very unlikely that a violent conflict could arise in the future between any two of the member countries but even in that very hypothetical case internalising the conflict is not an improvement.

Now let us go to our alternative. If the people of our imaginary country X are independent and sovereign, how can they avoid war? What arrangements are they making?

The people in the alternative want first of all to live in peace with all other nations on earth. To this end they are following some very simple principles:

1. They have clearly defined borders.
2. They do not claim any piece of land from their neighbours.
3. When they do not feel threatened, they do not participate in any military alliance.
4. If they feel threatened, they participate in a military alliance of their own choice. This alliance could be NATO, but could as well be any

other alliance if they thought that NATO was not suitable for their particular needs at that particular period of time.

It is the needs of the people for security that dictate participation in a military alliance and not the military alliance that dictates the needs of the people for security.

5. Most important of all, the people of country X know that prosperity and a high level of education are the best path to peace. Therefore, they try continuously to achieve for themselves the maximum rate of growth of income and the maximum possible education levels.

6. By applying in their country the Athenian democracy where every citizen has a democratic voice, they have made sure that their government can never attempt aggression against other countries without their explicit instruction to do so.

Widening democracy to give real decision power to the average citizen is the surest way for permanent peace. It is the ordinary citizen who would go to fight in a war and it is highly unlikely that he or she would decide to make war if they were given the real power to decide.

The evaluation of the argument is as indicated in Figure 55.

Figure 55

Option 1 Member of the EU	Option 2 The alternative
Grade: 50/100,000	Grade: 250/100,000

7. **Argument No. 7 (Political)**

   Within the EU my country will have a stronger foreign policy voice. This is certainly good.

First of all, within the EU no country has its own foreign policy. There is a common foreign policy. But common means something that belongs to everybody and therefore no country within the EU has its own foreign policy. In fact, a country within the EU does not have any foreign policy. It is the EU only that has a foreign policy. No individual country can have a foreign policy contradicting that of the EU on any matter. In this case, even the necessity of each country having embassies and consulates abroad is questionable. If a country does not have its own specific foreign policy (suited to the needs and democratic instructions of its people) what is the point of having embassies and consulates and even a ministry for foreign policy?

Furthermore, we should consider the following question: who has the stronger voice in foreign policy, the state of Arizona or Norway? Which of the two states can better express the voice of its people in international organisations and when dealing with other states? The answer is certainly Norway and Norway is not in the EU!

There is, however, another matter here. The voice of the EU in foreign policy is not the voice of any one country. But it is definitely a voice much stronger than the voice any country would have alone. But here we go to a completely different concept. It is a fact that the voice of the EU in foreign policy is extremely strong. But is the reason for any people participating in the EU their desire to create a very strong organisation (an empire) that will not speak with their particular voice on any matter but that will be so strong that it will be in a position to impose its huge voice on other nations? Is the desire for creating an autocracy that will not speak our voice but will be able to impose foreign policy solutions on third countries the reason that the people of a country participate in the EU? Do the citizens of Germany or Austria or Denmark have any real desire or real need to lose their own voice in foreign policy and be given a voice belonging to many different mentalities but which voice will nevertheless be so strong that it will equal or surpass that of the USA? Is the thirst for power (even if it is not mine or if it does not serve my needs) the motive behind any state participating in the EU? Maybe it is in the mind of a very small minority of people (who in the distant past have created many wars) but certainly it is not in the mind of the average person. The world does not need more empires. The world needs more countries expressing their own peaceful positions and aspirations. The world does not need the suppression of foreign policy voices, but peaceful expression by 'real' voices, i.e. voices of real people not voices of artificial empires.

And what about the alternative? The people in our imaginary country X simply exercise their peaceful and trade-friendly foreign policy through their legitimate and democratic government. Having their own foreign policy does not necessarily mean that their policy or positions are different from those of other countries (in the continent of Europe or elsewhere). It simply means that their foreign policy is made on every matter to suit their particular needs or aspirations. If their foreign policy on every particular matter coincides with that of any other country the better for everybody. However, identity of foreign policy with that of other countries is not a prerequisite for them in order to feel correct or justified or secure. For security, if they need to resort to anything they resort to their military alliance. For correctness and justification, since their foreign policy is made through very wide and very democratic procedures (Athenian democracy) they do not need to resort to others. Most of the time their foreign policies are similar to those of other nations over the continent of Europe. But if they need to be different then they are different.

Identity of foreign policies between fifteen different peoples would be desirable only if they had a common enemy. But this enemy does not exist. Therefore, identity of foreign policies is not compulsory for the same reasons that fifteen families living in a village do not need to have exactly the same relations with another family living in another village.

Being yourself and sometimes making some mistakes is better than pretending to be yourself and pretending not to make mistakes all the time. This aphorism summing up the argument leads to the grading in Figure 56.

Figure 56

Option 1 Member of the EU	Option 2 The alternative
Grade: 0/100,000	Grade: 500/100,000

8. Argument No. 8 (Political)

> The absence of border controls between EU member states does not help my country in reinforcing law and order, especially in the long run.

Within the EU there are no border controls between member countries. The reasoning for this is that elimination of border controls facilitates the speedy exchange of people and goods. But this is only one side of the coin. And even this side is not so very important because travellers today take a typical two minutes to get through border procedures. The same applies to traders passing through customs. They follow a very simple procedure at customs of no more than ten minutes' duration to make sure that their goods are legal and that there is nothing suspicious.

Now let us see the other side of the coin. The elimination of border controls greatly facilitates all those who either want to enter a country illegally or carry with them something illegal (say illegal drugs or guns). It is obvious that any person dealing with illegal things will feel much better when travelling across fifteen countries without any check either for identity or for the goods traded. It is equally obvious that the law enforcement agencies of any particular country become almost powerless to perform one of their main duties: to check and control any illegal good, service or person entering their country. This is a very high price to pay for the convenience of gaining a few minutes every time one needs to cross borders.

There is, however, one more consequence associated with the elimination of border controls. In the long run, the authority exercised collectively by the people of a country over their geographical area is eliminated. If the people of a country do not exercise control over their borders, they have in effect eliminated their collective authority to check the inflow and outflow of people and goods over their area. They in effect dismantle their country. Dismantling the people's ability to collectively and democratically exercise control over their geographical area through their legitimate authorities is not a service to the people. It is a disservice.

Now let us go to our alternative. The people there exercise quick and effective controls over their borders. Travellers do not delay at the border for more than a few minutes and transporters of goods and services do not delay for much longer. Effective border control does not mean time-consuming controls, especially with today's technology (computer databases, cooperation between national authorities, etc.). The people in country X have instructed their government through their vote to keep law and order within the country and to minimise illegal goods or persons coming from other countries. This is one of the main reasons they are paying taxes to their government – to minimise illegal activities. They are not paying taxes for the policemen and customs personnel just so that they can receive their salaries every month. They want results and efficiency from them. Exercising efficient control over the country's borders is one of the basic requirements for keeping law and order at a satisfactory level, for peace of mind and to enable people to go about their lives happily and without fear that at every step a drug baron or robber may be waiting. Quality of life is dependent on many things and one of those things is the ability of the average citizen to go around in his country without excessive fear or without facing problems. This is one of the prerequisites for a happy life. And the people in country X want to have a free and happy life, both for themselves and for future generations. Figure 57 grades this argument.

Figure 57

Option 1 Member of the EU	Option 2 The alternative
Grade: 50/100,000	Grade: 250/100,000

9. Argument No. 9 (Political)

> Within the EU my country is not represented as an entity in any trade deals, in the World Trade Organisation, in direct aid to other countries and increasingly in foreign relations. In the long run, this deprives me of my nationhood.

It is a fact that in all trade deals in the World Trade Organisation, there is no country named Germany or France or the United Kingdom or Italy. There are countries like Japan, South Korea, Egypt, Brazil, etc., but there is no Germany, France, United Kingdom or Italy. There is a 'country' named the EU. The same applies to direct foreign aid. It is no longer Sweden or Denmark or Belgium or Holland or Finland that appear to give foreign aid (government to government) to third countries (like Syria, Ethiopia, Pakistan, Bulgaria, Albania, etc.) every year. It is a 'country' named the EU which gives foreign aid and this aid is given through the 'government' of the EU named the Commission. In foreign relations in various hotspots (Bosnia, Palestine, etc.) there is a representative of a 'country' named the EU. There are no representatives of any particular member state.

In the long run, this increasing tendency will deprive the typical citizen of a typical member state of his or her present nationhood. The people in other countries will no longer regard them as countries and downgrade their names to just 'states'. The 'country' for them will be the EU or Europe. Within the EU the next generation will only occasionally say that they are Spaniards or Portuguese or Italians. They will usually say that they are Europeans. In effect, within the EU nationhood is gradually and systematically being dismantled in favour of a new wider Europeanism. There are huge philosophical implications in this, but here we note only that, politically speaking, people in general like to have a particular country and nation. Depriving them of their nation is depriving them of something which belongs to them collectively, which they love (to a smaller or a greater degree) and for which they want just to be proud of. People have asked for an increased rate of material growth and happiness. They have not asked for the erasing of their present nationhoods. Figure 58 grades the argument.

Figure 58

Option 1 Member of the EU	Option 2 The alternative
Grade: 0/100,000	Grade: 2,500/100,000

10. Argument No. 10 (Political)

> Within the EU my national flag as well as other national symbols are being gradually and steadily replaced with those of the EU. This is something I have not asked for.

It is a fact that gradually and steadily the national flag of any member state is being replaced with a nice blue flag with yellow stars in a circle. The official plan is that initially the two flags shall coexist and later on the EU flag will be the national flag in the 'country' named the EU or the Union or Europe. But what is in a flag? Does it represent the desire for aggression against others? Or is it the desire for particular identity? In today's civilised world it is the latter. In a flag we see our sovereign powers; we see our legislature; we see our judicial system; we see our ability to govern ourselves. In a flag we see our history, our culture, our particular customs and habits, our lakes and mountains and rivers. We see, in effect, our particular identity. To have a piece of cloth symbolising all these ideas and many more and to feel proud of it does not at all imply aggression against others. It means the connection of our past with our future in a rapidly changing world. It means stamina and a point of reference. For this piece of cloth in every country rivers of blood have flowed. Therefore to abolish it in favour of a more beautiful or a stronger or a bigger one is at least doing an injustice to the citizens of a country. However, the changing of the flag as well as of all other national symbols (national anthem, unit of money, passport, etc.) is only a natural consequence of the loss of sovereignty for any nation within the EU. It is very doubtful whether the people of any member state have ever asked for the elimination of their national symbols. But this is only one of the thousands of natural consequences of being in the EU.

No grading will be given for this argument since the matter of substance, which is the loss of sovereignty, has been dealt with elsewhere.

11. Argument No. 11 (Political)

The transfer of the powers of the people to a new country named the EU or the Union or Europe has been done in an unconstitutional and undemocratic manner. It will therefore be challenged by the people of each country in the future until the voice of the people decides on this matter.

In the beginning people thought of the EU as a free trade area in the form of the Common Market. Then came the Common Agricultural Policy (CAP) and the Common Fisheries Policy (CFP). Then came the Customs Union. After that came the European Economic Community (EEC) followed by the European Community (EC). Then in the mid-80s came the Single European Act (SEA) and with it the European Union (EU). In 1992 came the Maastricht Treaty and in 1997 the Amsterdam Treaty. All those steps were slow and gradual, all leading to the final result: the transfer of the powers of the people of each country to a new entity called the EU or the Union or Europe. The fifteen previously independent and sovereign countries became member states and the sovereign and independent power now is the EU.

All the above steps were usually taken unilaterally by the legislative bodies of each country and only in a very few circumstances in a few countries by referenda. We will examine here the constitutional validity of those actions.

One thing must be clarified here before anything else. The sovereignty of a group of people is not a matter like increasing or decreasing taxes or spending less for infrastructure or making a treaty with another nation. The people of each democratic country have three inalienable powers (legislative, judicial and executive), which powers they transfer to their representative politicians with their vote. Their representatives use those powers for a specific period of time and at the end of the period they return all the powers to the people who then vote for new representatives. The representatives of the people are not authorised (they do not have the right) to transfer all or part of the three powers of the people to others whatever those others might be (Commission, Europarliament, European Court of Justice). The three powers belong to the people of each country and not to their representatives, who are only temporary custodians of the powers of the people for a period.

To use an imaginary situation which sheds light on the above, let us for a moment suppose that in 1940, just after the German troops had occupied France, the previously democratically elected parliament of France had convened peacefully and, after extensive debate, had decided with a vast majority to pronounce that it would be to the benefit of the French people for France to become a permanent part of a pan-European empire since the people would in the long run be better off and would belong to a bigger and stronger country named Europe. All three inalienable powers of the people would now reside permanently outside France and, it was alleged, peace and prosperity would now prevail indefinitely for the French people. Now suppose that this was really the decision and conclusion of the representatives of the French people (the legislators) who had been democratically elected well before the war started. We do not examine here why or how they had come to this imaginary conclusion or decision. We just assume that the members of the French legislature voted democratically and decided at that time to remove the three inalienable powers from the French people. A huge question now arises.

Would such a hypothetical decision by the French parliament be legal or illegal? Would such a hypothetical decision stop the French Resistance for sovereignty as expressed from 1940 to 1945?

The answer is obvious. The decision would be illegal and nothing would stop the French people in the long run from regaining their sovereignty. The same would apply to another, again hypothetical, example.

Imagine that during the Cold War years the West German legislative bodies had decided to transfer the powers of the German people to the Soviet Union and for West Germany to become in effect part of the Soviet Union. The German people could have been told that belonging to a big and strong country would be a good thing in the long run. It would give them stability, peace and prosperity. The question again is the same. would such an imaginary decision by the German Bundestag be legal or illegal?

The answer again is obvious. The representatives of the German people are always temporary custodians of the three powers of the people for a limited period of time. They are not entitled to transfer any of those powers in part or in whole to anyone else but back to the German people at the end of each period of office.

The conclusion from the above is that all treaties about the EU – the Single European Act, the Maastricht Treaty and the Amsterdam Treaty – are illegal.

Before proceeding further a crucial note should be made here. One naturally could ask: were the parliamentarians or government officials voting or signing for illegal actions badly intentioned or arrogant or even traitors? My opinion on this very important matter is as follows. The parliamentarians voting for the Maastricht Treaty or for the Amsterdam Treaty or the government officials signing the Single European Act simply did not know what they were signing. They did not know what they were entering into and what the consequences would be. Those consequences have only now started to appear to the average member of parliament. No parliamentarian in his or her right mind could have had bad intentions against his or her own people.

But this is a case of treaties having been decided by legislatures. Is there not a possibility for the people of a country to decide to abolish their sovereignty? Is there not a way for a group of people to decide to lose their three inalienable powers in favour of being absorbed in another country? The simple answer is yes, through a well-informed and impartially organised referendum. The decision for a nation to in effect abolish itself is a decision that can be taken by all its people through a referendum. But deciding to abolish a country's powers and in the long run its very existence requires special conditions for the referendum. Some of the special conditions are outlined here below.

Condition 1
Since the people of the country would have to decide on an extremely serious matter, it is imperative that the referendum should take place at least three years after its announcement. Only this period would be enough to give the people in every corner of the country the chance to be informed of what exactly is at stake. It is very easy with today's market research methods for any government to find with a mathematical accuracy of about 2% what the outcome of a referendum will be at a certain moment and, therefore, manipulate the timing of the referendum.

If, for example, a government found that today the outcome of a referendum would be inconclusive it could choose not to raise the matter, but if after one year the government found again through polling organisations that the referendum could be won then it could decide only at that time (after one year) to proceed with the referendum and make it fast (say, within three months after the announcement). Most of the constitutions of countries all over the world do not have such provision because they were written well before technology and the science of statistics made polling very inexpensive and very accurate.

Therefore, the first condition that a fair referendum would have to fulfil is that the date and the wording of the referendum on abolishing the powers of the people should be fixed at least three years in advance. This would give all citizens of a country the chance to be informed on what is at stake and to think carefully and peacefully. Poor and rich, university professors and illiterate people, men and women, young and old have the right to be informed from every point of view, for the short and long run, about a decision to reduce their sovereign country to a state absorbed in a greater entity and in the long run lose their particular identity.

Condition 2
During the three-year period before the referendum, no outside money should

be allowed to influence public opinion directly (through advertisements) or indirectly. This means that no EU money should reach the country through any channel. And since this is impossible if the government of the country contributes any money to the yearly budget of Brussels, this means that for the whole period of the campaign no contribution from the government to the budget of Brussels should be made and no money from Brussels should be accepted.

If the farmers receive price support from the EU, they will be influenced in their decisions (thinking that the EU is giving them support and not their fellow countrymen). When the construction companies' personnel undertake projects funded by the EU, they will be influenced in their decision (thinking that the EU is giving them the funds and not their fellow countrymen). When various research organisations personnel receive funds from the EU, they will be influenced in their decisions (thinking that the EU is giving them the funds and not their fellow taxpayers). When various cultural organisations receive funds from the EU, they will be influenced in their decisions (thinking that the EU is giving them the funds and not their fellow taxpayers). When the members of the Europarliament or the Commission or the direct employees of Brussels receive their salaries, medical benefits and pensions from the EU, they will be influenced in their decisions (they will tend to think that the EU is giving them the money, not their fellow countrymen).

Therefore, during the three-year period before the referendum, no money should go from the government of the country to the EU and no money from the EU should come to the country, subject to very strict checking by the country's judicial system. All funds previously given by the EU to farmers, construction projects, research organisations and cultural events organisers should be given directly by the government of the country.

Condition 3
During the three years' campaign, no money from outside the country should be allowed to contribute to the various parties' campaign funds. If this is not enforced then it is possible (some would rather say certain) that EU funds going directly or indirectly to private or public organisations, companies or parties could be very easily channelled to influence a referendum. Again, the judicial system should strictly supervise the campaign funds of any party, organisation or media establishment.

One might ask here: why should funds coming from the EU to influence public opinion in a referendum be excluded? The answer in short is twofold. First, because the people of the country should decide by themselves without any outside influence, and second, because EU funds are public funds (taxpayers' money) and in any democratic country it is absolutely illegal for anybody to use taxpayers' money to influence the outcome of the decision of the people in an election or a referendum or even simply to brainwash the people to support any government policy. More about this huge matter will be discussed in other chapters where it will be shown that the constitutions of all countries are being continually violated when EU funds are used for direct or indirect advertisements.

Condition 4
During the three years' campaign the activities of the European Investment Bank (EIB) and the European Bank for Reconstruction and Development (EBRD) within the country should be strictly supervised as to where they lend money or invest. Both of those banks are owned by the EU and their set-up capital belongs to the public at large (they are public institutions used as financial arms by the Commission in Brussels). Without strict supervision of their activities during a referendum campaign they could in theory lend money under soft conditions to various private or public organisations in order to influence the votes of the people. They could as well invest directly into media empires with the implicit assumption that the media empires would suppress any unfavourable voices.

Condition 5
The outcome of the referendum should require not just a majority of those who voted, but a majority of the whole electorate of the nation. On such a serious matter as the decision of a nation to abolish the three powers of its people and in the long run to abolish even its particular identity, it is obvious that if, for example, 70% of the eligible voters bothered to vote, then a 52% majority represents only 36.4% of the eligible voters or total electorate (52% x 70% = 36.4%). But 36.4% of the total electorate cannot decide either way on such an important matter.

Up to now no country has voted in a totally fair referendum regarding the EU using as a minimum the above mentioned minimum conditions for fairness, non-use of public money and in-depth familiarisation of the average citizen with the subject. The argument therefore that the transfer of the three powers of the people to the EU has been done in an unconstitutional and undemocratic manner is correct. However, the present argument will not be given any grades because it concerns the way (the method) the powers were removed from each individual group of people and not whether this removal of powers is a good or a bad thing for the average citizen. The latter has been examined and graded elsewhere.

12. Argument No. 12 (Political)

> Within the EU, I will belong in a huge country named the Union or Europe, which could compete successfully with giants such as the USA or China in every field (political, economical, cultural, athletic, military). My self-confidence and pride are thus increased, whereas if I continued being a citizen of my relatively small nation-state, I could not have this chance.

The argument is very strong and especially attractive to people with some kind of hunger for imperial power and needs thorough consideration. First of all, let us quickly see the philosophical point of view of the argument. For each human being, a nation or country is something like a big family. It is a group of like-minded people sharing some common linguistic, cultural and historical characteristics (not necessarily racial characteristics) and living over some defined geographical area. This group of people or geographical area could be large or small but one thing is certain. No one chose which country he or she was born in the same way that no one chooses which parents he or she was born from.

Now the argument runs like this. Because I happened to have been born in a relatively small nation, it is better for me if somehow I change my nation and I adopt a new much bigger one. Intellectually and philosophically this is equivalent to someone saying, 'Because I just happened to have been born from poor or weak or ill educated or socially unrecognised parents, I will feel better if I change my parents,' or, 'Because I was born in a small or weak family, it is better for me to be adopted by another fourteen families so that I feel stronger and more secure.'

It is obvious that the argument is philosophically incorrect because our parents should be honoured for whatever they are and should not and cannot in fact be exchanged for others! The same applies in general to our family. Our family as well as our personal friends are not objects to be abandoned or exchanged on grounds of strength or glory or wealth or social recognition. People who have attempted to do that have always ended up unhappy. And no one wants to be unhappy.

This is as far as the philosophical considerations go. But let us come to the practical considerations.

Everyone, given the choice, would like to belong to a powerful or strong nation. The reasons for this are not clear and they may be irrational or relics of centuries of rivalries and wars between nations, but let us see where today the real strength lies.

On the economic front the USA has certainly a greater Gross National Product than Switzerland or Singapore, but this is not what counts for the individual. It is the Gross National Product per person that counts as a measure of wealth and on that count both Switzerland or Singapore have more wealth than the USA. The notion that countries are rich or poor by considering only total wealth is completely wrong and it amounts to people believing in the existence of irrational entities. It is the wealth per person (or per citizen) that defines the strength or weakness of country on the economic front. On that count several small countries are economically stronger than huge countries such as the USA (not to mention other huge countries like China or India).

On the military front, if military strength is what the people of a small or medium country desire (which is very doubtful in today's pacifist and well-educated world), then they can become militarily stronger than China (if this is what they wish) by simply participating in NATO, or they can compete militarily against the USA (if this is what they wish) by making a military alliance with the newly democratic Russia and so on. The people of a small or a medium-sized country do not need to dismantle their country in order to belong to a militarily strong entity. They just need to participate in a military alliance of their choice and from which they can withdraw at any time in the future.

On the economic competition front, it is not countries or governments that compete internationally today. It is individuals and private firms that compete. The era of governments competing against each other in the international arena is over because they have ceased to be economic agents or actors. It is private companies who compete in the global arena where increasingly tariffs, quotas and other bureaucratic obstacles are eliminated. Companies from small countries like Taiwan or South Korea or Singapore or Switzerland have no problems competing and expanding as long as markets become increasingly accessible and open to free trade.

On the political strength front, if by political strength one means political 'clout', then one can consider the question, which state has greater political clout in the United Nations, the state of Mississippi, which is part of the USA, or the sovereign state of Norway which decided in a referendum not to join the EU? Or which state has greater political clout in the World Trade organisation, the state of Alabama which is part of the USA, or the sovereign state of Switzerland which decided in a referendum not to join the EU?

If by political strength one means strength of political institutions and democratic traditions, then the political institutions of Switzerland or Norway are at least as healthy and strong as those of the USA (not to mention other very large countries like India or China). In fact, the people of Switzerland, with their frequent use of referenda, most probably have the strongest and healthiest political institutions in the world today.

On the athletic or cultural strength front, there are people (and I am one of those people) who feel a deep satisfaction whenever they see their national flag being raised in an athletics competition because one of their athletes has received a medal in a competition. Those people would very much like their own country to be first in collecting medals in any competition. But obviously a country like Italy or France with a population of about 60 million people cannot hope to collect individually more medals than the USA, which is a country of 270 million people.

This is a matter of simple arithmetic and the probability of having top-rate athletes within a certain number of people taken as a sample. It is, for example, impossible for Italy to overtake the USA in medals won in the Olympic Games unless we assume that the Italian people decide to specialise in athletics the way East Germany did in the past. But this is highly unlikely to happen in a pluralistic country. Therefore many people who crave for national glory tend to think, My country cannot beat the Americans when it is alone. But if I submerge my country into a group of fifteen countries and then gradually the group as a whole becomes my country, then it is very probable that I will be able to beat the Americans in every kind of athletics competition and in any case the competitors will always be between teams of comparable ability. I will thus feel self-confident and very proud.

The same kind of thinking applies to cultural creation and scientific research. No single European country can compete against the Americans regarding the total number per year of technological innovations or Nobel prizes. But if fifteen European countries counted together their yearly total of technological innovations or Nobel prizes then they stand a good chance of competing as equals with the USA. No one can accuse people who have such thoughts of being badly intentioned. The desire of any human being to see his or her nation attain the greatest possible achievements in an absolutely peaceful manner is definitely the good face of nationalism.

However, these well-intentioned thoughts are missing the point and are simply wrong. The reason is that the strength of any nation in any field (athletic, cultural or scientific) is not reflected simply in the total number of achievements by its people. The correct indicator is the number of achievements per million of citizens of the nation. It is not how many Olympic medals France collects that counts. It is how many medals per million of French population that counts. This is the true indicator of the athletic abilities or inclinations of the French people. This shows their level of interest on average or their levels of achievement on average. To take the argument one step further. If in the next Olympic Games China (with 1,200 million population) collects more medals than Italy (with 60 million population) will this mean that the average Chinese citizen is more interested in athletics or more capable in athletic achievements than the average Italian citizen? The answer is obviously no. It is the average individual that counts, not the total. The achievements of the average individual is the unit upon which any democratic society is built and upon which the society monitors itself for its rate of progress, strengths or weaknesses. Total achievements and total numbers count for very little or for nothing in democratic countries and somehow they 'smell' of totalitarianism. The same arguments apply for the number of technological breakthroughs, the number of Nobel prizes, the number of cultural prizes or achievements and so on.

But what about those peculiar people in our alternative? Do they need to feel proud about their country in every respect (economic, political, cultural and athletic)? Do they feel weak competing against very large countries like the USA or China? Do they feel self-confident about the strengths of their society?

The people in country X believe first of all that, in the same way that competition between individuals is a healthy sign, so peaceful competition between nations in the international arena is a healthy sign for the continuous progress and improvement of all human beings.

However, in all units of international competition the people in country X translate all statistics on the basis of achievements per million of population. Their statistical services are always producing this kind of indicator after compiling all the data. Therefore, they judge the strengths or weaknesses of their country exclusively on this kind of indicator. Their self-assessment as a nation then becomes really meaningful for them since it refers to the achievements or weaknesses or indications or specialisations of the average citizen of the country. The people in the alternative do not wish to exchange their country for a bigger or stronger one. They simply know that their country can in real terms be the strongest on earth even if it happens to be the smallest!

Based on the above, it is suggested that in the 2004 Olympic Games in Athens the committee organisers measure the medals won by each participating nation using the proper and statistically modern indicators. Some surprises may then arise! The argument as a whole is graded in Figure 59.

Figure 59

Option 1 Member of the EU	Option 2 The alternative
Grade: 0/100,000	Grade: 250/100,000

13. Argument No. 13 (Political)

Within the EU, if all member states pooled their armed forces they could enjoy economies of scale in both manpower and expenditure. This will be beneficial for me.

Suppose for a moment that the fifteen states of the EU created an absolutely unified and homogenised army: a 'common' army (like the common foreign policy) or a 'single' army (like the single currency). They could thus create armed forces comparable in strength and numbers to those of the USA or China. The question is would the countries then spend a smaller percentage of their Gross Domestic Product on defence?

The answer is no. The reason is that when you become a military superpower you tend to attract super-enemies or super-adversaries. But super-enemies or super-adversaries require super-expenses in equipment and firepower. On average today the militarily superpowerful United States of America spends a much higher proportion of its Gross Domestic Product on defence than the average country in the EU. Regarding savings in manpower it is also highly doubtful whether the creation of a military superpower by itself can save manpower because superpowers tend to attract super-terrorists (apart from super-enemies). This is especially true for countries in the continent of Europe which tend to be near various hotspots or unstable areas simply because of geography. But super-terrorists or other super-illegals coming from all directions require increased manpower for defence, not reduced manpower. The other problem with creating a military superpower is that superpowers finally end up being super-policemen of the world and need to be present in all oceans and continents. But becoming a permanent super-policeman of the world is not a step towards reducing the manpower of the armed forces.

Another line of argument is that already there is a huge and powerful military alliance named NATO. If reductions in manpower or yearly military expenses can be made (and I believe they can be made for many countries), then the way forward is for a country in NATO to start reducing its military expenditures. There is not any military scope in creating a United States of Europe within NATO.

What then is the way forward regarding military expenditures? Is there not a possibility of reducing them in the near future? And what is the position of the people of the alternative on this very important subject?

First of all, the people of the alternative do not wish to be a military superpower. If they suffer from military insecurity, they participate in a military alliance of their own choice (not necessarily NATO) for as long as they wish to participate in the alliance.

Second, the people of the alternative believe that it is the spread of democracy and pluralism and education in all nations that creates the necessary conditions for defence expenditure reductions. It is not the creation of artificial military superpowers, but the deep roots of democratic procedures in all countries that will reduce military expenditures. In this respect, narrowing of democracy through centralisation in Brussels goes in the opposite direction.

Third, the people of the alternative believe that by giving every country or nation the absolute ability to govern itself without interference from others and without interfering in the affairs of others, only then will conditions for peace and harmony and happiness flourish. And with these conditions comes the reduction of the armed forces. Absence of these conditions creates fertile soil for continuous suspicions, anxiety, demands and conflicts of interests which in turn create the need not only for keeping strong armed forces but also for keeping unnecessarily large internal security forces (with their associated expenses) in order to suppress any agitation for national self-determination.

Briefly the people in the alternative believe that all fifteen countries in the continent of Europe need to be absolutely free to run their own affairs in a peaceful and democratic world in order to continually reduce their military expenditures. They do not need to eliminate themselves and create a superpower in order to reduce their military expenditures. They believe that the era of military superpowers is fast approaching its end and that the era of a few hundred small, self-governing, democratic and voluntarily cooperating powers all over the earth will soon dawn. The grading is in Figure 60.

Figure 60

Option 1 Member of the EU	Option 2 The alternative
Grade: 50/100,000	Grade: 100/100,000

14. Argument No. 14 (Political)

> Within the EU, the governing politicians of my country will never dare take any difficult decisions. They will leave all difficult decisions to the EU so that they avoid any political damage from the opposition parties. This is no good for me or for democracy.

The argument is generally correct. Within the EU, the politicians in any government do not need to take the heat for any decision which could be even slightly difficult or slightly unpopular. They do not need to risk making structural reforms in their country even if they got a mandate for this or they see that the reforms are needed for the benefit of their countrymen and women. Why should they risk anything and risk being kicked out of power? It is much easier to leave the reforms to the EU. They can wait a few years or a few decades until the reforms come to their countrymen in the form of legislation or regulations or instructions or policies or advice from the EU. In this way it will not be they who appear to be responsible for the decision and any adverse or unpopular consequences. It will be the EU, 'our partners' who suggest those ideas or reforms and we have to follow 'otherwise we will be left behind' or 'we will be considered as not cooperating'. At the end of its term the government can then claim as its own only the measures that have proven to be popular. The rest can be given to the public as 'general measures from the EU which are unavoidable' and for which the governing parties should not be held responsible. This is another form of 'trying to have your cake and eat it' or 'having a free lunch' or elevating the 'free rider's problem' as is known in microeconomics from the level of the individual to the level of the national government! In a few words it is a mixture of irresponsibility, opportunism and cowardice on the part of the government.

In conclusion, the argument is correct but we will not pursue it further, neither will we give grades to it. This is because the argument is a direct consequence of the simple fact that the three inalienable powers of the people do not reside with their government or their parliament any more. They reside outside the country and it is only natural that a government hesitates to govern because even if it decided to try it could not do so! Why then try?

15. Argument No. 15 (Political)

> The EU institutions have become a bureaucratic organisation governing de facto 360 million people and trying to conquer their hearts using various handouts. This is not healthy.

It is a fact that EU institutions as a sum (Commission, Europarliament, Court of Justice) are a huge bureaucratic organisation. But is it bureaucratic because the people who run it are not very efficient (and therefore with some change in the particular faces or with some internal reforms could stop being bureaucratic), or is it bureaucratic because of something more fundamental? It is the latter case. Whenever in the world any organisation has proven to be bureaucratic, the underlying reason is never the particular people. It is the system that is always the root of the problem and, in most cases of bureaucracy, it is the vagueness of the raison d'être of the organisation that is the deepest and strongest cause. The reasons that Brussels is hugely bureaucratic are very simple and very fundamental.

1. Brussels, like any government, tends to be bureaucratic simply because it tries to handle all the public affairs of the people (i.e. to handle a portion of their wealth with the purpose of redistributing it, to handle their new legislation, to handle their regulations, official foreign aid, foreign affairs, environment, justice system, etc.). We know that government of any kind naturally tends to create some form of bureaucracy. But whereas a national government handles the affairs of a relatively small number of people, with greater homogeneity and living over a relatively small geographical area, the Commission and parliament in Brussels try to govern a much bigger group of people. At the same time a national government is all the time under the spotlight of its national electorate, opposition parties and media. There is very little or nothing of this in Brussels simply because of geographical distance and centralisation. It is therefore natural that Brussels is a huge bureaucracy. It is not the particular people running Brussels who are at fault. It is the system.

2. A bureaucratic organisation once formed tends always to feed on itself (using the energies of others) in order to grow and to grow. At present the Commission collects yearly from fifteen national governments (i.e.

from the subjects of those national governments) approximately 100 billion US dollars and redistributes those back to the governments as well as to foreign governments in the form of official foreign aid. This tendency to collect money and redistribute it can only grow because the administration of the money (of others) is what feeds the need for projecting a popular image and self-importance. But, more importantly, it is the non-financial areas of policy (and legislation) that tend to grow in a bureaucratic organisation. Almost all kinds of policies (from foreign policy to humanitarian affairs to transportation to culture) are already concentrated in the hands of the Commission and all legislation in the hands of the Europarliament.

3. There is, however, a more fundamental reason why an organisation can become hugely bureaucratic. This is when the raison d'être of the organisation has ceased to exist (or even never existed!). Whenever and wherever in the world an institution has become hugely bureaucratic it has been proven historically that the reason for the existence of the institution had faded or it never existed in the first place. It could be the case that if the EU institutions are hugely and undoubtedly bureaucratic then their reason for existence is not very clear!

The second point of the argument that the Commission is using various handouts with the EU label (instead of national government labels) in order to conquer the hearts and minds of the people is also correct. Any funds for infrastructure, for farmers support, cultural support and research support always come either from within the same country or from governments of other countries. The funds are simply repackaged with the label and the flag of the EU so that the hearts and minds of the people (especially the younger generations) may be conquered by the Commission.

The economic consequences of this phenomenon have been examined elsewhere. Here we can only note that such disingenuous behaviour is not a healthy sign for any bureaucratic organisation. It is a sign of a lack of transparency and of having intentions to establish, enforce, develop and perpetuate something shady. We can only note here that these signs are not only bureaucratic but rather unethical!

In conclusion, it is not the particular people running the EU institutions that make the EU a huge bureaucracy. It is the system that is at fault and more specifically it is the simple existence of the system that creates bureaucracy.

When grading this argument in Figure 61 we assume that 'less bureaucracy' is for the average citizen better than 'more bureaucracy'. The people in the alternative have to suffer the bureaucracy only of their own government and therefore we assume for them less bureaucracy.

Figure 61

Option 1	Option 2
Member of the EU	The alternative
Grade: 0/100,000	Grade: 100/100,000

16. Argument No. 16 (Political)

> Within the EU, I am bombarded every day with direct and indirect advertisements on the merits of the EU. All this advertising is done with public funds to promote political aims. This is a direct and continuous violation of one of the basic laws of any truly democratic society that no public funds will be used to influence the public for any political aim even if everyone agrees with this aim. This is equivalent to the continuous raping of democracy and I do not feel good about this.

In every *truly* democratic nation, there are very strict laws prohibiting absolutely the government of the day from promoting any political aims, whether these aims are right or wrong. The reason for this is simply fairness, i.e. the citizens should decide on any public matter (whether political, economic, cultural or environmental) by themselves and not with the aid of government money (which is owned by the public at large and not by any political or private organisation).

And even after the citizens have decided on any matter, they have the absolute right to change their opinion on the same matter in the future. Therefore, the government cannot use taxpayers' money to try the influence the views of the public on any of its initiatives, positions, plans or philosophies. Moreover, it cannot use public money to help the citizens to remain of the same opinion on a matter or a policy that another government adopted in the past or the citizens themselves decided on in the past through referenda. This has nothing to do with the policy or measure or philosophy being wrong or right. This has to do with democracy whereby no public money shall be used to advertise the aims of the government even if 100% of the electorate agrees at the moment with the particular aims of the government. Let us give some hypothetical examples to clarify things.

Example 1
The government wishes to 'educate' the voters that continued membership of NATO is good for them. The government cannot use even one dollar of taxpayers' money even if 100% of the citizens of the country agree at the moment that continued membership of NATO is a very good thing.

Example 2
The government wishes to 'educate' the public that socialism is not a very fashionable thing to believe in today. It cannot use even one dollar of

taxpayers' money even if the mood of the public would be conducive to such a campaign at the moment.

Example 3
The government wishes to reduce the value added tax on a great number of items and to fix the exchange rate of the currency against a basket of other currencies. It also wishes to make use of free trade agreements with India and impose quotas on imports of Japanese cars. All these intentions or policies of the government are in the economic sphere of activities. The government can implement the policies perfectly, but it cannot use even one dollar of taxpayers' money to convince (through direct or indirect advertisements) the citizens of the country that the measures are correct or that they will be beneficial to them.

If it wishes to advertise anything, it has to use money from the budget of the party (or parties), not the budget of the government. Parties are organisations that have every right to inform the citizens on their positions or philosophies but the government collects money from every citizen whether or not he or she supports the government and so this money cannot be used to 'brainwash' any group of people. Otherwise, for example, a right of centre government using the money of left of centre people could continuously 'brainwash' them and theoretically remain in power for ever. This would be, of course, equivalent to the death of democracy and the pluralistic society.

Now let us come to what is happening today within any of the fifteen member countries regarding the EMU and the EU. Everybody knows very well, and it has been stated by a great number of officials, that the EMU is a political project (and an economic project as well) and that the EU is a political project. In particular, the EU is a complete political and economic union of a number of countries. This political and economic union has, from every practical aspect, been de facto since 1992. But both at that time as well as today, there is a considerable portion of the population who oppose it. In some countries this portion of the population is growing and in a few the majority believe that the EU is not a good thing. Therefore, the matters of participation in the EU and also in the EMU are highly debatable and highly political. But even if they were not debatable at all, even if everyone in a specific country agreed (in 1992 or today) that 'the EU is a good thing', the matter is political. It is a matter of political decision (by the government or by the people) and as such is subject to the laws about public funds.

The majority today (if it exists) does not have the right to use taxpayers' money (coming from both the majority and the minorities) to propagate that the EU is a good thing. Instead of this, in all fifteen member countries, the following things are happening almost daily and have been happening at least for the past eight years:

- Step 1: The citizens of the country pay taxes to their government.

- Step 2: Approximately 4% of the taxes go automatically from the government to the Commission (in Brussels).
- Step 3: The Commission uses a significant portion of this money for advertising the merits of the political decision to be within the EU. The advertisements are direct or indirect and in 1995 the total amount for direct advertisement was officially 250 million dollars for the fifteen countries. But this money is public money. It comes from the taxpayers of the country (if the country is a net contributor to the EU budget) and from the taxpayers of other countries (if the country is a net receiver from the EU budget). In this second case things are even worse. The money for political advertisement comes from foreign governments who are in effect brainwashing the citizens of the recipient country with the full knowledge, assistance and active participation of their government.

It is worthwhile here to see at a glance a very small sample of advertisements (or 'messages') that are propagated in every country within the EU.

Direct advertisements

- Spots on TV describing the merits of the EU funds.
- Flags bought with public money and on display everywhere.
- Various infrastructure projects where it is obligatory that big boards display who is contributing the funds (EU) as well as the EU emblem.
- Stickers on cars or keys accessories with the EU flag distributed freely, but produced with taxpayers' money.
- Research projects in universities or other scientific institutions, where it is displayed on big boards and in all announcements that the EU is sponsoring or subsidising them.

Indirect advertisements

- Subsidising wholly or in part cultural events that promote the 'spirit' or 'philosophical aspiration of the EU' vis-à-vis union of the fifteen different peoples together with the relevant signboards and announcements in newspapers.
- Subsidising in all or in part of weekly television productions promoting the union of the fifteen nations, always displaying the fifteen flags, with some productions especially targeted at children.
- Advertising in all media about EU citizens' rights.
- Tourist promotion advertisements by the national governments in non-EU countries' newspapers and media where in prominent positions the strides and successes of the specific country towards EMU membership and

criteria are displayed.

- Producing thousands of statistics every year through Eurostat and then distributing the statistics to all kinds of media worldwide. Eurostat is the statistical organisation of the EU and all its running expenses are paid for with public money. Its statistics refers almost always to member countries as a group and give various group indicators (e.g. unemployment rate of the EU, average life expectancy in the EU, births per 1,000 people in the EU, total imports of the EU, total exports of the EU, per cent increase of car sales in the EU, and so on). These statistics are then given to the media worldwide, who are only too happy to receive them for nothing and usually present them in comparisons with other countries like Japan, the USA, Canada, Australia, Russia, Taiwan, Singapore, Argentina or South Korea. If Japan or South Korea or Argentina are countries, then, of course, in the subconscious of the average reader or viewer the EU has to be a country too (especially if the viewer or reader is a very young person).
- Subsidising of film productions with politically correct messages promoting the idea that we are 'Europeans'.
- Subsidising training courses for professionals or managers where the politically correct messages are channelled.
- Subsidising language courses in the fifteen countries where the teachers are supposed to be inclined towards the politically correct message.
- Giving foreign aid to third countries as the EU, not as any individual member. Therefore, the people in these third countries receiving foreign aid are thankful to an entity called the EU and in the long run will consider that the EU is a country.
- Imposing passports and identity cards of the same kind, shape, dimensions and colours. In the long run, people in other countries seeing one kind of passport will naturally think of a single nation. The same applies to the people in the member states especially in the long run.
- Advertising in the newspapers of the financial arm of the EU, the European Investment Bank (EIB) where also the map of the EU is displayed.

The list of indirect advertisements or promotions or announcements is actually endless. And all this is done with public money.

We are clearly seeing a gross and continuous violation of the law about public funds used for promoting political aims, and maybe we are witnessing the continuous and systematic rape of democracy in countries with deep democratic roots, traditions and cultures. Any citizen of any country could sue his or her government on that particular matter, and provided that the judges were really independent, could nullify all actions of his or her government regarding the EU, at least since 1992.

In the grading of this argument in Figure 62, we assume that continuous violation of the laws and the raping of democracy are bad things and consequently give the relevant credit to the alternative whose citizens do not permit even the slightest use of public or foreign funds for persuasion, advertisements, education, or brainwashing regarding the shaping of public opinion on political matters, economic matters, and even philosophical convictions.

Figure 62

Option 1 Member of the EU	Option 2 The alternative
Grade: 0/100,000	Grade: 2,500/100,000

Chapter XIII
PHILOSOPHICAL ARGUMENTS

Introduction to the philosophical arguments

Some people believe that economics defines politics. Others believe that politics define economics. It is without doubt, however, that both politics and economics are defined by philosophy. It is the philosophical convictions of men and women that give rise not only to their political preferences and convictions but to their everyday economic behaviour as well.

It may strike one as absurd to say that the philosophical convictions of a human being define or even influence his or her everyday economic behaviour. But, as the science of microeconomics teaches us, economic behaviour is mostly about getting maximum utility, the maximum level of personal satisfaction from our everyday life. Concepts such as 'utility', 'satisfaction', 'wealth', 'public good', or even simple 'good' are indispensably connected to philosophical concepts such as happiness, liberty, self-determination, culture, identity, freedom of choice, community spirit and competition. All those concepts are philosophical concepts without which the economic behaviour of humans would not differ at all from the economic behaviour of animals. It is those concepts that define political beliefs and in turn economic behaviour. All people wish to become as wealthy as possible or as famous as possible – with extremely few exceptions.

But why do people want wealth or fame? Clearly they want them to feel happier. A poor person without food or home cannot be happy. But even if he gets enough food and a home, he still needs many other things in order to feel happy. *It is this desire for happiness that drives the lives of people.*

Any political or economic model ultimately has to be consistent with this desire of human beings for maximum happiness. The EU model as such has to comply with this rule, otherwise it will certainly create unhappiness and revolt. If this revolt finally happens, it will not be the first time in human history that a politico-economic model has created unhappiness and revolt. In the next several chapters we will critically discuss various philosophical arguments about the EU examining questions like:

- Is unity or diversity the way through which human civilisation has progressed and how it should progress further: through unity or through diversity? Through homogeneity or through variety? Through singularity or through plurality? Through centralisation or through decentralisation?

Through widening the representation of the individual in public affairs or through narrowing the representation of the individual in public affairs?
- Do humans need to have an individual identity only or do they need also some kind of national identity? Is a human being happy living alone with his or her family only or do they need to feel part of a similar-minded group of people known as a nation or country?
- Is dismantling the different nation-states and with them the different national identities necessary for avoiding wars in the future? Is peace incompatible with group identity? And if so, which is preferable: the distant and infinitesimal probability of a future war between civilised nations or the near certainty of losing one's identity?
- Is maximum prosperity incompatible with sovereign groups of people known as countries or nations? Can unhappy individuals give rise to the maximum rate of material growth? Does competition or cooperation create maximum material progress?
- Is not the gradual elimination of the various cultures and national identities a million times more environmentally dangerous than the elimination of various kinds of endangered animals and plants? Is not the diversity of human beings as important for the equilibrium of the environment as the diversity of plants and animals?
- Would it be better or worse if we had one common government all over the world instead of 170 as we have at present? Would not peace, prosperity and happiness be served better if after, say, one hundred years all the different governments, parliaments and judicial systems on earth had been replaced with a single one, a common one?

Those questions will be discussed and attempted answers given in the next several philosophical arguments. It is my impression that within those arguments lies the final answer to the question whether the EU is a good or a bad thing especially in the long run.

1. Argument No. 1 (Philosophical)

We are in a hurry for EU and EMU integrations to be completed so that we put under a common roof all nations of Europe. Only then will we be sure that there will be no more war in Europe and peace will prevail for ever.

The argument has been repeatedly projected over the past few years by many government officials and other public figures. We examined the same argument from the purely political point of view on page 199. We considered, for example, whether or not war between democratic and civilised nations is unlikely in the future; what the best way to avoid future wars would be and still store decentralised and widespread democracy and sovereignty, and whether any eventual conflicts would be any milder by being internalised instead of being external.

We will examine the same argument from its more general and more powerful view: the philosophical view. We repeat the argument here in simplified terms but also in detail. In the past, the argument runs, we had many different countries in Europe, each one going its own way. This resulted in many instances in the countries fighting each other with millions of dead and economic ruin. By building a common state for every people we will definitely avoid wars because everybody will be inside the same house in the same big family. We will all live in peace, harmony and cooperation and by living in peace we will attain in the long run very high rates of growth in personal income because we will not suffer the economic damage of wars.

The argument likens each country to a 'family' with its own 'house' (the independent nation-state). It implicitly compares the continent of Europe to a village with, say, fifteen different 'families' each one living in its own independent house up to 1992. But, the argument runs, the families in the village sometimes fought each other in the past (especially the neighbours) for insignificant reasons or even non-existent reasons. Sometimes it was property in doubt, sometimes it was a family vendetta, sometimes it was just the aggressive and unreasonable behaviour of a crazy chief of a family that created trouble between two or more families. As a result, fights broke out and members from each family were brutally killed. Some of the houses were bigger, some were smaller, some were richer, some were poorer, some were inhabited by highly educated people some were inhabited by hard-working farmers. But all houses had a common characteristic: they were all independent and each one pursued its own objectives. This characteristic of independent behaviour was always the root of the problem of war. Now, if this independence were removed from each family, it would certainly eliminate any possibility of future fighting between neighbours.

Therefore, it was decided to proceed to the following project: we would first try to make the disposable income of each 'family' roughly comparable (see the EU transfer of funds to 'poor' countries). We would then gradually dismantle the fences and the outside walls of all fifteen houses in our village (the continent of Europe). We would then build instead a big common fence external to all the village houses. Then all the different families in the village would live under the same roof inside the same big house. Each member of each previously independent family would get up in the morning and go to work exactly as before and return in the afternoon to the same common single house bringing one day's earnings from hard and honest work. In the evening, all fifteen families would sit around a big table for dinner together with all the children. We would enjoy community spirit and camaraderie, and have nice discussions in the huge living room late in the evening. We would have regular parties on birthdays or namedays occasions. All our children would stay in the same house and feel like brothers and sisters. Naturally, no member of this big new family would ever attempt to fight against another member, thus avoiding conflicts between independent families.

Furthermore, within this big house there would be a common budget because of common expenses and facilities. This would mean that each working member of every previously independent family would contribute to the common budget at the end of the month all his or her monthly earnings. We would thus have in our new big single house a huge common purse out of which each member of any family would be able to withdraw money for his or her personal expenses. The withdrawal of money would be according to a fair system so that each one covered his or her needs as much as possible and each working member of any family would keep a fair portion of his or her hard-earned money for their personal plans. Alternatively, we could devise a scheme in which each family automatically retained a portion of its earnings and contributed only the rest of its earnings to our common single budget for running the house.

We would also have common objectives for investments and projects in nearby areas or villages. We would have a common stance on the affairs of the new big family when we dealt with people in other villages. We would thus be in a stronger negotiating position when dealing with any single villager in another village. Each family, sharing a huge common budget, would have much greater financial security. We would also be more secure against attempts by burglars to steal any of the previously independent and isolated houses.

All our children would in the long run get the same culture since they would be living under identical home conditions. This culture would be named the 'European' culture. Moreover, when running our families under a common roof, we would permanently and significantly reduce each family's running expenses due to economies of scale. We would be buying bulk quantities of food, consumables and medicines and therefore we would obtain lower prices. We would have common installations for power supplies, water, telephones and sewage and this would make our infrastructure needs cheaper. When the utility supplying companies saw that we bought bulk quantities of electricity or water, they would most probably give us lower prices. We would be buying bulk quantities of computer programs for the kids (software) and, therefore, get them cheaper. We would make the books for the children more or less common so that we get good discounts. We would have economies of scale on almost anything when running this big new family and this would reduce our costs especially in the long run. We would have as much fun as each family likes at night and in the way that each family likes (alone or together with another family) without prejudicing the values of the other families but according to the free will of each family. It would be a nice big family, strong, secure, dynamic, peaceful and eventually we would attain much faster rates of material growth. Peace, prosperity and happiness would thus prevail over our nice village.

And the argument concludes that we started the actual dismantling of the walls of our houses with the Single European Act in 1985 and we expect to finish the construction of the new big common house in 1999 with the EMU. By that time all fifteen families will be able to have a common roof and eventually all the families of the wider village will come under the same roof. We have named this nice, peaceful and big house the 'European Union'.

This is the argument about war and peace in the EU. It is very powerful at first glance, but we ought to have a second glance (and maybe a third and fourth glance in later arguments!). It is absolutely true that in any village the neighbours sometimes fight each other. It is also absolutely understandable for the villagers to want to live a life without fighting and any other disputes. But is this a reason to dismantle each independent house and put every family in the same big house? Obviously not. Fighting can be prevented in the long run only by having educated families obeying the rules of living next to each other, which is translated into having fully democratic nations with highly educated people. Full independence for each family is actually a precondition for a successful and happy village. An independent family is the building block of any society, even if the family consists of a single parent or even a bachelor. This is simply because of the nature of the human being and not because of the grand design of any one engineering social system.

From the economic point of view, only when a household looks after its own affairs will it attain its maximum potential. Only if the family controls its own house, its own yearly budget, its own destiny, only then has the family real interest and real incentives for maximum material progress. If the family lives in a common house, with a common budget and common facilities, the family will be disinterested in its own affairs, it will not have incentives for progress. In the big new house there might be at the beginning some economies of scale in the running costs. But this is only in the beginning. Sooner or later, with the passage of time, great dynamic inefficiencies will evolve. The administrative costs will rise while the flexibility of the individual family unit will have been lost. No one in the big house will be interested in saving on electricity or water because everybody will pay at the end of the month ('free riders problem' or 'moral hazard'). The same goes for food, for the fire alarm expenses, for insurance for the house, the same for every type of expense. But worst of all, each family, having lost its individuality and exclusive economic rewards for its hard work, loses interest in attaining the maximum material progress in the long run. It loses interest in economic effort. It also loses interest in economic innovation or risk, since the individual family will not reap the fruits of its efforts. The benefits of any risky but successful economic efforts will be enjoyed (at least in great part) by all other families. This is the basic, the fundamental practical economic reason why successful villages have always been built on the fully independent individual household having its own house and running its own affairs. The families trade with one another exchanging their goods or services, but at the end of the day each family member returns to its own economic unit: its own self. Economic trading, competition, cooperation are all part of the normal natural way of life, but they are all based on the existence of an independent family-household as the building block of any village, market or society.

But the big new common house also has many other repercussions apart from the economic repercussions. Replacing fifteen previously independent houses with one big family house is in the long run equivalent to replacing fifteen individual family mentalities-inclinations-cultures with one single mentality-inclination-culture. In time, since everybody lives every day under the same roof, it will be natural for the next generation to have just one culture, the common culture. But having one culture instead of fifteen, having one mentality, one way of thinking instead of fifteen is the worst thing that can happen to the villagers. It is through diversity of cultures, histories, ideas, hopes and aspirations that a village becomes more civilised and generation after generation is elevated to higher levels of civilisation.

Translated into the continent of Europe the above metaphor is equivalent to replacing many cultures with one, reducing the diversity of human civilisation by forcefully engineering the homogenisation of cultures. Being diverse means being different and being different is not to be confused with being superior or inferior. The idea of being culturally superior is a sin and the idea of being culturally inferior is simply wrong. But the idea of being different is neither a sin nor wrong. It is simply a natural fact and should be looked on as a blessing rather than as a menace. If preservation of the diversity of animals and plants is an urgent and environmentally good thing, then diversity of human cultures is also an environmentally friendly and natural thing. In fact, returning to Europe, the homogenisation of all family cultures into a single one is equally serious – some would say more serious – than the economic consequences of the single house.

There is, however, a third problem in this big single house that has been created. The name of the problem is, in one word, unhappiness. In the long run each individual family, having lost its economic incentives for material progress, having lost its independence to run its own affairs, having lost its particular culture, having lost its particular family background, having lost its particular way of living, loses its identity altogether. But human beings are by definition made to have one and only one identity and this identity is by definition unique. The identity of a family cannot be the same as the identity of another family otherwise it has no meaning. Loss of the individual family's identity creates unhappiness. But unhappiness is the worst thing that can happen to humans, worse even than being poor or weak. It is the pursuit of happiness that drives the actions of humans as individuals, families or groups. Remove this possibility of happiness and people are driven to death. Remove their identities and people have no reason for existence.

But what about the alternative model? How is it organised? The alternative is simply organised by nature and not by grandiose social engineering ideas.

The people in the alternative have their own independent, detached houses. There are houses small and large, rich and poor, but they are their own. The houses have their individuality and each one is pursuing its own objectives. It is individuality and the pursuit of personal objectives that make the alternative villagers enjoy very high rates of growth and real happiness.

What, then, about the camaraderie and community spirit that the people living in the big single house enjoy? Isn't it at least a very nice aspect of their model? It is, but the people living in the alternative individual houses enjoy the same kind of camaraderie and community spirit. They simply invite their neighbours to have parties (or any other type of fun) but the invitations and parties are happening at their own convenience and at their own pace – and this is maybe a reason why they are much more enjoyable events. *Individuality of each family (nation-state, country) is not incompatible with community spirit and fun. It is a precondition for true community spirit and fun.*

In order to make the examination of the argument of the single big common house complete let us look at the experience and historical evidence. Since in real life there is no law prohibiting all families in a village creating and living in a single house, why has this type of family not evolved naturally? Simply because it is unnatural. And unnatural things do not flourish or prevail in the long run. During the past one hundred years there have been many attempts by well-intentioned people to live in big common properties. They have all failed and been abandoned because the biological family is the building block of human societies and is in fact the most efficient building block. And it is the most efficient building block of societies because individualism drives human nature. And individualism drives human nature because people have one and only one brain each. The importance of the argument is reflected in the grading in Figure 63.

Figure 63

Option 1 Member of the EU	Option 2 The alternative
Grade: 0/100,000	Grade: 5,000/100,000

2. Argument No. 2 (Philosophical)

The creation of huge political units creates in the long run the possibility of huge wars. This is bad for peace.

Undoubtedly the EU is a huge political unit. It can exercise tremendous power when dealing with other countries. But this tremendous power will only push other nations to create their own huge political units simply by natural reaction. We may see in the next generation, for instance, all the sub-Saharan

Africans combining into one huge political unit, all the Arabs or even Muslims combining into one huge political unit, the Asians combining into one huge political unit and the South and Central Americans doing the same. Humanity could thus end up with five or six huge centres of political and consequently military power. Instead of having more than 170 independent centres of political and military power, humans would be reduced to just a handful of huge military-political powers. But the mere existence of huge military powers opposed on all fronts (political, economic, etc.) increases tremendously the possibility of huge wars between superpowers, wars that would have devastating consequences and would be very difficult to extinguish. Other things being equal, a huge nuclear war is more probable given the pre-existence of huge political and military powers.

Now the question arises: does the world need the existence of more political superpowers or fewer? Does the world need more military superpowers (or even military alliances) or fewer? And if a political superpower emerges or exists, against whom is it emerging or existing? You need political enemies in order to exist as a political superpower. But who at present are the political enemies of any of the fifteen countries within the EU? And who will be the political enemies after ten or twenty or fifty years? Does the average citizen of any of the fifteen countries today feel he has strong or dangerous political enemies in other countries, and who are they? The end of the Second World War, the rapid spread of democracy, the increase in living standards, the increased level of education, the spread of tourist travel, business travel, telecommunications, television, e-mail and the Internet are all developments that point to one and only one direction: there are no political enemies. Even if a few relatively weak pariah states exist today, they may not after ten or fifteen years be political enemies. Therefore, what is the reason for creating a huge political power? Simply there is no rational reason.

On the contrary, the creation of one huge political power near Asia and Africa will inevitably lead to the creation of corresponding and opposing political powers, especially in the Middle East. The same logic applies to creating a huge military power and it is needless to say that a large political power is by default also a huge military power. By extension, the recent eastward expansion of NATO to include former Soviet bloc countries means that NATO will gradually become a larger and stronger military alliance and power. But is there an increased threat to NATO justifying increased firepower? Does world peace need the expansion of NATO or its gradual and continuous contraction?

One of the fundamental laws in physics is that any action causes an equal reaction in the form of a force of equal magnitude but opposite direction. The same law applies in general in politics and in many other human fields. The emergence and continuous existence of a huge political force inevitably leads in the long run to the emergence and existence of a huge political anti-force. This is a result of the simple fact that nations do not like to be pushed around or dictated to in any field. A trading bloc creates other trading blocs to counter its weight in multilateral trade negotiations. A political superpower creates another opposing political superpower to counter its weight in foreign relations. But all this creates huge and unhealthy antagonisms in the form of oligopolistic situations worldwide. When oligopolistic situations develop in economics this damages the economic interests of everybody. But when oligopolistic situations develop in politics, this is bad news for long-term peace worldwide. Polypolarity, not oligopolarity,[1] is the way forward for minimising the probability of huge wars in the future. Hence the assessment of the argument in Figure 64.

Figure 64

Option 1	Option 2
Member of the EU	The alternative
Grade: 0/100,000	Grade: 2,500/100,000

3. Argument No. 3 (Philosophical)

> History and simple reason prove that human societies attain faster material progress and greater levels of happiness when they are the exclusive controllers of their own affairs. Within the EU, by definition, no country can run its own affairs. This is bad for the rate of material progress and the level of happiness of the average citizen of any country.

It is historically true and it is also a matter of simple logic that a human society is happier and achieves faster rates of growth when it can run its own affairs. This is a simple consequence of the natural fact that distinct human groups have an interest in running their own affairs only when they have full control over them. Loss of this full control over their affairs automatically removes their interest. In losing interest, they greatly reduce their collective efforts towards improving their society. Reduction of collective effort means (especially in the long run) that the rate of economic growth and especially the rate of increase in the level of happiness will be much lower, other things being equal. As long as a family feels as a family, as long as an individual feels as an individual, they need to be able to run their own affairs. In the same way, as long as a country feels as a country, as long as a nation feels as a nation, they need to be able to run their own affairs. But, by definition, this is impossible within the EU where no country can have its own laws, its own judicial system and its own government policies. Having been denied the opportunity to run their own affairs, to be masters of their own fate and destiny, people start being

---

[1] 'Poly' in the Greek language means 'many' and 'oligo' means 'a few'.

cynical and disinterested about their own public affairs. This leads to slower rates of growth, a reduction of the sense of community and eventually to lower levels of happiness. In turn, lower levels of happiness bring greater proportions of all kinds of psychological problems in any society.

We said that countries need to be self-governed entities. But does Germany feel as a country? Does France feel as a country? Does Spain feel as a country? Does Italy feel as a country? The answer is an unequivocal 'Yes' and this 'Yes' is not a result of arbitrary definitions, but a result of culture, history, geography, customs and language.

The simple conclusion is that a distinct human group needs self-government as a necessary (though not sufficient) condition for maximum continuous improvement, for attaining always its maximum potential. But the EU model is by definition not compatible with self-government.

What then about the alternative? Simply put, the people in the alternative are peacefully running their own affairs with full respect for their neighbours' ability and wish to run their own affairs. Hence the grading in Figure 65.

Figure 65

Option 1	Option 2
Member of the EU	The alternative
Grade: 0/100,000	Grade: 2,500/100,000

4. Argument No. 4 (Philosophical)

> Homogeneity of laws, judicial systems and government policies or practices greatly reduces the chances of new improved forms of government because it eliminates the 'democratic laboratories for experiment' known as 'sovereign states'. In the long run this is very bad and very inefficient.

It is beyond any doubt that today the EU has eliminated fifteen sovereign states and replaced them with one de facto huge sovereign state. But let us assume that what has happened during the past fifteen years over the continent of Europe, happens during the next generation or so over all the other continents on earth. If elimination of sovereign states is practically or theoretically correct then one can reasonably conceive a situation where, say, by 2050 the whole world has been reduced to five or six huge sovereign states. Is this development good for experimentation with new forms of government policies? When are the chances of producing successful political or economic experiments greater: when humanity has five or six laboratories of democracy or when humanity has 185 laboratories of democracy? Obviously in the second case.

Government systems and practices can never be constant through time simply because the needs of the people change with time. Let us see some practical examples.

In the early 1980s the British government introduced the concept of privatisation. This concept has since spread successfully almost all over the world. But assume that in 1980 the EU had already been completely formed and that its laws in the Europarliament did not permit such a concept at that time. Then, the concept of privatisation would have never been born (or it would have been born very late). It is not a matter of whether privatisation was a rather successful idea. The point is that the British parliament as an independent laboratory of democracy (at that time, not today) could perform the experiment.

Moreover, let us go for a moment many decades back in history. Let us transfer ourselves to the beginning of the twentieth century when the role of government was very small all over the continent of Europe but assume further that by 1900 the EU had already been formed as a huge sovereign state where, according to its laws, nationalisation or almost any kind of social protection for the people were not compatible with the laws of the Europarliament. Would the ideas of social protection have been evolved and spread? Would socialism (or even communism) have evolved as a viable political system or philosophy? Would the tendency of governments to expand their scope by giving extensive protection to the weaker members of the countries have evolved as rapidly as it did? The answer is simply no. The reason is that instead of thirty-five independent countries as models of social or economic change, instead of thirty-five laboratories for experimentation over the continent of Europe there would have been just one laboratory. Again, it is not a matter whether socialism or communism or protection of the weak by taking money from the strong is a correct or wrong idea. The point is that people continuously need new ideas and that in the long run the more laboratories for experimentation they have, the greater the chances for new ideas to flourish. New ideas are not always correct and new experiments are not always successful. But humanity needs new ideas in order to move to higher levels of governance or prosperity or happiness. New ideas have to be tried to be proven or disproved. This was true in the past and will be true in the future. Trial and error is the surest method for social, economic or political change.

At present almost all countries in the world have a problem with the future provision of pensions for their elderly. There are however five or six countries that have already experimented or are experimenting by privatising their pensions system (Chile, Argentina, Mexico, Singapore and New Zealand are involved, I believe). But assume that the EU model of one parliament, one judicial system and one government had been applied planet-wide and all 170 sovereign states had been replaced by just one huge sovereign state and one world government. In such a situation would the experiment with the pension system be taking place in those countries? It would not have, because there would be one worldwide pension system and only one laboratory for experiment. Again, it is not a matter of whether the experiments with privatising the pension systems are successful or not. The point is that at this moment five different experiments are taking place in five different independent and sovereign countries. The most successful of those may sooner or later be imitated by many other independent sovereign countries. If none of the current experiments on the pension systems proves successful, then surely another sovereign state will make its own experiment. Somehow the best new form of providing pensions will emerge and spread worldwide. There is only one thing needed for this to happen: to have available as many laboratories for trials as possible, because trials will bring errors but trials will also bring successes.

The situation here reminds us of something from the science of microeconomics, namely the various forms of organisation of industries with the most prevalent among them perfect competition, oligopoly and monopoly. Perfect competition exists in an industry when there are a great number of competitors. Oligopoly exists when the number of competitors is reduced to 'a few' (say three to eight) and monopoly when there is just one monopolist competing against nobody. According to standard microeconomic theory monopolistic and oligopolistic situations are much inferior to perfect competition, especially when the element of time is taken into consideration (dynamic inefficiencies). The golden rule is that the greater the number of competitors, the better for consumers. By using the metaphor from microeconomics, one can clearly see where the model of the EU leads humanity in the long to very long run. It leads to the creation of a few huge political-economic sovereign states. Each of the huge sovereign future states can clearly be compared to an oligopolist in the political-economic-cultural arena. And then one can easily envision a situation where the oligopolists merge into a worldwide single monopolist in the arena of political-economic-cultural development.

But is oligopoly or eventually monopoly preferable to perfect competition? Clearly, from the philosophical point of view as well as from the practical long-term point of view, it is to the benefit of humanity to have as many individual autonomous sovereign geographical groups of people as possible living in peace with all the other groups, but at the same time striving to provide for humanity the best example of governance, the best example of a set of laws, the best example of a judicial system, the best example of culture and civilisation. But isn't this best example already found in any of today's existing sovereign states? Isn't the best example already the model of the USA or maybe the EU or Japan or Switzerland or Norway or Canada or Australia or New Zealand or China or Malaysia or Argentina?

The answer is simply and unequivocally that the best example will never be achieved by humanity because, by definition, you can never achieve perfection through time. In the same way that in Euclidean geometry you can walk for ever on a straight line but never find its end point (the point at infinity), in the same way humanity will never achieve the 'ideal' society ('politeia' according to the ancient Greek philosopher Plato) even after infinite time.

The message in this argument is clear: If humanity wants to avoid oligopolistic and later on monopolistic situations, if humanity wants to have at its disposal incentives for peaceful and creative competition in all fields, then merging between sovereign countries is not the way forward. On the contrary, the way forward is keeping and protecting the independence and sovereignty of all those countries who wish to be independent and sovereign entities. Moreover, if some huge sovereign states of today want in the future to de-merge (or split) into various smaller more manageable units, humanity should not present an obstacle to that.

Now a crucial and revolutionary philosophical, but also practical question, arises: if merging of sovereign nation-states is damaging to the long-term interests of the international community, should the United Nations draft regulations, or rules, or laws, prohibiting such mergers? If the government of a country can prohibit the merging of two companies on the grounds that with the merger they become too strong for meaningful competition, then why should the United Nations not make laws that will prohibit the merging of many sovereign nations on the grounds that they will become too strong as a political entity which will be able to impose its will (or outcomes favourable to its will in general) on the other nations on earth, and also on the grounds that the existence of as many players as possible is to the long-term benefit of everyone? The answer to this thought is a huge and simple no. The moment the United Nations issued such a prohibition or law, at the same moment the UN itself would have become the de facto worldwide government, the de facto monopolist having erased from the face of the earth all the sovereign nation-states. By definition, a sovereign nation-state cannot accept instructions or laws from any other entity except its own people and at the moment it became subject to the instructions or laws or prohibitions of the United Nations, at that very same moment the sovereign nation-state would have been eclipsed as an independent entity. And if a number of sovereign nation-states want to abandon their sovereignty and independence and become a huge new sovereign state, then humanity (or the United Nations or the international community) should respect that merger.

Mergers of sovereign nation-states should not be regulated by anyone except the people of each state. The same, of course, applies to any future de-mergers (or spin-offs or splits as they are currently known in the fashionable tendency of huge business conglomerates to de-merge into more focused and specialised business units!) The importance of the argument is reflected in the grading in Figure 66.

Figure 66

Option 1 Member of the EU	Option 2 The alternative
Grade: 0/100,000	Grade: 7,500/100,000

5. Argument No. 5 (Philosophical)

The EU model undoubtedly leads over the long term to the loss of national identity. This is not good as a model for humanity.

Over the long run for any country within the EU national identity will be lost. Gradually, year after year, the words German, French, British, Italian, Spanish, Portuguese, Dutch, Belgian, Irish, Danish, Swedish, Finnish or Greek will lose their meaning. We will see in other chapters how this happens and we will try to see whether this loss of national identity is simply a side effect of the pill named the EU or if it is a deliberate and well-organised and executed effort by well-intentioned people who believe that national identities are obstacles to peace or prosperity. Here, in this argument, we will accept as a fact that the EU model has as a long-run side effect, the loss of national identity (say, within one or two generations), and we will try to see purely from the philosophical point of view if this loss of national identity is simply negligible, or if it is detrimental. Specifically we will project and extrapolate the EU model to the whole world and examine the following situation.

Assume that everyone follows the EU model and that after one hundred years all sovereign nations have lost their sovereignty through some well-intentioned and grand social engineering design and that after two hundred years all national identities are lost. There are no more Americans, Canadians, Argentinians, Egyptians, Greeks, Italians, Israelis, Russians, Algerians, Iranians, Australians, Chinese, Japanese, etc. and that there are simply human beings living peacefully with one another. Is this a better world or is it better to envision a world where after two hundred years (and with all other material conditions the same as in the first case) people are still living peacefully side by side but have retained their national identities, their colourful ways of life?

The words 'colourful ways of life' in the last sentence provide one of the keys to the answer. Once the national identities are lost, once all humans have the same national identity (as 'citizens of the world'), at that very moment their life by definition will have become much less colourful almost to the point of being dull because the various national identities for humanity today, even if we don't realise it, are the factor that gives more colour to the lives of the people. Having a more colourful world is far superior, much more interesting than having a world without any colour. A versatile world is more interesting than a dull one.

But this is the point of view of the cosmopolitan or businessman who travels widely from place to place or on an international television channel showing events all the time from a continent-wide or worldwide point of view. Let us try to see the same from the point of view of the average citizen of any nation today. Does the ordinary human being need to have a national identity or only his or her personal identity and biological family of wife, children, parents and relatives? First of all, not all human beings happen to have a family or choose to have one for various reasons. So for those without a biological family a world without the nation would be a world without any family. This is a loss for them compared to the present situation where they at least have a virtual family: the nation or the country.

But let us come to the most common case where a person has a biological family. Does this person need another much larger family in the nation? To answer this question we need to go back in time in ancient Greece and specifically in the northern part of Greece, Macedonia, where the great philosopher Aristotle lived (very near a city called Thessaloniki which is the second largest city of Greece today). This great philosopher once said, 'Man is a socialising creature.' By that he meant that humans in general do not like to live alone, with only themselves or with their biological family. They need to be active in their society, they need to feel part of that society. Therefore, Aristotle said in essence that humans need to feel part of something bigger than themselves.

But does this 'bigger than themselves' exist in a world without national identities? It exists in the form of the pan-human society in general, but at the same time it does not exist because it is very vague, it has lost its reference point. To define a football team and to support its play in the league we need other football teams as well. If the league contains just one football team, then it is not worth watching or supporting the team because there are no other teams for contrast; there is no reference point. To define a large family like a society or country or nation, you need other large families as well. To define a specific mathematical set of objects or numbers, you also need to know that there are other mathematical sets of objects or numbers. If the only mathematical set available is the set called Q, the all-inclusive infinite set (it includes all objects or all numbers), and you say that you are part of this infinite set, then essentially you are part of no particular specific set; you are alone. This is because one of the fundamental ways in which we make sense of the world is through comparing and contrasting or looking for similarities and differences.

Today loneliness is endemic; increasing numbers of people live alone and community spirit is in decline. The hypothetical event of deliberately erasing national identities, erasing the nation-states, erasing those huge families with the homogeneity of interests or culture or history (the real community with all its intrigues and problems) will inevitably increase our loneliness.

To conclude, one could use the words of Pope John Paul II about the biological family and see what they mean for the large families or countries: 'The first and fundamental structure for "human ecology" is the family, in which man receives his first ideas about trust and goodness and learns what it means to love and be loved, and thus what it means to be a person.' Today we are 170 large families in the 'global village' and if we imagine that we are just one, then we have somehow downgraded 'human ecology'. Without national identities we somehow lose our reference point on earth.

From the above discussion it is clear that a world without national identities is a world with much less happiness than a world with national identities. Since happiness is of the utmost importance for the average human being, one can easily say that the side effect of losing national identities is not simply a negligible side effect of a harmless pill named the EU model. It has very strong side effects making the pill poisonous.

But what if, say, after 1,000 years or 10,000 years it becomes unavoidable that, owing to technological developments, national identities would be lost? Should we try to stop that?

It is a fact that today's world is characterised by an unprecedented rate of change – change driven by an accumulation of knowledge. Nationals of various countries definitely communicate more with each other in all sorts of ways (from the telephone, to the Internet, to tourist travel, to satellite television) and this inevitably leads to a gradual reduction of the different characteristics between the various national identities. But this phenomenon is a natural, very gradual change which is welcome simply because it is natural. There is no reason why people should be forced to expedite a change that could happen in 1,000 years (or 10,000 years) or make it happen in two hundred years through an inter-governmental grand design of worldwide social engineering. On the contrary, because all this technological change brings to each person huge changes in how she and her children see the world and what amount of information they receive daily (even if they don't want to), it is rational to say that humans will adjust better to this rapid change of technology around them if they do not at the same time live through the forced unnatural change of losing their most basic reference point on earth: their national identities.

One could even proceed further and offer the strange and maybe revolutionary thought that if humans always need a contrasting point for definition and reference and if, by simply natural technological developments, humans are going to lose this contrasting point after, say, 2,000 years, then maybe people should delay that date by a few thousand years so that in the meantime they can inhabit other planets and thus at that time create contrasting worlds? If contrasting national identities are necessary for happier and more stable lives, would it be better to delay the natural way of things until we of the old world on planet Earth create a new world on another planet and then abolish national identities on earth?

The answer to this is very hard. What is, however, very easy to answer is that we should not try by artificial government-induced measures to lose our national identities by any kind of grand inter-governmental social engineering. The easiest way to cope with information and technological change is by not changing whatever needs not to change and by keeping with us the reference points needed for psychological stability and happiness. The argument grading is in Figure 67.

Figure 67

Option 1 Member of the EU	Option 2 The alternative
Grade: 0/100,000	Grade: 2,000/100,000

6. Argument No. 6 (Philosophical)

> The evolution of the history of public affairs of people is characterised by movement from authoritarianism and slavery towards more and more power for the individual, towards wider representation of the individual. The EU model is a model going in the opposite direction.

Regarding public affairs, people started thousands years ago living under dictatorial chiefs of tribes or living under slavery and gradually moved towards representative democracy where they elected their lawmakers and administrative leaders. Since 1992 the lawmakers for the people of each member of the EU have been in effect their representatives in the Europarliament and the actual administrators are those in the Commission in Brussels. In earlier chapters we discussed how this is a fact and in later chapters we will see more evidence of examples of this de facto situation. Philosophically speaking, the Europarliament is a representative, democratic body, but with two major differences when compared to the national parliaments that existed in each member country up to 1992 (today they exist more or less only as talking forums, but not as lawmaking bodies).

The first difference is that the electorate making the laws for each country has changed. Before it was the electorate of the individual country. Now it is the electorate of fifteen countries that decides the laws of any particular country. This is a simple consequence of the fact that even if all the representatives of a particular country agree on a specific matter they are still a small minority in the Europarliament. This colossal change in the electoral base and its implications have been examined previously.

The second difference is that whereas before 1992 the population of a country was represented in its national parliament with a number of lawmakers, now it is represented with a substantially smaller number of lawmakers in the Europarliament. In simple terms, the Europarliament is representative democracy, but with a much more distant representation. There is much less contact between, say, the average citizen of Finland and her representative in the Europarliament simply because there are fewer representatives and they are far away in terms of distance.

On the other hand, the executive body in Brussels, known as the Commission, has centralised almost all the administrative powers of the fifteen member countries.

The EU model is in effect a model that is still democratic, but by definition with less representation of the average person in the decision-making process and more centralisation of powers. But if history is any guide, what was required before 1992 or even 1985 is decentralisation of powers from the national capitals to particular areas of each country, not centralisation of power from the national capitals to Brussels. And regarding the national parliaments, what historically was required was more direct representation of the people of each country in their lawmaking process, not less representation by having available a smaller number of representatives in Brussels or Strasbourg and neutralising the role of the national legislators.

Again from the point of view of history, developments that go against the tendency to give more real legislative and administrative powers to the average citizen are sooner or later overturned by the tide of human civilisation. The words 'Commission', 'Brussels' or 'Europarliament' are alien to the average person in any country and most of the time synonymous with the words 'bureaucracy' and 'ineffectiveness'. Those may be the early indications of the tide of history on a collision course with unnatural institutions and creatures.

There is no grading for this argument because the practical implications have been examined in detail in previous chapters.

7. Argument No. 7 (Philosophical)

> Today 'the village' is de facto the whole world; therefore, to try to create a fortress village named Europe is counterproductive and in the long term a futile exercise.

During the last two decades the whole world has changed profoundly. The ease of travel, the telecom revolution, the spread of television and the information technology revolution have produced a world where everybody trades with everybody regardless of geographical distances and where anyone communicates with anyone even in the most distant places on earth. It is a fact that we already live in a global village consisting of all 185 countries.

This global village has not been produced by some grand social design or enlightened engineering, but simply by natural, technological, economic and political developments, which have led to people trading or communicating with each other, not on the basis of race or religion or geographical area, but purely on the basis of their mutual private interests in the pursuit of maximum material progress and happiness. In such a global village there is not any philosophical reason for a group of people to try to create Fortress Europe. Creating fortresses is in essence a defensive, reactionary and counterproductive move compared to the vision of a global village of 185 houses communicating and trading in all directions. A fortress based on geography is implicitly on a collision course with free trade and unimpeded communication regardless of geographical distances. On the other hand, a fortress based on culture is doubly wrong, first on practical grounds and second in principle.

On practical grounds it is distortion of the truth to speak about a 'European' culture. Europe is a continent of at least forty different, deeply rooted and historic cultures, proud of themselves and of their histories. To say that there are not forty different cultures but only one culture is simply an unnecessary lie. The Greek culture has as many common elements with the culture of Germany as it has with the culture of Syria or Australia or Russia, and the Spanish culture has as many common elements with the Swedish or German cultures as it has with the Argentinian or Mexican cultures.

Second, and most importantly, to try to create an artificial European culture on the grounds of philosophical principle is related to a sense of cultural superiority (in the worst case) or cultural distinctiveness (in the best case). But cultural distinctiveness, when it is artificial and not natural, and especially when this distinctiveness is promoted by spending vast sums of money is against the tide of history. The whole notion of creating a 'European' or an 'Asian' or a Pan-American culture is contrary to the fact of the global village, which is already a reality today.

8. Argument No. 8 (Philosophical)

> In an ideal world and in the global village, there are no collective property rights or collective liberty for particular groups of people because we are all children of Mother Earth. Therefore, abolishing the sovereignty or independence of individual countries within the EU is a step in the right direction.

There are some people (a relatively small minority within each country) who are ideologues though well intentioned and who believe that, since we are all human beings and since we all inherited the earth, there is not much meaning in phrases such as, 'This area (the country known as Germany) belongs to the German people,' since the Germans are in reality brothers and sisters of the French and the other people on the continent of Europe. In other words, they say that the Germans cannot exercise collective property rights over a specific geographical area since we have all inherited the same continent.

When someone then argues that, by extension of the above, the continent of Europe has been inherited by all mankind and therefore there should not be collective property rights even over the whole continent of Europe in the form of EU citizenship, and in the form of Fortress Europe, they essentially agree and suggest that this is the first step towards a more just world where, at a distant time in the future, no nation will exercise control over a particular geographical area. The same, they say, applies to the expression of collective liberty by a group of people. There can be no collective liberty of a particular group of people to do whatever they like with their own lives because, they say, expression of such a collective liberty contradicts the collective liberty of the one and only group of people that exists, the international community or humanity. In other words, the group is the whole of humanity consisting of a great number of individuals. In the long run, they say, a nation cannot exercise collective free will within the whole group of humanity in the same way that today the people of a city cannot exercise collective free will independent of the will of the whole country within which the city exists. Individuals have rights, but in the long term people living in geographical areas known as countries should not have collective rights because the only actual country is the whole world. Thus, the argument runs, since there should not be collective property rights and collective liberty, there is no point in talking about the sovereignty or independence of countries.

The argument is very powerful, philosophical and therefore very difficult to answer. However, an attempt will be made here to give two short answers on two completely different grounds.

Firstly, on practical grounds, suppose for a moment that the argument is correct and that after 10,000 years, owing to natural, technological and other developments, no particular group of people will exercise collective rights over any area or over its own particular way of life because it will be subject to the general rights and will of the whole of humanity. But is there any reason why those natural developments should be expedited by grand social engineering in such a way that they happen in one hundred to two hundred years instead of the next 10,000 years? The assumption of the argument is that this development would happen naturally anyway over a very long period until there are no particular groups of people with particular rights. But if this development is to happen naturally by the free will of free people, what is the reason for tremendously expediting such a development? Here there is no rational explanation, because the moment the development starts being expedited and engineered by some grand social design, that very moment the development ceases to be natural and becomes unnatural. But unnatural developments are not welcome in general. Moreover, someone could suggest that if ageing for a human being is a natural development, is there any reason why a rational person should expedite his or her ageing? If death is the final outcome of any life, should a rational human being commit suicide today to expedite the natural end of life?

Secondly, on philosophical grounds, the argument about non-existent collective rights of a group of people is most probably wrong. In general, after several thousand years of human history, three rights are almost universally accepted as natural rights of the individual: the natural right to individual liberty, the natural right to own property individually and the natural right to the pursuit of happiness. But what is the collective liberty of a group of people known as a nation or a country? It is simply the sum of their individual liberties! And what is the collective property right of a group of people known as a nation or a country? It is simply the sum of their individual property rights! And what is the collective right to the pursuit of happiness of a group of people known as a nation or a country? It is simply their ability to live their lives the way they wish to!

In other words, if we accept the existence as natural rights of individual liberty, property and the pursuit of happiness, then we accept by default their collective expression, which in two words is known as sovereignty and independence. To accept individual liberty, property and the pursuit of happiness and not to accept their collective expressions is at least inconsistent and at worst could mean that deep inside one does not believe even in those individual rights.

But now we come to a very philosophical point. Do individual property rights exist as natural rights? Does individual liberty exist as a natural right? The answer to this is axiomatic. Either one believes or does not believe in those axioms. The axioms cannot be proven or disproven. They are simply axioms. So, some people are entitled to believe that in an ideal world there are no natural individual property rights and some other people are entitled to believe the opposite.

How can the civilised nations proceed in this crucial matter of axioms? Simply by using the utmost democratic principle: the majority of beliefs of the people is the way forward. And since the vast majority of the people today believe in the existence of individual rights in both property and liberty, we have then to accept them as axioms and live our lives accordingly.

Chapter XIV
THE VERDICT BETWEEN THE EU AND THE ALTERNATIVE

In the last four chapters we have compared, on theoretical and practical grounds, the EU as an option and the alternative as another option. Counting the grades in all the arguments (economic, political, and philosophical), we find that the alternative appears to win by a great margin on almost all fronts. The main advantages of the alternative as the best way forward are:

- Fully decentralised development instead of centralisation.
- Responsibility and incentives instead of non-accountability.
- Much wider democracy instead of anonymous and distant bureaucracy.
- Real decision-making power to the ordinary citizen.
- Free markets instead of a single market, singularity on anything is going backwards, plurality is the way forwards.
- Free trade not only between fifteen nations, but in essence free trade between 185 nations; freedom is good in all directions and there are no particular preferable directions.
- Keeping the peace for ever needs education and full democracy; it does not need the dismantling of the sovereignty or of the independence of countries.
- Cultural individuality, languages and distinctiveness of human societies are better preserved with the alternative as part of the general environmental and ecological effort for natural equilibrium through diversity.
- Happiness considerations make necessary the existence of particular groups of people known as sovereign countries; the simple existence of a pan-continental group of people or of the whole of humanity is not sufficient to make a person accept that he or she belongs somewhere or that he or she is not just a number.

Our discussion in Part Two was both theoretical and practical, but avoided hard and detailed evidence about what the EU really is today and where it will lead each member in the long run. This evidence is presented in Part Three with a great number of specific and scattered examples taken from the media and the press.

Part Three
What the EU Is Today – The Simple Facts

Chapter XV
HARD EVIDENCE

Introduction

Up to now we have tried to see if the EU and the EMU are beneficial to the average citizen of any country and we tried to compare the EU with an alternative model. During the course of our discussion we made claims such as: 'No country within the EU can be sovereign or independent' or that 'The EU or the Union or Europe is the sovereign and independent country and the fifteen members are simply areas or states.' These and many other similar claims may be obvious to political activists, but most probably are not at all obvious to the average person on the street. In this part (Part Three) we give a number of simple facts or cite events taken mostly from the daily press or the media in general and to each fact or event we attach some comments. The comments all highlight the short-term and especially the long-term implications of what the EU is today and tend to substantiate all our previous claims. They do not, however, attempt to discuss at all whether the EU is a good or a bad thing because this has already been examined before. Here we only give events or facts. In each example the comments are very brief and in most instances they are oriented towards the long-term consequences.

Whenever possible, the relevant press announcements are exhibited or highlighted. The examples are taken in all spheres of the public domain – economic, political, cultural, philosophical – and are only a very small number, a drop in the sea of examples that one could mention. They are nevertheless sufficient to make clear what exactly the EU is today.

The examples are taken mostly from factual statements, announcements or events during 1997 and are presented without regard to the discipline – monetary, economic, political, cultural, philosophical.

Example No. 1

A copy of a certificate of origin for two wooden boats is shown in Figure 68. The two boats were exported from Greece to Saudi Arabia in August 1996.

Figure 68

1 Αποστολέας (Consignor - Espéditer) TRADING SA ,DILIGIANNI STR. KIFISSIA	A 12461	ΠΡΩΤΟΤΥΠΟ ORIGINAL
2 Παραλήπτης (Consignee - Destinataire) TECHNICAL SERVICES S.A. P.O. BOX 516 JEDDAH 21422 AL MALEK ROAD OBHUR	ΕΥΡΩΠΑΪΚΗ ΚΟΙΝΟΤΗΤΑ - EUROPEAN COMMUNITY COMMUNAUTÉ EUROPÉENNE ΠΙΣΤΟΠΟΙΗΤΙΚΟ ΚΑΤΑΓΩΓΗΣ CERTIFICATE OF ORIGIN CERTIFICAT D' ORIGINE	
	3 Χώρα καταγωγής (Country of Origin - Pays d' origine) GREECE	
4 Ενδείξεις σχετικές με τη μεταφορά (μνεία προαιρετική) Transport details (Optional) Informations relatives au transport (mention facultative) BY SHIP	5 Παρατηρήσεις (Remarks - Remarques)	
6 Αύξων αριθμός, σημεία, αριθμοί, αριθμός και φύση των δεμάτων, περιγραφή των εμπορευμάτων Item number, marks, number and kind of packages, description of goods No d' ordre, marques, numéros nombre et nature des colis, désignation des marchandises		7 Ποσότητα Quantity Quantité
2 pcs WOODEN BOATS 4 meters 1,70 X 0,75 m		800 Kgr

8 Η ΥΠΟΓΡΑΦΟΥΣΑ ΑΡΧΗ ΒΕΒΑΙΩΝΕΙ ΟΤΙ ΤΑ ΑΝΩΤΕΡΩ ΠΕΡΙΓΡΑΦΟΜΕΝΑ ΕΜΠΟΡΕΥΜΑΤΑ ΚΑΤΑΓΟΝΤΑΙ ΑΠΟ ΤΗΝ ΧΩΡΑ ΠΟΥ ΑΝΑΦΕΡΕΤΑΙ ΣΤΗ ΘΕΣΗ 3
THE UNDERSIGNED AUTHORITY CERTIFIES THAT THE GOODS DESCRIBED ABOVE ORIGINATE IN THE COUNTRY SHOW IN BOX 3
L'AUTORITE SOUSSIGNÉE CERTIFIE QUE LES MARCHANDISES DESIGNEES CI- DESSUS SONT OROGINAIRES DU PAYS FIGURANT DANS LA CASE No 3

ATHENS CHAMBER
OF COMMERCE AND INDUSTRY
7, AKADEMIAS STR.
106 71 ATHENS GREECE
27 AUG 1996
Τόπος και ημερομηνία εκδόσεως, όνομα, υπογραφή και σφραγίδα της αρμόδιας Αρχής.
Place and date of issue: signature and stamp of competent authority.
Lieu et daté de délivrance. désignation, signature et cachet de l' autorité compétente

COMMENT

At the top and right of the certificate in large capital letters appears the phrase: EUROPEAN COMMUNITY. Below this, in much smaller letters the country of origin is mentioned. Now, let us imagine the Saudi customs clearance employee or, in fact, any person who reads this paper. The impression that one gets is that the two boats are in fact coming from the European Community and in particular from a sub-area called Greece. After maybe five years the words 'country of origin' could be changed to 'state of origin' (to be closer to the truth) but already the impression gained by any reader of this document is that the two wooden boats come from an entity called the EUROPEAN COMMUNITY or EU. If we imagine the same certificate issued in similar form for the next fifty years, it is easy to understand that, at least as far as the certificate of origin is concerned, the actual entity exporting is the EU, not Greece.

Example No. 2

EU WILL BLOCK FRENCH BID FOR END TO SUMMER TIME

Brussels, March 10 (AFP)

France's bid to have the twice-yearly clock change in continental Europe abolished will be blocked by its European Union partners at talks tomorrow, EU officials said. EU transport ministers are expected to agree in principle that the current EU rules governing time changes should be extended after 1998, when the current directive expires.

France wants to keep the same time all year around, arguing that the time changes disturb the biological rhythms of children and old people, increase air pollution and seriously disrupt farmers.

Tomorrow's decision on a common EU position will be taken by qualified majority voting, which means France cannot veto a deal on a renewal of the directive.

Arab News
11 March 1997

COMMENT

If French citizens, through their elected government, cannot set the time according to their own wishes, interests or preferences, if the same applies to the citizens of any other country within the EU, then on which matter can the citizens of any country decide for themselves what they perceive to be in their own interests? If the EU regulates time setting then is there anything that it does not regulate or that it should not regulate? Why can each country not set the time according to the wishes of its citizens as those wishes are expressed through their democratically elected government? Is Brussels wiser than the collective will of the people of any country? But even if Brussels is wiser than the collective will of, say, the Swedish or Finnish people, why should it impose this will on them? Democratic governance does not mean that the government of the people is always right. It simply means that it expresses the will of the majority of the people in a country and that the people are responsible to gradually correct any deficiencies in their governing regulations.

The only rational explanation for this directive to the French government about time setting is that, by all countries changing their time on the same days of the year and only according to the rules of Brussels, their citizens gradually, generation after generation, will feel like citizens of the same country and they will always know who is their real government.

Example No. 3

EDITORIAL
TAXING PROBLEMS

The latest proposal in Brussels is to abolish the different tax status of residents and non-residents. The target is not citizens of non-EU member states who live outside the EU but who may have deposits there. It is those who live in one EU state but place savings in another, where of course, they are non-resident and so avoid tax.

Ten years ago, it was reckoned that the tax authorities in Western Europe were together losing around $16 billion a year in tax revenue because of increasing mass mobility. For example, retired Danes living part of the year in Spain (but never long enough to be classified as resident) might have a tidy portion of their life savings in the UK where, of course, it was tax exempt. Or it might have been Frenchmen keeping quiet about investments in Luxembourg.

Today, the problem has grown out of all proportion. It is now estimated that EU member state treasuries could be losing as much as $100 billion a year. The mass movement of Europe's citizenry back and forward across its internal borders has shot way ahead of the member governments' ability to cope with it. Germany alone is said to be losing $12 billion worth of tax revenue because of Germans placing deposits in Luxembourg banks, where such investment enjoy tax-free status. Twelve billion dollars would be more than enough to solve Chancellor Kohl's financial headaches. He could meet the conditions for joining the single currency without the damage currently being inflicted on the German economy.

The matter could be dealt with by the simple procedure of the 15 tax authorities coordinating their information networks. However, it could equally be derailed by the Euro-standardisation lobby which wants to see tax harmonisation, with the same corporation tax, the same income tax and the same value-added tax from Orkney to Otranto, and a single tax gathering institution to boot. But this is not something that the British or Danes will countenance, and probably not even the French or Germans. Nor is there any reason why, even in a federal Europe, the standard tax regime should apply.

A harmonisation of information, however, is another matter. To exchange details about the financial activities of everyone within their borders (and that means everyone, citizens of the EU as well as non-citizens alike) implies no loss of sovereignty.

Arab News
9 March 1997

COMMENT

The editorial is about taxing the bank deposits of anyone anywhere in the EU. Firstly, the matter of taxing deposits of non-residents is at least controversial philosophically for two simple reasons: a non-resident is not using the roads, hospitals, schools, police, etc. of the country. Therefore it is rational that he or she should not pay taxes on the deposits in the bank. Secondly, and most importantly, a country may for many reasons wish to attract capital because capital is what is needed for its economy to grow. Why should this country be denied the option to attract deposits into its banks by not taxing them or by taxing at only a very small percentage? But the above two points are one million times less important than the following points.

Point 1

A country may wish today, for whatever reason, to tax the deposits in the banks by non-residents and residents. But suppose that tomorrow the people of the country, by working hard and making a lot of sacrifices, have achieved a budget surplus. Their public finances are thus in very good shape and, according to common sense and standard economic theory, they decide to reduce taxation starting by eliminating taxation on deposits in the banks of the country for both residents and non-residents. Can they eliminate taxation in their bank deposits? Can they reap the fruits of their hard work, of their collective successful effort to put their public finances in order? The simple answer is, *no, they cannot. They remain prisoners of the situation in all other countries as expressed by Brussels.*

Point 2

Harmonisation (which is another word for making things identical) of anything is not a precondition for success. It is a precondition for strangling any initiative; it is a precondition for not rewarding those who want to or who can move fast; it is a guarantee for moving slowly or a guarantee for long-term failure.

Point 3

The editorial speaks about 'harmonisation of information'; the expression is deceiving. The correct one is 'synchronisation of spying by government authorities on the activities of its citizens and especially of citizens of other countries'. (Or maybe they are not from 'other countries' but we are all in effect in one country?)

Point 4

The editorial says that 'To exchange details about the financial activities of everyone within their borders implies no loss of sovereignty'. It implies, however, loss of liberty for the individuals without any justifiable reason.

The end result of all this, as implied by the key words, will be: harmonisation of taxation on deposits so that everywhere they go the people will feel the same and therefore upcoming generations will not differentiate between their country and the others. Their de facto country will be the EU.

Example No. 4

EU CHIEF SLAMS G-7 STYLE CLUB IN EURO ZONE
Brussels, January 27 (AFP)

Belgian Finance Minister Philippe Maystadt said the fact that the launch of the Euro was only 704 days away made it urgent for the EU to step up the pace of *fiscal harmonisation*, particularly *in the taxation of companies and private investments held by non-residents*.

'It is intolerable that companies can switch from one country to another to take advantage of lower corporate taxation,' he said.'

Arab News
28 January 1997

COMMENT

Again we see the word harmonisation, which in reality means 'making things the same' and is the opposite of diversity.

The minister speaks about fiscal harmonisation. With the abolishing of national currencies there is automatically and by definition monetary harmonisation. If, in addition to monetary, there is fiscal harmonisation and, since fiscal and monetary policies are the only economic policy tools available to any government, then we come to the conclusion that all governments will have the same economic policies indefinitely. Then how is good government to be differentiated from the mediocre? There is no way to tell because all economic policies will be the same. In this case, instead of many governments, the participating countries should have just one and not tolerate the illusion that each state has its own government. Harmonisation is the death of contrast. And the death of contrast is the death of competition for the best practices in policies.

Suppose that the citizens of a country, owing to their hard work and diligent government, reduce their public debt or eliminate their public debt. This is not only possible, but highly desirable. In this case it is natural that, in order to attract employers and reduce unemployment, the people of the country can instruct their government to drastically reduce the taxation of corporations who can come from every corner of the earth and set up shop in the country. But according to the press announcement this would become impossible because taxation of corporations should be the identical (harmonised). In fact, any variation in taxation of corporations is, according to the excerpt, 'intolerable'. What should be, under rational thinking and under good economic practice, desirable is intolerable. In this case why should the people of the country try to work hard, to reduce their government spending, to reduce their total debt, to reduce taxation, to attract more foreign investment in order to reduce unemployment if, by definition, they cannot do that unless all other people in the EU decide to do the same, agree to do the same and finally achieve in practice the same reduction of government spending? You cannot differ from the others according to the finance minister because if you can differ then you will be better than the others and if you can be better than the others then you will attract more foreign investment. But in economic life being richer does not mean that the neighbour becomes poorer. On the contrary, the neighbour becomes richer. Being better, being more successful than the others, is what moves human history forward. Being harmonised, being identical, means being still, being stagnant.

Example No. 5

CUBA ROW TO DOMINATE EU TALKS WITH ALBRIGHT
Brussels, January 26 (AFP)

The transatlantic row over controversial US legislation on Cuba, Iran and Libya will dominate the first meeting *between the European Union and new US Secretary of State* [1] Madeleine Albright this week, officials said.

Albright, sworn in last week, will make her debut as Washington's leading voice on the international stage on Tuesday when she receives *Dutch Foreign Minister Hans van Mierlo, representing the EU's current presidency*, [2] *and European Trade Commissioner Sir Leon Brittan.* [3]

Prior to the meeting with Albright, Brittan is due to discuss Cuba and other trade related issues in meetings with Treasury Secretary Robert Rubin, top trade officials Charlene Barshevsky and Stuart Eizenstat.

Efforts to conclude a global deal [4] on the liberalisation of telecommunications by mid-February and progress towards eliminating non-tariff barriers to *EU–US trade* [5] are expected to dominate these talks.

Arab News
27 January 1997

COMMENT

Remarks correspond to the numbers inserted in the text.

Point 1

The impression that one gets is that the Secretary of State of a country named the US is to meet representatives of a country named the European Union. Similar phrases repeated over a number of years in the media (especially since 1992) are making the EU a de facto country. The subsequent generations will thus find it natural to think that the EU is a country.

Point 2

The representative of the president of the country named the EU.

Point 3

The Trade Minister (or Commissioner) of the country named the EU or Europe. We saw on page 182 why the word 'Commissioner' is somehow hiding the correct word which is 'minister'.

Point 4

We saw on page 134 that the individual states of the EU have been excluded from all kinds of global deals (and even from not so global deals). We see this now in action. In the very important deal for liberalising the worldwide telecommunications markets (valued at present at $700 billion annually at least) the trade ministers of countries like Germany or France or Italy are not participating.

But what would be the problem if everybody participated in the table discussing the liberalisation? The obvious answer is that the fewer voices the better for the deal. But this is against the most basic democratic principle that everyone should have their say and that if they agreed that the deal was beneficial for their people they should sign the deal, but if they thought that the deal would be not beneficial for their people they should either try to modify it or not sign it. There is not such a thing as the less the representation the better or the faster the deal simply because, by the same token, one parliamentarian from each party within an individual country could represent all other members of parliament of the same party on every matter, reduce the parliament to just a few parliamentarians and thus make speedier and easier the discussion and passage of every law. But this is narrowing the democratic representation, not widening it.

We should move in the opposite direction, giving if possible to each voter the power to decide on everything, not narrow his or her representation in parliament. The argument that collective representation of nations in trade deals is more effective or speedier is fallacious and contrary to the very principles of democracy. The individual representation of each nation in all international forums is safeguarding the true interests of each nation, reinforces its peaceful and democratic existence, produces outcomes more transparent and just and, in the long run, ensures the plurality and diversity of voices and opinions necessary for humanity to move forward with the maximum possible speed.

Point 5

EU–US trade. Since the US is a country there is no doubt that the EU must be a de facto country. At least this is what the incoming generations will understand and be led to believe. And they are right to believe so.

Example No. 6

MINORITY TONGUES ALTER EU'S LINGUISTIC COMPLEXION
Brussels

The spread of *English as Europe's lingua franca* [1] and the revival of more than 40 minority languages, some of which were close to extinction, are transforming the European Union's linguistic environment, a new report says.

The European Bureau of Lesser Used Languages [2], which published its annual report in Brussels this week, says that one in seven people in the EU speaks a minority language.

The bureau, a non-profit-making organisation based in Dublin and *supported by the EU*, [3] says it does not see its role as preserving a *European tower of Babel*. [4]

Arab News
25 January 1997

COMMENT

Point 1

In a single market a single language will sooner or later prevail. With the extinction of all other languages we will have the extinction of the great part of all other cultures. Without the single market but with many free markets, a single language is not necessary and in any case, if some languages become extinct owing to natural causes in, say, 1,000 years, with the unnaturally imposed single market they will become extinct in the next few generations.

Another very crucial question here is: since a single market requires a single language for obvious reasons, then why has the Commission not explicitly declared such an aim to make, say, English the single language of the single market? Obviously, the reason is not that the people in Brussels do not recognise or do not desire to impose a single language on everybody. The reason is that such a move, once understood, would be resisted fiercely and jeopardise the aim of creating a single country. Therefore, they have chosen the path of least resistance: set up the single market and the single language together with the single culture will come in one or two generations in a way that will appear to be natural.

Point 2

Does the average Italian or British or Portuguese citizen know about the existence of the Bureau? Obviously not. Would it be much more effective if a country wishing to preserve any of its minority languages had such a bureau within its own borders, under its own supervision and instructions? Preservation of minority languages and cultures is a very important aim to be left to a bureau a thousand kilometres away from the place where the minority language is spoken.

Point 3

'Supported by the EU' is an indirect way of saying 'supported 100% from the Commission's yearly budget', which is in turn the sum of automatic contributions from the yearly budgets of the fifteen national governments that collect all their yearly budget money from the taxpayers of each nation.

Point 4

It is very strange that the towers of Babel under the names of Commission, Europarliament, Euro-Court of Justice and EU do not wish to preserve a European tower of Babel. However, it is exactly this cultural diversity which should be preserved and which is day after day being destroyed by the single market. What the EU sees as a linguistic tower of Babel is actually the only way forward for humanity: independent, diversified and decentralised development of each culture in a world where everyone trades with anyone else on earth. But this cannot happen in a single market or in a single country.

Example No. 7

SINGAPORE TRADE GROWTH TAKES SHARP DIVE IN 1996
Singapore, January 20 (AFP)

Singapore said today that its trade growth took a sharp dive last year but expressed guarded optimism that 1997 would produce a modest recovery in line with an upturn in world electronics demand.

Growth of non-oil exports to three top markets – the *United States, European Union and Japan* – slowed to single digit-rates and declined for Malaysia and Hong Kong by 3.4 percent and 4.8 percent respectively.

Arab News
21 January 1997

COMMENT

In the subconscious of the average reader all over the world, the following message is translated as a side effect of the news. Since the USA, Japan, Malaysia and Hong Kong are countries, then the European Union must be a country. Especially for upcoming generations the message is very clear and when repeated over a period of time it will reflect reality. All this is possible because of Eurostat (see our argument on page 90). The taxpayers of all fifteen states pay through their governments to run Eurostat. In turn, Eurostat finds it natural to integrate all statistics, in effect eclipsing all fifteen member states (including Germany). Whether eclipsing fifteen countries is what the people have asked is a completely different question.

Example No. 8

RISING JOBLESS TOTAL WORRIES BUNDESBANK
Frankfurt, January 20 (AFP)

Bundesbank President Hans Tietmeyer confirmed today that unemployment is at the centre of the central bank's concern about the state of the economy *in Germany and Europe*. [1]

The German unemployment rate surged to 10.8 percent in December from 10.3 percent in November and many experts warn that the number is likely to rise from about 4.1 million now to 4.5 million next year.

Official data published last week showed that in November 18.2 million people, or 10.9 percent of the workforce, *were unemployed in the European Union*, [2] from 10.8 percent in November 1995.

Arab News
21 January 1997

COMMENT

Point 1

Europe here is obviously another name for the EU. The question is why the central bank of Germany is not focused only on unemployment in Germany, but is also focused on unemployment in other countries. The answer is that the German central bank knows very well what we said on the theoretical level on pages 108 and 178. Because of integration and the harmonisation of monetary and fiscal policies no single state has control over its unemployment rate (or any other major economic problem for that matter). Because of common legislation, common regulations and common fiscal and monetary policies no national government can exercise effective control over its own unemployment rate. But since when did the German people explicitly instruct their authorities (which are temporary custodians of the people for four years at a time) to abolish for ever their ability to exercise control over their unemployment rate?

Point 2

We see here again Eurostat in action (as we saw in the previous example) and the indirect but very effective creation of a country named the EU with one unemployment rate and in the process the eclipsing of the individual countries.

Example No. 9

WORLD'S TOP EMPLOYER URGES MORE FLEXIBILITY
Lisbon (AFP)

Tourism employs more people than any other industry in the world but to continue to create jobs, travel and hotel industries want greater flexibility in labour legislation, professionals meeting here said.

The World Travel Tourism Council (WTTC) which organised the two-day gathering at Vilamoura in the Algarve region of southern Portugal, also called on governments to pay more attention to the needs of tourism professionals, notably by liberalising the transport market and other exchanges.

However, the tourist industry remains convinced that it has a key role to play in fighting unemployment. 'Tourism creates jobs and wealth as jobs are created rapidly and at a low cost,' *said the European commissioner for tourism*, [1] Christos Papoutsis in a speech to the participants.

In the European Union, [2] tourism accounts for 5.5 percent of *gross national product [3] and six percent of jobs*. [4] Papoutsis said 2.5 million new jobs were expected to be created in the *15 member states* [5] by 2006.

Arab News
21 January 1997

COMMENT

Point 1
The correct word would be minister instead of Commissioner.

Point 2
The proper and complete expression would be, 'In the country called the European Union'.

Point 3
The Gross National Product of which nation? Obviously of the nation called the EU.

Point 4
'Six per cent of jobs' in which country? Obviously in the one called the EU.

Point 5
'Member states' is an appropriate expression for entities without sovereignty (like the states of Texas or Alabama). For entities with sovereignty one usually uses the word 'country' or 'nation'. Therefore here, the word 'states' reflects correctly the reality which is most probably unknown to the average citizen of any of those member states.

Example No. 10

On the following pages a copy of a statistical table about the movement of currencies is shown from the weekly magazine *Asiaweek* of 10 January 1997.

ASIAWEEK CURRENCIES

ONE UNIT OF	IS WORTH	UNITED STATES DOLLAR	JAPAN YEN	HONG KONG DOLLAR	SINGAPORE DOLLAR	MALAYSIA RINGGIT	PHILIPPINES PESO	THAILAND BAHT	INDONESIA RUPIAH	SOUTH KOREA WON	TAIWAN N.T. DOLLAR	CHINA RENMINBI	MYANMAR KYAT	CAMBODIA RIEL	LAOS KIP	VIETNAM DONG	INDIA RUPEE	PAKISTAN RUPEE
UNITED STATES	DOLLAR	1	116	7.74	1.40	2.53	28.30	25.64	2,363	844	27.50	8.30	164	2,686	950	11,094	35.85	40.08
JAPAN	100 YEN	0.86	100	6.67	1.21	2.18	22.66	22.09	2,036	727	23.70	7.15	141	2,315	819	9,560	30.90	34.54
HONG KONG	DOLLAR	0.13	15	1	0.18	0.33	3.40	3.31	305	109	3.55	1.07	21	347	123	1,434	4.63	5.18
SINGAPORE	DOLLAR	0.71	83	5.53	1	1.81	18.78	18.32	1,688	603	19.64	5.93	117	1,919	679	7,924	25.61	28.63
MALAYSIA	RINGGIT	0.40	46	3.06	0.55	1	10.40	10.14	935	334	10.88	3.28	65	1,062	376	4,388	14.18	15.85
PHILIPPINES	PESO	0.04	4	0.29	0.05	0.10	1	0.98	90	32	1.05	0.32	6	102	36	422	1.36	1.52
THAILAND	BAHT	0.04	5	0.30	0.05	0.10	1.03	1	92	33	1.07	0.32	6	105	37	433	1.40	1.56
INDONESIA	100 RUPIAH	0.04	5	0.33	0.06	0.11	1.11	1.09	100	36	1.16	0.35	7	114	40	469	1.52	1.70
SOUTH KOREA	100 WON	0.12	14	0.92	0.17	0.30	3.12	3.04	280	100	3.26	0.98	19	318	113	1,315	4.25	4.75
TAIWAN	N.T. DOLLAR	0.04	4	0.28	0.05	0.09	0.96	0.93	86	31	1	0.30	6	98	35	403	1.30	1.46
CHINA	RENMINBI	0.12	14	0.93	0.17	0.30	3.17	3.09	285	102	3.31	1	20	324	114	1,337	4.32	4.83
MYANMAR	100 KYAT	0.61	71	4.72	0.85	1.54	16.03	15.63	1,441	515	16.77	5.06	100	1,638	579	6,765	21.86	24.44
CAMBODIA	100 RIEL	0.04	4	0.29	0.05	0.09	0.98	0.95	88	31	1.02	0.31	6	100	35	413	1.33	1.49
LAOS	100 KIP	0.11	12	0.81	0.15	0.27	2.77	2.70	249	89	2.89	0.87	17	283	100	1,168	3.77	4.22
VIETNAM	1,000 DONG	0.09	10	0.70	0.13	0.23	2.37	2.31	213	76	2.48	0.75	15	242	86	1,000	3.23	3.61
INDIA	RUPEE	0.03	3	0.22	0.04	0.07	0.73	0.72	66	24	0.77	0.23	5	75	26	309	1	1.12
PAKISTAN	RUPEE	0.02	3	0.19	0.03	0.06	0.66	0.64	59	21	0.69	0.21	4	67	24	277	0.89	1
SRI LANKA	RUPEE	0.02	2	0.14	0.02	0.04	0.46	0.45	42	15	0.48	0.15	3	47	17	196	0.63	0.71
BANGLADESH	TAKA	0.02	3	0.18	0.03	0.06	0.62	0.60	55	20	0.65	0.19	4	63	22	260	0.84	0.94
NEPAL	RUPEE	0.02	2	0.14	0.02	0.04	0.46	0.45	42	15	0.48	0.15	3	47	17	195	0.63	0.71
SAUDI ARABIA	RIYAL	0.27	31	2.06	0.37	0.67	7.01	6.84	630	225	7.33	2.21	44	716	253	2,958	9.56	10.69
IRAN	100 RIAL	0.03	4	0.26	0.05	0.08	0.88	0.01	79	28	0.92	0.28	5	90	32	370	1.20	1.34
TURKEY	1,000 LIRA	0.01	1	0.07	0.01	0.02	0.24	0.24	22	8	0.25	0.08	2	25	9	102	0.33	0.37
RUSSIA	100 RUBLE	0.02	2	0.14	0.03	0.05	0.48	0.46	43	15	0.50	0.15	3	49	17	200	0.65	0.72
PAPUA NEW GUINEA	KINA	0.74	86	5.73	1.04	1.87	19.48	19.00	1,751	625	20.38	6.15	122	1,990	704	8,221	26.57	29.70
AUSTRALIA	DOLLAR	0.80	92	6.17	1.12	2.01	20.95	20.43	1,883	672	21.91	6.61	131	2,140	757	8,840	28.57	31.94
NEW ZEALAND	DOLLAR	0.71	82	5.48	0.99	1.79	18.62	18.15	1,673	597	19.47	5.88	116	1,902	673	7,855	25.39	28.38
CANADA	DOLLAR	0.73	85	5.66	1.02	1.85	19.22	18.74	1,727	617	20.10	6.07	120	1,963	694	8,110	26.21	29.30
MEXICO	NEW PESO	0.13	15	0.99	0.18	0.32	3.35	3.26	301	107	3.50	1.06	21	342	121	1,413	4.57	5.10
BRITAIN	POUND	1.69	196	13.07	2.36	4.27	44.42	43.31	3,992	1,425	46.45	14.02	277	4,537	1,605	18,740	60.56	67.70
FRANCE	FRANC	0.19	22	1.48	0.27	0.48	5.02	4.90	451	161	5.25	1.58	31	513	181	2,119	6.85	7.65
GERMANY	MARK	0.64	75	4.98	0.90	1.63	16.91	16.49	1,519	543	17.68	5.34	105	1,727	611	7,133	23.05	25.77
SWITZERLAND	FRANC	0.74	86	5.74	1.04	1.88	19.51	19.03	1,754	626	20.41	6.16	122	1,993	705	8,233	26.61	29.74
EUROPE	ECU	1.24	144	9.60	1.74	3.14	32.63	31.82	2,932	1,047	34.12	10.30	203	3,333	1,179	13,766	44.49	49.73

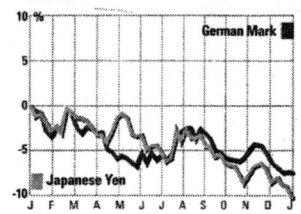

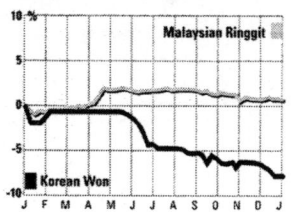

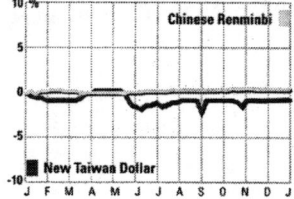

MOVEMENT OF CURRENCIES AGAINST THE U.S. DOLLAR

HARD EVIDENCE

DECEMBER 30, 1996

SRI LANKA RUPEE	BANGLADESH TAKA	NEPAL RUPEE	SAUDI ARABIA RIYAL	IRAN RIAL	TURKEY LIRA	RUSSIA RUBLE	PAPUA NEW GUINEA KINA	AUSTRALIA DOLLAR	NEW ZEALAND DOLLAR	CANADA DOLLAR	MEXICO NEW PESO	BRITAIN POUND	FRANCE FRANC	GERMANY MARK	SWITZERLAND FRANC	EUROPE ECU	IS WORTH	ONE UNIT OF
56.74	42.61	56.78	3.75	3,000	108,320	5,534	1.35	1.26	1.41	1.37	7.85	0.59	5.24	1.56	1.35	0.81	UNITED STATES	DOLLAR
48.89	36.72	48.92	3.23	2,585	93,339	4,769	1.16	1.08	1.22	1.18	6.77	0.51	4.51	1.34	1.16	0.69	JAPAN	100 YEN
7.33	5.51	7.34	0.48	388	13,999	715	0.17	0.16	0.18	0.18	1.02	0.08	0.68	0.20	0.17	0.10	HONG KONG	DOLLAR
40.53	30.44	40.55	2.68	2,143	77,371	3,953	0.96	0.90	1.01	0.98	5.61	0.42	3.74	1.11	0.96	0.58	SINGAPORE	DOLLAR
22.44	16.85	22.45	1.48	1,186	42,840	2,189	0.53	0.50	0.56	0.54	3.11	0.23	2.07	0.62	0.53	0.32	MALAYSIA	RINGGIT
2.16	1.62	2.16	0.14	114	4,119	210	0.05	0.05	0.05	0.05	0.30	0.02	0.20	0.06	0.05	0.03	PHILIPPINES	PESO
2.21	1.66	2.21	0.15	117	4,224	216	0.05	0.05	0.06	0.05	0.31	0.02	0.20	0.06	0.05	0.03	THAILAND	BAHT
2.40	1.80	2.40	0.16	127	4,584	234	0.06	0.05	0.06	0.06	0.33	0.03	0.22	0.07	0.06	0.03	INDONESIA	100 RUPIAH
6.72	5.05	6.73	0.44	356	12,837	656	0.16	0.15	0.17	0.16	0.93	0.07	0.62	0.18	0.16	0.10	SOUTH KOREA	100 WON
2.05	1.55	2.05	0.14	109	3,939	201	0.05	0.05	0.05	0.05	0.29	0.02	0.19	0.06	0.05	0.03	TAIWAN	N.T. DOLLAR
6.84	5.13	6.84	0.45	361	13,052	667	0.16	0.15	0.17	0.16	0.95	0.07	0.63	0.19	0.16	0.10	CHINA	RENMINBI
34.59	25.98	34.62	2.29	1,829	66,049	3,374	0.82	0.77	0.86	0.83	4.79	0.36	3.19	0.95	0.82	0.49	MYANMAR	100 KYAT
2.11	1.59	2.11	0.14	112	4,033	206	0.05	0.05	0.05	0.05	0.29	0.02	0.19	0.06	0.05	0.03	CAMBODIA	100 RIEL
5.97	4.49	5.98	0.39	316	11,402	583	0.14	0.13	0.15	0.14	0.83	0.06	0.55	0.16	0.14	0.08	LAOS	100 KIP
5.11	3.84	5.12	0.34	270	9,764	499	0.12	0.11	0.13	0.12	0.71	0.05	0.47	0.14	0.12	0.07	VIETNAM	1,000 DONG
1.58	1.19	1.58	0.10	84	3,021	154	0.04	0.04	0.04	0.04	0.22	0.02	0.15	0.04	0.04	0.02	INDIA	RUPEE
1.42	1.06	1.42	0.09	75	2,703	138	0.03	0.03	0.04	0.03	0.20	0.01	0.13	0.04	0.03	0.02	PAKISTAN	RUPEE
1	0.75	1.00	0.07	53	1,909	98	0.02	0.02	0.02	0.02	0.14	0.01	0.09	0.03	0.02	0.01	SRI LANKA	RUPEE
1.33	1	1.33	0.09	70	2,542	130	0.03	0.03	0.03	0.03	0.18	0.01	0.12	0.04	0.03	0.02	BANGLADESH	TAKA
1.00	0.75	1	0.07	53	1,908	97	0.02	0.02	0.02	0.02	0.14	0.01	0.09	0.03	0.02	0.01	NEPAL	RUPEE
15.13	11.36	15.14	1	800	28,881	1,476	0.36	0.33	0.38	0.36	2.09	0.16	1.40	0.41	0.36	0.21	SAUDI ARABIA	RIYAL
1.89	1.42	1.89	0.13	100	3,611	184	0.04	0.04	0.05	0.05	0.26	0.02	0.17	0.05	0.04	0.03	IRAN	100 RIAL
0.52	0.39	0.52	0.03	28	1,000	51	0.01	0.01	0.01	0.01	0.07	0.01	0.05	0.01	0.01	0.01	TURKEY	1,000 LIRA
1.03	0.77	1.03	0.07	54	1,957	100	0.02	0.02	0.03	0.02	0.14	0.01	0.09	0.03	0.02	0.01	RUSSIA	100 RUBLE
42.04	31.58	42.07	2.78	2,223	80,267	4,101	1	0.93	1.05	1.01	5.82	0.44	3.88	1.15	1.00	0.60	PAPUA NEW GUINEA	KINA
45.21	33.95	45.24	2.99	2,390	86,311	4,410	1.08	1	1.13	1.09	6.26	0.47	4.17	1.24	1.07	0.64	AUSTRALIA	DOLLAR
40.17	30.17	40.20	2.66	2,124	76,692	3,918	0.96	0.89	1	0.97	5.56	0.42	3.71	1.10	0.95	0.57	NEW ZEALAND	DOLLAR
41.46	31.15	41.50	2.74	2,193	79,181	4,045	0.99	0.92	1.03	1	5.74	0.43	3.83	1.14	0.99	0.59	CANADA	DOLLAR
7.2	5.43	7.23	0.48	382	13,792	705	0.17	0.16	0.18	0.17	1	0.08	0.67	0.20	0.17	0.10	MEXICO	NEW PESO
95.84	71.98	95.90	6.34	5,068	182,973	9,348	2.28	2.12	2.39	2.31	13.27	1	8.84	2.63	2.28	1.36	BRITAIN	POUND
10.84	8.14	10.84	0.72	573	20,688	1,057	0.26	0.24	0.27	0.26	1.50	0.11	1	0.30	0.26	0.15	FRANCE	FRANC
36.48	27.40	36.51	2.41	1,929	69,650	3,558	0.87	0.81	0.91	0.88	5.05	0.38	3.37	1	0.87	0.52	GERMANY	MARK
42.10	31.62	42.13	2.78	2,226	80,386	4,107	1.00	0.93	1.05	1.02	5.83	0.44	3.89	1.15	1	0.60	SWITZERLAND	FRANC
70.40	52.87	70.45	4.65	3,723	134,409	6,867	1.67	1.56	1.75	1.70	9.75	0.73	6.50	1.93	1.67	1	EUROPE	ECU

Note: The Brunei dollar is valued at S$1, the Macau pataca at about HK$1. Source: Dao Heng Bank, Asiaweek Research

COMMENT

In the first column on the left side, the names of thirty-four countries are exhibited. The last name is that of a country named Europe with a currency called the ECU. It appears that if a group of people have a currency they are a country and vice versa (if you are a country you have a currency). By extension if you don't have a currency you are not a country. Therefore, if, for example, France, Germany or Britain are within the EMU (and don't have their own specific currency) their names will automatically disappear from such tables (they were there in 1997 at the bottom of our example table). In the long run this disappearance of names will be considered by everybody to be natural since the countries will have been fully absorbed by the new country named Europe.

Example No. 11

BA–AMERICAN AIRLINES

British Airways (BA) rounded on threats from European Union (EU) competition authorities on Monday and said Brussels has no jurisdiction over its planned alliance with American Airlines (AA) under European law. The European Commission warned Britain on Monday it could face a European Court of Justice (ECJ) action if London clears BA's proposed link-up with AA without prior approval from Brussels. BA said that under article 89 of the EU's founding Treaty of Rome, Brussels has the right to investigate and report on important matters but it is up to national authorities to decide on them.

Arab News
14 January 1997

COMMENT

For any impartial person reading through this piece of news the impression is clear and nobody should be in doubt. For a proposed alliance of a British airline with an American airline, the authority to investigate compliance with competition laws is the Commission and the justice system that will prosecute the matter (if necessary) is the European Court of Justice. No one should doubt who is the actual (not the nominal) government of Britain and which justice system is the actual (not the nominal) justice system of Britain. Needless to say, if the USA or Japan or indeed any government agency or private company on earth wish to make an alliance or merger or acquisition or just open shop on British soil, they should know who the actual authorities are and whose laws apply.

Example No. 12

U.S. POSTS WORST TRADE DEFICIT IN EIGHT YEARS
Washington, February 19 (AFP)

The United States last year posted its worst trade deficit since 1988 as improvements in the *shortfall with Japan were offset by wider gaps with China, Mexico and the European Union*.

Arab News
20 February 1997

COMMENT

Since the United States, Japan, China and Mexico are countries, then the European Union must also be a country! This is the long term message taken from this news and this is actually corresponding to the de facto situation (i.e. to the true situation).

Example No. 13

ALGERIAN PARLIAMENT ADOPTS PROPORTIONAL REPRESENTATION
Algiers, February 19 (Agencies)

Algeria's interim parliament adopted a new electoral law today replacing the old majority voting system with proportional representation ahead of legislative polls slated for later this year, officials said.

The new law replaces a 1990 electoral code under which the Islamic Salvation Front (FIS) made sweeping gains in 1991 polls.

Meanwhile, *the European Union (EU)* [1] urged Algeria today to defuse its crisis by ensuring that the country returns to democracy.

Alone since the beginning of the year, 350 people not directly involved in the continuing conflict between the Algerian government and extremists have been killed, *the EU observed*. Michiel Patijn, representing the Dutch EU presidency, told the European Parliament in Strasbourg [2] that the continuing attacks by extremist forces were both 'immoral and senseless'.

The EU expected the Algerian government [3] to deal with the crisis with both wisdom and restraint.

'The only way out of the crisis is for Algeria to keep going down the path toward a democratically legitimate government,' Patijn said on *behalf of the 15 EU member states*. [4]

Important steps to this end were the presidential elections in 1995 and constitutional reform in 1996. Algeria would be well advised in 1997 to take another step by holding parliamentary elections.

The EU would continue to support the Algerian government and to insist that it observe human rights and maintain the process of democratisation, he said. [5]

Arab News
20 February 1997

COMMENT

Point 1

A country named Algeria is being advised by another country named the European Union (EU). The fact that the advice is absolutely correct does not alter the fact that the fifteen member countries cannot offer their individual advice and that they have lost their individual voice regarding foreign policy.

Point 2

The parliament of the country named Europe.

Point 3

This is the foreign policy on that matter and at that point of the country named the EU. Since the foreign policy is common, no individual state can deviate, act or say anything other. The question is why do the fifteen states each continue to have its own foreign ministry? The most rational answer is that if they abolished their foreign ministries (in order to reflect the truth) then the average man and woman on the street would start wondering why this is happening and when he or she voted for that.

Point 4

The term states is the correct one, like the states of California and Illinois in the USA or Westphalia, Rhine and Bavaria in Germany. But if Bavaria and Rhine are states and if the country is the EU or Union or Europe, then what is Germany? Is it a state? If it is a state then Rhine is a state within a state and this is strange.

Point 5

The country named the EU will continue to support the Algerian government towards democratisation and respect for human rights. It is natural then that the Algerian government will feel grateful in the future to the entity called the EU and not to the states called Britain, France, Italy, Germany. etc. It is also natural that, for the Algerian government, only the stance of the EU Commission and the EU parliament will matter in the future. The fifteen national parliaments are useless to the Algerian government and in the long term irrelevant. What would be wrong if each member state had the full power to exercise its own foreign policy line towards the Algerian government? What would be wrong if the Algerian people and the Algerian government knew which particular state is helping or not helping and where the real money or moral assistance (or pressure as the case may be) came from? If a particular state government feels afraid to have its own foreign policy line towards Algeria, if it feels that it is better that it hides behind Brussels, then the state government is simply not up to its basic tasks. Exercising foreign policy is one of the basic tasks of any government and fear to exercise that policy is fear to exercise one of the tasks the citizens of the state have instructed their government to perform.

Example No. 14

EURO MPS FLAY FRENCH LAW
Strasbourg, February 21 (AFP)

The European Parliament yesterday called for France to ditch its tough new proposed immigration law, following a full-session vote in Strasbourg. A majority of Euro MPs adopted the resolution, 'calling on the French government to withdraw the proposed Debré law'. The bill – named after its author, Interior Minister Jean-Louis Debré – would oblige French nationals lodging immigrants to tell authorities of their departure, tightening a 1993 law that only made them sign their arrival.

Arab News
22 February 1997

COMMENT

The matter whether the French immigration law was correct or not is irrelevant. The truth is that today France is simply an area within a country named the EU. As such, France cannot have its own immigration laws. The immigration laws are drafted and voted in the parliament of the country (Europarliament) and then sent to the fifteen area parliaments for rubber stamping. Countries have immigration laws, areas do not have immigration laws. Countries can exercise border controls, areas cannot exercise border controls.

On practical grounds, suppose that France had very strict criteria for immigrants while ten other member countries implemented very flexible immigration criteria. This means that, for example, one million legal immigrants coming this year legally to those ten flexible countries and becoming citizens of those ten countries after a period of, say, four or five years of hard and honest work, could then very easily go and search for work in France legally. Therefore it is a fallacy if any member state believes that it can have its own immigration laws or border controls.

Example No. 15

In Figure 69 a copy of the first page of my passport is shown. The following are observed regarding passports:

1. All passports of EU member states have the same dimensions and colour.
2. Any immigration officer or hotel receptionist looking at this passport gets the impression that the traveller is coming from a country named the European Community (or EU) and in particular from the state of Greece.

Figure 69

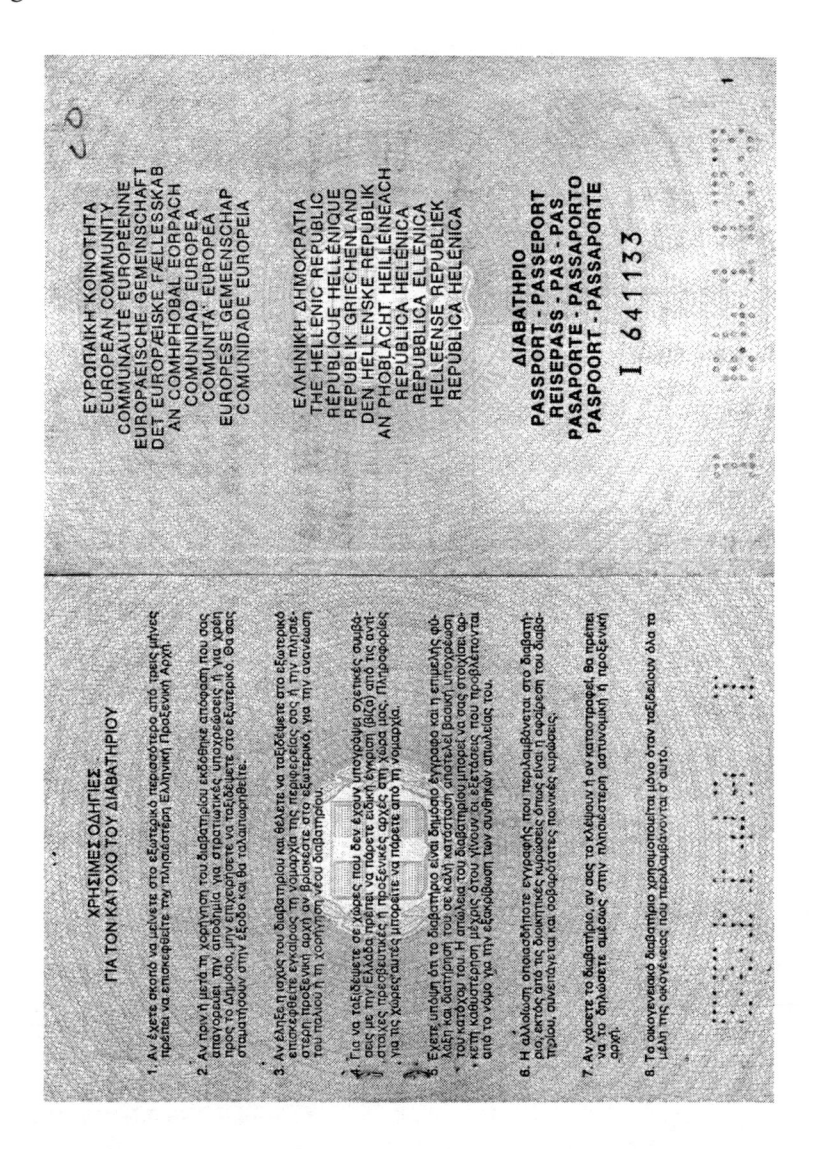

The above phenomenon, when repeated millions of times with many millions of people from all fifteen member states and for not more than one generation automatically creates the feeling amongst the people of all fifteen member states that their country is the EU. At the same time it creates the impression to all other nationals that the traveller is a citizen of a country named the EU. It is quite another matter whether this development is a good or a bad thing and it is also completely another matter whether the people of any of the fifteen member states have at any time voted explicitly and knowingly to abolish their countries in favour of a new larger one.

Example No. 16

EU ASKS TALEBAN TO RELEASE FRENCHMEN
Kabul, March 3 (AFP)

The European Union has demanded the release of two Frenchmen imprisoned by the Taleban in Kabul, a diplomat said today. 'We presented a message from the presidency of the European Union for the release of the two detained Frenchmen,' declared Didier Leroy, French chargé d'affaires for Afghanistan. Leroy said he and a senior humanitarian aid representative of the EU passed the message to the Taleban acting deputy foreign minister yesterday.

Arab News
4 March 1997

COMMENT

Why is the EU asking for the release of the two Frenchmen instead of the French government? Obviously because in practical terms France cannot have its own foreign policy, its own voice in international affairs. Foreign policy now has to be common. The very important message that the Taleban are getting out of this representation is that France is a region of a country called the EU. Even if the Taleban do not get that message, the children of the Taleban when they grow up will surely believe that France is a region of the country called Europe. And, at least as things stand today, these children will be correct in that particular belief.

Example No. 17

EU DONATES $1.2M IN FOOD ASSISTANCE
Islamabad, July 15 (AP)

The European Union has pledged $1.2 million worth of food aid for community development projects in rural north-west Pakistan, according to a statement released today. The EU will provide 12,895 metric tons (14,000 short tons) of wheat to a United Nations programme aimed at erosion and expand farmland in Malakand district, 160 kilometres north-west of Islamabad. Villagers who participate in the UN food-for-work programme will be paid in coupons which they can exchange for wheat, the statement said. The project aims to reduce soil erosion and flooding on 38,000 hectares of private land.

Arab News
16 July 1997

COMMENT

Giving food aid to the Pakistani people is a very good cause. In fact, giving humanitarian aid without any strings attached to any developing nation on earth is a worthwhile cause. But why should the aid money go from the various member countries to Brussels and then from Brussels be packaged as 'EU aid' and sent to developing countries, instead of each member state sending the corresponding aid to one particular country of its own choice? In this individualistic and specific way the people of Italy would know at any moment what kind of official aid and how much official aid they give per year and to whom they give it. The Italian people would be able to exercise control over their government as to what it does, why it aids and whom it aids. The Italian opposition, the media, the intellectuals and every other citizens' organisation would be in a clear position to know and to lobby the government. Instead, the citizens of Italy, the media, the opposition parties and most probably the Italian government itself are not aware of that particular official aid given by Italy to the Pakistani people. More importantly, they don't know how much of this $1.2 million comes out of their contribution to the EU budget for 1997.

In fact, it is very doubtful whether the average Italian citizen knows at all that every year the EU is giving official aid to many developing countries and that for all practical purposes Italy has stopped giving any official aid directly itself because Italy gives through Brussels. One might wonder why this indirect system of foreign aid is happening instead of a direct and transparent system. The answer is very simple. The country is the EU and the government of the country (the Commission) is the only official organisation normally authorised to give foreign aid. The government collects money from the citizens of the area named Italy, puts the money into a centralised purse and then distributes it as coming from the government, not from the particular area.

It is needless to say that the Pakistani government and the Pakistani people will feel grateful to the entity called the EU and not to the entity called Italy or Spain or Finland. In the long term (say, after ten years) if this system continues, any particular state of the fifteen in the EU will be irrelevant to the people of Pakistan regarding any official aid they may wish to receive.

Theoretical arguments regarding foreign aid were examined on page 201.

Example No. 18

EGYPTAIR SECURES $85 MILLION LOAN
Cairo, July 19 (AFP)

The European investment bank today granted EgyptAir a loan of 75 million ECUs ($85 million) to help buy two airbus 321s due to be delivered in the next two months. EgyptAir official Sabee Mikhail told AFP the loan will cover 'part of the price of the two aircraft', which will come to a total of $120 million.

Arab News
20 July 1997

COMMENT

The publicly owned European Investment Bank (EIB) (i.e. a bank controlled by the Commission or by an entity called the EU) is giving a loan to EgyptAir. There is nothing wrong with EgyptAir getting loans from any bank on earth, including from government-owned banks. The following are, however, noted:

1. Why does EgyptAir not get a loan from a bank owned, for example, by the French government or by the Greek government? The reason is that those governments have to be downgraded and the new government in Brussels upgraded.

2. It is obvious that EgyptAir, by getting that loan, will feel dependent or grateful (usually those loans are soft or subsidised) to an entity called the EU, not to any individual country. In the long term EgyptAir will feel that the EU institutions are relevant and that the national institutions of the fifteen countries are irrelevant to it.

3. The possibility of the loan being soft or subsidised is great since, if this were not the case, then EgyptAir could get a loan on purely commercial terms from any private bank in the world. But if the loan is subsidised, then it is subsidised by the fifteen national governments, i.e. by the citizens of the fifteen member countries. But in an era of fiscal austerity, have the citizens of any of the fifteen member countries given instructions for subsidised loans through, not their own government or government-owned banks, but through an EU-owned bank?

4. Usually government-owned banks give soft or subsidised loans to foreign government-owned companies in order to pursue some kind of foreign policy or economic policy with regard to that country. In this case the EU is trying through the European Investment Bank to conduct foreign policy or economic policy. But have the citizens of any member country given, to anyone else other than their own government, instructions to conduct foreign or economic policy vis-à-vis Egypt, or any other country for that matter, by using their own money? And if there is such a policy, who is pursuing it and who is monitoring it? Where is the democratic principle of a government conducting transparent foreign or economic policy with regard to foreign countries, and the opposition parties, the media and the citizens controlling that policy in a reasoned, peaceful and democratic manner?

5. What percentage of the citizens of any of the fifteen member countries know that their money is being used not for the foreign policy goals of their own government but for the foreign policy goals of the country called the EU?

Example No. 19

In various countries one can see some products on sale which have the label: 'Made in EU'.

COMMENT

Usually products have labels of sovereign states like 'Made in Germany'. The main reason for this is that the consumer or vendor or firm should know the country the product was made in in order to know under which legal system the product was made and to know very roughly the possible quality standards of the product, the standards being extracted from the general perception of the country.

Fifty years ago the logo 'Made in Japan' did not necessarily mean high quality or reliability. However, today, the same logo of the same country is usually associated with high quality, reliability and after-sales service. This change in perception is reflected in the general conviction of the consumers that Japan is producing good quality products in general.

It is therefore good for the buyer of any product (the buyer could be also a firm) to know by which country exactly and specifically the product was produced in order to form as correct an opinion as possible about the product, apart from whatever information or idea the buyer has about the specific brand or manufacturer of the product. To say to the buyer simply 'Made in EU' or 'Made in Europe' is like trying to hide from the buyer the exact place of manufacture as if, for example, Italy or Spain or Portugal or Greece are second-rate countries, or that they should be ashamed of themselves or that they should somehow try to improve their commercial image behind the general image of an entity called the EU.

This is a self-defeating attitude which tries to avoid hard truths about the ability of a group of people to improve their commercial image by simply improving the quality of their goods or services. None has ever gained by trying to hide his or her identity, whether he or she is an individual or a nation. The above action, however, (the action of hiding behind the logo 'Made in the EU') entails also a kind of moral hazard, as it is known in microeconomics, the tendency of someone perceived as a producer of lower quality goods to try to capture part of the image of someone else who is perceived as a producer of higher quality goods. Hard effort, truth and transparency are preferable to the producer than the short-term gains made out of confusing or hiding the exact origin of a product.

The second consequence of the logo 'Made in the EU' is that in the long term such a logo is one more practical way to erase from the conscious and subconscious minds of buyers all over the world the concept that the fifteen member states are independent and sovereign entities and replace it with the idea of a new country called the EU or the Union or Europe. The voters have not explicitly asked for this new country and they have not explicitly asked to erase from the map their own countries and identities. But this simple and innocent logo, when exhibited on millions of products for, say, twenty years, creates by itself in the minds of all people on the planet the new sovereign country called the EU.

A third reason why a logo should be as specific as possible is that if after buying a product there are found defects, or manufacturers' defaults in supplying parts to firms, or there are safety problems or health problems or environmental problems, then the buyer knowing the specific real country of manufacture, knows at the same time which legal system to concentrate his or her efforts on when going to court or to which commercial body or embassy or consulate to address his or her complaints. In other words, an exact logo gives to the buyer the ability to know the exact legal system with which the product should comply or under which it would be liable for prosecution. It is one thing to speak about the Italian legal system and it is another to speak about the Finnish legal system.

Here, however, one could suggest that the new country named the EU has a complete and detailed legal system and it has higher and lower courts. In fact, the logo 'Made in the EU' is de facto obliterating the legal systems of the fifteen member states and is de facto replacing them with the complete legal system of the EU. It appears that there are many ways to create a large new country by erasing fifteen smaller ones, even if the inhabitants of those fifteen smaller ones have never asked you explicitly or even implicitly to dismantle their countries or identities.

Example No. 20

During the last Sunday of October 1997 all clocks in Greece as well as all other fourteen countries of the EU went back by one hour. In the international TV news it was also mentioned that, after mutual agreement between Washington and Brussels, at the same date all clocks went one hour backwards in the USA. It was also noted in the media that this agreement between Washington and Brussels was permanent, i.e. both the USA and the EU would turn their clocks back by one hour every year on the last Sunday of October.

COMMENT

Point 1
The USA is definitely a country and is negotiating with another 'country' named the EU. A country speaks to a country, a sovereign state speaks to a sovereign state and a nation speaks to a nation.

Point 2
The fifteen areas or states constituting the sovereign entity called the EU obviously cannot turn their clocks back whenever they wish. They have to turn their clocks back at the same date as the other areas. They have different geographical locations (longitudes), therefore they certainly can have different

time zones, but they cannot change their clocks whenever they deem proper. Moreover, if the majority of the people in any of those countries decided that they wished to have the same time all year around (summer and winter) they simply cannot do that. If, for example, the French people judged that the costs of changing time outweighed the energy savings and they therefore wished by a vast majority not to change time (i.e. to have constant time) then they simply could not do just that. They have to follow the instructions from Brussels.

Point 3

On the substance of this administrative action, the people of a country can first of all decide whether they wish to change time when winter approaches in order to save energy or to not change time because the energy savings are smaller than the disturbance caused to their lives and schedules. This is up to them to decide. They have a government and a parliament. But even if the people of a country decide to leave the time unchanged this year, nothing precludes them from making another decision next year and so on.

On the date for turning the clocks backwards or forwards and on the amount of turning (by one hour or two hours), it is again a decision that the people of a country could take by themselves. If the object of changing time is to save energy, this depends on sunrise and sunset and this in turn depends on the exact geographical location (longitude) of a country. Sunrise and sunset are independent of the EU since the sun has been rising in all countries before the EU was created and certainly the sun will continue to set long after the sunset of its empire. Therefore, the date for changing clocks in any country wishing to save energy should be different simply because the longitude of every country is different (even by a few degrees of longitude).

There are certainly some material benefits if all fifteen countries change time on the same date, but it is very doubtful whether they outweigh the costs of energy lost due to not changing clocks ten or twenty days earlier or ten or twenty days later (depending on the geographical location). There is, however, one hidden cost here. The hidden cost is not material, but in the long run it becomes a material cost. It is the cost of losing one more piece of the independence, sovereignty and identity of a country. This loss of independence and sovereignty is only a psychological or happiness cost. But this loss of happiness, this loss of independence and separate identity is by itself a loss as far as humans are concerned. In the long run the loss of independence leads to the rise of feelings of dependence, the loss of identity leads to a rise of a feeling of loss of purpose and loss of orientation and this certainly leads whole groups of people to slacken their material progress (slower progress than otherwise). If you don't know who you are, then you have no reason for being and if you have no reason for being, then you have very little reason for fast material progress.

Point 4

Changing the clocks of 360 million people all at the same date for many years to come is one more practical step to changing their identities and especially the identities of the coming generations in order to create a new identity, the European, and a new country, Europe.

Point 5

The thought that somehow the fifteen countries should change time together because they trade more or less together is self-defeating because it ignores the fact that the future is in trading increasingly with everyone in the world and there are 185 countries in the world (170 real countries and 15 nominal countries).

Point 6

The fact that Washington and Brussels have decided to change their clocks yearly on the same date and by the same amount is most probably unknown to both US average citizens and by the average citizen of any of the fifteen member states of the EU. It is an indication of a capital of a country talking to a capital of a country but it gives also a hint of 'two entities trying to synchronise the rhythm of their heartbeats' and this is somehow strange for two sovereign entities.

Example No. 21

On 6 December 1996 there was a report on an international TV station regarding a nuclear fusion reactor. The reactor was being built in Austin, Texas, USA, had a construction budget of $10b and was to be completed by 2010. The reactor was being built with money from four donors: the USA, Russia, the EU and Japan. There was also on the screen a nice symbol with the four donors and their flags on a circle as shown in Figure 70.

Figure 70

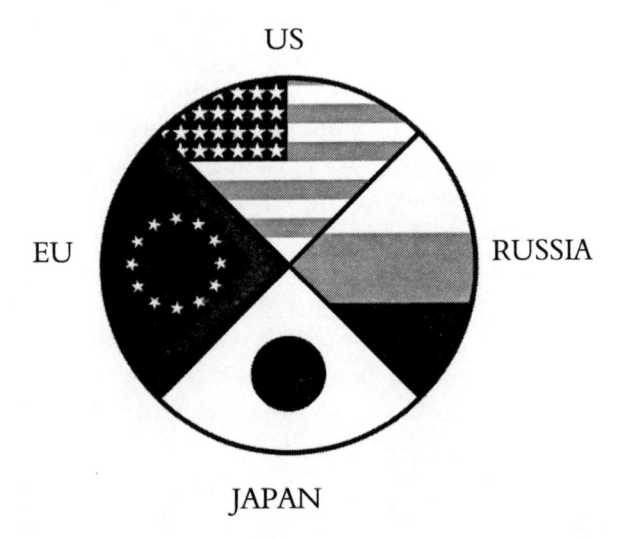

COMMENT

Point 1

In the mind of the viewer (especially the young ones) the following association is necessarily made. Since the USA, Russia and Japan are sovereign nations, the same must apply to the entity called the EU, with the nice blue flag bearing the fifteen yellow stars.

Point 2

What would be the problem if instead of the EU the names of real countries were mentioned? What would be the problem if the names of Germany or France or Britain or Italy or any other real donor nation appeared on the TV screen? Obviously something like this would reflect the actual, the real situation but this is incompatible with the long-term aim of very gradual and step-by-step elimination of the real countries as independent and sovereign entities and their transformation into areas or states.

Example No. 22

On 10 December 1996 when I visited the Greek consulate in Jeddah, Saudi Arabia, in the office of the Consul General there were two small flags on a desk (obviously as per instructions by the government): the Greek flag and the flag of the entity called the EU.

COMMENT

Since you cannot be a country within a country, it is obvious that Greece has become a state of the federal country called the EU or the Union or Europe. But what does a flag in a public office mean? It simply symbolises the allegiance of public employees to a country, its instructions and, most importantly, the people of the country whose flag it is. Therefore, one has to assume that the foreign ministry personnel now owe allegiance to two flags and therefore to two entities: a sovereign country called the EU and a state or area called Greece. Which of the two allegiances is stronger? It is very hard to go into the soul of a man or a woman but in the long term (say, after a generation) the allegiance to the independent and sovereign entity has to prevail for everybody. Allegiance to the dependent and small entity called Greece would have to be gradually absorbed by the allegiance of the large and glorious entity, which in any case contained the small entity.

But then, what is a country? Is it a shirt or a suit to change when it becomes old? Is it a house to sell for a larger one? Is it a wife to abandon when she is not young any more? Is it a friend to abandon when he is not rich any more? Is it a political party to abandon when it is not in power any more? Is it a couple of old pensioners to abandon because they are not useful any more? Most probably a country is nothing like these things and, again most probably, the allegiance of the citizens of a country, even a small and relatively poor one like Greece, the allegiance to the democratic institutions of a country and to the history of a country cannot be replaced or dumped or superseded.

But why serve two entities at the same time? Obviously, you cannot serve God and Mammon at the same time. But the EU is not Mammon, it is rather more God. But then you cannot serve two gods! You usually serve one god unless you are in ancient Greece where you could serve twelve gods! But then the EU today has fifteen small gods and a large one instructing all the small ones. Obviously the ancient Greeks when they spoke about the twelve gods on mount Olympus were not aware of the EU or the Union or Europe. But, no, they knew about Europe because, according to their mythology, she was carried off by the king of the gods, Zeus, and she was brought in a cave on Mount Idi on the island of Crete! By coincidence, I was also born near this mountain; I knew the Greek mythology very well, I knew about the pretty woman called Europe; but I also knew that we finally always have to make a distinction between mythology and history, between lies and truth, between imaginary and real numbers, between fake and original entities, between a continent and a country.

When I was ten years old, the teacher in an Athens elementary school told us to put on a short theatrical sketch and she gave me the part of Zeus, the father of all ancient Greek gods, for a few minutes. But when the sketch was finished I became myself again and I knew that I was not the father of the gods. However, at that time, I also believed that I was a Greek, but this belief of mine appears now to be wrong because, according to the new nice flag in the office of the consul in the Greek consulate in Jeddah, Saudi Arabia, I must have been basically a European all those years. The Greek identity will gradually be absorbed and diminished within the great European identity. It is rather curious to find after four decades of life that you have been living with the wrong identity or at least with an identity that is only a small part of your real identity.

Example No. 23

At various EU institutions for the past five years many actions, laws and regulations were justified by the officials of the EU in the name of European 'integration'. In general the word 'integration' is being used today by pro-EU politicians very often and the same word is as a consequence aired today in various media very often. The frequency with which the word is used in public life (in order to characterise or justify a political or economic measure) is at least a thousand times greater than the frequency that the word was used in public life say twenty-five or thirty years ago. It is therefore instructive to investigate what this word actually means.

The average person listening to the word 'integration' or 'European integration' is more or less thinking of some kind of summation. Summation of nations maybe, or summation of markets, or summation of parliaments and so on. However, the word 'integration' has a totally different linguistic, practical and philosophical meaning. Integration does not mean summation or the simple association of things, markets or human beings.

According to a standard dictionary 'integration' is 'the act to combine parts into a whole' or 'complete something that is imperfect or incomplete by adding parts'.

In the first definition the verb 'to combine' is used, not the verb 'to sum'. In the second definition the verb 'to complete' is used. Both definitions refer actually to taking individual (independent) things (or entities) and transforming them into another thing. This thing is called 'a whole' in the first definition (which means that before it was not a whole) and in the second definition we see clearly that the new thing is now complete whereas before it was 'imperfect' or 'incomplete'. In other words, with integration a new state of things is created, a new entity is created by using various parts. In the case of the EU, the various parts that were combined were the fifteen previously existing independent and sovereign states, and the new entity is the EU or the Union or Europe. Briefly, integration is not the same as the summation of fifteen independent and sovereign nations, but is a process or transformation of those fifteen nations into a new large, independent and sovereign country called the EU.

A much more accurate and detailed description of the word 'integration' can be derived from the science of mathematics and more specifically the subject of calculus. According to standard calculus definitions, 'integration' is a 'transformation' where a 'function' (of one or more variables) is 'transformed' into another, completely different function. The word 'different' here is important. The integral of a function is a different function, not a better function or a worse function. It is simply different.

Now we can describe in a mathematical way and in very simple terms what exactly has already happened to the fifteen member states when they were transformed by 'European integration' (which started primarily in 1985 and was to be practically completed by 1999). A country is mathematically and philosophically speaking a function of the legislative, judicial and administrative powers of its people; it is a function of its culture, identity and economy.

If we use, for the sake of the completeness of the mathematical argument, symbols such as:

legislative power of the people:	l
judicial power of the people:	j
administrative power of the people:	a
culture:	c
identity of the people:	i
economy:	e

then we can symbolise the European 'integration' with the following equation!

$$\iiiint\limits_{l\ j\ a\ c\ i\ e} (G+F+B+I+S+N+Bel+D+A+Sw+Fi+Ir+P+Gr+L)\ dl\ dj\ da\ dc\ di\ de = EU$$

where G = Germany, F = France, B = Britain, I = Italy, S = Spain, N = Netherlands, Bel = Belgium, D = Denmark, A = Austria, Sw = Sweden, Fi = Finland, Ir = Ireland, P = Portugal, Gr = Greece, L = Luxembourg.

In simple calculus terms fifteen entities (functions) have been integrated with respect to legislative power (l), judicial power (j), administrative power (a), culture (c), identity of the people (i) and economy (e) and a new function has resulted on the right-hand side of the equation. This new function is named EU and, according to standard calculus, is completely different from the function within the integral on the left side of the equation. In other words, the function (G+F+B+I+S+N+Bel+D+A+Sw+Fi+Ir+P+Gr+L) is not equal to (not the same as) with the function EU, *until it has been integrated*.

Someone could argue that the mathematical meaning of the word 'integration' is not applicable to the case of European integration. However, mathematics is, in essence, in its highest form and in its beginning, part of philosophy. In fact, higher mathematics and philosophy have the same starting point and use the same principle: the principle of rational thought.

In the case of European integration the mathematical concept of integration mirrors precisely the philosophical concept where fifteen functions (countries) are integrated with respect to all their characteristics and were transformed into a new function (country) called the EU. This new country (function) is by definition completely different from the countries (functions) integrated. In fact, the fifteen countries do not exist because they have been transformed into the EU. Whether the people of those countries asked explicitly and with full knowledge to be transformed, whether countries and people can be used as functions for experimental transformation and whether the result of the integration, the EU, is better or worse than the transformed parts is a completely different question discussed in previous parts of the book.

A final related question is whether the people of the fifteen countries can transform the EU into its constituent parts if they so wish in the future. In simple words, can the 'integral' called the EU become the functioning sum of fifteen democratic and sovereign countries?

Mathematically speaking, this can be achieved easily by the process known in calculus as 'differentiation', i.e. one simply has to 'differentiate' the EU with respect to legislative power, judicial power, administrative power, culture, identity of the people and economy in order to get the fifteen independent and sovereign countries. Using symbols from calculus one can easily write:

$$\frac{\partial^6(EU)}{\partial l\, \partial j\, \partial a\, \partial c\, \partial i\, \partial e} = G+F+B+I+S+N+Bel+D+A+Sw+Fi+Ir+P+Gr+L$$

Concluding the examination of this example, one can suggest that through the process of European integration fifteen countries have become areas or states of a new country that contains all of them. As to the question whether the EU will ever be transformed itself, the answer is not known. But if we ever hear in any media the words 'European differentiation', then the process of transforming the EU into its real constituent parts will have begun. It may then be the first time in human history when differential calculus will have transformed the lives of 360 million people.

Example No. 24

On 3 October 1997 on *Asia Business News* (time 13:05 GMT), the TV channel presented data about new motorbike registrations in Europe. There were numbers for registrations in Germany, Italy, the UK, France, and so on. At the bottom of the table the following was written: 'Source: *European* Transport *Ministry*.

COMMENT

'Tongue in confusion speaks the truth.' (Ancient Greek proverb).

Example No. 25

From the news on 24 October 1997 on an international TV channel regarding a summit at Kyoto, Japan, about the environment. The summit was to take place in December 1997 and almost all countries in the world were to take part.

> The EU would cut the emissions of its member nations, but would count the fifteen nations as one country. The Japanese disagree because this would put poor and rich countries into the same basket.

COMMENT

The summit in Kyoto was about setting limits or reducing the greenhouse gases to specific levels within a specific time framework (up to 2010).

Improving the environment in every country and over the world as a whole is a very worthwhile aim. It is, in fact, one of the most worthwhile causes. But why should the fifteen EU nations not each be responsible for itself regarding greenhouse emissions? Why should each nation not be able to put on the table in Kyoto its own well thought out proposal? Why, after the summit was over, did each nation not assume responsibility to monitor itself? Are there not in each nation opposition parties, media, intellectuals, environmental groups and citizens to monitor the progress of their government in keeping the promises given at Kyoto? Why should the EU speak for those fifteen nations? And why should the EU then give quotas to the people of each nation as to what amounts of emissions they should have each year? The rational answer to all those questions can be only one. That the EU is already a country and it is natural that its administrative body (the Commission) should instruct the areas or states as to how much total greenhouse emissions each one can have per year. At the same time, the EU, by presenting itself as one entity regarding emissions of harmful gases, is projecting and reinforcing worldwide the idea of one country. Also at the same time, the EU administrative body becomes 'the monitor and policeman of the environmental behaviour of each one of the fifteen nations'.

But if the government of a nation needs a policeman regarding its environmental behaviour, this policeman should be its own people and more specifically the opposition parties, the parliament, the media, the intellectuals, the environmental groups and the citizens. By having the EU institutions as monitor and policeman, all the above factors representing the people of a nation are in the long run neutralised regarding environmental awareness, democratic controls and vigilance. If the people of a nation cannot monitor the deterioration or improvement of their environment, if the people of a nation cannot keep their environmental promises given at a summit, if the democratic and civil institutions of a nation cannot check the environmental behaviour of its government, if the lawmakers of a nation cannot make laws limiting or improving the emissions from power plants, factories and cars then who else can improve their own environment?

Example No. 26

EU SIGNS $40M AID PACKAGE FOR SYRIA
Brussels, May 30 (DPA)

The European Union today signed a $40 million (31 million ECUs) aid package for Syria as part of a drive to build closer aid and economic relations with Mediterranean countries. Officials at the EU Commission said the money would be used for a telecommunications project, the tourism sector and to modernize municipal administrations. Ten million ECUs of the total package will be given to the Syrian telecom establishment for undertaking technological change in the sector and to implement training schemes to upgrade human skills.

Arab News
31 May 1997

COMMENT

Giving official aid to Syria and indeed to any nation on earth is a humanitarian gesture worth every effort. However the important comments made on page 201 (theoretical considerations) and in example 17 on page 268 (practical considerations) are identically applicable. Hence, they will not be repeated here.

Example No. 27

AUSTRALIA'S CENTRAL BANK SEES NO RISK TO INFLATION
Sydney, August 19 (AFP)

Australia's central bank said today that its easy monetary policy was supporting economic growth without risking the country's record of low inflation.

Arab News
20 August 1997

COMMENT

The existence of a central bank appears to be important for economic growth and inflation for an economy the size of Australia. Within the EMU, economies of much greater size like Germany's or France's will not have their own central bank. Furthermore, the EMU philosophy suggests that central banks are not needed for short-term economic growth objectives and therefore twenty-four countries over the continent of Europe could have just one central bank. Maybe the Australian central bank should hand over its functions to an Asian central bank operating, say, in Hong Kong or Singapore and taking care of the short-term and long-term economic problems of the Australian citizens!

Example No. 28

FRENCH DEPUTY TO OPPOSE AMSTERDAM TREATY
Paris, August 18 (R)

An influential Socialist member of the French parliament has vowed to oppose ratification of the Amsterdam Treaty, saying it would open the way to the decline of the European Union.

In an article published today in the daily, Le Monde, Jack Lang, chairman of the National Assembly's foreign affairs committee, called the accord signed at last June's EU summit in Amsterdam 'a rump treaty' papering over cracks. He demanded that the EU be turned into a federation to retain its momentum. [1]

Lang said the European Commission, Parliament, central bank and Court of Justice were already virtually federal institutions. [2]

Arab News
19 August 1997

COMMENT

Point 1
The EU does not need to be turned into a federation. It is a de facto federation regardless of whether this is to the benefit of the people or not and regardless of whether the people knew what they were entering under the names of 'single market', 'Maastricht Treaty' and 'Amsterdam Treaty'.

Point 2
The member of the French Parliament is right in the sense that the Commission has centralised the executive powers of the people of each country, the Europarliament has centralised the legislative powers of the people of each country and the Court of Justice has centralised the judicial powers of the people of each country. Those are de facto (as opposed to de jure) federal institutions and the EU is a de facto federal country with fifteen states or areas. The de jure announcement of the foundation of the country named the EU or the Union or Europe is scheduled for much later (after ten to twenty years) so that the people will have been used or accustomed or brainwashed to the new situation (and the older people who remember their previous country will have died anyway). In this way there will be no reaction on the part of the people to changes in their identities. This appears to have been always the plan of the social engineers who conceived the idea of creating a new country called Europe, and it appears to be a wise plan, at least for them.

Example No. 29

EU TO FINANCE INDIAN HEALTH CARE OVERHAUL
Luxembourg, September 2 (AFP)

The European Union and India today signed an accord under which the EU will provide 200 million ECUs ($216 million) over five years to help overhaul India's family health care system. The money, which represents the EU's biggest ever aid programme in Asia is to be concentrated on improving family planning through maternal education, pre-natal care and contraception. The accord was signed on the sidelines of an EU–India meeting here by Kamala Sinha, the Indian minister of state for foreign affairs, and Manuel Marin, the European Commission vice-president.

Arab News
3 September 1997

COMMENT

The same comments regarding official aid to foreign countries that were said in examples 17 and 26 on pages 268 and 280 apply also here.

Example No. 30

CHINA SLASHES CUSTOMS TARIFFS BY 26 PERCENT
Beijing, September 14 (AFP)

China announced today an average 26 percent cut in import and export duties on more than 4,800 items from Oct. 1. The cut will mean a drop in the overall tariff rate from 23 percent to 17 percent, the Xinjua news agency said, citing the Customs Tariff Commission (CTC) of the State Council.

Arab News
15 September 1997

COMMENT

As we said on page 148 all nations are moving towards lifting all tariffs, quotas and other restrictions (usually bureaucratic restrictions) so that by 2010 there will be completely free trade everywhere. The North and South Americas will be free trade areas in 2005 and the whole of Asia Pacific area by 2010.

In such a world:

1. There is no place for customs union areas (like the EU).
2. There is no place for trade blocs areas (like the EU or ASEAN or Mercosur).
3. There is no place for blackmails such as 'if you are outside our club you will face trade or investment barriers' and hence 'you had better join our nice club' or 'don't even think to leave this nice club'.

The era of reckoning is fast approaching. A few years are a blip in the eyes of the time scale of human existence.

Example No. 31

October–November 1997 stock market upheaval. Many currencies were devalued and some depreciated slightly. In the midst of the turmoil the US dollar was slightly down but the Swiss franc was slightly up since it was considered a safe haven. Currencies of small but healthy economies like Norway or New Zealand or Chile were also unaffected.

COMMENT

During the turmoil we saw that currencies of huge economies like Japan or Brazil or even India depreciated. However, currencies of small but healthy economies like Switzerland, Norway, New Zealand and Chile were either strengthened or unaffected. The same applies for medium-sized countries like the United Kingdom whose currency was outside any Exchange Rate Mechanism. For all those countries during the financial turmoil their currencies were either unaffected or actually strengthened. What was the reason?

Simply the sound fundamentals of their economies. This proves one more time in practice that the size of an economy does not have any correlation to vulnerability to attacks on the part of pure 'market forces' or even 'determined speculators' with definite financial motives, with or without political motives. What counts for the stability of a currency is one and only one thing: the soundness or otherwise of the economic and financial fundamentals of the country. There are many factors defining those fundamentals, but size of the country (or of the economy) is not amongst those fundamentals. You can be a huge country like the USA and during the crisis see your currency depreciate slightly against the Deutsche Mark from 1.80 to 1.71, but you can be the tiny Switzerland or Norway and see your currency stable or slightly appreciating. Therefore the claim that 'you need to be within the EMU in order to have a stable currency owing to the size of the money supply' is theoretically and empirically wrong. We have examined the above argument a little more theoretically on page 50.

Example No. 32

During the autumn of 1997 there was stock market and currency turmoil. The crisis started in Thailand then spread to South-East Asia and on to North-East Asia, Latin America, Eastern Europe, Russia and, in essence, affected every currency and every stock market in the world. There were a number of firms failures, brokerage houses failures and bank closures as well as bank runs. The markets appeared to be something like 'communicating vessels', but nevertheless the strong and healthy markets were finally able to support the weak ones and avoid a global financial collapse and complete meltdown. Would this be possible if instead of 185 markets we had one worldwide market? Would this be possible if, instead of more than 170 different currencies and central banks, we had just one currency and one central bank?

COMMENT

The currency and stock market crisis spread during October–November 1997 to many countries, but with different intensity. Markets with unhealthy fundamentals were very vulnerable, but markets with healthy fundamentals were not. Finally, the healthy markets kept stable and within a few months transmitted their stability to the vulnerable markets. Where does all this lead us?

One conclusion is that all markets and all economies today are interconnected. If a particular economy is 'weak' and is affected by a 'virus', then this economy gets 'flu' or 'pneumonia' and this 'flu' can contaminate other 'weak' economies because 'weak' economies are susceptible to attacks by viruses. However, 'strong' economies are much less susceptible to attack and, in fact, the 'strong' economies can finally beat the virus in the body of the weak ones.

A second conclusion is that the economies and the markets have different degrees of financial health simply because their management over the last few decades has been in the hands of different governments and central banks.

Therefore, the markets today are interconnected, but at the same time they are under different economic and financial management. These different managements provide for diversity of strength and this diversity of strength in turn provides stability in the form of allowing various degrees of 'contamination' once troubles start in one country or in one area.

Now what would happen if, instead of 185 essentially different markets, we had all over the world a single market with one currency, one central bank and one management team in the form of an economic policy ministry? If trouble started in one part of that single market with a bank run, it is obvious that there would be no isolating safety valve to stop the general feeling of panic or instability. In essence, the different central banks and different governments provide the only safety valve to prevent the automatic transmission of financial trouble (real or imaginary) spreading with the speed of light from one place to another. To put it another way, since, owing to many technological factors, owing to increasingly free trade and owing to increasingly free investment (in both real and financial assets), the markets are interconnected, the only safety valves available to partially stop troubles spreading in a few days over the whole planet is the diversity of economic and financial management.

The diversity of economic management is achieved through the independent governments (economic policies – economic ministries – legislation – fiscal policies). The diversity of financial management is achieved through the different central banks (or equivalently the different currencies). The philosophy and practice of the single market and the EMU (and the EU in general) is to replace this diversity in economic management with a single economic management (single legislative structure, single fiscal policies, coordinated economic policies) and to replace the diversity in financial management with a single currency, a single central bank and a single interest rate. This is a recipe for making the whole world much more susceptible to total financial collapse. If a smaller number of currencies is practically a good thing, then one day there will have to be all over the planet just a few currencies and then finally one. This is a recipe for greatly increasing the probability of one day in the distant future having a total financial collapse all over the planet.

Fortunately, in the autumn of 1997, there were more than 170 different currencies and central banks all over the earth and the total financial collapse was avoided. The tendency for financial collapse could be increased in the future by the recent fashion for many central banks to reduce or remove from their foreign reserves the only real asset they usually possess, which is gold. In this case a financial panic and a bank run could in the future be spread more easily since the people would know that their cash is not supported by real assets. Fortunately there is a very recent embryonic development where people, private citizens, are creating their own cash or money in the form of electronic money units mutually acceptable in their transactions over the Internet. It appears that some governments are destroying currencies, but private citizens are creating new currencies. It could be that the mythological Greek bird, the phoenix, was not the only thing that can be reborn. Maybe we will see currencies reborn and multiply in number. It could also be that private citizens have a greater instinct for survival than governments.

Example No. 33

In the offices of ministers, deputies, etc. of various countries, two flags have been installed: the flag of the state (say, Greece) and the flag of the country (EU). When the officials speak to reporters or give interviews, obviously those two flags are displayed to the viewers.

COMMENT

Point 1
The target is not to show that, for example, 'we are members of a club like NATO or the UN.' The target is the subconscious part of the minds of the viewers and especially the subconscious part of the minds of the young viewers, the new generation. The adult viewers already know very well which is their country. The upcoming generations, though, will naturally tend to believe that their country is the EU and one or two generations afterwards they will have no doubt at all about this.

Point 2
It is debatable whether the initiative for the installation of these two flags came from the national government of any country or was in instructions from Brussels. It is also debatable whether the money for buying all those flags came from the budget of the national government or the budget of the EU. It is, however, unquestionable that in either case the money came from the taxpayers of each country who in effect are giving part of their money to propagate the opinion that they have changed country and that most probably they will have to change identity and culture.

Point 3
Displaying the flag of an institution or displaying the political choice of a government of the moment, even if this political choice of the moment is assumed to be consistent with the wishes of the majority of a country, is not consistent with the democratic principle that no public funds, no public buildings and no public institutions should ever be used to exert covert or outright political persuasion or spread propaganda to the people of the country. This is a major violation of that democratic principle and the national justice system of each country, if it is presented with complaints by the citizens, should find such displays illegal and unconstitutional (provided, of course, that the judges are independent from the national government and national

parliament).

Example No. 34

On 5 November 1997, in the various news media it was announced that the French truck drivers were on strike and were blockading many roads. [1] The Commissioners were meeting urgently to try to press the French government [2] to stop the strike. Other EU member states said that the strike violated EU law [3] about the free movement of goods.

COMMENT

Point 1

Anyone can have his or her opinion about whether blocking roads is a legitimate political action. However, if we accept that blocking French roads was a breach of French law, then it is the French authorities and no one else who should act. If, on the other hand, blocking roads was not a violation of French laws, it is again the French authorities and the French people who should try to tackle the problem and no one else.

Point 2

The expression 'to press the French government' legitimises the view that others can dictate to the French authorities what is good or not good for the general French public. It is the French people, the French media and the French opposition parties who should 'press' the French government if they felt that this was to the benefit of French society.

Point 3

If the strike violated EU law, it should be irrelevant. What should have been considered was whether the strike violated French law or not. And two final questions: which law is applicable on French soil? French or EU law? And which of the two sets of laws prevails on French soil?

Example No. 35

On 7 November 1997 the Greek employees of the National Organisation for Medicines (the authority in Greece that checks and approves new medicines) were protesting (in fact, the farmers were also on strike) against the abolition of some special small tax that had existed for many years on the price of each drug. This small tax was to cover the running expenses of the Greek agency that researches, checks and approves or disapproves new drugs, medicines, etc.

COMMENT

The real reasons behind the abolition of that special tax and which reasons nobody dared to tell the people protesting or on strike are:

1. The approval or disapproval of any new drug is now centralised in

Brussels under a 'federal' authority. The various national drug approval authorities have in effect become superfluous. Whether those national authorities for drug approvals know or ignore this fact is another matter. Whether the health sensitivities of each particular nation are preserved or flattened is also another matter. The Greek government simply was not straightforward with the striking members of the agency for checking and approving drugs and did not say, 'You have been superseded by the Central Agency in Brussels.'

2. The special tax which was providing funds for the Greek medical approval agency had to be abolished because of the plan of the EU for 'value added tax harmonisations' or to put it straight, VAT should be identical for all products and services across the member states.

This is the philosophical concept of single country, single market, single taxation, single value added tax, and single authority for drugs approval. Whether this philosophical 'singularity concept' is right or wrong has been discussed in Part Two.

Example No. 36

TAIWAN JOBLESS RATE STANDS AT 3.03%
Taipei, September 23 (AFP)

Taiwan's unemployment rate stood at 3.03 percent in August down 0.16 percentage points from a year earlier, the government said today. A total of 287,000 people were out of work in the month, an increase of 18,000 people over the previous month, the Directorate General of Budget, Accounting and Statistics said. The agency attributed the increase to a rise in the number of first-time job seekers, which totalled about 10,000. Some 9.45 million people were in work in August, it said.

Arab News
24 September 1997

COMMENT

It is very strange how a small island of 20 million people, far away from the main Western rich customers, with a high population density, without energy or other substantial mineral resources, without many archaeological sites to attract tourists, without rich agriculture, without receiving foreign aid or structural funds from anyone, without imposing its laws to harmonise a single market, without subordinating its judges to the European Court of Justice, without accepting instructions from the Commission, without being subject to the Common Agricultural Policy, without being subject to the Common Fisheries Policy and with a language that makes it inherently difficult for the natives to learn the main Western languages of trade and science, it is very strange how this country can have an unemployment rate of only 3.03%! The answer certainly does not lie in membership of the EU. It simply lies in two things: hard work and free trade. Loss of sovereignty, integration, single markets and Commissions do not produce wealth and do not reduce unemployment.

Example No. 37

CHINA CUTS TARIFFS ON 4,784 ITEMS
Beijing, September 26 (AFP)

China unveiled the extent of its upcoming tariff cuts today with a list that showed a 20-point cut on luxury cars and a 15-point reduction on microwaves, air conditioners and televisions.

Zinc, plywood, milk powder, alcohol and fish also received significant cuts, according to General Administration of Customs figures released by the Economic Information Daily.

In total, some 4,784 targeted products which make up 73 percent of commodities subject to import taxes, will have their rates cut from Oct. 1.

This reduces China's average tariff rate from 23 percent down to 17 percent and is aimed at reaching the goal of 15 percent average tariff levels by the year 2000.

According to the figures provided, average tariff on agricultural products will run at 21.2 percent after Oct. 1, while industrial products will average 14.4 percent and oil imports some 7.9 percent.

Arab News
27 September 1997

COMMENT

As discussed on page 148, it is inevitable that by 2010 at the latest, almost all nations on earth – bar the poorest of the poor – will have cut all tariffs to zero and there will be completely free trade in goods and services. A small number of the remaining very poor nations (mainly in Africa) are to make their tariffs zero at the latest by 2020. Within such an environment common customs areas or free trade blocs are rendered meaningless. The future is with every nation trading freely (in goods and services) with every other nation on earth. The future does not lie in locking a nation within a bigger artificial entity and creating barriers around that entity. This 'locking' of a nation may initially give a sense of economic security, but the reality is different. If you want to prosper, you have to trade with the cheapest source available. If you want to be secure, you have to be equally friendly to everyone else. If you want to be dynamic and self-confident, you have to be yourself and look after your interests in a peaceful and ethical way.

Example No. 38

EU PROJECT TO CURB MALARIA IN VIETNAM
Hanoi, October 10 (R)

The European Union will back Hanoi in a four-year malaria control project which will begin in 1998, the official Vietnam News Agency (VNA) said today. It said that the $19 million project will be carried out in seven provinces, where over 76,000 people – 25 percent of nationwide cases – were reported to have contracted malaria in the first nine months of this year.

Arab News
11 October 1997

COMMENT

Foreign aid to Vietnam to curb malaria is an absolutely worthy cause. Why, however, should those $19 million go first to Brussels, be repackaged in Brussels as 'EU aid' and then be sent to Vietnam? Would it not be much more practical and realistic if each country sent its corresponding amount to Vietnam under its full responsibility, control and accounting, especially by the opposition parties and media? Moreover, it would be even more practical if only one of the fifteen countries sent the $19 million to Vietnam and the rest of the member countries contributed more corresponding aid to other developing nations. Foreign aid as a total yearly sum is the same whether each member state gives to Vietnam or some member states skip Vietnam and contribute more to other developing countries. One intuitive and serious objection to each member country sending its yearly total amount directly to developing countries is the following: 'If each country is left to decide and implement the foreign aid by itself, then many countries will be reluctant to send anything.'

The reasoning is faulty. It is correct in the implicit assumption that the governments of the fifteen member states are at the moment contributing money to the EU budget for foreign aid without the full knowledge or the explicit and specific authorisation of the electorate or the national parliament. The reasoning is, however, wrong in that the free will of the people of any country to give foreign aid to a developing nation will not change when this aid is given directly and under the full light of publicity and the control of the established democratic institutions of the people, the media and the pressure groups. Directness is always better than indirect ways, transparency always preferable to avoiding publicity and the full exercise of the people's power is always preferable to distant and concentrated representation.

Why then is the EU giving the foreign aid packaged as EU aid? The only reason is because the long-term aim is for the people of third countries (in this example Vietnam) to think of the EU as a country, to be grateful to the EU and not to any particular member nations. In this slow, indirect, but very efficient way, the members will gradually lose their 'personality' and be absorbed into a new personality: the 'European'. The method may take one or two generations to achieve its results but it is a sure way to create a new large country out of fifteen smaller ones.

We have discussed the theoretical arguments about foreign aid in more detail on page 201.

Example No. 39

BONN PARLIAMENT APPROVES EUROPOL
Bonn, October 10 (DPA)

Reacting to calls for better means to fight organised crime, the German parliament today approved the creation of Europol, the European Union's fledgling police force. 'National police alone are no longer capable of effectively fighting the cancer of organised crime,' said Michael Stuebgen, a deputy from Chancellor Helmut Kohl's CDU.

Arab News
11 October 1997

COMMENT

The new country named the EU or the Union or Europe must have its own police force or federal police force. Centralised power requires always a centralised police force and there can be no country without its own police force. This is the true reason for Europol and all the rest of the reasons are simply excuses.

Example No. 40

SPCPD GETS $25M LOAN FROM EUROPE
Cotabato City, October 14

The cash-strapped Southern Philippines Council for Peace and Development (SPCPD) has secured more funds from foreign sources to sustain its socio-economic thrusts, bolstering efforts of rebuilding the war-devastated economy of Muslim-dominated areas in Mindanao.

Muslimin Sema, SPCPD's executive director, said one of the huge cash inputs for Mindanao's special Zone of Peace and Development (ZOPAD) is a P768 million loan *($25 million) from the European Investment Bank (EIB) for the expansion of the airports in nearby Datu Odin Sinsuat town and Puerto Princesa, Palawan.*

Sema said an agreement on the infrastructure package was signed recently in Hong Kong by EIB Vice-President Rodulf de Korte and Finance Secretary Roberto de Ocampo.

> *The EIB loan is the fourth special grant of the European Union to Mindanao's SOPAD where President Fidel Ramos and the Moro National Liberation Front (MNLF) are implementing a multi-pronged peace process.*
>
> Arab News
15 October 1997

COMMENT

Whatever was said about foreign aid and about the role of the EIB in example 18, page 269, is also applicable here. It is also worth noting the word Europe in the title of the article.

Example No. 41

LABOR'S 4 MPS FACE EUROPEAN PARLIAMENT PROBE
Strasbourg, France, October 22 (R)

> *European Parliament President Jose-Maria Gil-Robles has ordered a probe into threats by Britain's ruling Labor Party to punish four Euro-MPs defying orders to keep quiet about reform of the voting system.*
>
> *He was reacting to claims by British Labor Euro-MPs Ken Coates, Michael Hindley, Hugh Kerr and Alex Falconer that a new binding Code of Practice, approved by the Labor Party's ruling National Executive Committee last month, breached the Euro-assembly's own rules.*
>
> *The four have been given until 1400 GMT today to give assurances that they will recognise and abide by the code or face disciplinary action.*
>
> Arab News
23 October 1997

COMMENT

Under which party were the four MEPs elected? Which country do they represent? To which country's voters are they supposed to give allegiance? Which law is the supreme law on British soil?

Example No. 42

APEC IDENTIFIES POTENTIAL AREAS FOR LIBERALIZATION
Singapore, October 27 (AFP)

> *APEC economies today offered more than 40 product sectors for tearing down tariff and non-tariff barriers earlier than scheduled under the grouping's timetable for free trade and investment by 2020.*
>
> *The sectors were offered for the so-called 'early sectoral voluntary liberalization' under APEC's proposed second route for member economies to achieve free trade and investment.*
>
> *The blueprint requires the 18 member economies to begin dismantling tariffs from Jan. 1 1997 to achieve free trade and investment by 2020.*

Developed economies such as the United States and Japan should achieve the target 10 years earlier.

APEC's proposal for early sectoral liberalization stemmed from the group's success last year in sewing up a pact to scrap tariffs on information technology (IT) products. It set the pace for a World Trade Organisation agreement to eliminate tariffs on most IT products by 2000.

Arab News
28 October 1997

COMMENT

As was discussed on page 148, the plan for complete worldwide free trade in goods and services is to be achieved by 2010 for the vast majority of the countries and by 2020 for the rest (the poorest countries). In such a free trade environment worldwide there is no economic meaning for a bloc like the EU and there will be no incentives for outside countries to join the bloc and there will be no disincentives for inside countries to leave the bloc. Some people would describe those incentives and disincentives as well thought out political blackmail, but in politics the lines between incentives, disincentives, deception and blackmail are usually blurred! However, 2010 is very fast approaching and then those blurring lines may become very clearly defined.

Example No. 43

DIMITRA IS AS UNPOPULAR AS EVER
Athens, October 31 (AFP)

An official of the Women's Rights Observatory, an inter-party group funded by the European Union, called Avriani's campaign deplorable.

Arab News
1 November 1997

COMMENT

Each country should have its own women's rights organisation or organisations funded by public money to as high a degree as the citizens of the country indicate with their votes. There is no practical reason for the EU budget to fund such groups which could be funded more efficiently on a national level. Public money for women's rights is a worthy cause, but money is much more efficiently used when it is under national control (no expenses for hotels, travel, long-distance calls and, most importantly, greater transparency and accountability).

Example No. 44

A few extracts from the Maastricht Treaty follow.

Regarding any country that does not join the EMU, its central bank must subscribe to the capital of the European central bank and transfer 'foreign reserve assets and contribute to reserves on the same basis as the national central bank of a member state whose derogation has been abrogated'. Furthermore, the amount of European central bank capital can be increased by majority vote.

This means that even if a member state stays outside the EMU it will have to contribute capital to the European central bank and to again contribute capital whenever the majority of the members decide so.

Another extract, from Article 102a, runs: 'Member states shall conduct their economic policies with a view to contributing to the achievements of the Community.' (Note: not the objectives of individual member states.) And 'Member states shall regard their economic policies as a matter of common concern and shall coordinate them within the Council [of Ministers].'

COMMENT

Within the EU no country can have its own economic policies. It has to 'contribute to the achievements of the Community' to 'coordinate with the Council' and to treat them as a matter of common concern. The theoretical arguments regarding this loss of independent economic policies were presented on pages 85-162. Here we can only note on an empirical level that since the Single European Act was enacted (1986) and especially since Maastricht the rates of growth in the member states have been considerably lowered on average and unemployment has taken off. This may be not a coincidence.

Example No. 45

AUSTRIA JOINS SCHENGEN, SAYS SCHLOGL
Vienna, November 10

Austria is joining the Schengen, according to Interior Minister Karl Schlogl.

'From April 1, 1998 the principle free travel for free citizens applies for Austrians too,' Schlogl announced here after a recent meeting with his European colleagues in Vienna.

With this, the Schengen schedule has been settled after months of delays, and interruptions from the Bavarian regional government and threats of a veto from the Greeks. 'We are very happy *that there will be a common visa*,' said Walter Friedle, consul in Jeddah. When telephoned for his comments and what it means for Saudi Arabia, he told *Arab News* that many Saudi businessmen who go to Germany, France and Italy to participate in international exhibitions usually also visit Austria.

'The common visa will facilitate their visits,' Friedle said, and added, 'the common visa is very helpful. It will facilitate the trips of Saudi businessmen, as well as leisure travellers from the Kingdom "dramatically", and mean a saving in visa fees, because instead of 3 or 4 visas, they will need only one.' The aim of the Schengen agreement is the abolition of passport controls on the borders within the Schengen states, and the increase of controls on the exterior borders. The announcement gives the green light to travellers from countries where

the Schengen agreement applies, mainly France, Germany, Spain and the Benelux countries, beginning December.

Arab News
11 November 1997

COMMENT

The abolition of border controls has the obvious advantage of making travel easier between countries. It has, however, the following drawbacks:

1. Unavoidably for outlaws and criminals travelling becomes much easier.
2. It removes from the national government any ability to control the immigrant population. For example, an immigrant can come to Austria over its borders with Germany or Italy. Legal immigrants should be welcome in any country and even the illegal ones should be considered owing to humanitarian or political persecution circumstances. However, the fact remains that within the EU the people of a nation have no control over the number of legal or illegal immigrants they receive each year.
3. Historically, a nation that does not exercise some control over its borders ceases to exist as an independent and sovereign entity.

The above very serious drawbacks, if weighed against slightly easier travel, point to conclusions other than the ones mentioned in the press extract regarding the Schengen accord. It could be proven, for example, that it is preferable for a country to keep its border controls and simply make extremely easy, fast and cheap visas available for third country nationals or for citizens of member countries to cross borders. Possible delays at the borders of one or two or three minutes are an infinitesimal price to pay for keeping effective control of a country's borders. More theoretical arguments on the matter of border controls have been presented on page 108. Free travel for free citizens is not equivalent to unchecked or uncontrolled travel since a group of people has a collective right to check or to control who is entering its 'house'.

Example No. 46

APEC TO PRESS FOR FREE TRADE
Singapore, November 17 (AFP)

APEC economies are to forge ahead with tariff cuts in their zeal to achieve free trade and investment in the region even as many of them are embroiled in financial turmoil, officials say.

The members of the Asia–Pacific Economic Cooperation (APEC) forum will include fresh tariff reductions under 'individual action plans' (IAPs) and pledge to participate in a new accelerated liberalization program involving specific product sectors, according to the officials.

The commitments will be announced when APEC trade ministers and leaders meet in Vancouver, Canada from Nov. 21–25. IAPs are the keys to the implementation of APEC's free-trade blueprint, adopted at the group's 1996 summit in the Philippines, which required the *18 member economies to begin dismantling tariffs from Jan. 1 1997 to achieve free trade and investment by 2020. Developed economies such as the United States and Japan should achieve the target 10 years earlier.*

Officials said that host Canada would circulate a document in Vancouver explaining fresh tariff and non-tariff liberalization offers made by APEC economies in their IAPs.

'Every economy has improved their IAPs and they have also reported to us how they have implemented their undertakings,' Leonard Edwards, Canada's assistant deputy minister for trade and economic policy, told AFP.

He said that the IAPs would remain the primary vehicle for trade liberalization even though APEC would open up a new channel for freeing trade through a so-called *'early sectional voluntary liberalization' (ESVL) program.*

Arab News
18 November 1997

COMMENT

By 2010 almost all trade in the world will be done without tariffs, quotas and other bureaucratic restrictions. The era of trading blocs will be then over.

Example No. 47

BRUSSELS SET TO COMPENSATE CJD VICTIMS
Strasbourg, November 19 (GNS)

The European Commission was on the verge last night of making an unprecedented commitment to financial compensation for victims of Creutzfeldt-Jakob disease, in the wake of the mad cow crisis.

The move, which would be the first time the EU has offered compensation for an illness, is to be voted on by the European Parliament in Strasbourg later today.

Although he stopped short of suggesting what form the compensation should take, Mr Santer told MEPs: 'More than 20 people have been victims of the new variety of the disease. Their families deserve our solidarity.

'The Commission has decided to rally to their aid with concrete help, which the parliament wants to bring them.' A resolution before the parliament yesterday called for the Commission and member states where there are CJD cases *'to put in place the financial resources required for the provision of assistance to families affected by CJD rapidly and with a minimum of red tape, in the light of the recent findings of scientific research which demonstrates a close connection between BSE and CJD'.*

Arab News
20 November 1997

COMMENT

The one thing not said is that the Commission does not have its own money. The money of the Commission comes from the national governments. It is those governments who should give direct assistance to CJD victims.

Example No. 48

EU LEADERS AGREE ON NEW JOBS STRATEGY
Luxembourg, November 21 (AFP)

In an announcement timed to coincide with the summit, *the European Investment Bank announced the creation of a new 125 million ECU ($137 million) venture capital fund for small, high-tech companies.*

The move represented the first step in a programme under which the EU's long-term lending arm plans to make up to one billion ECUs ($1.1 billion) available to support the creation and growth of small and medium-sized enterprises (SMEs) over the next three years.

Arab News
22 November 1997

COMMENT

The European Investment Bank (EIB) was formed with capital from all national governments. In other words, it is a publicly owned bank. We see this at a period when, in almost all member countries, nationalised banks are being privatised in the same period. Let me emphasise, fifteen nations are downgraded to areas or states and therefore their nationalised banks are being privatised. At the same time a new country is being created with the name of the EU together with its two nationalised banks – the European Investment bank (EIB) and the European Bank for Reconstruction and Development (EBRD). Those two banks are the official financial arms of the new country-nation.

Conclusions

In this chapter a number of examples were presented. All the examples were taken from the media (mainly from the daily and weekly press) over a period of only one year. They are only a small sample from a much, much greater number of examples that could have been taken from the media over the same period. The purpose of the examples was not to say whether participation in the EU is a beneficial thing or not. This has been critically examined in Part Two of this book. The sole purpose of the examples was to establish clearly what the EU is today by laying out simple facts. In summary the simple facts are:

1. The legislative power of the people of each member country (their power to make laws) has been transferred to the Europarliament.
2. The judicial power of the people of each member country has been transferred to the EU High Court of Justice in Luxembourg.
3. The executive-administrative power of the people of each member country [their power to govern themselves] has been largely transferred to the Commission (government) in Brussels. The small part of the executive-administrative power that has not yet been transferred to the Commission is being transferred with the abolition of the country's currency.
4. Centralisation of decision-making and of action is one of the main characteristics of the EU.
5. The democratic process has become narrower since to each member of Europarliament corresponds a much larger number of voters than the number of voters corresponding to each member of a national parliament. Also the distance between the people and the Commission in Brussels, or the people and the High Court in Luxembourg, is much greater than the corresponding distance between the people and their national government or national courts.
6. More than 3% of the taxes paid by the citizens of each member country are automatically transferred each year to the Commission. Part of this money is spent for the operation and maintenance of the EU institutions, for advertisements of the EU political ideals, for official aid to other countries and the rest (the greater part) is repackaged as 'EU funds' and sent to all member countries (for agricultural funds, structural funds, research funds, etc).
7. The words 'common' or 'single' have been extensively used to reflect the complete and peaceful removal of the individual policies of each country. No country has its own agricultural, fisheries, environmental, immigration, foreign or monetary policies. There is a common agricultural policy (CAP), common fisheries policy (CFP), common foreign policy and with the abolition of national currencies a common monetary policy.
8. The borders between member countries have in effect been abolished.
9. There is an EU flag, an EU anthem, an EU budget, an EU passport, an EU currency (ECU or euro), an EU central bank (issuing the currency) and two EU-owned (publicly owned) banks – the European Investment Bank (EIB) and the European Bank for Reconstruction and Development (EBRD). Those two banks are in some sense 'nationalised', they are used as the financial arms of the Commission and the huge sums of money they lend yearly to various firms, institutions or foreign governments have nothing to do with the EU budget.

10. There are considerable barriers to trade between the EU member countries and other countries in the form of quotas, tariffs, regulations or other bureaucratic restrictions.

11. The word 'harmonisation' has been extensively used to imply that exactly the same set of laws and regulations would be in force at all times in all member countries and in all spheres of activity. This is a natural consequence of the concept of a single market which was established with the Single European Act and enforced officially with the Maastricht Treaty in 1992.

12. The word 'common' has been extensively used to imply the removal of the power of the people to set their individual policies country by country (Common Agricultural Policy, Common Fisheries Policy, Common Immigration Policy, Common Environmental Policy, Common Value Added Tax Policy, Common Capital Taxation Policy, Common Foreign Policy, Common Tariffs Policy, Common Quotas Policy, Common Trade Policy, Common Drugs Approval Policy, Common Measurements Standards Policy, Common Mergers and Acquisition Approvals Policy and so on).

13. The word 'single' has been extensively used to imply the removal of differences amongst many things, systems, ideas or policies and their replacement with one which must be identical in all member states. In that sense the word 'single' has in many instances a similar meaning to the word 'common', but usually it implies the removal of even the slightest difference or peculiarity and its replacement with one single concept, identical everywhere.

14. The ideals, political aims, economic aims, practices and policies of the EU institutions have been advertised and promoted and marketed year after year both directly and indirectly and always by using taxpayers' money.

15. The two 'nationalised' banks, EIB and EBRD, have been used extensively as the financial arms of the Commission in order to promote and achieve its short-term and long-term internal and external political and economic aims and policies. The capital base of these two nationalised banks is publicly owned.

The above main facts, amongst other things, substantiate the claim made in Part Two that the fifteen member countries have lost their independence and sovereignty and have been downgraded to simply areas or states. In their place a new huge independent and sovereign country has been born. Its name is the EU or the Union or Europe. Some might argue that the EU is not a country since there are many languages inside it and there is no common national identity. However, the existence of many languages does not exclude the possibility of belonging to the same country as the examples of Switzerland or India readily can prove. As to the absence of a common national identity, this is something that under the present system of the single market will come in one or two generations (provided that the single market conditions and concept do not change).

Some might claim that the member countries are still independent and sovereign. However, this is incompatible with the EU being an independent and sovereign entity since, by definition, you cannot have an independent and sovereign entity within an independent and sovereign entity.

A final question remains to be answered. If fifteen historical and democratic nations have been abolished in a gradual and peaceful way with or without the full knowledge and consent of the vast majority of their citizens, why and how did all this process happen? This process happened under the false pretence of European integration and will be examined in a brief but essential way in the next (and last) part of this book.

Part Four
How and Why the EU Was Created – A Rational Approach

Chapter XVI
MOTIVATIONS

Introduction

In Parts Two and Three it has been established that fifteen previously sovereign and independent countries have in effect reduced themselves to simply areas or states in favour of a huge new sovereign and independent country named the EU or the Union or Europe.

In Part Four we will examine how this was done and why this was done. The examination will not be from a historical perspective with dates, names of treaties, names of acts, and so on. The examination will be from the point of view of the average citizen of any of the fifteen member countries. In other words, when answering the question 'How?' we will try to see the facts as they were seen (or as they were presented to) by the average person. We will try to see the various treaties, not from their legal or formal or scientific perspective, but from the perspective of the common man and woman. As to answering the question 'Why?' we will try to use rational explanation to show why a parliament or a government or a people might decide to essentially strip themselves of their powers and downgrade themselves. We would like, however, to point out here that in real life as well as in science not all questions have answers and not all problems have solutions.

The essential steps

Early in the 1950s, the European Coal and Steel Community (ECSC) was formed between West Germany, France, Belgium and Luxembourg. From the point of view of the average citizen, this meant establishing some kind of cooperation between countries that had been at war just six years before. That seemed to be a good step towards peace and reconciliation and no one can object to moves that promote peace. From the point of view of the economists, this meant the elimination of tariffs when trading in coal and steel between those four countries and establishing common external tariffs. From the scientific point of view (the theoretical and practical international economics point of view), the elimination of tariffs between the four countries was a beneficial thing, but the establishing of common external tariffs was a damaging thing that in most circumstances negated the benefits (trade diversion negates trade creation and the balance can be slightly positive or slightly negative).

However, at that time (1951), when all nations were burdened with tariffs, quotas and other bureaucratic restrictions on trade, when half of the world had governments that did not pay attention to any economic theories or were following the wrong economic practices, when East was suspicious of West and vice versa, free trade in steel and coal between the four countries seemed to be a beneficial thing to most economists and the idea of cooperation through binding together two very basic industries was naturally acceptable and desirable. This was the first essential step which from the purely economic-scientific point of view was rather neutral, but from the political point of view was desirable.

The second essential step was the establishing of a Common Market by the Treaty of Rome in 1957. The average citizen understood the Common Market as the elimination of tariffs, quotas and any other restrictions to trade, increased competition, access to a greater variety of goods and services and in the long term lower prices and more employment. This on balance seemed to be a good thing and from the scientific-theoretical economic point of view it was a very good thing.

What, however, the average citizen did not notice at that time, and does not notice even today, is that the trade barriers that were being eliminated between the participating countries were transferred and erected at the periphery of the participating countries (at the 'external' borders). A common market meant common external barriers to trade. But those common external barriers to trade according to standard international economics theory cancel almost all positive effects from the elimination of the internal barriers and in many cases can on balance produce negative results. For the trained economist at that time, the whole exercise of a common market seemed to be a pro-free market and pro-competition exercise and since the common external barriers to trade were to be, in the long term, gradually reduced until eliminated, most economists did not seriously object. No one at that time noticed that economic theory does not speak about a *common* market, but about *free* markets. The average citizen believed at that time (and most probably believes even today) that the Common Market meant simply free trade between independent, sovereign and democratic groups of people and therefore did not have very serious objections to the initiative of the specific governments of the time.

As to the governments themselves who signed the Treaty of Rome, they appeared to consider the whole initiative as a free trade and free markets initiative, going contrary to the very strong prevailing Marxist or hard-line socialist ideology. There were, incidentally, some very long-term and vague intentions mentioned about binding obligations and moving towards integration, which intentions seemed to be irrelevant in the midst of the Cold War. This fact, together with the fact that usually very few government officials trouble to read a treaty carefully, meant that most believed that the treaty would never materialise and lead to the establishing of a Common Market concept as an effort coming from the governments to the people of the participating countries, or as an initiative from the top to the bottom of their societies.

The third essential step was the introduction of the European Economic Community (EEC) concept where the Common Market was to be transformed into an area where products, services, capital and labour were to be able to move freely to find their most productive uses. This, according to standard economic theory, is a very beneficial thing on balance and therefore most of the economists did not object to the concept. From the perspective of the average citizen, it seemed a move towards freely exchanging his or her currency for other currencies and being able to seek work freely in many other countries. This certainly seemed on balance a reasonable and beneficial new possibility, especially since most of the countries participating in the EEC at that time were of roughly similar income per person.

Therefore, the average citizen did not seriously object to the EEC concept since it appeared to give to the people more choices or, in essence, something for nothing. In addition, it would bring people from different cultures closer to each other through free trade and this certainly appeared good from both the cultural point of view and for the maintaining of peace and cooperation.

To the various government officials at that time, the EEC concept seemed to be beneficial, not only from the economics point of view, but from the political cooperation point of view, especially since the Cold War was at its height. In the East there was a common powerful opponent and therefore any move towards more political cooperation in Western Europe would be beneficial for reinforcing stability.

This step (the third essential step) lasted roughly during all the 1960s and 1970s. During that period for the countries that were outside the EEC, there were two huge incentives to get inside: the elimination of all barriers to trade with the EEC member countries and political reinforcement through having many powerful, peaceful and democratic partners. Thus the EEC was gradually enlarged with the accession of various countries.

In 1974, the powerful Council of Ministers was established, in 1979 the Europarliament and in the same year the European Monetary System (EMS). The Council of Ministers was to resolve common political problems at high levels, the Europarliament was to discuss and introduce legislation in some areas of common interest and the European Monetary System was to make the various currencies relatively stable against each other so that trade between the member countries would be facilitated by erasing sudden currency fluctuations.

Again, the average person did not seriously object to establishing those institutions or measures. Only people in special governmental positions or with special education or special interests could start detecting that gradually administrative powers were being transferred from the government of each country to the Council of Ministers, that legislative powers were being gradually transferred from the national parliaments to the Europarliament and that judicial powers were being transferred from the national High Courts of

Justice to the European High Court of Justice in Luxembourg. Very few people, those with knowledge of economics, could know that the fluctuation of currencies, according to standard economic theory, is not necessarily a bad thing.

One additional but very important fact at that time was that all aspects of political, economic and intellectual life of any member country were basically revolving around the main argument of the time: to be in the broader pro-socialist camp or to be in the broader pro-capitalist camp. All other aspects of political, economic and intellectual life were far behind this main argument in all EEC member countries. Therefore, no one was really worried that the Council of Ministers said this or that or the Europarliament said this or that. The political parties were concerned with their opposing parties within each country and there was no time for any serious thought as to what was happening in the EEC institutions. The EEC appeared on balance to be a good thing, even if trade barriers were alive and well at its perimeter. After all, all nations outside the EEC had trade barriers on their borders.

The fourth essential step was taken during the 1980s. During that decade the EEC was renamed the EC (European Community), which to the average citizen meant nothing. It was simply a change of name of an international body, but to those closely following politics, it meant that the EEC was now becoming an entity concerned not only with economics, but also with other things. It was becoming a Community of peacefully coexisting and cooperating independent and sovereign countries. It was not just an *economic* Community. It was becoming gradually apparent that some selected economic, political or judicial powers were being transferred and centralised in Brussels. The farmers realised that it was the EC institutions that were subsidising or assisting them, not their national government. Many infrastructure works in almost all participating countries were being funded wholly or in great part by the Commission in Brussels. A lot of legislation was being signed by the national parliaments because it was simply coming from the Europarliament. Some wrong decisions by the national courts were being challenged and overturned by the European High Court of Justice in Luxembourg and this brought satisfaction to the public. The words 'Brussels', 'Community', 'European', 'Common', 'Structural', 'Funds' and 'Commission' were appearing with increasing frequency in the press, TV and radio stations.

In 1986, an act was signed in Brussels, called the Single European Act. Its aim was to establish a single market all over the European Community. To the average citizen this was simply another change of name. The Common Market was being renamed the Single Market. To the various government officials, economists and journalists, this Single Market meant an effort to make the Common Market a more homogeneous market with more or less the same economic conditions applying to all participants so that increasing competition and privatisation would be fair for everybody. Extremely few people at that time could foresee the colossal and explosive implications that would unfold as the simple philosophical consequences of one word: the word 'single'. However, at that time all these developments meant very little to the average citizen, politician, economist or philosopher of all member countries. The decade of the 1980s was approaching its end with upheaval over all of Eastern Europe and beyond, and everybody was busy looking to the sudden and rather orderly and peaceful collapse of one of the two main political systems and ideologies of the world.

The fifth essential step towards the creation of the EU started and lasted all through the 1990s. In 1991, the Maastricht Treaty was signed where it was envisioned that internal borders had to be eliminated, everybody would be able to work in any other member country (even at its public institutions) and that the countries should be united economically and monetarily (Economic and Monetary Union or EMU). In 1997, the Amsterdam Treaty was signed where all countries were to adopt a common foreign policy. The fifth essential step was to be completed in 1999 with the introduction of the single currency or euro.

Early in the 1990s, it became known to the average citizen that the European Community was being renamed the European Union (EU). It seemed merely another renaming of an international body of peacefully cooperating, democratic, independent and sovereign states. During the decade, a great deal of legislation and regulation came from the EU institutions to every member national government and was rather easily accepted in a drive to achieve the goal of a single market. It became, however, evident to a portion of the population of every country that all major administrative, legislative or judicial functions concerning their country were gradually being taken over by the EU institutions.

At the same time, in all countries, a lot of new flags with yellow stars on a blue background were being flown on a great number of public buildings and in private establishments or companies. Stickers with the same flag were put at the back of many cars; direct and indirect advertisements of the EU institutions and ideals were appearing in all the media; all passports were given the same colour and appearance; all new driving licences were displaying the same flag; all new identity cards were to have a bar code connected to a central computer in Brussels; the checks on the internal borders were being abolished; the immigration policy was becoming common; the visas of third country nationals visiting any member country were starting to get the same appearance; interest rates were being made to converge; currency exchange rates were becoming more or less fixed; and finally, in 1999, most of the national currencies were to be abolished and a new unit of money was to be born: the euro, strong, great and glorious.

With the euro, a new, huge and powerful country was to be born called the EU or the Union or Europe. The only strange thing about this new country was that the vast majority of its inhabitants were not aware of its existence. They mistakenly believed and they still insist on believing in the illusion that this EU is just a free travel zone and that their countries are the fifteen previously existing entities with the names Germany, France, Britain, Italy, Spain, Holland, Belgium, Sweden, Austria, Finland, Denmark, Ireland, Portugal, Greece and Luxembourg! But perceptions do not alter the facts, and the fact is that in 1999 a huge and powerful country named the EU was to be born and the fifteen member countries have been downgraded to simply areas or states. This entity has all the essential characteristics of a sovereign and independent country. It has a parliament (legislative body), a government under the name of the Commission (executive body), a judicial system, (High Court of Justice), a yearly budget, a system for yearly collection of taxes (VAT), a system for spending those collected taxes, a statistical service (Eurostat), an auditing body, an agricultural policy (CAP), a fisheries policy (CFP), a competition policy, a body for approving drugs, a health and safety policy, an environmental policy, a capital (Brussels), a central bank (in Frankfurt), a unit of money (euro), a full legal system, a taxation policy regarding taxes on capital and on value added (VAT), a foreign policy, an immigration policy, a citizens' rights policy, a police force (Europol), a passport, an identity card for almost all its citizens (treaty of Schengen), a well-defined external border, a budget for official annual aid to third countries, two nationalised banks (European Investment Bank (EIB) and European Bank for Reconstruction and Development (EBRD)), an official newspaper (*Government Gazette*), a flag, a national anthem and regular and full democratic elections for its legislators every four years.

The government is not directly elected, but it is elected indirectly since the Commissioners are appointed by the national governments which are elected democratically. The only essential thing or characteristic missing from this new country is the culture or national identity. But as a new baby develops his or her identity slowly while growing up, in the same way it is expected that the citizens of this newly born country will develop their new identity and culture (the European identity and culture) simply as time passes by generation after generation. The old national identities and cultures will necessarily have to be erased, set aside or downgraded by fusion into the new European culture and identity. And since this new culture and identity is wider and more inclusive than all the others it will surely be a superior culture and identity.

In order for this fusion and transformation of cultures and identities to be expedited, a number of incentives have been given in the form of subsidised TV or radio productions promoting pan-European themes; by introducing into the schools subjects about the history of a 'European' civilisation, by considering nationalism as chauvinism and hence something to be condemned, by subsidising the teaching of foreign languages, by subsidising the European Football League, by subsidising the 'European capital of the year', by subsidising European exhibits, European projects, and by indirect or direct advertisements of the various European projects or ideals. It may take a few decades but the European identity and culture are expected to be fully fledged and thriving by the gradual fusion (or, if necessary, over the ashes) of fifteen smaller or narrower or redundant cultures and identities.

We saw above the main historical and essential steps to the birth of the EU from the perspective that counts: the perspective of the average citizen, the perspective of that unknown voter without whose full permission, consent and authorisation nothing can be done in democratic countries. Now, let us try to revisit the 'how' question using a logical rational reduction process: we will reduce the question of 'how the EU was born' into a number of standard, essential characteristics – attributes – facts. Thus the many characteristics of the event of forming the EU are the following:

1. The forming of the EU was not an event of a specific moment. It was a *process*. This process lasted approximately fifty years (from 1951 to 1999).

2. The process was *designed*; it was not spontaneous or random. The aim of creating a new country over the whole continent is evident in the works of various people right after the Second World War and it is evident in the Treaty of Rome (1957), especially if one reads the treaty between the lines.

3. The designer or designers of the project had *deep knowledge of economics, politics, philosophy and social evolution*. They knew, for example, that free trade in all directions is a beneficial thing for any country, but that if free trade was permitted in the periphery of the then European Economic Community, then one of the incentives for the countries outside to come inside would be eliminated. They knew, as another example, that a common set of laws is a condition that in the very long term inevitably creates a common identity for the citizens of the new country.

4. The process was implemented *very slowly and gradually (step by step)*. If the same process had been implemented over a period of, say, only ten or fifteen years, then it would undoubtedly have failed, since the same generation of people when subjected to a lot of radical changes usually reacts (and many times it reacts violently).

5. The process was a top-to-bottom one and never vice versa. Throughout the fifty-year period the initiative belonged always to high-ranking government officials and it was never a result of popular demand. There had never been a popular demand for the transfer of the legislative powers of the people of any nation to a place outside that nation or of the transfer of parts of its government to a centralised body called the Commission or even the Council of Ministers. With the Maastricht Treaty the countries were, in effect, being united, but there had never been demonstrations or strikes by the people in France or Germany or elsewhere for those countries to be united or lose their independence.

However, the fact that the process was always top to bottom and that the EU is an entity formed by government officials without any popular demand or initiative by the average citizen does not by itself justify any criticism as to the merits of the process or its ends. After all, people elect their representatives who, in turn, think about measures that generally improve the lives of everybody and there were in history a vast number of initiatives taken by elected officials that were beneficial to the people. Legislators and governments do not always respond to popular demand. They sometimes respond to their own ideas, which in most instances are right.

6. The process was not the initiative of any specific country. Since 1951 there were always involved, in every essential step, more than two countries.

7. The creation of the EU was not the result of acts by a specific political party. Throughout all those fifty years there has not been a specific party in any country that had in its manifesto from the beginning the creation of a new country. There was not a single party in any country rallying its supporters consistently, clearly and unequivocally during all that period towards the creation of a new powerful entity called the EU, towards the transfer of legislative, administrative and judicial powers outside of the country and finally towards the abolition of the sovereign country and its transformation into an area. If there had been such a party it ought to have declared its aims clearly to its supporters in 1951. There has never been in any of the member states any party with such a consistent, clear, explicit and declared programme, especially a programme of fifty years duration.

8. The fifty-year process was not a construction of political parties exclusively from the right of centre (pro-capitalist camp) or from the left of centre (pro-socialist camp). In all essential steps and in all treaties, there were involved governments from all kinds of political persuasion and parties in power alliances from all parts of the political spectrum.

9. The creation of the EU was not the result of a single person, politician, philosopher or idealist. There has not been a Karl Marx to form a theory or an ideal to energise either popular masses or politicians. There had been in the 1940s and 1950s a small number of well-intentioned people not directly involved in politics who spoke or wrote about uniting the various nations in the continent of Europe, but their ideas were very general or vague and, most importantly, there had not been powerful government officials to openly declare and suggest that they were following those ideas or ideals.

While during the past one hundred years there have been hundreds of millions of people following the ideas of Karl Marx (rightly or wrongly), while there have been millions of democratically elected legislators or government officials rightly or wrongly following the Marxist ideology or other established political theories (socialism, liberalism, conservatism, free markets and so on), there has not been during all those fifty years a single powerful politician to openly advocate to his or her supporters a specific theory of creating the EU. The Soviet Union was created by Lenin, based on the theories of Marx. China was created by Mao Tse Tung, based again on the theories of Marx. But there has not been a single prime minister or president who will be known as the creator of the EU After all, it is highly unlikely that any specific democratically elected official could have been in power for fifty years.

10. The fifty-year process operated on countries with completely different cultures, languages, main religions, stages of development, specialisation of economies and work ethics. The process worked on countries as diverse as Portugal to Finland and Britain to Greece. Therefore, the EU cannot have been a construction of any specific religion or any homogeneous expansionist or imperialist force or nation.

11. The transfer of the powers of the democratic institutions of each country to the corresponding democratic Euro-institutions (Europarliament, Commission and Euro-Court of Justice) had been done very gradually, very slowly but also very effectively. Parliaments, justice systems and governments were stripped of the vast bulk of their powers without too much debate in the legislatures or in the media. The transfer of powers was done in such a skilful way that even today the vast majority of the citizens of each of the fifteen member nations are simply not aware of this transfer of powers. One would expect that at some stage of the process an institution such as a national parliament or a national government would react to transferring its powers to another institution outside the country. But this has not happened.

It requires a lot of skill, effort and organisation to convince members of any parliament that they can be stripped permanently of their legitimate powers in favour of members of another parliament outside of the country. It requires a lot of conviction on the part of a government to remain silent when it receives instructions or even fines from an executive body residing outside the country. It requires a lot of patience on the part of the judges of a nation when they see that their decisions in the highest of the courts in their own country are overturned by other courts outside the country. It requires a very effective campaign in all the media to convince serious journalists, political and economic commentators and columnists that, in order to make fast economic progress, you have to give up permanently your people's right to independent economic and political decisions. It finally requires something more than an effective and long-term campaign to convince serious philosophers in any nation that centralisation of decisions, power and economic structures over a whole continent is the way forward or that free markets are equivalent to a single market.

12. One other characteristic of the fifty-year process is the progressively greater ease with which independent and sovereign governments submitted themselves to signing accession treaties or other treaties which would certainly have great impact on their people, especially in the long term. At the early stages of the Cold War it was extremely difficult for even only two sovereign and democratically elected governments to stop arguing between themselves over very simple matters. Progressively however, not two, but many governments started signing treaties easily such as the Maastricht or the Amsterdam Treaty without any obvious kind of fighting and serious disagreements between them.

13. The process of the forming of the EU was also characterised by the signing of treaties of colossal importance *without proper information and debate*. Democratically elected governments, and especially those in Western Europe, usually tended to inform all concerned parties in advance and have debates before introducing relatively simple laws. For example, a government, before introducing a new law on trade unions, advised all concerned parties in the country, took their input and then acted. For such relatively simple laws, there are usually great debates before they are introduced. In the case, however, of accession treaties, and most importantly on the treaties of Maastricht or Amsterdam, such a proper, impartial and lengthy information campaign and debate were absent in almost all member states. For relatively simple subjects such as a new tax or the yearly percentage increase in public employees' salaries, there was usually plenty of information and great debates which in many instances resulted in paralysing strikes. However, when the subject was the signing of treaties or laws regarding the EU formation process, such information and debate was either totally absent or skilfully given a very low profile. Thus we have seen fundamental powers of the people being taken to Euro-institutions, borders being eliminated, economic policies being dictated, currencies being abolished, foreign policies being abolished, national identity cards being bar-coded to a central supercomputer in a Euro-institution and hundreds of colossal changes taking place either without information and debate or with a minimal amount of both.

14. Throughout the fifty years, public money (taxpayers' money) has been used as the main tool for forming the new country. Taxpayers' money goes quietly from the nations' capitals to the Euro-institutions and then with a lot of noise goes back to the nations' capitals. It is clearly public money that is received by the farmers, by construction companies for infrastructure projects, by universities for research projects, by city

councils for cultural events and by the 20,000 direct employees of the EU. It is clearly public money, those loans given to member states companies by the European Investment Bank (EIB) with lower than the market interest rates. It is clearly public money, those loans given to other countries (especially in North Africa, the Middle East and Eastern Europe) by the European Bank for Reconstruction and Development (EBRD) and by the European Investment Bank (EIB) again in the form of loans with lower than market interest rates. It is clearly public money, that foreign aid given by the EU every year to countries all over the world. It is clearly public money, those vast annual sums spent in all fifteen member states and beyond to market or advertise, directly or indirectly, the benefits and merits of the process.

15. The second most extensively used tool for the creation of the new country has been the *uniformity of conditions* doctrine. It is well known to historians and political analysts that the citizens of a new country can gain a new identity or culture only in the long term and only if they are continuously subjected to the same conditions of laws, regulations, policies, political structures, economic structures and so on. Those uniform conditions have been put in place by continuously using terms such as 'harmonisation', 'common', 'single', 'level playing field', 'fiscal dumping', 'integration', 'union', 'meeting of criteria', 'process', 'inevitable', 'European' and so on.

16. The third most extensively used tool for the creation of the new glorious and powerful country are the Euro-institutions themselves from the Commission, to the Eurostat, to the Europarliament to the European Court of Justice. Once a central institution is set up over a continent it is evident that even if its members happen to have the best of intentions, it will tend in the long term to assume powers from the member countries. Institutions need power to survive and to project themselves and since the total amount of power is constant (it is in effect the mathematical sum of the unalienable powers of all the citizens of each nation), the only way that Euro-institutions once established could project themselves was by taking as much power as possible from the national institutions and projecting it to 360 million people. But once the power is projected from a central point, the 360 million people will naturally think in terms of a common central identity. This is especially true in the long term (say, in one or two generations).

17. Another characteristic of the process for the creation of the EU is the insistence that governments strictly follow the dates of the various steps and the readiness to use harsh or unpopular measures in order to follow the schedule. We thus see weak and otherwise reluctant governments insisting on the date of 2 January 1999 for abolishing their currencies and taking (especially after the 1992 Maastricht Treaty)

unpopular measures in order to follow the targets and aims of the process. This insistence on following the set dates and the readiness to accept harsh or unpopular measures in order to follow the aims of the process by otherwise weak governments has a continuity even when the government in power changes hands to the opposite side of the political spectrum.

18. *Readiness to project or accept false or partly false statements* on the part of various national governments and Euro-institutions in order to further the process or market its aims to the public is one more characteristic of the fifty years leading to the creation of the new country. For example, it is scientifically false to suggest that the size of a currency, as measured by the total assets held in that currency, has anything to do with the inflation rate and the interest rates or the stability of the currency. Another example that is partly false is the idea that in order to prevent future wars you have to restrict or erase the ability of human communities, known as countries or nations, to make fully independent and sovereign decisions.

19. *Cooking of the government books* (which is legally and morally equivalent to fraud) in order to achieve economic targets is one more characteristic. It is widely known that from the date of signing of the Maastricht Treaty until 1997, many government books and data have been officially 'cooked' in order to present the picture of compliance with the conditions for abolishing the national currencies.

20. *The curious or strange downfall of Eurosceptic leaders and arm-twisting of whole Eurosceptic nations* in order to bring them in line with the process is one more characteristic. In 1989, the then socialist and rather Eurosceptic or Maastricht-sceptic government of Greece was brought down under curious circumstances. In 1990, the then conservative and Eurosceptic (or Maastricht-sceptic) prime minister of Britain was suddenly brought down, again under sudden and strange circumstances. In 1992, the Danish people rejected by referendum the Maastricht Treaty but their arms were somehow twisted and after only one year they were again given a referendum on the same subject.

21. The main underlying philosophical argument throughout the fifty-year process appears to have been the idea that in the same way that within a given market small firms need to merge in order to survive and grow through economies of scale and market power, so whole countries need to merge in one big single country in order to achieve for their people maximum material progress and to survive the competition of huge and powerful countries – economies like the USA or China or even Japan.

The second main philosophical argument throughout the fifty-year process appears to have been the idea that the various nations over the continent of Europe, in spite of their various small cultural differences, have in essence the same overall or prevailing 'European' culture and therefore they ought to all live within the same country.

Why the new country was formed

Having examined in a rational reduction process the question of *how* the EU was formed, we will attempt now to answer the very important question *why* it was formed.

1. If there has not been a popular demand on the part of the citizens of any nation to abolish their inalienable political and economic powers in favour of anyone else, then why were the fundamental powers of the people transferred and centralised to the Euro-institutions?

    The only rational answer to this is most people even today ignore that this transfer of powers has happened.

2. If there was not a popular demand to abolish fifteen nations in favour of a new one, then to whose demand were the successive government officials responding? The only rational answer to this is that they were responding to their own enlightened ideas. Successive government officials in all fifteen member countries believed rightly or wrongly that there were obvious and strong merits in abolishing their democratic and historic countries in favour of a much larger and equally democratic one.

    Therefore, enlightenment of successive government officials believing that they were acting on behalf of the long-term public good of their people could be the answer here.

3. The next question to come to is why the whole integration process, which lasted over fifty years, was not fully explained by the enlightened leaders to the citizens of each country right from the beginning. If, in other words, the enlightened successive government officials of fifteen independent and sovereign countries acted on what they perceived to be for the public good of their people, then why did they not try to take political advantage of a bright idea right from the start and inform all of their people properly about their intentions and plans and ask for the people's explicit, unequivocal and fully informed support?

    The rational answer one can give here is that in many instances leaders chose not to fully inform their people about measures which could create strong or unexpected reactions if fully explained.

4. However, if political measures are taken in relative secrecy by governments due to their short-term difficulties or unpopularity, the same cannot be said when the measures are about abolishing a country or

transferring the powers of the people to centralised continental bodies outside the country. The assumption that government officials wanted to hide the truth from their people because they were traitors is completely illogical because no one really wants to betray his or her country, especially officials who have made it a purpose of their lives to serve their people and spend a lot of effort, energy, time and even their own wealth in order to be elected.

The only rational answer to this question is that until very recently (say until 1997) the government officials could not predict or clearly see where all this process would eventually be leading to and that now they feel that it is too late to admit ignorance or mistakes or to change direction.

5. If taking away powers from the national institutions and centralising them in the corresponding Euro-institutions was happening during the process, then why did the various national institutions not react to this erosion of their powers? Did they not have self-interest in preserving the status quo, or were they altruistic and idealistic enough to downgrade or marginalise themselves in favour of an ideal they perceived as the long-term public good?

Altruistic and idealistic behaviour could be one rational explanation, but one more probable explanation could be that until very recently the members of the various national institutions did not realise that they were being stripped of their powers.

6. One could make the assumption that the EU was created by the leaders of a large European nation, trying to control the whole of the continent by peaceful means.

But if the creation of the EU was the result of a nation such as Germany intending to exercise hegemony over the continent, then the structures of the Euro-institutions would have been chosen in such a way that the German representatives would be in a majority in the Europarliament and in the Commission. This is clearly impossible since the German representatives will always be a small minority. Especially for Germany, which has a federal structure, there will be obviously very little meaning for a German government or a German parliament when those will be squeezed between the Euro-institutions and the corresponding institutions of the German states.

7. Could the creation of the EU be the result of efforts by a specific pan-continental party?

If the creation of the EU was the result of a single political party or a single politician working over a period of fifty years, we would all know that. But this is not the case.

8. Could the creation of the EU be the result of some kind of Euro-chauvinism?

If the creation of the new country was the result of some kind of Euro-chauvinism on the part of governments, then we would have seen countries being governed by chauvinistic or militaristic politicians. But this is not the case. During all those fifty years the vast majority of the governments of member nations were anything but chauvinistic. No government of a member state in recent memory could be characterised as chauvinistic. Most importantly, a chauvinistic leader, by definition, would not exchange his country for another and would not strip himself of his powers.

9. Could the creation of the EU be the result of Europeans trying to counter-balance the military or political powers of the USA?

    If the creation of the EU was the result of a desire by fifteen governments to antagonise the military or political might of the USA by creating an even bigger country than the USA, then we ought to have seen progressively increased military spending in Europe and we ought to have seen European governments that believed in political antagonisms and in creating empires. But we have not experienced governments willing to create political empires. On the contrary, most of the contemporary government officials are pacifists willing to reduce the size of government and projecting the image of full cooperation with countries such as the USA or even Russia or China.

10. Could the creation of the EU be an effort by the Europeans to match the economic power of the USA?

    If the creation of EU was the result of successive governments wanting to counterbalance the economic might of the USA, we ought to have experienced national governments under the illusion that economic might rests with governments and not with private companies and therefore we would have experienced expansion of the public sector as a declared aim of the EU. This, however, is not the case.

11. Could the creation of the EU be the result of successive national governments wishing to counterbalance the huge private companies of the USA by creating huge private 'European' companies? There can be many objections to this approach.

    Firstly, in order to create huge private corporations you simply need a free trading world, as can be easily seen from the huge corporations of Japan, South Korea, Taiwan, Switzerland, Canada, Australia or Brazil. In a free trading world even the smallest of the countries can create the biggest corporation with offices, operations and factories in almost every country.

    Secondly, if antagonising the huge private corporations of the USA was the aim, then the EU would not permit even one merger between US- and EU-based corporations.

Thirdly, in the global markets even huge US corporations are very small compared to the size of the total global market.

Fourthly, in the strict international economics sense, there is no scientific meaning in counterbalancing any huge corporation from abroad. You simply need to have anti-monopoly laws within your own country to make sure that no company (regardless of whether it is local or foreign) has a prevailing share of the market.

Fifthly, it appears to be a very high price to pay to be willing to transfer the powers of your people and abolish your country in order to counterbalance the huge private corporations of the USA.

12. Could the creation of the new country be the result of creating pan-continental democratic institutions with very limited powers initially, but then gradually the Euro-institutions became self-motivated bureaucracies and gradually became bigger and bigger by feeding on the powers of the corresponding national institutions in a perpetual unending process as always happens with bureaucracies?

    This could explain only a very small part of the process, since if such were the case then very early the various national institutions would have quickly reacted to the erosion of their powers and in order to support their position they would at the early stages have mobilised their people. Additionally, every democratic nation has institutions such as the defence force, police force, secret services, foreign office and so on whose first and foremost obligation is to preserve the integrity of the nation and the inalienable sovereign powers of the citizens of the country. Those institutions at some stage would have detected the process, informed the national government and, since each government is first and foremost interested in preserving its power or equivalently preserving the powers entrusted to it by its people, then we would have seen at some stage all national governments reacting badly to the Euro-institutions. But such a thing has not happened except in an extremely limited number of cases and in a very mild and rather passive manner.

13. Finally, could the creation of the new country be the result of cowardice? Could it be the case that successive national governments were afraid to take hard and unpopular steps that were nevertheless correct and beneficial to their people and chose to hide behind mantras such as, 'The Commission said this,' or 'The Europarliament voted that'? Could it be the case that successive national governments thought that they had to reduce the public sector or reduce the government deficit or increase competition, and in order to do that they preferred to act collectively instead of acting individually, so that they could better withstand the short-term reaction of their people? This is quite a plausible explanation but it cannot be reconciled with the following rational objections or facts:

- During the past twenty years, which have been the most essential in the process, the overall size of the public sector as a percentage of GDP has not decreased in almost every member country. In fact, the size of the public sector as a percentage of GDP has slightly increased in most member countries.
- Regarding reducing the government deficit, or reducing inflation or reducing the total public debt, those are not subjects justifying abandoning a country or transferring the powers of its people to centralised Euro-institutions.
- Regarding free markets, increasing competition, reducing red tape, reducing bureaucracy, making the labour markets flexible, reducing unnecessary subsidies, eliminating distortions to the laws of supply and demand and so on, these again are hardly reasons justifying the creation of huge bureaucratic Euro-institutions and the systematic creation of a new country with all kinds of common policies such as foreign policy, agricultural policy, immigration policy, fisheries policy or nationalised banks in the form of the EIB and the EBRD. In short, you don't need to transfer the powers of your people in order to promote free market or pro-capitalist economics. Moreover, until very recently, such free market policies have been promoted by rather Eurosceptic national governments while the great majority of the national member governments were following implicit or explicit pro-socialist views and practices.
- Elected democratic government officials who have been fighting for many years to climb within the structures of their own political party, who have fought elections, who were brave enough to stand in front of crowds and give speeches, who are comfortable when giving interviews to dozens of journalists, who are courageous enough to withstand the usually unjust accusations of their opponents or of the media, who have the managerial ability to lead huge organisations like the public sector machines, who are ready to lead their defence forces in case of war, who are continuously sacrificing their personal or private lives in order to serve their people, those government officials and leaders are very unlikely to be cowards and to be afraid to look their people straight in the eyes and tell them what is the true situation and what has to be done.
- To support the fact that successive government leaders and other officials preferred to deceive their people in order to take unpopular measures out of cowardice is even statistically impossible. It can happen under extreme circumstances to one particular government at a particular point in time, but it cannot happen to most

of the governments in all of the fifteen member countries most of the time during the past twenty years at least. Cowardly leaders can be found in a country only as a very, very rare exception and not as a rule over a period of twenty years and in fifteen specific countries which happen incidentally to be geographically neighbours! It is statistically much less possible than lightning striking twice the same house over a period of one hour!

In conclusion, having tried in a rational manner to give an answer to the question as to why the new powerful and glorious EU was created, we have not found any satisfactory one. In other words, using logic one cannot find plausible explanations of the fact that fifteen historic and democratic countries have abandoned their independence voluntarily in favour of a new one whose existence is almost ignored by their citizens!

It was said, however, in the introduction to this part that in real life, as well as in science, not all questions have answers and not all problems have solutions. For instance, the mathematical problem of 'squaring the circle' (i.e. finding a square whose area is exactly the same as the area of a given circle) has no solution, and the question of why and by whom the universe was created has no answer in the strictly scientific world, although it has answers in the axiomatic-philosophical world.

There is a proverb that 'if everything else fails, try logic'. We have tried logic and we failed on every possible attempt to explain why. We will therefore modify the above proverb into the following: 'If every logical path fails, try fiction!' We have thus to try to make a future effort by writing a clearly fictitious work on the subject, which might satisfy the minds of readers who definitely require an answer to every question even if the answer is in the sphere of political fiction.

However, I am satisfied at simply having tried and failed to find a rational answer to the 'why' question since I fully accept the limitations of the human mind.

Part Five
Epilogue and What Lies Ahead

Chapter XVII
QUICK REVIEW – SUMMARY

> I have tried to be honest. To be honest is to confront the truth. However unpleasant and inconvenient the truth may be, I believe we must expose and face it if we are to achieve a better quality of American life.

Those were the words of the American civil rights leader, Martin Luther King Jnr. I believe that the same words should be applicable when one tries to examine the truth about the EMU and the EU. I do not know whether the examination of the whole subject in this book is scientifically correct or even unbiased. I know one thing, however: that I tried to be honest. I tried to examine from every possible angle a subject of colossal importance for the lives of the people in fifteen historic, democratic and peaceful nations. I tried to be unbiased as much as possible, to the degree that a person can be unbiased when he sees (or thinks that he sees) unjust or wrong things being done to millions of people in a rather deceptive manner.

At the same time, an effort was made to present an alternative to the EU as a way forward, as a way towards a more prosperous, more decentralised, more peaceful, more democratic, more diversified future for every nation in Europe or elsewhere.

In Part One, the arguments regarding the EMU and its pros and cons, as well as the corresponding pros and cons of the alternative, were examined.

In Part Two, the arguments regarding the EU and its pros and cons, as well as the corresponding pros and cons of the alternative, were examined.

In Part Three, a great number of examples from the media and press were given in order simply to describe what exactly the EU is today and what exactly is happening.

In Part Four, a quick answer was given to the question as to how the EU was formed and an unsuccessful attempt was made to answer the questions of who created the EU and why.

The last question most probably remaining in the mind of the reader could be: what lies ahead? The answer here is that if the arguments presented in this book were, objectively speaking, correct, then the EU will be peacefully dissolved into its constituent parts within the next generation or so and some form of the Athenian democracy will prevail. If, however, the arguments presented in this book were, objectively speaking, wrong, then the EU will continue to exist. Only time will tell. In the meantime, this book will wait on the shelves of those readers who are convinced that the arguments presented here were correct, or it could be consigned to the dustbin of history by those readers who are unconvinced by the arguments. One thing is certain, however. In the long term, the correct ideas always win over the wrong ideas, even if the wrong ideas are supported by all the armies in the world and all the money in the world, because ideas have consequences.

Appendix 1

SIMPLIFIED FORM OF CENTRAL BANK OF SWC BALANCE SHEET FOR JUNE 1997

(All figures are in billions of SM)

Assets (Sources)		Liabilities (Uses)	
Type of asset	Amount (b)	Type of liability	Amount (b)
Foreign exchange and gold	60 SM	Deposits held by commercial banks at central bank	80 SM
Central bank credit	937 SM		
Loans and discounts 1b SM		Currency held by the public 840b SM	
Government securities 930b SM		Vault cash 80b SM	920 SM
Net other credit 6b SM			
Net other assets	3 SM		
Monetary Base M_O (Sources)	1,000b SM	Monetary Base M_O (Users)	1,000 SM

Notes:

1. Foreign exchange and gold include:
    - Foreign currencies
    - Reserve position in the International Monetary Fund (IMF)
    - Special Drawing Rights (SDRs)
    - Gold
2. Loans and discounts item is the high-powered money lent to commercial banks.
3. 'Government securities' are government bonds of the country SWC (sovereign government bonds).
4. The central bank issues currency (SM), but all 'other banks' (commercial banks) are prohibited by law from doing so.

Appendix 2

In Figure A, the French economy is originally in equilibrium at point E_1 with the interest rate on the French franc at i_1 and the National Income of the French economy at Y_1. The IS curve is the equilibrium curve of the French economy in the 'goods' market and the LM_1 curve is the equilibrium curve in the 'assets' market. In Figure B, AD_1 is the original demand curve for the French economy before the French central bank decides to increase the money supply in order to reduce unemployment.

When the French central bank increases the nominal money stock this implies a higher real money stock at each level of prices. The LM_1 curve thus shifts to the right to the new position LM_2. Interest rates decline to induce the French public to hold light real balances. The decline in interest rates, in turn, stimulates aggregate demand and thus raises the equilibrium level of income and spending in France. For constant price level P_1, the new income (output of the French economy) is at point Y_2, which is directly below point E_2. The new AD curve (shown as AD_2) is therefore passing through point E'_2. In a similar manner, we can derive all points of curve AD_2. In fact, it can be proven that 'An increase in the nominal money stock shifts the Aggregate Demand schedule up exactly in proportion to the increase in nominal money'.

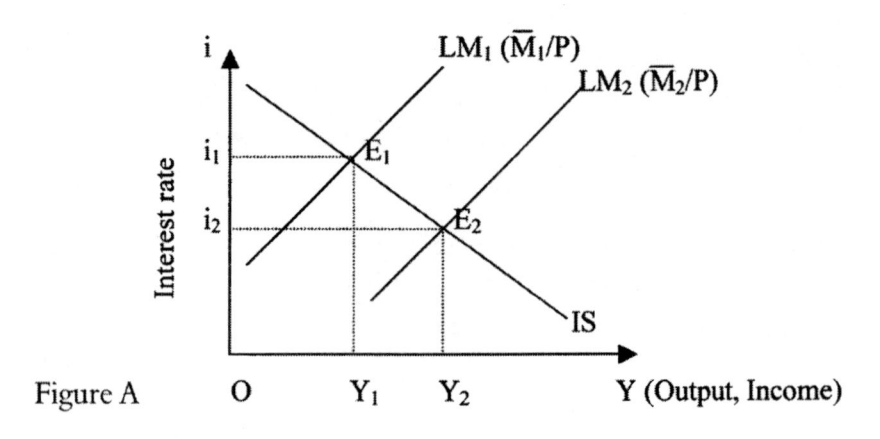

Figure A

Figure B

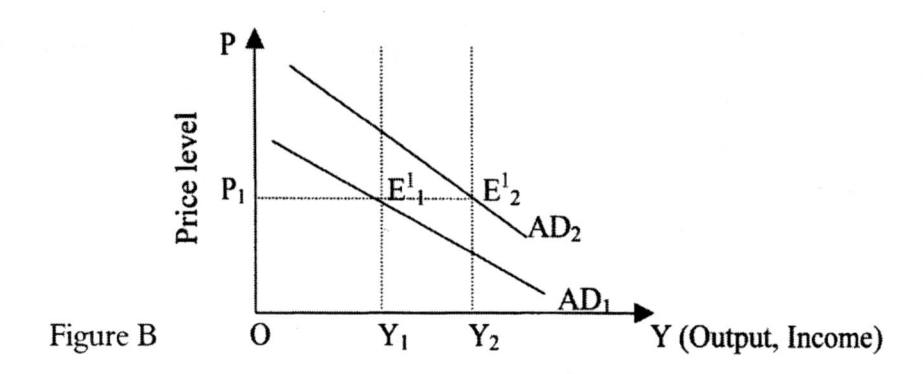

Index

B
BA– American Airlines, 263

C
central bank, 17, 18, 22, 26, 29, 41, 64, 72, 281, 294, 325
  Bundesbank, 259
  European, 294
  Frankfurt, 17, 18, 59
  loans, 56, 270, 313
commercial bank, 19, 20, 23, 41, 325
Common Agricultural Policy (CAP), 91, 92, 141, 179, 206
Common Fisheries Policy (CPF), 179, 288
Creutzfeldt-Jakob disease (CJD), 296
currency, 20, 26, 32, 46, 52, 58, 59, 62, 64, 67, 70, 72, 263, 284, 314
  common, 13, 14, 30, 31, 45, 50, 56, 65, 68, 74
  dollar, 71, 283
  ECU, 263, 298
  euro, 17, 18, 39, 56, 57, 62, 74, 254, 298, 307, 308
  exchange rate, 19, 22, 50, 52, 53, 95, 179, 220, 307
  franc, 64, 90, 326
  shekel, 71
  single, 7, 15, 66, 117, 252, 307
  smart card, 46, 47, 170
  Swiss franc, 71, 283

E
economic arguments, 100, 106–62
economics
  agent, 29, 118, 119, 123, 212
  convergence, 43, 109, 159
  debt, 19, 27, 44, 56, 59, 66, 144, 254
  economic policy, 44, 65, 70, 117, 120, 121, 254, 294
  fiscal policy, 22, 23, 26, 30, 31, 32, 51, 117, 158, 159, 259
  global market, 143, 160, 318
  indicator, 22, 53, 55, 111, 213, 222
  internal market, 143, 150
  stability, 52, 168, 284, 285
  White, Lawrence H, 46
EgyptAir, 269, 270
EMU, 29, 30, 31, 33, 35, 37, 41, 42, 43, 47, 48, 55, 56, 58, 60, 66, 73, 76, 225, 281
Europarliament, 117, 143, 164, 166, 167, 168, 209, 218, 240, 282, 298, 305, 313, 316
  Council of Ministers, 305, 309
Europe, 79, 180, 185, 205, 206, 211, 215, 216, 225, 226, 229, 234, 241, 259, 265, 291
  Austria, 294, 295
  Belgium, 56, 58
  Britain, 263, 292, 314
  Denmark, 29, 58
  France, 100, 251, 266, 292
  Greece, 58, 109, 118, 152, 175, 238, 249, 314
  Ireland, 58
  Norway, 40, 44, 70, 202, 212
  Portugal, 58, 260
  Sweden, 29
  Switzerland, 40, 70, 99, 103, 109, 211, 212
European Bank for Reconstruction and Development (EBRD), 210, 297, 298, 299, 308, 313, 319
European Coal and Steel Community (ECSC), 303
European Commission, 139, 140, 143, 144, 263, 296
  de facto government, 178, 188
  lobbies, 121, 129, 186
European Community (EC), 206, 251, 306, 307
European Economic Community (EEC), 79, 206, 305, 306, 309

328

European Investment Bank (EIB), 210, 222, 269, 292, 297, 299, 313
European Monetary System (EMS), 305
European Union, 44, 51, 85, 88, 90, 96, 98, 100, 102, 104, 106, 108, 115, 133, 134, 142, 144, 145, 148, 153, 154, 155, 156, 157, 158, 160, 161, 163, 173, 178, 196, 199, 201, 203, 204, 205, 206, 211, 214, 216, 217, 219, 224, 225, 228, 230, 232, 233, 245, 247, 251, 255, 258, 260, 263, 264, 265, 280, 282, 307, 323
  advertisement, 92, 95, 154, 219, 221
  Brussels, 35, 36, 81, 90, 92, 93, 117, 137, 140, 146, 269, 288, 306
  budget, 95, 120, 140, 209, 221, 290
  bureaucracy, 35, 38, 140, 217, 218
  centralisation, 117, 121, 137, 138, 166, 174, 182, 241, 312
  EU model, 84, 114, 150, 153, 224, 234, 237, 240
  foreign aid, 92, 98, 141, 204, 218, 222, 269, 290
  foreign policy, 198, 201, 265, 298, 307
  funds, 139, 152, 154, 187, 209, 218, 298, 306
  health care, 110, 118, 144, 282
  law, 66, 116, 117, 125, 127, 158, 164, 165, 166, 168, 169, 171, 173, 263
  Patijn, Michiel, 264
  pensions, 119, 144, 153, 158, 234
  public funds, 151, 209, 219, 222
  single European tax code, 144
  Strasbourg, 81, 117, 153
  time setting, 251–52
  Trade Commissioner, 134, 135, 136, 255
  unemployment, 27, 54, 109, 110, 111, 151, 259, 288, 294
Eurostat, 222, 258, 259, 313
Eurotax, 67
Exchange Rate Mechanism (ERM), 27, 31, 283

F

financial market, 71, 159
foreign exchange market, 48, 71

G

global village, 239, 241
  conglomerates, 161
  harmonisation, 158, 252, 253, 299
  synergies, 161
government, 22, 23, 26, 32, 37, 38, 43, 53, 56, 58, 62, 67, 80, 117, 118, 121, 136, 137, 139, 158, 159, 163, 178, 179, 186, 193, 217, 233.
  bilateral agreements, 135, 142, 157, 194
  bonds, 17, 19, 20, 32, 38, 55, 56
  budget, 32, 35, 36, 37, 62, 66, 111, 119, 133, 190, 220
  Bundestag, 168, 207
  election, 130, 177, 191, 193, 308
  foreign reserves, 17, 20, 55, 65, 73, 285
  interest rates, 18, 22, 24, 25, 34, 37, 66, 95, 159
  ministry of economics, 137, 138
  securities, 20, 159, 325
  sovereignty, 63, 81, 164, 182, 196, 199, 206, 236, 242, 253
grading system, 15

I

immigration, 111, 112, 153, 181, 266, 308
international economics, 40, 50–60, 85–100
  economics, 54
  exports, 52, 111, 154, 156
  Factor-Price Equalisation theorem, 109
  imports, 52, 109, 111, 142
  short-term policies, 51
International Monetary Fund (IMF), 73, 194

J

justice system, 81, 83, 117, 125, 174, 176, 190, 263, 286
  European Court of Justice, 156, 158, 173, 175, 217, 263, 282, 288, 306, 313
  judiciary, 80, 195
  Socrates, 175

K

King, Martin Luther Jr, 15, 323

L

legislation, 101, 102, 149, 158, 164, 165, 166, 167, 172, 216, 305
  electronic referendum, 112, 113, 124, 127–29

Electronic Voting System (EVS), 128, 129, 192
French immigration law, 266
lawmaking, 124, 127, 156, 166, 170
legislative body, 61, 81, 117, 163, 178
reform, 216, 217, 264

M

macroeconomics, 22, 26–44, 32, 36, 37
   aggregate demand, 24, 326
   aggregate supply, 24
   balance of payments, 19, 22, 55
   foreign policy, 31, 179, 180, 198, 201, 202, 265
   GDP, 22, 37, 44, 56, 59, 62, 90, 100, 145, 146, 193, 319
   inflation, 19, 22, 27, 39, 40, 52, 66, 72, 281, 314
   interest rates, 22, 24, 27, 30, 34, 42, 49, 313, 326
   investment, 50, 55, 88, 89, 135, 141, 150, 154, 255, 292
   labour force, 29, 70, 111, 154
   monetary base, 20
   national capital, 154, 182, 183, 241
   National Debt, 19
   national income, 22, 326
   natural resources, 29, 72, 136
   privatisation, 132, 234, 306
   recession, 23, 32, 33, 42, 145
   tax, 31, 33, 90, 91, 94, 95, 96, 97, 101, 106, 107, 118, 119, 120, 123, 133, 137, 139, 144, 151, 158, 159, 179, 193, 220, 252, 253, 254, 287, 298
   tourism, 29, 95, 108, 114, 122, 260, 280
mathematics, 116, 277
   integration, 277, 278, 279
Maystadt, Phillipe, 254
microeconomics, 45–49, 93, 99, 102–6, 102, 133, 151, 185, 224, 271
   disposable income, 30, 32, 145, 226
   farm support, 151
   minimum wage laws, 151
   monopoly, 70, 92, 138, 149, 185, 235
   oligopoly, 70, 93, 149

N

National Organisation for Medicines, 287
nationalism, 213, 308
   athletics, 212
culture, 106, 180, 196, 225, 227, 229, 242, 308
language, 164, 257
national flag, 79, 205, 212, 275, 286
national identity, 237, 238, 299

P

philosophical arguments, 69–75, 224–44
   Aesop, 15
   collective liberty, 242, 244
   collective rights, 243
   dynamism, 71, 125
   Heraclitus, 132
   history, 57, 62, 166, 174, 180, 232, 243
   Plato, 69, 236
   Pope John Paul II, 238
   Socrates, 17, 175
policy tool, 22, 24, 26, 28, 36
   economic, 14, 254
   exchange rate, 54
   fiscal, 22, 23, 30, 32
   monetary, 14, 22, 23, 25, 26, 29, 30, 52. See
political arguments, 61–68, 163–223
   democracy, 62, 92, 117, 169, 174, 188, 216
   Lenin, Vladimir Illyich, 311
   Mao, Tse Tung, 311
   Marx, Karl, 310, 311
   socialism, 219, 234

S

Schlogl, Karl, 294
science of economics, 7, 22, 50, 65, 70, 88
   Common Market, 206, 304, 305, 306
   free market, 38, 54, 79, 99, 100, 132, 150, 257, 304, 319
   single market, 115–17, 118, 119, 120, 122, 132, 138, 145, 149, 157, 158, 257, 285, 299, 306
Single European Act (SEA), 206, 207, 228, 294, 299, 306
Southern Philippines Coucil for Peace and Development (SPCPD), 291
special drawing rights (SDR), 73, 325

T

technology, 46, 168, 170, 172
   computer, 48, 124, 125, 169, 170, 171, 172, 174, 192, 307

television, 128, 169, 170, 172, 192, 193, 272, 308
the Internet, 48, 97, 112, 124, 127, 128, 129, 148, 169, 170, 192
trade, 50, 51, 52, 82, 83, 85, 87, 99, 134, 142, 148, 156, 197, 204, 274
   barriers, 85, 86, 89, 99, 135, 142, 289, 304
   bureaucratic restriction, 85, 99
   competition, 70, 79, 99, 102, 104, 115, 130, 149, 157, 185, 235, 263
   deficit, 264
   European Trade Commissioner, 134, 135, 255
   EU–US, 255, 256
   free trade, 79, 83, 86, 99, 105, 109, 113, 142, 148, 154, 156, 206, 283, 292, 295, 304
   Hong Kong–China, 110
   inflexibility concept, 86
   multilateral trade negotiating, 232
   Singapore, 110
   stock market, 283, 284
   tariffs and quotas, 82, 85, 87, 99, 120, 134, 135, 142, 148, 157, 181, 194, 212, 280, 283, 289, 299, 303, 304
   trading bloc, 85, 86, 148, 160, 232
treaty, 206, 304
   Amsterdam, 207, 281, 307
   Maastricht, 43, 79, 206, 207, 293, 299, 307, 309, 314
   Maastricht treaty, 66, 67
   of Schengen, 308
   regarding financial services, 87
   regarding information technology, 87
   regarding telecommunications, 87

Treaty of Rome, 263, 304, 309

U

United Nations (UN), 27, 61, 212, 236, 268, 286

W

war, 73, 199, 200, 201, 225, 228, 319
   Cold War, 207, 304, 312
World Bank, 141, 194
world economy, 109
   Algeria, 264, 265
   Australia, 144, 281
   Brazil, 40, 70, 283
   Chile, 144, 283
   China, 100, 110, 283, 289
   Hong Kong, 47, 58, 100, 103, 110, 258, 291
   India, 70, 282, 283, 300
   Japan, 89, 100, 105, 258
   Nicaragua, 40
   Philippines, 291
   Singapore, 40, 58, 100, 110, 114, 258, 292
   South Korea, 89, 100, 105
   Soviet Republics, 27, 64, 231
   Syria, 280
   Taiwan, 40, 70, 100, 288
   USA, 41, 89, 111, 138, 211, 274, 317
World Trade Organisation (WTO), 87, 89, 93, 108, 134, 135, 142, 155, 204
   GATT, 87, 157